HOW
THE
WORLD
WAS
WON

Peter Conrad

HOW THE WORLD WAS WON

The Americanization of Everywhere

 Thames & Hudson

This is the seventh book of mine published by Jamie Camplin.
He has enlivened and encouraged me for almost three decades,
with more faith in me than I have in myself. Much as I value his
friendly support, I also respect his clear-eyed judgment, and
have come to realize that when we disagree, he is always right.
As in every previous case, it has been a pleasure and a privilege
to work with Jamie's colleagues at Thames & Hudson, who set
themselves to make books that are things of beauty, meant to be
handled rather than scanned on a cold grey screen. I have also
benefited from the expertise of two freelancers – my minutely
conscientious copy-editor Richard Mason, and Marian Aird
who prepared the index. It was a joy to discuss the project with
Gloria Loomis, and as well with Walter Bernstein, who wrote the
scripts for two of the Hollywood films I have referred to here.
Caroline Dawnay at United Agents, braving a grim market, has
represented me with tenacity and bright-eyed enthusiasm.

How the World was Won © 2014 Peter Conrad

First published in 2014 in hardcover in the United States
of America by Thames & Hudson Inc., 500 Fifth Avenue,
New York, New York 10110

thamesandhudsonusa.com

Library of Congress Catalog Card Number 2014932784

ISBN 978-0-500-25208-6

Printed and bound in China by Everbest Printing

Contents

1 | Looking to America

Like many others who arrived in the world after 1945, I often need to remind myself that I am not American.

I happened to be born in Australia, which in my childhood was a remote outpost of two successive empires. Officially we were sustained by a colonial connection to Britain, and at school we were taught English history and told as little as possible about our origins as a penal colony. But that craven loyalty had begun to fray. At the end of 1941, seven weeks before the Japanese captured Singapore and pushed south to bomb the city of Darwin, Prime Minister John Curtin briskly exchanged protectors and announced – 'without any inhibitions', as he said, and with no 'pangs' about embattled Britain – that 'Australia looks to America'.

I belonged to the first generation to have its gaze forcibly redirected. I grew up juggling the borrowed cultures of two foreign powers: I educated myself by reading English books borrowed from the local library, but sidled off to watch American Westerns and screwball comedies at the cinema every Saturday afternoon. The books told me about an old world that was eccentric and insular, crooked and cranky, groaning under the weight of its antiques. The films showed me an alternative – a landscape as anamorphic as a Cinemascope screen, its expanses patrolled, unlike Australia's scorching deserts, by chivalrous cowboys; a society of scarcely credible gloss and glamour, with buildings that shot into the sky like fireworks and people who conversed in volleys of crackling witticisms. My dreams were colonized by an imaginary America.

I came to understand that Australia lived on sufferance, remotely dependent on the United States, which – as Hubert Humphrey said in 1948 – offered itself to 'the whole two billion members of the human family' as 'now, more than ever, the last best hope on earth'. The offer to take patriarchal responsibility for the human brood was a reassurance, but the proviso about being the last hope sounded alarming. Shortly before the presidential election in 1960, John Kennedy warned in a speech in New York that 'to be American in the next decade will be a hazardous experience'. The rest of us had to share in those hazards, whether or not we found them as exhilarating as Kennedy did. In 1962, aged fourteen, I remember lessons being interrupted by an announcement over my school's public-address system to report that Russia was withdrawing its missiles from Cuba. This was an unglobal world where news was myopically local, so I had little idea what that meant; the relief of the teachers, I later realized, made it clear that we had been granted a stay of execution. I wish I had known the Cold War slogan of the historian Arnold Toynbee, who adapted the catch-call of American liberty to demand 'No Annihilation Without Representation'. If we were all the subjects of American power, why shouldn't we react as the colonists in the 1760s did when taxed by Britain?

In November 1963, Kennedy was assassinated. It was early afternoon in Dallas but already night in Australia; when I awoke my mother broke the news and added 'There'll be a war now' – a bright thought for a Saturday morning in the antipodean spring, but a reasonable assumption. Fights were picked above the equator, where history happened. Australians would eventually be obliged to join in – or else we would patiently, passively wait until the nuclear fallout drifted down to make an end of us. My adolescence was overshadowed by Nevil Shute's novel *On the Beach*, in which the last human beings messily succumb to radiation sickness in Australia after a brief, unnecessary war in the upper hemisphere. Among them is an American naval officer who, since those who outrank him are all dead, becomes the Supreme Commander of his country's fleet. Beached in Melbourne, he deals tactfully with the local sense of unworthiness by accepting eucalyptus as the equal of New England's deciduous trees. However, he is 'unreasonably suspicious of Australian whisky', and he ridicules Australian provincialism when he visits an art gallery and sees a version of bombed New York painted by an untravelled surrealist who has reassigned the Brooklyn Bridge to New Jersey and planted the Empire State Building in Central Park. At the end, he sails his submarine back across the Pacific, expecting that he and his crew will expire on the way home. 'I guess the United States is me, right now,' he says. Given that symbolic burden, to die in Australia would hardly be proper.

In exchange for protection, Australia compliantly contributed troops to America's war in Vietnam; along with a few Koreans, we constituted what were known as 'Free World Forces'. The truth of the matter is illustrated in a photograph by David Moore, taken at the airport in Canberra during President Lyndon Johnson's visit in 1966. Johnson stands at the microphone, paying gravel-voiced compliments to his ally. Two paces behind him is Harold Holt, then the prime minister, bent in an attitude of broken-backed obsequiousness. Shamingly, I can understand Holt's bowed head. In 1968, when my number came up in the conscription lottery, I was indignant at having my immediate future taken away by America's executive whims – yet it was also thrilling to be hauled out of obscurity at the bottom of the world and made to contribute to this grand ideological showdown between the United States and its doctrinal enemy.

Some stories by Frank Moorhouse, published in 1972 as *The Americans, Baby,* catch the mood and mentality of the time, with sex as shorthand for Australia's willing submission to imperious, glamorous America. In one story, Carl stops writing anti-war speeches to let a suave American called Paul Jonson – allegedly a journalist, probably a CIA agent – buy him beers and seduce him. Twenty-year-old Cindy moves in with thirty-year-old Hugo, a hippie from Nebraska who has come to Australia as a 'nuclear refugee'; he orders her to read *The New Yorker,* by which she is utterly mystified. A recurrent character called Becker takes umbrage when people mistake him for a GI on leave from Vietnam: he is a sales executive sent out from Atlanta to convince recalcitrant Australians to drink Coca-Cola, and he considers Sydney a hardship posting, good only for 'ten-dollar screws'. In this case the colonials retaliate, and he is raped by a transvestite. The initiation turns out to be a mercy. Becker forgets about his born-again Christianity, and rather than returning to Atlanta starts a new life as a jazz pianist in the Queensland resort of Surfer's Paradise. Another story describes an Australian tour by the poet Kenneth Rexroth, introduced by an inept host as Rex Kenroth. Moorhouse's Rexroth, homesick for drugs that are unobtainable in this deprived place, says that 'everything here is some sort of damn imitation of America' – not of America now, but of 'the States in the forties'. Sad to say, that was probably true.

As it turned out, a Rhodes Scholarship saved me from having to take up arms, and I left for England with my military service deferred. At my college in Oxford I met my very first real Americans, who impressed me almost as much as those I had seen on big and small screens in Australia. They ambled through ancient quadrangles with casual grace, larger and louder than life, conversing as sassily and savvily as characters in a sitcom. And ah, those diamantine teeth and panoramic smiles! They brought America with them – its amplitude, its confidence, its relaxed egalitarianism. Their country was not marginal, like mine; it had grown to be a digest of the entire world, so they felt at ease wherever they were. They also took their invincibility for granted: one of them said to me about a forthcoming examination, 'I'm gonna shoot it right out of the water.'

Among these prime specimens was Bill Clinton, also a Rhodes Scholar, who told me to knock on his door if ever I was passing through his college. 'That's not a French invitation,' he added, sensing my scepticism. At the time I had no reason for remembering Clinton, whose chubby bearded face faded from my memory until the 1990s, but I never forgot the phrase – so worldly-wise, and so subtly critical of deceptive European manners. Of course I did not take him up on the non-French invitation, but I did befriend a philosophy graduate from Massachusetts who once remarked, when we were exchanging reminiscences, that he could not conceive of growing up outside the United States: no Disneyland, no Little League, no ice-cream parlours, no driving licence at the age of sixteen, no Senior Prom. I suppose I should have been offended, but I accepted America's centrality and its bear-hugging universality. I had played baseball as well as cricket, I told him defensively; I even owned a cap pistol for games of cowboys and Indians, though during the Davy Crockett craze I pleaded in vain for a coonskin hat (trimmed, since we lacked raccoons, with rabbit fur); and I remembered my first taste of Coca-Cola, its carbonated fizz exploding from the bottle like the spirit of America.

In the summer of 1969 I finally visited the homeland of so many fantasies, and in a used car with some equally unkempt friends spent two accident-prone months making a road trip from New York to California and back. It was almost a delayed rite of passage into adulthood and – after my first year in crumbly, cosy England – into the revved-up stresses of modernity. I warmed to the American conviction that life should be equated with liberty or perhaps with sheer vivacity, and should be spent pursuing happiness rather than dutifully trudging down a time-worn furrow; I began to resent the way I had been discouraged from wanting an existence less middling and resigned than that of my own browbeaten family. Still, on the back roads we sometimes took in rural states and in the urban flophouses where we stayed, many people did not look free, and quite a few seemed abjectly or eruptively unhappy. While we were on our travels, Americans stepped onto the moon and left their flag behind: the high point, literally, of their advance through the universe. At the same time, they sank deeper into the slough of Vietnam. During the week we spent in Los Angeles, Charles Manson and his feral accomplices roamed through the canyons above Hollywood, slaughtering bourgeois householders they denounced as 'pigs'. Back in New York I watched Richard Nixon arrive at the United Nations, grinning from inside his bulletproof black car at the citizens who cursed and heckled him.

I returned to Oxford at the end of the summer, feeling that I needed to convalesce. I didn't revisit America for a couple of years, but then began to find it irresistible. Arrival in New York made my nerves jangle and jived up my speech, though in my down-in-the-mouth way I never managed to end every sentence with the eternally hopeful rising inflection that was becoming compulsory. In the 1970s it may have been danger that excited me, both personal fear – the city was then notoriously unsafe – and the sense of imminent crisis and collapse, which made me feel that I was alive in interesting times. In 1945 the United States, profiting from a war that had bankrupted Europe and Japan, undertook to be the world's benefactor and guardian. A quarter of a century later, it was American society that seemed to be menaced, ripped apart by civil strife, its constitutional promises belied by desperate poverty. The South Bronx was a graveyard of charred, gutted tenements, bag ladies trundled their shopping carts of scraps down Manhattan avenues that were cratered with potholes, and troglodytes lived among the rats in sooty tunnels beneath Grand Central Station. Angry, lurid graffiti coated subway carriages, so you seemed to be travelling in metal cells recently vacated by a ward's worth of lunatics equipped with spray-paint canisters. Beyond the rotting concrete pilasters of the obsolete West Side Highway, the buckled piers on the Hudson River were orgy rooms for young men with their own interpretation of what it meant to live free and pursue happiness. Everything was in a state of decay, and decadence had its pleasures as well as its perils.

In 1980, when New York was near to bankruptcy and real estate prices were low, I bought an apartment in Greenwich Village and began to spend several months there every year. It became a base from which I could travel across the rest of the country, sometimes to give lectures, more often on journalistic assignments, occasionally just for sightseeing; it made me a part-time resident of the United States and brought me closer to the glories, fads and follies of the greatest show on earth.

Not long before I moved into my lookout on the corner of Bank and Hudson Streets, Ronald Reagan announced that 'America is back'. Had it ever gone away? And given its omnipresence, where could it go? But it did seem periodically to disgrace itself, usually at the time of presidential elections; then it would return to favour, at least until the next disillusionment.

The reconstruction of the battered world after 1945 was meant to inaugurate a new moral order, described by the magazine publisher Henry Luce as 'the American century', when the nation would inspire and guide 'the progress of man'. For most of its history, the United States had followed George Washington's advice to remain isolated from the fractious world. Now it had imperial duties, though in 1947 Simone de Beauvoir noted that America was an empire of a new kind, driven less by the love of power than by 'the love of imposing on others that which is good'. Despite this faith, events in America often turned out not to be testimonials for goodness: Joseph McCarthy's persecution of activities he considered 'un-American', the assassinations of the Kennedys and Martin Luther King, the villainy of Nixon. In recent decades there have been the diversionary oil wars of the Bushes, the sadism of 'enhanced interrogation' at Abu Ghraib, the shaming aftermath of Hurricane Katrina, and massacres at schools in Colorado and Connecticut. But always America redeems itself, or is forgiven. Like the banks that were bailed out in 2008, the United States cannot be allowed to fail.

Growing up in Austria in the early 1950s, Arnold Schwarzenegger took stock of changed geopolitical priorities, and added his ego to the new empire's arsenal. 'America was the most powerful country,' he decided, 'so I would go there.' Having arrived, he set about 'finding an apartment building to buy and move into': ownership came first, residence second. Next he acquired a tract of desert outside Los Angeles, the supposed site for a supersonic airport that was 'monstrous, very futuristic, exactly what I imagined America was about'. He lost money on the investment, but his vision had a certain plausibility: America administered growth hormones to our underdeveloped world, and pumped up reality as if with steroids.

For others, American power meant spectacle, which conquered by stunning the senses. In 1953 in New York the Egyptian philosopher Zaki Najib Mahmoud sampled Cinerama, a short-lived novelty that hoped to outwit television by projecting film onto a curved, circumambient screen. The occasion was a sunburst or thunderclap of virtually religious revelation. 'Henceforth,' Mahmoud declared, 'God has destined these people to lead, and us to follow. He has destined them to produce, and us to consume.' His act of submission was nothing less than *This Is Cinerama* expected as it made America's destiny manifest. A camera attached, significantly, to a converted bomber soars above bristling Manhattan, sweeps across the Pentagon and its acreage of car parks, passes Pittsburgh with its smoking factories, swoops over plains gilded by their crops, glides above the Rockies, glances at the craggy pantheon of Mount Rushmore, plunges into an open-cut copper mine in Utah, skids beneath the Golden Gate, veers inland to follow the Colorado River through the Grand Canyon, then looks down admiringly on the 'stupendous masterpiece' that is the Hoover Dam and at the 'agricultural paradise' that blooms in the desert at Imperial Valley. Meanwhile the Mormon Tabernacle Choir chants patriotic hymns and a narrator hails the grandeur of America, exemplified by architecture, military might, agriculture, industry, geology, engineering, and perhaps above all by the cinema. *This Is Cinerama* ends with that aerial tour; it begins, a little more turbulently, at Playland in Rockaway Beach in the New York borough of Queens, with a screeching vertical trip on a shaky rollercoaster. America is first and foremost a ride, and a wild one.

The images that dazzled Mahmoud and so many others were accompanied by a parade of commodities. President Johnson, explaining in 1966 why he thought that the homeland was imperilled by covetous Asian hordes, said 'We have what they want.' Here was where all desires could be satisfied, in a continent-sized department store. Dispensing with Johnson's paranoia, Linda Ronstadt rephrased his boast when she sang 'Anything you want, we got it right here in the USA.' Ronstadt rejoices when the wheels of her plane bump down on the runway, and mentions the delights she has missed while overseas: a drive-in, a jukebox, a diner where hamburgers sizzle on the grill. 'Ah we're so glad,' she bawls, 'we're living in the USA.' If that is how America is defined, all of us are resident there. Around the corner from my house in London, people wearing baseball caps and T-shirts stamped with the names of American football teams they do not support and American colleges they did not attend line up to buy fried chicken that claims a connection with Tennessee (Kentucky is copyrighted, therefore off-limits). McDonald's has its largest branches in Moscow and Beijing, and even the most hostile regime cannot resist the swanky trappings of Americana: in North Korea in December 2011 the embalmed corpse of Kim Jong-il travelled to its mausoleum balanced on top of an armoured black Lincoln Continental.

Runaways and detractors find that America is inescapable. William S. Burroughs lived abroad from 1948 to 1974, but never defined himself as an exile. 'One can hardly say that one is in exile from the United States as a whole,' he explained; it would be as absurd as claiming to be in exile from the world. The Danish director Lars von Trier has made films set in Washington State, Colorado and Alabama, but he priggishly refuses to enter the United States. Still, the gesture hardly guarantees his immunity. In 2005 von Trier estimated that 'Sixty per cent of the things I have experienced in my life are American', which led him to conclude that, despite his dogged disapproval, 'In fact I am an American.' To be more precise, he is fractionally or virtually American; inside our heads many of us possess the same hyphenated nationality.

Occasionally it looks as if our Americanized world has no room for other countries or cultures. The cover of *The Whole Earth Catalog*, launched in 1968, did not show the whole earth, only the continent partially occupied by the United States. At the cinema, Universal brands the globe by letting it revolve until the so-called western hemisphere basks in the sun: now it can rest, ensuring that America is never on the dark side. Every October, baseball teams compete in a championship that is called the World Series even though it is confined to North America. Near the end of his life, Steve Jobs took his family on holiday to Turkey. In Istanbul he hired a local historian as a guide, but soon became irritated by lectures about the rites of the Turkish bath and the preparation of Turkish coffee. To himself, he said 'So fucking what?' Out loud, he commented that kids in Turkey apparently drank what every other kid in the world drinks, wore clothes that might have been bought at the Gap, and of course used cell phones. 'They were like kids everywhere,' he concluded, meaning that they were like kids in California. Is globalism actually the universalization of the United States?

Proclaiming the advent of the American century in 1941, Henry Luce noted the country's jazz, slang and patented products were 'the only things that every community . . . from Zanzibar to Hamburg, recognizes in common'. Inevitably, the entire world became America's market. But some Americans were keen for this era of omnipotence to end. Arthur Miller thought he had slowed its progress in 1949 with his play *Death of a Salesman*, which blasphemed against Luce's cult of success by examining a single case of failure, the career of a shabby, deluded commercial traveller. In the 1960s the student agitator Todd Gitlin expressed the hope that 'an *anti*-American century' had begun, instigated by protests against the war in Vietnam, and in 1968 Norman Mailer heard Nixon deliver a speech about a friendlier foreign policy that 'seemed to be calling for an end to Henry Luce's American Century'. By 1980, after the bungled rescue of the hostages in Iran, Hunter S. Thompson warned that the Arabs, unafraid of the United States and aware of the advantages their oil gave them, were 'looking beyond "the American century"'. During the course of his confession in 1998 about his sexual peccadilloes, Bill Clinton said that he would prefer to spend his time preparing for 'the next American century': the phrase now sounded as hollow as his quibbling self-defence. The American century began shortly before I was born, and it seems likely to last about as long as an average human being does.

Politicians keep boasting, though their assertions are increasingly windy. In 1998 Madeleine Albright, the American ambassador to the United Nations, justified an attack on Iraq by claiming a fortune-teller's uncanny powers. 'We are the indispensable nation,' she said. 'We stand tall and we see further than other countries into the future.' In July 2011, during the squabble about the debt ceiling, the Speaker of the House of Representatives spelled it out. 'We are the greatest country that ever existed in the history of the world,' declared Nancy Pelosi. Maybe so, but the assessment seemed retrospective, and it had undertones of disgruntlement and regret, since with greatness come onerous responsibilities and tragic perils. Early in 2014 President Obama edged around the usual superlative when he carefully referred to the United States as 'the largest organization on earth' and added that the country still had the power to do good, whether or not – he added, with a telling proviso – anyone was paying attention.

Today even Superman has been stripped of his role as the superpower's muscular embodiment. In 2011 Action Comics decided that in an interconnected world he could no longer go on defending 'Truth, justice and the American way', a motto first heard on the radio in August 1942; to prove his change of heart, he undertook an exploratory flight to Tehran. An improvident nation currently casts nervous glances at the rivals who underwrite its excesses. The skyline of Shanghai makes Manhattan look stumpy, Bollywood is in ruder health than Hollywood, and in the autumn of 2012 the latest dance craze originated in Korea. Although the Universal logo still allows the United States to enjoy the warming sun, the company was sold in 1990 to Matsushita Electric/Panasonic, then to the Canadian liquor firm

Seagram, and finally to the French water utility and media conglomerate Vivendi. In the luminous gulch of Times Square, a glaring totem pole continues to advertise Coca-Cola, but American brands are jostled by Hyundai and Samsung. Climbing towards the top of the pole is the billboard of the Chinese state news agency Xinhua, which in October 2013, days before a possible financial default by the United States government, called for the construction of a 'de-Americanized world'. I shivered when I heard that on the CBS television news in New York: the adjective was new to me, but I expect to be hearing it again.

The philosophical farmer Hector St John de Crèvecoeur, the first European to recognize Americans as human beings of a new kind, said in the 1780s that they were 'Western pilgrims', whose mission was to follow the sun and carry on a culture that 'began long since in the East'. In due course, he expected them to 'finish the great circle' by returning the impetus to the East, where it originated; we are now living through the start of that closing phase. It is time to look not towards America but back at it, retraversing three-quarters of a century that began with its promise to raise up bruised, battle-sore humanity and renovate our world.

2 | A Coming of Age

'We Americans are unhappy,' wrote Henry Luce at the start of his editorial on the nation's destiny, published in *Life* in February 1941. For others, unhappiness may be a normal condition, but Americans pursue happiness with a will and expect to attain it. Written into the Declaration of Independence, the aim was a novel one: now, as John Steinbeck put it in his essay 'America and Americans', there was a select group of people who wanted more than 'food and warmth and shelter', those ancient human desiderata. Once begun, the pursuit could not be interrupted, so Luce therefore briskly prescribed a cure for the country's malaise. The United States, he said, should take charge of human affairs.

Luce's manifesto for the American century doubled as an announcement of his availability for high office: although Franklin Roosevelt was still in the White House, Luce fancied being appointed Secretary of State in a future Republican administration. That never happened, and he had to exercise influence indirectly – as the husband of the playwright and journalist Clare Boothe Luce, a fervent anti-communist who became President Eisenhower's ambassador to Italy in 1953, but more significantly as the founder of three magazines that set an American agenda for the next phase of history. *Fortune* celebrated the achievements of business; *Time* and the supplementary newsreel *The March of Time* ensured that progress maintained its steady tempo; *Life* illustrated the news and in its photographs showed the human face of history, preferably graced by a smile. Magazines like these, as the journalist Clifton Fadiman commented in 1956, catered to America's 'mint-fresh sense of world leadership with its iron mandate that we be mentally as well as chronologically up-to-date'.

Nevertheless, the American century was slow to begin, and Luce complained in his editorial that the United States remained on the sidelines of history, 'like an infinitely mightier Switzerland'. Having seceded from Europe, its founders treasured their geographical isolation, so that Oswald Spengler in his apocalyptic chronicle *The Decline of the West* called America 'rather a region than a state', a peopled wilderness that was politically and culturally negligible. What exasperated Luce was that his stay-at-home countrymen could still not 'accommodate themselves spiritually' to their nation's new status as 'the intellectual, scientific and spiritual capital of the world'. When Roosevelt attempted to caution Hitler in 1939 by hinting that America might take sides in the European quarrel, he was defied by Senator William Borah from Idaho, who specialized in foreign affairs but opposed membership of the League of Nations, never travelled abroad, and believed that America should retain the world's respect 'by minding her own business'. Borah's ideal America was not only neutral but self-neutered.

The hero of Sinclair Lewis's *Babbitt*, published in 1922, is an exemplary citizen of a country that was self-sufficient to the point of solipsism. Content in his industrious mid-Western city and proud of its similarity to 'Detroit and Cleveland with their renowned factories, Cincinnati with its great machine-tool and soap products, Pittsburgh and Birmingham with their steel', Babbitt abhors 'foreign ideas and communism', which to him are one and the same, and has therefore 'never yet toured Europe'. In Anita Loos's *Gentlemen Prefer Blondes*, published in 1925, the gold-digging Lorelei does venture across the Atlantic, but is unimpressed. She finds the Tower of London dwarfish, stubbier than an office building at home in Little Rock. In Paris she approves of the Eyefull Tower, as she calls it, and enjoys the American jazz bands in Momart, but she finds European men unattractive, despite their fancy titles: they kiss your hand without giving out diamond bracelets like American millionaires. 'Civilization is not what it ought to be,' Lorelei decides, 'and we really ought to have something else to take its place.' The alternative might be the bracing American outdoors, where Babbitt spends his vacations.

Of course, as Luce recognized, the current international emergency was bound to shock Americans out of their isolation. Winston Churchill, in his speech in June 1940 about defending Britain on the beaches, admitted that the plucky islanders might fail in their efforts to resist Hitler. In that case, he said, the struggle would be continued by 'our Empire . . . until, in

God's good time, the New World, with all its power and might, steps forth to the rescue and liberation of the Old'. Churchill politely blamed American procrastination on God, and concluded his sentence in the present tense to bring forward the moment when the stepping forth would occur. That advance into history was surely inevitable because he personified the United States as a young hero – sprightly, still fresh, bound to be invincible – just as Luce demanded that his countrymen summon up the 'nobility of health and vigour' they would need for their new role in the world.

The shared emphasis on physique was revealing: adolescent America had outgrown parental Europe, as the director Jean Renoir realized when, on his arrival in Hollywood in 1941, he was told that MGM had an annual turnover three times that of Portugal. After Roosevelt's declaration of war in December 1941, Robert Stevenson directed a propaganda film that introduced Americans to their new allies. The subject was Joe Britain and his eccentric habits (such as hiding from neighbours behind hedges rather than lounging on a porch to greet them, like sociable Americans); seeking out this obscure, diminutive fellow, Stevenson first located the United Kingdom on a map, and then – to illustrate its puny size – transferred it across the ocean and ignominiously squeezed it into the state of Idaho. Churchill took a calculated risk when he invoked America's 'power and might': what if, while defeating Hitler and Mussolini, it almost incidentally overran and absorbed the entire continent?

Three months before Luce's essay on the American century was published, Eleanor Roosevelt and the poet Archibald MacLeish took part in a radio discussion with Clifton Fadiman, during which Fadiman announced that 'We are through as a pioneer nation; we are now ready to develop as a civilization.' This development was sparked by America's role as a 'sanctuary' – Herbert Hoover's word – that gave shelter to intellectuals, artists and scientists who fled from the Third Reich. But it was no longer enough to offer a safe haven to nay-sayers; the nation now needed to acknowledge its responsibility to a world on which the founders of the republic had turned their backs.

A similar reappraisal was required of Europeans, who were accustomed to disparaging the country whose help they desperately needed. The old continent's scornful attitude is summed up by a sign in a shop window on the French Riviera in Ernst Lubitsch's film *Bluebeard's Eighth Wife*, released in 1938: 'English spoken. Si parla Italiano. Man spricht Deutsch. American understood.' Americans were rejects and renegades, of whom Europe was well rid. If they returned to brandish their wealth, it was enough to take their money; they could hardly expect to be treated politely. At their most supercilious, Europeans saw their current political turmoil as a badge of superiority, a credential of case-hardened wisdom. In Lillian Hellmann's 1941 play *Watch on the Rhine*, a venal Romanian count who is an informer for the Nazis mocks his ingenuous acquaintances in Washington. 'We are Europeans,' he drawls, 'born to trouble and understanding it' – and also profiting from it, as he does when he blackmails a political hostess whose daughter is married to a German refugee. After the affronted matriarch departs to fetch the money, he sniffs 'The New World has just left the room.'

Europeans could not forgive Americans for running away to a better, more prosperous life. Maxim Gorky, on a fund-raising trip for the Bolsheviks in 1906, denounced New York as the headquarters of Mammon, and found no evidence of beauty or intellectual vitality anywhere else in the country. Gorky thought that culture was engendered by discontent, and believed that America, stupefied by its wealth, had never felt 'the pangs of the dissatisfied spirit'. Instead of spiritual stresses, it produced gross bodily ailments: Sigmund Freud attributed his lifelong dyspepsia to the meals he was fed during his tour in 1909, the low point being a barbecue in the Adirondacks hosted by William James. He grumbled as well about the inaccessibility of American toilets, and when he finally located one scoffed because it was so ridiculously palatial. With their outdoor cooking and their over-opulent sanitary engineering, these people were at once barbarous and ridiculously genteel. They were also childishly ignorant of history and its guilt-ridden residue. Freud ridiculed Woodrow Wilson's decision to intervene in the First World War in 1917 and his plan for post-war harmony: only a fool or an American would imagine that it was possible 'to free the world from evil'. In 1926 he went further by informing Max Eastman that his homeland was a 'Missgeburt', a monstrous birth, like a warped experiment in science fiction. He sourly joked about the aptness of American behaviourism, which treated people as bundles of conditioned reflexes lacking soul or mind. 'Consciousness,' Freud told Eastman, 'quite obviously exists everywhere – except in America.' That for a long while was the received opinion. Teaching in Kansas City before his return to France in 1946, André Maurois classified Ernest Hemingway as a 'post-Christian' writer, whose heroes, like the majority of Americans, ate, drank and fornicated but ignored all loftier pursuits. Such an elemental exist-ence, Maurois said, 'could never satisfy a Russian or Frenchman'.

Stefan Zweig in a 1925 essay regretted 'Die Monotonisierung der Welt', and asked where this bland, pallid averageness came from. Answering his own question, he replied 'Anyone who has ever been there knows – America.' Two years later, the social scientist Richard Müller-Freienfels reported on the emergence of a new human type, resembling a product of Henry Ford's fac-tories: the world had filled up with platoons of interchangeable clean-shaven men – he might have been describing the Standardized Citizen or Regular Guy admired by Babbitt – accompanied by chorus lines of doll-like women with painted faces. Müller-Freienfels saw this as a consequence of 'Fordism', which to Europeans seemed less a mode of streamlining industrial output than a totalitarian social theory. Also in 1927, the French economist André Siegfried, taking stock of what he called 'America's coming of age', identi-fied a division in the newly enlarged world, a conflict between matter and spirit. Ford and Gandhi, according to Siegfried, represented the two sides of the argument. Should we forcibly regiment the world, or rise above it by 'renouncing comforts and fortune', those uniquely American boons? Siegfried feared that America's bathrooms and automobiles came at 'a tragic price'. Productivity demanded that the individual sacrifice his 'manhood' to machines; in return, when released by the factory siren, he consumed the goods turned out on the assembly line. That, for Siegfried, was not a fair exchange (though since then we have sweetened it by delegating the sweated labour of manufacture to the remote societies that Gandhi wished to liberate).

The French critic Georges Duhamel never pardoned America for the abruptness with which an immigration inspector thrust a thermometer into his mouth when he stepped ashore. Still indignant, he broadcast the bad news in 1930: the 'far western land' was 'already mistress of the world. . . . Behold, people of Europe, the new empire!' Duhamel believed that America, just as implacably as Soviet Russia, was effacing the individual by treating man as a collectivized insect, and to his dismay he found evidence of the same tendency in Germany, where Frankfurt had been reconstructed as a pile of blocks to house 'disciplined little animals'. Recovering from his American trip in his French garden, Duhamel shuddered when he recalled the 'demoniac uproar' of Chicago, sniffed at the memory of the 'marshy odour' of Lake Michigan, and stopped his nose altogether when he thought about the degradation of the Mississippi, obscured by levees as if it were the excrement-choked Cloaca Maxima.

Gamer than Babbitt, the novelist Henry Miller moved to Paris in 1930 and lived there until the outbreak of war. 'Shit,' he said, 'the French are a great people, even if they're syphilitic.' Civilization for Miller had its mucky foundations in 'vice, disease, thievery, mendacity, lechery', and America lacked that seasoning. He relished the earthiness of France, savoured its food and wine and, after the 'toasted sawdust' of American tobacco, delighted in the toxins of its Gauloises Bleues. Here was a culture derived from the soil and rooted in it; America by contrast could exhibit only the 'hypnagogic, chthonian' south-western desert with its dinosaur prints and meteor craters, a waste where nature had 'gone gaga and dada', making man 'just an irruption, like a wart or a pimple'. Miller's enforced homecoming in 1940 confirmed this prejudice. On the docks in Boston, he saw nothing but dregs and debris, flung together in 'a delirium of greed'. In Times Square he found the Great White Way to be an asbestos Elysium without fire or heat, lacking the sensuality of Montmartre. Were the people in the streets, fed on condensed milk and canned food, turned out by some scientific laboratory 'with the aid of a chain-store cloak and suit house'? All that these humanoid specimens could make, Miller sighed, were knobs and bulbs, screws and pulleys, 'comforts and luxuries'. It did not occur to him that this might be no mean achievement, and that in time everyone else, including the French, would want to share those utilitarian benefits. Instead he lamented that 'The whole fucking world is going a hundred per cent American. It's a disease.'

Luce saw the prospect differently. Rather than wanting America to be corrupted by Europe, he expected America to win Europe's war for it and then to savour rewards that would be both moral and financial. He urged the United States to support the British in their fight against Germany, and as a recommendation added that war was good for civilian morale: without citing sources, he alleged that in London there had been fewer than a dozen mental breakdowns since the Blitz began. He knew that Americans would dislike the idea of propping up Britain, as if forgetting the victory that secured their independence in 1776. He therefore stipulated that in any alliance the young United States would be the 'senior partner', though he admired the journalist Clarence Streit's proposal for Union Now, a scheme for federally integrating the democracies on both sides of the Atlantic. Almost a year before America was jolted into entering the war, Luce made premature plans for a post-war international community which would feel 'the full impact of our influence, for such purposes as we see fit and by such means as we see fit'. The unilateral swagger of those phrases has an edge of menace, and in his prescription for the time still to come when 'America enters dynamically upon the world scene' Luce specified that there should be a free-trade agreement to ease exports, and cast a covetous eye on the unexploited Asian market.

America, Luce said, was to be a 'powerhouse', although instead of an electrical charge it would emit 'the ideals of Freedom and Justice', which were to be beamed around a benighted world. As the son of a Presbyterian missionary who spread the faith in China, Luce instinctively drew on biblical analogies: invoking the Good Samaritan, he suggested that Americans should give away 'all that we cannot eat', and in a rousing conclusion to his *Life* editorial he defined the national task as the 'mysterious work of lifting the life of mankind from the level of the beasts to what the Psalmist called a little lower than the angels'. That elevation duly came to pass, but only in a fantasy. In 1946 Frank Capra's *It's a Wonderful Life* recalled a war that was won, symbolically at least, by recruits from the New England village of Bedford Falls, a snug repository of patriotic virtue. The cop earned a medal in the North Africa campaign, the taxi driver was parachuted into France, and the bartender single-handedly recaptured the railway bridge across the Rhine at Remagen. Only the hapless George Bailey, played by James Stewart, lacks a heroic record, having been judged medically unfit for service. Bankrupt, depressed, having abandoned his dream of seeing the world outside his hometown, he considers suicide on Christmas Eve. Just in time, an angel swoops down to dissuade him and insists that 'No man is a failure who has friends' – a message that Capra addressed, he said, to the poor, the downtrodden, 'and those behind Iron Curtains'.

It took more than a single emissary from above to exalt mankind, but the National Aeronautic and Space Administration made angels of the Americans it selected to ride rockets into the stratosphere, representatives of the nation's valour and scientific prowess. *Life* paid the first seven astronauts half a million dollars for exclusive access to their private lives, and after their parade through New York in 1962 Luce gave them dinner atop his corporate headquarters. That meal in the Tower Suite may have been the consummation of his hopes for America. Then, with a flurry of minders and bodyguards, the astronauts scuttled back to ground and dashed to Broadway for a performance of the musical *How to Succeed in Business Without Really Trying*, in which a clueless window cleaner, helped along by some farcical mix-ups, ascends to the presidency of the World Wide Wicket Company and then makes plans to graduate to the presidency of the worldwide United States. Were Americans rightfully ascending to the sky or scrambling up shaky ladders of self-advancement? Luce's preachy editorial told one version of the story, the Broadway satire another, and both were true.

Ten months after Luce's exhortation, the Japanese attacked Pearl Harbor. As anticipated, America joined the world and undertook to manage it.

In a country whose beginnings were Eden-like, erasing the European past to start afresh, Pearl Harbor seemed like an anti-creation, a mockery of Genesis or the Big Bang. The background of diplomatic squabbling, official confusion and unheeded warnings was elided: in popular understanding, the attack came out of nowhere, unprovoked and therefore unforgivable, and war stories obsessively re-enacted it, trying to comprehend the sudden alteration of normality. In Fred Zinnemann's 1953 film of James Jones's novel *From Here to Eternity*, soldiers breakfasting in Hawaii comment on the fine weather as church bells chime. They are startled when what they think is dynamite explodes on the nearby airfield: surely no engineers are working on a Sunday? Roosevelt said that the date would live in infamy, and it was soon so infamous that it could be alluded to quite unspecifically. Edna Ferber's *Great Son*, a saga about Seattle published in 1945, referred simply to 'that Voice on the radio': the capital letter turned the announcer who broke the news into an oracle, megaphonically booming from the beyond. In 1952 Ferber's *Giant*, about the twin Texan empires of cattle and oil, mentioned 'that Sunday morning in December' without needing to say more. This was the zero that marked the inception of a new calendar.

The event became mythical, but it occurred in a modern world where myth was indistinguishable from fiction. The radio announcements that hustle the hung-over Montgomery Clift out of bed in *From Here to Eternity* therefore have to specify that 'This is a real attack, not a manoeuvre.' In Howard Hawks's *Air Force*, released in 1943, John Garfield is travelling from San Francisco in a B-17 Flying Fortress bomber when the radio picks up gunfire and gabbling Japanese voices from the control tower in Hawaii. 'Who you got tuned in, Orson Welles?' Garfield asks, remembering the spurious panic stirred up at Halloween in 1938 by Welles's radio play documenting a Martian invasion of New York. And what if the news remained unheard? Would the peacetime idyll then continue indefinitely? In *They Were Expendable*, John Ford's 1945 film about a flotilla of torpedo boats in the Philippines, the drinkers at a party switch off the radio just before the bombardment begins. But after an uneasy interval the information is passed round the room in whispers, the dancing slows to a halt, and the piano tentatively strikes up 'My country 'tis of thee'. For all our wishful thinking, history cannot be stopped in its tracks.

Pearl Harbor was a blooding, and it licensed a newly ferocious response to one part of the foreign, inimical world. Told in retrospect, the story of the war in Asia and the Pacific called forth a vindictive rage not heard before from Americans. In Raoul Walsh's 1945 film *Objective, Burma!*, Americans are awarded sole responsibility for the reconquest of that country. Leading the charge, Errol Flynn – an Australian, here cast as an architect from Maine – calls the Japanese 'slope-heads' and 'monkeys'; a war reporter accompanying his troop, who stumbles on the corpses of some tortured Americans, gives a more highbrow paraphrase of that abuse when he reviles the enemy as 'degenerate moral idiots' and demands their extermination. In Fritz Lang's *American Guerrilla in the Philippines*, released in 1950, Tyrone Power and his naval team are beached on Leyte by a monsoon. They vegetate in the jungle, eating bananas and combing their beards, but cheer up when they meet an enemy patrol. 'That was the first moment of real satisfaction we'd had in seven and a half months,' Power reports. 'We'd killed our first Japs.' Doubts remained, especially about Burma, which was Britain's war. Digging the journalist's grave in Walsh's film, one soldier says 'Funny how he was always trying to find out what we were fighting for.' His partner adds 'Maybe now he knows.' The laconic remark is not especially optimistic: could death be the aim?

In a huge, disparate country, local loyalties now had to be replaced by a sense of shared identity. The crew of the B-17 in *Air Force* engage in territorial banter as they leave the mainland on the way to Hawaii. A New Yorker disparages the sunny tedium of California, someone else touts the charms of Minnesota. Their rivalry ends when they hear Roosevelt's declaration of war, which emphasizes that 'our *whole* nation' will rise up against the Japanese. Garfield the disgruntled gunner and a showy pursuit pilot who prefers to fly alone are told to forget their personal gripes, because 'We all belong to this aeroplane', which for the duration is a flying United States. When a pet dog that has been smuggled aboard is discovered, the pilot asks 'What is this, Noah's ark?' Yes, in a way – a container not for all breeds in copulatory pairs but for every type of American, though there is room only for one of each (and none are women). A touching scene in *They Were Expendable* questions whether this regimentation actually worked. In Manila, John Wayne exchanges mnemonic snapshots with Donna Reed, who plays a nurse, as they sit on a verandah in the evening. 'Rather like home,' she says. 'Porch, hammock, fireflies.' 'Where?' he asks. 'Iowa,' she replies. 'Tall corn. Where?' 'Upper New York State,' he answers. 'Apples.' The telegraphing of essential information is beautifully tender, though it acknowledges that if these two people were at home they would have as little in common as the prairies and the eastern seaboard.

The Japanese were aggressors; it was harder to rally Americans against Hitler, who – despite his reveries about New York in flames, with skyscrapers buckling under bombardment from the Luftwaffe – had not trespassed on American territory. He had apologists like the aviator Charles Lindbergh and the support of the German-American Bund, whose members marched along East 86th Street in Manhattan, pilloried FDR as Frank D. Rosenfeld, and referred to his welfare policies as the Jew Deal. The Bund summoned its adherents to demonstrate in favour of 'true Americanism' at Madison Square Garden in February 1939. In October 1941, during the campaign to coax the United States to take up arms, the Committee to Defend America hired the same arena to mount the patriotic pageant *Fun to Be Free*, with skits by Ben Hecht and Charles MacArthur and music by Kurt Weill, who had fled from the Third Reich in 1933 and was now a naturalized American. A caricature in the programme showed an iron-helmeted Hun strutting across Russia to stomp on American soil with his hobnailed boot. Hecht had no qualms about vilifying the Germans, fat-necked and puffy-faced, 'as if they had grown four legs and a snout'.

Personifying America was not so easy: whether or not the states were united, Americans did not constitute a unitary, purified race. Seeking a common denominator, the pageant's organizers decided to equate ideology with entertainment and treated freedom as a synonym for fun. One of the narrators was the notoriously racy Tallulah Bankhead, more an embodiment of licentiousness than of liberty; her colleague Burgess Meredith described the crisis as an exercise in theatrical politics, arguing that 'Democracy's Show Must Go On!' or else the world would become a stage for 'a daffy and ruthless playwright'. But Hitler's ambitions were far from daffy, and to mock Germans for their ugliness and obesity was to underestimate their efficiency and resolve. Americans were still finding it hard to imagine the mad, bad world they were shortly to enter.

When the United States declared war two months later, Weill wanted to organize a '"cultural attack" on Germany by short-wave radio', a blitzkrieg whose missiles would be 'the great literature and music of all countries'. In the event, his contributions were aimed at the home front, and he used music to reinforce the meaning of the hallowed texts that defined American identity. In 1942 he composed a new orchestral accompaniment to the national anthem and the pledge of allegiance, framed by 'The Battle Hymn of the Republic' and his own setting of Walt Whitman's poem about mobilization for the Civil War, 'Beat! Beat! Drums!' The suite was recorded by the unstentorian Helen Hayes, which was a mercy: bellowed by a male speaker, these would have been bloodthirsty rants. But despite Hayes's restraint, the words are a reminder that America was created by one war and almost torn apart by another. In the hymn, it is an armed God whose 'truth is marching on', and the anthem – here performed complete, not in the version bowdlerized for daily use – thrills to the clamour of bombs and the flaring of rockets, takes pleasure in the blood that washes away the pollution of the foe, and insists 'Conquer we must'.

Whitman's poem is a call for total war, as a percussive drum invades church, school, courtroom and private home. Weill offered this and his setting of two other Whitman poems to the bass Paul Robeson, whose sepulchral voice had the requisite tones of anger and grief; Robeson never performed the pieces, perhaps feeling that it was tactless to recall the Civil War at a time when the country needed to be unified. Whitman's 'Oh Captain! My Captain!' rejoices at victory, but regrets that the loss of Lincoln mars the festivity, while 'Dirge for Two Veterans' contemplates a double grave containing a father and son. To these Weill added 'Come Up from the Fields, Father', about two parents on an Ohio farm who receive a letter telling them their son has been wounded and assuring them that he will get better, though in fact he is already dead. The mood of the accompaniments is mournful, even ghoulish: the tattoo of the drums makes corpses sit bolt upright in their hearses. Later in 1942 Weill set MacLeish's 'Song of the Free'. The words recognize the laid-back informality of the American libertarian

– 'We will live the way we choose and we'll talk the way we please' – but the rhythmic battery of the music is better suited to the lines about keeping rifles clean and powder dry in case it is necessary to teach the enemy how to die.

Starkness like this was unwelcome: the troops sent overseas after Pearl Harbor needed to be cheered up and emboldened by memories of a homeland and heartland. In Margaret Buell Wilder's novel *Since You Went Away*, published in 1943, a housewife in Dayton, Ohio, writes letters to her absent husband, sustaining him with news of domestic routines and seasonal celebrations from May to Christmas. She is a mid-Western Mrs Miniver, though unlike her prototype in the English Home Counties she does not have to tackle a Nazi airman who lands in her back garden after being shot down. The addressee of her letters is also far from the fray: in Miami on a training course, he is staying in a hotel and has time off to go swimming. She tells him about other letters received by a friend, whose husband is a civilian engineer in the Pacific. 'Neither of you has yet seen action, of course,' she admits, 'but just leaving the country makes the difference' – or, in her husband's case, just leaving the state: war for this American means having your freedom taken away from you by the meddlesome, impersonal state. When the novel was filmed, it was introduced as a study of 'the Unconquered Fortress, the American Home'. True, the fortress is not conquered, but despite the portentous capital letters the film shows it quietly capsizing under the pressure of social change. Claudette Colbert goes to work as a very elegantly uniformed riveter in a factory, and when one of her daughters, played by Shirley Temple, suggests renting a room to a stranger to make ends meet, the other daughter shrilly protests that this sounds like communism. Taking in a lodger would violate the privacy of their property, as if they were living in one of the apartments into which the Russians herded multiple families, with curtains strung up in the middle of a room to divide the groups. Babbitry was not eradicated overnight.

In 1942 the photographic album *Fair Is Our Land* was published to supplement two earlier volumes entitled *This Realm, This England* and *France Will Live Again*, which respectively saluted a country the Nazis were attacking and another they had overrun. The books about England and France assumed that the armies were defending or attempting to reclaim a natal landscape. In the case of America, the emotional appeal was not so easy: the land may sometimes be fair but it is also torrid or frigid or rugged, often uninhabitable and not always lovable. The selection of images looked away from the sources of the country's power and emphasized farms not cities, agriculture not industry. The survey includes combine harvesters in Washington, a logging camp in Oregon, a lettuce factory in Salinas, and a genteelly derelict sugar mill overgrown with Spanish moss in Florida. Otherwise the expected views of New England villages and Yosemite, Yellowstone or the Grand Canyon are supplemented by only one or two urban vistas. Boston is represented by an upside-down reflection in its harbour, and the New York skyline ablaze after dark is sarcastically captioned 'Civic Insomnia': all good Americans are presumably asleep on the unstimulating prairies.

Donald Moffatt's introduction to *Fair Is Our Land* begins by acknowledging that 'for the first time in our history we are suffering shock' – the numbed aftermath of that infamous Sunday – but then backtracks to lament the wrong choice made by the country in 1919, when Americans rejected the Treaty of Versailles, refused to participate in the League of Nations, and embarked instead on a 'holy debauch' of gluttonous consumption. Moffatt tallied the consequences of that error with wincing disgust. The automobiles turned out in Ford's factories were killers, and the cities that thrust their white pinnacles into the sky belonged to gangsters and grafters. Western forests were butchered to produce 'our favourite reading matter, pulp', the granaries on the plains refined wheat into 'insipid fluff' that gave bread the consistency of cotton wool, while drugstores sold 'icy syrups guaranteed to wreck the health'. Moffatt even admitted that the photographs in *Fair Is Our Land* might fail to encourage patriotic sentiments because the average American lacks 'the peasant's fierce love of his land – he's too much of a migratory critter for that'. Americans worshipped an immaterial idea, not the ground beneath their feet, and that idea, Moffatt hinted, could be a delusion. His compatriots needed to experience a moral reformation to prepare them for going to war. When their century began, would they be ready, and did they deserve the authority they inherited from moribund Europe?

3 | 'The Meaning of America'

To be an American, Henry James once reflected, is 'a complex fate'. Fate is doom, as deterministic as your genetic code; although James added that Americans questioned 'a superstitious valuation of Europe', he spent his adult life as an expatriate and finally took British citizenship during the First World War. In 1872, when he made the statement, the fate to which he referred was a simple matter of family ties and regional roots. As the huddled masses welcomed by the Statue of Liberty began to arrive at Ellis Island, it became much more complex. For those uncountable people from divergent backgrounds, dispersed across a country that contained icy mountains and sweltering tropics, forests and deserts, a common American identity could be no more than a legal formality.

A 1945 film called *Where Do We Go From Here?*, which had musical interludes by Kurt Weill and Ira Gershwin, joked about the slipperiness of American identity by pointing out that the sacred adjective was a misnomer. Bill, a befuddled patriot who is physically unfit for the army, appeals to a genie to help him contribute to the fight against the Nazis, but the magic spell is muddled and he is despatched to the past instead, bumping down on Columbus's ship as it sails towards America in 1492. There is a mutiny on board, which Bill quells by telling the disaffected sailors what they – or their descendants in the twentieth century – will find onshore: girls in tight sweaters, tangy pickles, and other such treats. They relent, and allow their commander to proceed towards what he expects will be called Columbia Land. Bill feels obliged to blurt out the bad news to Columbus: the new country took its name from his rival Amerigo Vespucci, one of whose female descendants, called America Vespucci, actually appealed to Congress in the nineteenth century to reimburse the family for infringement of copyright. In *Where Do We Go From Here?* the piqued Columbus wants to turn back, leaving America undiscovered. But it is too late: land has been sighted, history must run its course. In retreat from an uncertain future, the fantasy suggested that the past was a succession of accidents, not the manifestation of destiny. It also cheekily asked whether Americans would love their country as much if it were called something else. Perhaps patriotism was merely onomastic. Admission to America did not necessarily reinvent the newcomers; once inside the Statue of Liberty's golden door, they had to be Americanized. Saul Bellow – doubly an immigrant, since he was born in Montreal soon after his parents migrated there from St Petersburg, and was taken to Chicago as a child – remembered his father extolling Americanism and its advantages at the dinner table while his elder brother exemplified 'total Americanization' by quitting the ethnic back streets and hanging out downtown in the Loop. Despite these efforts, some Americans still felt or looked more American than others. 'O America! America!' sighs the adolescent hero of Philip Roth's *Portnoy's Complaint*, suspecting that the country belongs to boys called Johnny, Billy and Jimmy, not to the Aarons and Marvins of his acquaintance. James Baldwin likewise explained his migration to France by saying that at home no black man could think of himself as an American citizen.

By the mid-1950s, the travel writer James Morris noticed that only 'islands of Europeanism' remained in America, singled out by shops that sold Swiss cheese or Cornish pasties in Wisconsin or by remote Scandinavian outposts in Minnesota. In New Mexico, Spanish mores still prevailed, though the old folkways were menaced by 'the advancing American civilization from across the mountains'. 'Razzle-dazzle Americanism' had overtaken Hawaii and effaced all memory of the Polynesian monarchies. Morris, metaphorically releasing a gasp of European dread, likened this ravenous assimilation to the appetite of a boa constrictor. Once America had been Americanized, would the rest of the world be swallowed whole?

Soon after the war, André Maurois published a history of America, hoping to allay French suspicion of the United States. He admitted that his countrymen had petty, petulant reasons for their mistrust. They were still annoyed that their Atlantic sailors had been overtaken by Spanish navigators in the sixteenth century, and that the Anglo-Saxons had squeezed them into odd corners of the New World such as Quebec and Louisiana. He made amends by personifying America as Don Quixote: like the crackpot idealist in Cervantes' novel, the country had travelled far from home, shed blood and spent money to redress wrongs and free captive nations, yet it had not received the gratitude that was its due. Maurois gave his book the flattering title *The Miracle of America*; that miracle, he explained, derived from the fact that Americans, no matter what their origins, came together in agreement on the propositions set forth in the Declaration of Independence. What Maurois called 'the beautiful dream of Americanism' – whose articles of faith were deliverance from history, an egalitarian redefinition of humankind, and adventuresome progress in illimitable space – depended on the lack of borders or limits. A frontier in Europe was the fence that divided you from the adjoining country, whose citizens you probably disliked; in America it was an uninhabited horizon or, when the trek across the continent was completed, a shining sea. 'The Good Neighbour Policy', as Maurois pointed out in a *Reader's Digest* article in 1946, 'could only be an American expression.' Without the recidivist conflicts that had torn Europe apart, America, as he put it in his history, was 'the hope of the world'.

Even so, Maurois had to ask what united the states. It could not be language or heritage or religion, which in Europe were divisive forces; was it then the 'love for a certain way of life'? That was what the troops were told when they asked what they were fighting for. Yossarian in Joseph Heller's *Catch-22* illogically assumes that GIs enlisted for the sake of hotdogs, Mom's apple pie and the Brooklyn Dodgers, all of which were supposedly threatened by European fascism and Japanese militarism. Yet that excommunicated those Americans who hated hotdogs, had mothers who were bad cooks, and supported other baseball teams. Maurois worried that a faceless, savourless national identity was currently being imposed by mass production, which decreed that every month all Americans should drink the same fizzy beverage, go to the same films and tell the same jokes, after which they would 'pass on to next month's craze'; he did not foresee that Europeans, subjected to the same economic imperatives, might soon begin to behave in the same way. More positively, he pointed out in *Reader's Digest* that life across the length and breadth of America was standardized by the mass media, which evened out social and economic disparities and made the amalgam governable. Europe, by contrast, was an unsynchronized mess, with some countries living in the twentieth century while others were becalmed in the thirteenth or sixteenth. No European Union could ever be as cohesive as the United States.

In a special issue of his magazine *Les Temps modernes* in 1946, Jean-Paul Sartre analysed 'the complex monster of myths, values, recipes, slogans, figures and rites' which 'over there, they call "Americanism"'. The purpose of this doctrine, he believed, was to erase individuality; the melting pot melted down European traits, and unlike Maurois he did not see this as an advantage. In the lobby of the Plaza Hotel in New York, Sartre noted the affectedly 'nasal twang' and studiously immobile face of a European who was undergoing assimilation, and thought he was watching an Ovidian metamorphosis. The man used to have 'a French face', but soon he would be 'a tree or a rock', American and therefore no longer quite human. For Sartre, Americanism was less about pursuing happiness than about needing fantasy, since the country was so insecurely chimerical. This craving, he argued, was satisfied every day by Marvel Comics: Superman was the Nietzschean Übermensch Americanized, and what made the immigrant from Krypton so uniquely American was his banal democratic camouflage as the nerdy Clark Kent. Among the other exemplary national figures analysed in *Les Temps modernes* were Wonder Woman and Plastic Man, creatures at home, according to an essay on comics included by Sartre, in a country whose people were 'phenomenally stupid', cowed by superstition and in awe of machines. America was indeed a monster, complex only – in this prejudicial view – because its primitive simplicity was so out of touch with atheistic modern times.

Ignorance entitled the contributors to *Les Temps modernes* to fabricate tales about the oddity of Americans, particularly in sexual matters. Sartre reported that schoolgirls took classes in which they learned about dating protocols and received tips on manoeuvring boyfriends into proposals of marriage, thus ruling out the pernicious French practice of free love. The Dadaist Philippe Soupault claimed that teenagers had cramped, awkward sex on the back seats of their cars because defloration on wheels rather than under a roof did not count as intercourse, and in his analysis of divorce rates he declared that alimony payments were regarded by these guilt-ridden puritans as a deserved penalty for the crime of adultery. Tampering with what Europeans took to be normal behaviour, Americans supposedly jeopardized the sanity of the human animal. Soupault assigned psychiatric ailments to each American region – neurasthenia in the cold north-east, flaring lunacy in the hot south, megalomania in the empty spaces of the west. North-easterners, he asserted, had a propensity to commit suicide, southerners were inclined to be rapists, and the west produced religious maniacs. Seen from a distance, the country was a blank slate on which such crackpot generalities could be scrawled.

Yet even at home, America was less a place than a state of being. Sartre was right about its mythical nature, which meant that it was endlessly susceptible to interpretation. Everything depended on how Vespucci's forename was glossed; with no other pedigree to anchor it, the treasured word could be co-opted by any ideology. Citing the equality proclaimed by the Declaration of Independence, the Communist Party organizer Earl Browder declared that 'We are the only true Americans', while Senator Joseph McCarthy, persecuting those same communists for being un-American, defined McCarthyism as 'Americanism with its sleeves rolled up'. While the adjective was imprecise and promiscuous, the noun formed from it sounded dogmatic and prescriptive. Dwight Eisenhower said in his inaugural address that 'recognition of the Supreme Being is the first, the most basic expression of Americanism'. The truth is that Americans, then as now, believe in many different gods, or in none at all; the Supreme Being was a convenient fiction, dreamed up by eighteenth-century philosophers who discredited the idea of a creator but wanted to assert that the universe was orderly, and it was only in 1954 that the sanctimonious phrase 'under God' was inserted into the pledge of allegiance to distinguish the United States from godless Russia. Cecil B. de Mille went further, expounding Americanism as a moral code and a religious creed. De Mille, who abhorred the sophistication of the east and west coasts, thought that 'ancient pieties' were honoured only by 'the Buttes, the Burlingtons and the Biloxis' in the hinterland; he therefore set up a Foundation for Americanism to defend unfashionable values and virtues. 'In the real America,' he said, 'honour, decency, patriotism . . . are still real.' The repetitiveness of the language betrays the vacuity of the idea: some parts of America are more real and therefore more American than others. De Mille endowed Americanism with divine favour in his 1956 film *The Ten Commandments*, with Charlton Heston like a biblical George Washington who rallies the chosen people to cast off their bondage. Holding up the tablet on which the commandments were carved, Heston also resembled the Statue of Liberty, uncrowned but wearing similar sandals.

Whether or not the sea parted to make way for the migrants, to become American was and still is a cause for jubilation. The new arrivals may have saved their lives; certainly they expect new lives – virtual reincarnations – to begin. Therefore in 1940, as the United States was reconsidering its fortunate isolation from the rest of the world, Congress established a spring holiday to be known as I Am An American Day, later renamed Constitution Day and transferred from May to September. On the appointed date in 1941 Harold Ickes, Roosevelt's Secretary of the Interior, gave an address in Central Park that asked the immemorial question 'What constitutes an American?' His answer looked outwards not within: he offered the American idea to the rest of the beleaguered world. Who was entitled to say 'I Am An American'? Not people of any particular colour or race or religion, not even those who happened to be citizens. 'An American,' Ickes declared, 'is one in whose heart is engraved the immortal second sentence of the Declaration of Independence.' In 1941 that assertion of faith in life and liberty was likely to mean more to the British, the French and Europeans in countries overrun by 'the Nazi Attila' than to the merry-making crowds in Central Park. The truths propounded in 1776 were universal, and Ickes sought to revivify them by forming 'one great democratic international' which would include 'our friends and allies everywhere', in Asia, Africa and South America as well as Europe. Americanization meant the gift of hope, the promise of eventual freedom, and not, Ickes cautioned, merely the annexation of 'new markets or territories'. He challenged his countrymen to 'gird spiritually for the battle' and then, even before their war began, jumped ahead to envision the era of plenty, security and goodwill that would ensue as soon as it was won.

But military victory was far from immediate, and in the Pacific it required the use of atomic bombs, which compelled Americans to think again about the power they wielded. Were Little Boy and Fat Man agents of righteousness, or of vengeance? Hadn't some of the thousands incinerated in Hiroshima and Nagasaki been 'temporarily enslaved', as Ickes said of the Germans? America's military success had to be portrayed as a moral triumph, making what Hubert Humphrey called its 'democratic practice' a model for all other societies. James A. Michener's novel *Hawaii* contains a subplot that captures this hasty revaluation. Shigeo Sakagawa, a Japanese American, enlists after Pearl Harbor and when wearing the uniform he advertises his 'newly won Americanism'. In 1946 he is sent to Yokohama to interpret for a Harvard academic who is supervising land reform. He is aghast at the destruction he sees, but the professor cheers him up by saying that 'few nations are lucky enough to lose a war to the United States'. He means that the irradiated earth will now be Americanized; Shigeo remains unpersuaded.

By 1948, *Time* had to ask Ickes's question all over again in an editorial that coincided with I Am An American Day. It began by drawing attention to the advent of a new empire. Once, when Roman laws and legions prevailed, men everywhere were proud to say they were Roman citizens; in the mid-nineteenth century, in 'the earth's far corners', people could be heard identifying themselves as British subjects. Now the statement that carried with it 'the most arresting tones of history' was 'I am an American.' Uttered thus boldly, it was more than an affable introduction, spoken with hand extended; it staked a claim, perhaps issued an ultimatum. Asking 'What did the phrase mean?', *Time* began by clarifying what it didn't. Americans were not subjects of a monarch like the British, and unlike the Romans they did not belong to the state: they tolerated a government only if it did their bidding. They knew well enough that collectively they amounted to 'the greatest power on earth'; the problem, however, was the response of a 'friendly and unfriendly' world to that power. *Time* showed off America's economic might and technical eminence in a barrage of images and statistics that looked and sounded positively Soviet. On the plains, tractors clanked through fields where farmers celebrated 'a bumper wheat crop – the fifth . . . in a miraculous row'. Highways and bridges had sprung up to span the land, and at the University of California there were plans for 'a 6-billion-electron-volt atom-smasher'. Against this impersonal rumble of engines, the magazine set a smattering of anecdotes that vouched for the muscle-bound country's kindness and sense of kinship with the world. Townspeople in Aiken, South Carolina, were collecting food and clothing to send to their counterparts in the French city of Morlaix. The ladies of the Mormon Church in Indianapolis had contributed forty homemade frocks, and students at a Missouri college sent off 'a carload of clothing for Europe'. Those acts of charity did not quite drown out the noise of the massed tractors or dampen the voltage of the atom-smasher.

Nor did it occur to *Time* that Europeans might resent having to accept alms. Critics there found it hard to forgive America for its superfluity, and construed handouts as insults. In *The Quiet American*, Joseph Mankiewicz's 1958 film of Graham Greene's novel about the CIA in Vietnam, the British malcontent Fowler asks Pyle, the generous, ingenuous American, for a cigarette. Pyle tells him to keep the packet, and says he has a carton to spare. 'I asked for one cigarette,' snaps Fowler, 'not economic aid. I don't want to be impressed by how many packs you've got.' After the war, it was not necessarily more blessed to give than to receive.

Time's editorial concluded by recognizing that pre-eminence was a burden, and that privilege carried a concomitant load of obligations. Americans, it argued, were becoming aware that to be American 'meant more than owning the atom bomb, or having steak for dinner, or the inalienable right to yell "Kill the ump"'. Those telling phrases – the meaty diet, the chant at the baseball game, above all the casual reference to owning a bomb as you might own a car or a fridge – characterized an America that was happiest at home, enjoying its surfeit, practising its rites, and protecting its monopoly of destructive force. As for what being American meant beyond the country's borders, *Time* could not yet say, because the rest of the world was still making up its mind.

Historical precedents had to be used with caution. After pointing out that the United States had inherited the global task once discharged by Rome and by Britain, *Time* said that no American could ever be 'a spokesman of imperialism'. Roosevelt urged the European powers to free their colonies after the war; Americans neutralized the word 'empire' before using it within the United States. New York is called the Empire State because of its size and wealth, not because New Jersey and Connecticut are its colonies, and Imperial Valley in California owed its name to the harmless puffery of a land company attracting settlers to the region. Empires are primed to prevail over subordinate cultures, but allusions to a clash of civilizations proved to be equally tricky. Eisenhower got away with describing the D-Day invasion as a 'Great Crusade', though George W. Bush was chastised for calling his campaign against Al Qaeda 'this crusade': the crusaders were mercenary warriors not knights of faith, and in any case they failed to rescue Jerusalem from its Muslim occupiers.

Despite such reservations, in 1946 Walter Lippmann predicted that America would consolidate the only true world order since classical times – a unification of east and west, with the Atlantic not the Mediterranean at its centre. The Sicilian bandit Salvatore Giuliano, who organized a separatist movement after the war, actually petitioned President Truman to request the annexation of his fuming volcanic island as the 49th state. Truman demurred, but in 1947 General George Marshall, his Secretary of State, called on Americans to 'face up to the vast responsibility which history has clearly placed upon our country' and announced a programme of European aid to rescue the levelled continent; it came to be known as the Marshall Plan, though Henry Wallace – Roosevelt's Vice President and a Progressive Party candidate in the 1948 presidential election – called it 'the martial plan', suggesting that those starred and striped packages were conducting ideological warfare by other means. Between 1945 and 1951, the United States contributed $26 billion to the economies of Europe. Greece received a special benefaction of $400 million in 1947 to preserve it from communism, though when Truman's proposal was debated in Congress, Senator Glen Taylor of Idaho wondered whether the ulterior motive of this aid was to ensure the supply of 'oil for the American monopolies – the oil that lies in the great lands just east of Greece and Turkey'. Two rival empires mobilized to compete for Europe, and Dean Acheson, who succeeded Marshall as Secretary of State in 1949, warned of 'a polarization of power on earth', the starkest since Rome's showdown with Carthage.

Soon after Marshall's announcement, the economist Henry Hazlitt published a tract asking *Will Dollars Save the World?* in which he decried the Plan as the 'sincerest flattery' of the economic management practised in five-year instalments by the Soviet Union. Hazlitt thought that Europe's problems were created by over-regulation and price-fixing, rather than by a 'dollar famine'. Against the fad of a 'dictated economy', he recommended the harsh justice of capitalism and a free market: once European currencies sagged, the balance of trade would be restored. Otherwise, without a gold standard to determine value, other nations would be permanently begging for handouts from the United States. *Pravda* had recently claimed that America was giving away its surplus to stimulate a domestic boom. In that case, Hazlitt asked, why not dump goods in the sea rather than sending them to Europe, or lavish 'free overcoats, free lunches and free automobiles' on the needy at home? Besides which, the starving populations of India, China, Africa and Latin America had 'superior claims on our charity'. Alarmists feared that without assistance Europe would go communist; Hazlitt grimly chuckled that this reminded him of a poor relation's threat to commit suicide: he was inclined to call the snivelling pauper's bluff.

Pointing out that a union leader in socialist Britain had warned against extortionate American moneylenders, Hazlitt advised that 'it will be a profound mistake to count on gratitude' from Europeans. Stephen Spender, however, was lavishly grateful. In 1948 he contributed to *The New York Times* an article entitled 'We Can Win the Battle for the Mind of Europe', in which he described the investment of all those dollars as a means of bolstering 'the old civilization of the West in Europe with the faith and the experience and the knowledge of the new Europe which is America'. Only three years after the war's end, a millennial change had occurred. In Spender's view – which endeared him to the Congress for Cultural Freedom, established with CIA funds to combat communism – America had not merely taken over custody of Europe but had taken its place.

The Marshall Plan was boisterously set to music by Irving Berlin in *Call Me Madam*, staged on Broadway in 1950 and filmed three years later, with Ethel Merman as a socialite who is given an ambassadorial post and sent to bank-roll the remote European country of Lichtenberg. 'Can you use any money today?' she sings on arrival, delivering the line with trumpet tones that make a donation sound like an armed assault. To her surprise, a dapper minister, played in the film by George Sanders, rejects the $200 million she thrusts on him and says that Lichtenberg must learn to live more frugally – exactly what Hazlitt's tract advised. Smooching with Merman in between negotia-tions, Sanders tells her she is 'the most American American I have ever met'. Immune to ironic European double-talk, she thanks him for the compliment. 'There are more valuable things than money,' he sighs. 'That's what money's for – to buy them!' Merman growls. But perhaps the Lichtenbergers are more materialistic than this visiting plutocrat. Rich in assets though lacking cash, Europeans hoard funds and convert them into heirlooms that can be transmitted between generations. In America, money still symbolizes effort and virtue, which makes its purchasing power almost incidental: big spend-ing gives expenditure an airy nonchalance, and extra moral credit can be earned by giving money away, as Merman's charitable tirade makes clear. Luckily she is able to display American wealth without disbursing it, and – truer to Hazlitt's recommendations than to Marshall's – she returns to her revels in Washington and leaves Lichtenberg to fend for itself.

In February 1951, a decade after Henry Luce's preview of the American century in *Life* magazine, *Fortune* expounded 'the meaning of America' to a world that remained sceptical. A long essay by Russell Davenport conceded that Europeans had the wrong ideas about Americans, but blamed the coun-try's lowbrow propaganda for those misconceptions. Determined to be upbeat, America had made it seem that the GIs were fighting 'The War That

Refreshes', while popular culture, as Sartre noted in *Les Temps modernes*, offered only the consolation of fantasy, either wistful or crazily violent. A photograph in *Fortune*, captioned 'Europe: autumn of 1950', showed a row of bombed buildings with two advertising placards in front of them – one a scaremongering appeal for an accord about nuclear weapons, the other a poster for *Der Hexer von Oz*. Davenport regretted that Sartre and his existentialist cronies were fans of 'Stateside sadism', convinced that the trashy crime novels of the 'Série noire', founded by Marcel Duhamel in 1945, contained parables about the quest for meaning in a murky universe; he added that the Russians could easily prove the iniquity of America by allowing a few Hollywood gangster movies to be exhibited in the territories they occupied. Then, cleverly co-opting a Trotskyist phrase, Davenport said that America owed its economic success to a 'permanent revolution'. In Soviet parlance this enjoined the proletariat to complete what the bourgeoisie lacked the courage to carry through. *Fortune*, appropriating the term, applied it to the functioning of consumer capitalism. Davenport castigated the European fondness for 'state socialism', and drew attention to the rewards of a free market. Another photograph illustrated those benefits: in it, three soldiers from the Russian zone in Berlin stare in amazement at a full-sized American suburban house on display at an industrial fair, with a television set in the living room and a Chevrolet in the garage.

Though Europeans coveted such marvels, they cheered themselves up by surmising that America's industrialized plenty had resulted in a bland or bleak dehumanization. This was a time when, as Leslie Fiedler wrote in a joking paraphrase of *The Communist Manifesto*, 'the spectre . . . haunting Europe – is Gary Cooper!' Cooper represented an American archetype, lanky, taciturn, decent, socially awkward despite his skill at gunfire. Yes, perhaps he had confounded Marx and Engels by fending off communism, which had no such handsome, amiable, unassuming model citizens to present to the world – but seen through European eyes, Cooper the typical American did look spectral, or like a freak designed by perfectionists in a scientific laboratory. Audrey Hepburn, playing a Parisian girl in Billy Wilder's 1957 film *Love in the Afternoon*, views Cooper as a member of an unfamiliar species. 'When they're young they have their teeth straightened, their tonsils taken out, and gallons of vitamins pumped into them,' she says. 'They become immunized, mechanized, air-conditioned.' A friend wonders whether she is talking about a creature just landed from outer space. 'No,' replies Hepburn, 'he's American.'

Unified but also rendered uniform by the war, Americans had begun to think of themselves in the same way. Dana Andrews, playing a demobbed bombardier in William Wyler's *The Best Years of Our Lives*, released in 1946, pays a peculiar compliment to a nurse he fancies when he says 'They oughta put you in mass production.' Ironically, he then visits the drugstore where he was a soda jerk before the war and discovers that it has been bought up by a chain and made over into a standardized emporium, with ceiling flags touting bargains and piles of unnecessary novelties. Were human beings too, as Europeans feared, being turned into factory products? Paul Newman jokes about this in the 1963 comedy *A New Kind of Love*. He is a philandering sports journalist, who toasts 'the bachelors of the world – may our tribe increase!' A buddy asks how that can possibly happen. 'Automation,' Newman replies: it is the organization man's answer to the emotional mess of procreation.

Davenport could not accept this version of the future. In a dizzy rhetorical flight, he rose to the challenge of demonstrating that a society regulated and enriched by machines could still possess spiritual grandeur. In the eighteenth century, John Adams declared the settlement of America to be a 'grand scheme . . . in Providence' for the liberation of mankind, and in the 1950s that humanitarian bequest seemed to be reaching its final stage. The 'special cosmic assignment' of Americans nowadays, Davenport said, was to amplify man technologically – to equip him with wheels, wings and telephonic or televisual antennae, emancipating him at last from the downtrodden earth. So much for American materialism!

Seen at ground level, the prospects for this take-off looked less certain. At the end of the war, the philosopher William Barrett said that he had witnessed 'European Man reduced to his extreme situations'. He was using a slogan of the new French existentialists: extreme situations were psychologi-cal and spiritual crises that made individuals think again about the status of the creature flatteringly known as 'homo sapiens'. Before returning to America, where human self-esteem had not been damaged, Barrett made a trip to Tunisia to visit the crumbled remains of what once was Carthage. His guide showed him an ancient commemorative stele which when turned over disclosed the scrawls added by American soldiers, 'the familiar hiero-glyphs of the public lavatory' back home, and described the Carthaginians as philistine men of commerce, 'the Americans of antiquity'. Barrett could not disagree, and the obscenely defaced slab gave him a preview of what might become of an empire that as yet hardly existed.

James Agee, reporting for *Time* towards the end of 1945, also brooded on 'man's hope, man's fate', which teetered in the balance as 'the atomic age' began in earnest. Packs of displaced persons wandered across Europe and bulldozers gouged mass graves for anonymous cadavers. Farmlands beside the Danube or in Holland were 'sterile as salt'. Nuns in France rifled through garbage for scraps of food. Harder-hearted, *Time* in 1946 called those scav-enging Europeans 'modern pagans', belonging to a self-destructive, godless race that needed spiritual instruction as well as food packages. An ultimate reckoning seemed to be near, which prompted repeated appeals to a deity no one any longer believed in – or, failing that, to his representatives on earth, the Americans. Concluding her tour of the United States in May 1947, Simone de Beauvoir said that 'America is a pivotal point where the future of man is at stake.' At the end of 1948 Jean Cocteau spent three weeks in New York. On his return flight to Paris he sat up all night in a dark limbo, vigilant while his fellow passengers dozed, and composed an open letter that paraphrased de Beauvoir. 'Americans,' he wrote, 'the dignity of mankind is at stake!'

Agee worried that the 'homesick and purposeless' American troops await-ing repatriation were not upholding the dignity of mankind. As they roistered and randomly copulated, he warned them of their obligation to behave alle-gorically, since 'it was not the Americans, but America, that Europe judged'. During the same months, Edmund Wilson travelled through ravaged Europe on an assignment for *The New Yorker*. His judgement of his compatriots was more severe – the liberators, he saw, were doubling as black marketeers and rapists – and despite the wreckage he became uneasily aware of how thin and provisional American society was. A young female compatriot who worked for a relief agency drove him round Aquila in Abruzzo. Though she missed Woolworths and the A & P, she praised the piazzas of the hill town, which created a forum for the mingling of citizens rather than laying out the plan for a presumptive future like the Manhattan grid or Washington with its alphabetical streets. Wilson initially called the Colosseum in Rome 'the old Madison Square Garden', then had second thoughts. The grand facade was at least an 'official mask', dignifying or at least concealing the brutality of what happened in the arena. Is civilization then merely a screen? Perhaps so, but the war demonstrated our need to be protected from the knowledge of our own bestiality. The high-minded mission of the troops amounted to little more than a clean-up of domestic pests and was over-reliant on alliteration: outside Naples, Wilson noticed signs warning that FLIES FOUL FOOD, FLIES FEED ON FAECES.

Freedom, meanwhile, meant less to Europeans than a full belly. Neapolitan urchins stole sacks of flour from American trucks, and if the bags were ripped the spilled powder was scraped off the ground to be sold. The French actor Stéphane Pizella, writing in the journal *Minerve* in September 1945, clucked his tongue about Americans who discarded a cigarette after smoking half of it; their negligence tempted shamefaced Frenchmen to kneel and surreptitiously collect the butt. People who not long before seemed supremely civilized were abased, perhaps debased, by their economic plight. In 1946 Vittorio De Sica's film *Shoeshine* viewed the world from below, from the vantage point of Roman waifs who buff the boots of American soldiers. Their pidgin catchphrase is 'Sciuscia, Joe?' All Americans are interchangeable Joes: their faces are far away, what matters is the feet which the Italians service. Locked up as delinquents, two of the boys are misty-eyed as they watch a newsreel of the American campaign against the Japanese in Bougainville, Papua New Guinea. But their tears have nothing to do with politics or warfare; they cry because they glimpse the ocean, which means an escape from their starved peninsula. Europe pays an equally hopeless homage to America in De Sica's *Bicycle Thieves*, released in 1948. An impoverished man is hired to glue posters of Rita Hayworth's sleek body onto crumbling, bullet-pitted Roman walls, but while he is patting her down, flattening lumps in the paper by caressing her flanks, the parked bike that he needs to do the job is stolen. America in one case is gleaming shoe leather, in the other tanned, nubile flesh. Either way, it exists to be serviced or worshipped but remains unattainable.

Talking to the *Life* photographer Margaret Bourke-White, a GI said that 'We've seen the poor Eyetalians, and they don't even have shower baths.' She thought the remark bathetic, but there was a certain moral logic to it, as Edmund Wilson made clear in 1954 when he said that he had derived 'more benefit of the civilizing as well as the inspirational kind from the admirable American bathroom than ... from the cathedrals of Europe'. Wilson was contrasting the joy of refreshment and reinvigoration with the stale orthodoxies of communal religion, and setting a society that valued domestic ease against one that cared more for public grandeur. The war made Americans aware that their way of life was indeed superior, above all in the smallest rooms of their houses, and the vision of ceramic sanitation persisted: the Guatemalans who risk their lives to enter California illegally in Gregory Nava's 1983 film *El Norte* do so because they have been assured, on the evidence of some faded copies of *Good Housekeeping* magazine, that 'in the United States even the poorest people have toilets'. Theirs is not an unworthy aspiration, but it redefines civilization and promotes plumbing to one of its most admired amenities.

On his travels Wilson met the crusading journalist Dorothy Thompson, famously expelled from Germany by Hitler in 1934. She told Wilson that it was time for the United States of Europe to be founded, and suggested work should begin on designing the flag. Playing a character based on Thompson in the 1942 film *Woman of the Year*, Katharine Hepburn is made in a small way personally responsible for Europe when she adopts an orphan (though she sends him back because he proves to be too much trouble); Thompson, brisker than Hepburn's version of her, simply gave the continent its orders and awaited results. Her impatience was widely shared. *Fortune* complained that Europe was a 'nest of obsolete autarchies' that ought to be swept away, replaced by 'a new supermarket' managed by Americans. But it would take more than a flag to unify a congested continent made up of states that were apt to turn political disputes into racial vendettas. For Wilson, Europe's problem lay in the concept of the nation, inhabited by natives who defined themselves eugenically and disliked other breeds, like the French- and Dutch-speaking populations of little Belgium. America's good luck lay in being 'not a *nation* at all . . . but a *society* in the course of construction'; Americanism referred to shared habits, not a biological essence. Wilson pressed his argument too far by claiming that the USSR, like the United States, was synthetic and therefore frictionless, making it too a more 'advanced system' than the rivalrous European jumble. Events after the collapse of the Soviet Union in 1991 show how difficult it is to live down nationalism and cast off the clan mentality; even the subsequent history of the American union – strained by civil unrest during the 1960s, now split into inimical groupings of red and blue states – has called Wilson's confidence into question.

The easy remedy for European ills was to export Americanism. But comparisons between folkways led to bafflement, since freedom meant different things in other countries. In 1946 the historian Denis Brogan remembered being told by an American student in Oxford that England was not truly democratic because no one ever punched a policeman in the nose. Davenport in his *Fortune* essay cast doubt on the attempt 'to Americanize people' by persuading them to drink Coke and chew gum – foreign tastes that, according to a diatribe in *Le Monde*, threatened 'the entire French moral landscape!' In Neufchâteau, Agee watched an American sergeant making maladroit efforts to pick up a passer-by. With an eye on the same transaction, the crabby female garage mechanic who was repairing Agee's jeep grumbled that only 'bad girls' had offered sexual solace to the Nazis, and they were punished by being paraded through the streets with heads shaved to be heckled and spat at. But at least these women had the excuse of belonging to a population demoralized by defeat, and they perhaps feared reprisals if they resisted German entreaties. To give in to a friendly American seemed somehow worse, because it was a voluntary sacrifice of cultural integrity.

Billy Wilder disposed of the problem in *The Emperor Waltz* in 1948 by citing canine behaviour, blessedly free of scruple and prejudice. Bing Crosby plays a gramophone salesman from Newark, travelling in Europe with his fox terrier Buttons. Trying to interest the fuddy-duddy Habsburg Kaiser in his wares, he finds the Viennese courtiers preoccupied with arranging a match between the Kaiser's pet poodle and a thoroughbred bitch called Scheherezade owned by the stuffy Stolzenburg-Stolzenburg family. Buttons, bumptiously American, gets in first, and the pampered bitch bears an impure litter. A horrified baron sentences the pups to drowning; Crosby saves them, and the Kaiser – who, unlike Agee's mechanic, improbably adapts to a society levelled by casual sex – dotes on the mutts. Among humans, exogamy was trickier. Howard Hawks's 1949 comedy *I Was a Male War Bride* enjoys the bureaucratic farce engendered by liaisons within the Allied ranks. Ann Sheridan, cast as a lieutenant in the American army, marries a French officer played by Cary Grant, and then has to smuggle him home on a troop ship that only has space for war brides, not war husbands. She manages it by requiring him to wear drag. 'American women!' scowls Grant, grimacing beneath a wig that not long before was a horse's tail. Sheridan wears pants and drives a motorcycle with Grant, symbolically emasculated, crammed into the sidecar: a wry acknowledgement that Europeans were being demeaned – in effect feminized – by new masters, or by trousered mistresses.

In 1959 William Bradford Huie looked even more astringently at the changed balance of power in his novel *The Americanization of Emily*. Emily is a uniformed Englishwoman who drives American naval officers around London during preparations for D-Day in 1944. Her passengers laze in the best hotels, entertain each other at black-market banquets, and expect their drivers to double as comfort women. With the war still unfinished, Americanization is already a dirty or at least a smutty word. 'Has Pat been Americanized?' asks the novel's narrator, a lieutenant commander called James Madison, about one of Emily's colleagues. 'Thoroughly,' replies a salacious admiral, delighted by her capitulation. Pat always carries a diaphragm, and makes simple demands: she expects to be fed first and insists on a bedroom, refusing to stretch out on the back seat of a car. Emily, by contrast, will not give in, and is reputed to be 'anti-American'. Most of her countrymen, she says, would have preferred to be occupied by the Germans – charming individually, dangerous only when they form groups – rather than the crass Americans. The liberators are equally unimpressed by their genteel English hosts. 'Why didn't we let the Germans take this bunch of snots?' asks a member of the admiral's entourage.

Huie was born in Alabama, and edited H. L. Mencken's conservative *American Mercury*, to which he invited J. Edgar Hoover and Billy Graham to contribute; in his novel he treats the Americans as marauding Yankees, carpetbaggers who carry stocks of Hershey bars and Palmolive soap to use as love potions, and he pities the English as if they were genteel relics of the Old South. Madison, who shares Huie's provenance, says that southerners know what military occupation means, so although they may be fighting for the flag, 'we also goddam the United States'.

All the same, he flagrantly asserts his imperial rights. 'We Americans,' he brags, 'are the modern Romans.' They are fighting a vehicular war, and Madison cannot help it if American tanks and trucks are too broad for the quaint, crooked English streets and country lanes down which they lumber, killing assorted livestock along with numbers of local civilians – more of whom, he jokes, died under American wheels than in Luftwaffe bombing raids. In Normandy, where beaches were renamed Omaha and Utah in advance of the invasion, farmers complain as the Americans thunder by. An old man says that at least the Germans built fortifications on the coast, which improved the land; Americans claim to be saving the world, but what about the corn they crush as their armoured cavalcade rumbles on towards Paris? Antagonism has to be allayed by a potlatch ceremony, with a formal exchange of gifts. The farmer presents Madison with six Camembert cheeses, and gets a carton of Camels in return.

Madison of course does Americanize Emily, gently not rapaciously, and marries her after the war. But he is also anglicized by contact with her, recognizing her as one of his refined 'Anglo cousins', and he receives a lecture on Anglican values from a canon who walks him around Westminster

Abbey at the end of the novel. Madison assumes that the war was won, both in Normandy or at Stalingrad, by mass man, who – as Sartre feared – is man Americanized, indomitably mechanized. The priest points to the Abbey as 'a fortress against the depersonalizers of man' who want to turn him into 'a cog, or a number, or a producer, or a consumer'; with its honoured graves and memorial tablets, it upholds the sanctity of the individual. Madison is too polite to point out that the qualifying individuals have to be great artists or holders of high office to earn admission. After this he receives a warning about the future from his disenchanted admiral. Together in Honolulu they watch a Superfortress B-29 take off, loaded with the bomb it will drop on Hiroshima. Madison fears the worst and – still thinking like a member of the southern Confederacy – foresees that, in the forthcoming 'revolt of coloured men against white', America will be punished for using the weapon against Asians. The next war has already begun, and it will conclude only in stalemate or even humiliation. 'The age of victory is over for America,' declares the admiral as the bomber disappears into the distance.

When *The Americanization of Emily* was filmed in 1964, with a script by the satirist Paddy Chayefsky, this prediction was even more startlingly pertinent. The United States had blundered into Vietnam, and war was now – for Chayefsky's version of Madison, as for Yossarian in *Catch-22* – at once an absurdity and a business opportunity. The booty in Madison's private supermarket far exceeds the wares he trades in the novel: he stocks Lanvin perfumes, Mumm champagne and Kentucky bourbon, with boxes of merchandise from Lord & Taylor, Bonwit, and Saks arriving on every military flight. Julie Andrews, cast as Emily, sneers at James Garner's Madison: 'You Americans are really enjoying this war. . . . It's just one big Shriner's Convention to you Yanks.' He snaps back with equal ferocity, though without flying the flag. Don't blame our Coke bottles, he says. Europe has been a squalid, disruptive brothel for two thousand years; Americans may be hicks, but their society is incapable of creating a Hitler. 'So lay off, Mrs Miniver,' he growls. Rather than listening to the admonitions of the Westminster Abbey custodian, the film's Madison finds his own way of stopping the war and getting off. He turns into a good soldier Schweik or a Falstaff, recommending cowardice as a means of saving humanity from self-destruction. Having muddled through the Normandy landings and survived a barrage of friendly fire, he vows to sabotage the victory celebrations by denouncing the insanity of war. Emily teases him for threatening such a futilely virtuous gesture. She was terrified of being Americanized, she says; now he, with his moral posturing, has turned into a bloody Englishman!

Otherwise the film makes few references to Americanization. The women are free-spirited hedonists who need no bribes, and even the prim Andrews freely offers herself to Garner. America's run of military successes may have ended, but the culture unpacked from those crates and cartons in the racketeer's headquarters had prevailed. By 1964 the whole world had been Americanized, so the capitulation of the innocuous Emily hardly mattered.

During his reconnaissance trip at the end of the war, Edmund Wilson found himself ineffectually wishing that Europe could be more like America – a federation, not a jumble of egotistical nation states. Political change was slow, yet when the cultural change occurred by stealth, Wilson disliked what it produced.

In 1945 he was disgusted by the craven British – less hungry than the Italians but greedier, gobbling up the demotic culture to which the GIs had introduced them. They 'feed themselves on our banality without catching our excitement,' Wilson observed. 'Many of them,' he added, 'now chew gum.' In 1963, returning to Paris for a year's stay, he found the city to be commonplace, no longer tragically glamorous as it was during its occupation by the Germans, smoothly merging into 'a more and more standardized, a more and more Americanized world'. The cultivated American abroad had come to lament the universal reach of his own society. President Kennedy was assassinated not long after Wilson's sabbatical began, and he adopted a disdainfully dismayed European attitude to the event. Linking Lee Harvey Oswald to the indiscipline of beatnik writers and Abstract Expressionist or Pop painters, he saw the killing as a revolt against both the patrician superiority of the dead president and the prestige of the classical European canon.

Another disillusionment followed in 1966, when the war in Vietnam prompted Wilson to think again about his country's conduct in the world. Ralph Waldo Emerson said that 'the office of America is to liberate' – to overthrow kingcraft, priestcraft, and the obfuscations of caste and monopoly. Now his terminology was adapted to justify an expansionist foreign policy that pretended to be defending freedom. This, Wilson decided, was just 'Anglo-Saxon hypocrisy', a canting alibi for commercial conquest, still soiled from its use by the British in the nineteenth century. The world had been slickly Americanized, but in the process America may have forfeited its soul.

4 | 'Have We Any Friends?'

Early in its career as a global power, the brawny United States sometimes sounded like an unrequited lover, inclined to whimper about the lack of reciprocation. Warning about resentment of the Marshall Plan, Henry Wallace bluntly informed his countrymen in 1947 'We are not loved in Europe.' More querulously, *Fortune* in 1951 asked 'Have We Any Friends?', and admitted with a pang that 'we are offended terribly when love is not forthcoming from others'. The sense of hurt could lead to fuming retaliation. Walter Winchell, for instance, bristled when he read an article in *Paris Match* in 1956 that speculated about why Europeans detested America on principle. In his syndicated column, Winchell snarled that the same foreigners who hate us 'certainly love our money. And our Armed Forces – when they are in a fight with a bully.' As evidence of prejudice further afield, he noted that police in India recently stopped crowds from greeting John Foster Dulles, the Secretary of State, although flags had been distributed so that multitudes could welcome Nikita Khrushchev. Winchell also reminded Raymond Cartier, who wrote the offending essay, that America had recently spent $52 billion on aid to an unappreciative world.

Generosity, however, cannot purchase affection. The Swiss photographer Bernhard Moosbrugger, in a survey published in 1959 as *USA – Europa sieht Amerika*, recalled that on his travels he and his companion Gladys Weigner were everywhere plaintively asked 'Why don't people like us overseas? We help everybody.' The problem, Moosbrugger and Weigner explained, was that Americans thought '*of* others but not . . . *as* others'. They could not conceive of alternative ways of life or systems of belief, and assumed that all problems would be solved by a brisk course of Americanization. Although at the centre of the world, they knew little enough about it: even now, less than 10 per cent possess passports. Russell Davenport admired the self-satisfaction of the British, who ruled their empire without caring what their subjects thought of them. Americans, however, could never be so self-possessed. A sojourn in a Swiss village in 1948 made James Baldwin painfully aware of the average American's desperation 'to be liked *as a person*', which Europeans – who defined themselves as members of a class or community, not as tenuous, autonomous individuals – found odd; writ large, the personal foible became a national trait.

Sartre explained this emotional hunger by arguing that, despite their wealth and power, 'Americans have an incredibly acute inferiority complex'. Incredible indeed, and also untrue, though Americans are certainly eager for others to share their pride in a society that is their collective creation. In Edna Ferber's *Great Son*, Dick Melendy sits in the train from New York to Seattle, watches the states roll by, and tells himself – as if making an amplified public announcement – that the United States is 'the damnedest, thrillingest country in the world'. His son Mike feels that he has a duty to convert Regina Dresden, a teenage Jewish refugee from the Nazis. He takes her up in his private plane to circle the mountains and swerves back down over the water; then, during lunch at the Farmers' Market, she gapes at truck drivers eating apple pie with ice cream. 'I am a greedy girl,' she admits as she samples the treat. Exploring Seattle, Regina notices the frequent use of Olympic as a business name, and reflects that this is truly 'a place of the gods'. 'It's a sale?' asks Mike to conclude the trial run. It is; she buys the mystique of America.

What underlay European hostility was a fear of being overtaken by America, outstripped in the historical race. This disquiet appears at its most flurried and farcical in Jacques Tati's *Jour de fête*, made in 1947 in a somnolent French village that is stirred into life when a slapstick film about the United States Postal Service is shown in the market square. Everything in America seems to be freakishly revved up: letters are sorted by impatient machines, then consigned to postmen who in their zeal to get the mail delivered leap into helicopters that buzz between penthouses, dive from the sky and wriggle down industrial chimneys, or drive sporty vans through hoops of fire. Tati, the village postman whose vehicle is a wobbly bicycle, is mortified by this glimpse of the future, and by the mocking customers who advise him to drink Coca-Cola if he wants to compete with the supersonic Yanks. He practises streamlining his gestures while he makes giddy circuits on a carousel, and hurls missives like missiles at workers in the fields as he zooms down dusty, overgrown lanes. He even multitasks by taking along with him a telephone whose cord has been cut, and while he pedals he makes gabbling calls to non-existent interlocutors. Two American military policemen – still on duty in the countryside so soon after the war – give chase, to the accompaniment of a jitterbugging soundtrack. Their jeep crashes: has plodding France caught up with America? Not really. Tati's bike veers into a creek, and when he climbs out he accepts a lift home in a donkey cart driven at a hobbling pace by a hunchbacked crone, the wise woman of the village. She tells him that the Americans are exhausting themselves in vain, because they will never make the world revolve any faster. Relieved, Tati abandons his mailbag, and instead helps a family of farmers to bring in the harvest, readjusting himself to the steady, implacable rhythm of the seasons rather than behaving like a machine gone mad.

As predicted here, the shock of American life was its acceleration. Visitors from the older, slower world were exhausted by its pace and wrong-footed by its unforgiving edicts; instead of speeding up their physical responses, they concluded that this was a future with no further use for human beings. The editor and critic Cyril Connolly, visiting New York late in 1946, was permanently flustered. He lacked the technical skill that pedestrians needed: he did not jump into action fast enough when the traffic lights changed, and was elbowed aside by the locals. Mutely ordered about by those red and green signals, he was also noisily nagged by the telephone in his hotel room, which jangled endlessly and summoned him to unnecessary appointments. On a drive around San Francisco, Simone de Beauvoir got into trouble because she asked her friend to stop on the Golden Gate Bridge. A sign barked its disapproval; retreat was impossible, because the car was forbidden to turn back. 'American machines are perfect,' de Beauvoir sighed – but because they could not conceive of human error, they did not permit adjustments and corrections. Her friend escaped the impasse by knocking down a barricade.

Connolly flunked another test by failing to unriddle the subway system – probably a good thing, because it was Sartre's opinion that when you inserted a nickel to operate the turnstiles on the platform you were undergoing a grimly American rite of passage, sacrificing individuality in order to be 'elevated . . . to the impersonality of the Universal'. A further rebuff to personal identity lay in wait at the Automat where, Sartre told his readers, you removed refrigerated sandwiches and pies from glass compartments in the wall rather than ordering them to be brought to your table as in a Paris café. Human agency seemed irrelevant, as men – or at least waiters – were shunted into obsolescence. The Swiss photographer Robert Frank, who arrived in New York in 1947, was similarly taken aback by self-opening doors, electric toothbrushes, the chutes in skyscrapers for posting letters, and the treacly music piped into elevators. Jean Cocteau claimed to be mystified by water that gushed from taps jutting out of the wall, and fondly remembered an old Europe where people trudged to the well with buckets. De Beauvoir, who presumably had the services of a maid at home on the Left Bank, found an ontological fatality in the American habit of 'sweeping the floor with a vacuum cleaner': a broom, she said, at least allowed people to feel that they existed organically. Other sanitary habits could not be compromised. In François Truffaut's *Baisers volés*, Jean-Pierre Léaud sniffles while sitting with his girlfriend on a park bench in Paris. He fumbles in his pocket, then asks to borrow her handkerchief. All she can offer is a Kleenex, but the American innovation prompts a shudder of disdain. 'Oh no,' he replies, 'I never blow my nose onto paper.' The efficiency of the process and the disposability of the product are alike repugnant. In 1958 François Reichenbach told Jean-Luc Godard that he intended to make a documentary film about the daily life of an average American, who by operating at top speed could cook a meal, eat it and wash up in five minutes. 'In America,' Reichenbach said, 'that's what poetry is. They say exactly the opposite to us: "I am, therefore I think."' Were people across the ocean really wired in such an unCartesian way?

Looked at like this, Americans received little credit for their good humour, which ought to have vouched for their humane elasticity. Connolly attributed their cheerfulness to an overdose of vitamins and calories, just as Babbitt in Sinclair Lewis's novel praises 'the Real He-Man, the fellow with Zip and Bang' – qualities borrowed from the effervescent or ammoniac products on sale in pharmacies. The fortified bodies of Americans had no room, Connolly said, for 'art, remorse and introspection', those apparently unexportable European staples, and when he reached California he opined that its climate created 'giants not genius' and remembered that a wit once said that Americans had no faces.

The French continued to complain about the conveniences of American life, which replaced the servant class with gadgets. As late as 1972 in *The Outside Man*, Jean-Louis Trintignant plays a hit man far from home who wanders through the Greyhound Bus terminal in Los Angeles suspiciously inspecting its mod cons: a machine to change dollar bills, another to take your photograph, a coin-operated shaver in the toilet (which the stubbly Trintignant uses), and television sets, also with slots for coins, welded to plastic bucket seats in the waiting room. Is he visiting a space station? As the director Jacques Deray sees it, this is a city not of angels but of automata or animated cadavers. At a roller derby, Angelenos with wheels on their feet whirl in circles at high speed, battering each other like cars in a freeway pile-up. In a go-go bar, naked women listlessly jive, their flesh greased and glistening like gunmetal. At a funeral home, a murdered mobster stiffened by embalming sits bolt upright in an armchair, a cigar protruding from his rigid mouth, his cracked skin turning purple in the tinted light of the viewing chapel. Trintignant, stumbling towards his own death, is already experiencing a morbid American sequel to human life.

Contradicting the ingrates, a single European extolled America's benevolence. The Catholic philosopher Jacques Maritain lectured throughout America in the years after 1933, took refuge there when the Nazis invaded France, and in 1948, following three years as the French ambassador to the Vatican, moved to Princeton; he is currently a candidate for sainthood, and his view of America was positively beatific. He disposed of aphorisms like Connolly's comment about dumb, big-bodied Californians by reflecting that Europeans overrated intelligence. In France a good person was, by implication, a simpleton, but Americans esteemed 'good will, devotion, help-fulness' rather than competitive mental skills. Maritain sympathized with the question asked by *Fortune*: Americans, he said, 'need to be loved', but that need was for him innately Christian, 'the mark of a soul which lies open to the sense of brotherhood'. He loved to watch Americans as they unmilita-ristically marched or even gambolled in 'big processions with resounding bands and girls in fancy dress' – pageants, like the Macy's Thanksgiving Day Parade, whose purpose was not to display power but to diffuse joy. Evidence for Maritain's encomium about American virtue can be found in the travel notes made by Moosbrugger and Weigner, who acknowledged Maritain as their 'honoured adviser'. They were startled to discover that the report cards issued by high schools gave grades for behaviour as well as for learning, and quoted one which commended a student who 'behaves in a friendly way and is ready to help others'.

Sociologists in the 1950s complained about the tyranny of adjustment in a society where individuals were, as David Riesman put it in *The Lonely Crowd*, increasingly 'other-directed'. Maritain stood out against this fashionable pessimism, found 'a strain of Gospel love' in the amiability of Americans, and thought that their dazzling smiles were almost 'evangelical'. De Beauvoir, by contrast, diagnosed lockjaw, while Connolly was relieved to relax at a dinner in W. H. Auden's messy New York apartment, where the guests reas-suringly displayed 'European teeth', as carious as their decadent continent. During Maritain's time in the midwest, a dentist attempted to Americanize his teeth, assisted by soothing nurses who, once he had a whiff of chlo-roform, seemed to be angels with rustling wings, ready to transport him instantly to heaven. For a Catholic, inured to suffering as a divinely ordained trial, this was a little too much. Did we deserve to be clinically perfected? Wasn't the body supposed to rot? Maritain cancelled future dental visits in order, he said, 'to protect within my mind the Christian idea of death'.

Connolly shuddered in the 'ferrous-concrete' crevasses of New York, and scowled at Rockefeller Center, 'the sinister Stonehenge of economic man'. Maritain did not feel oppressed by Rockefeller Center because he knew it to be impermanent. It was built, he pointed out, on land leased for ninety-nine

years: Americans were pilgrims bound for a celestial city, so even towering Manhattan was a temporary resting place. Europeans have always been
amused and alarmed by the wooden houses of Americans, since anything
not made of stone, like the tombs of the Pharaohs, surely cannot be relied on
to last. For Maritain this did not matter; he was reminded of St Paul's remark
about the faithful, who are detached from earthly things as if 'dwelling in
tents'. Photographs in Moosbrugger and Weigner's book – an encampment
of trailers, or a clapboard house mounted on a truck ready for relocation by
rail – illustrate the point, showing how the spirit continues its trek across the
desert, pitching and dismantling shelters as it travels on towards eternity.

In 1947, when Connolly devoted an issue of his magazine *Horizon* to
the phenomenon of America, he included an essay in which Christopher
Isherwood recalled his first cross-country trip from New York to Los Angeles
in the summer of 1939. After passing through saline wastes and flimsy towns
that consisted entirely of advertising billboards, Isherwood's arrival was a
bracing disillusionment. 'California,' he immediately decided, 'is a tragic
country – like Palestine, like every promised land.' A detour to the Mojave
Desert, so averse to life, supplied him with his own mystical insight, which
was hardly consistent with Maritain's belief that America was 'the Fortunate
Isles, the land of promise here below'. 'Accept it,' Isherwood told himself as
he contemplated the furnace of sand, 'and you will be happy.' This, however,
was not the kind of happiness that Americans were pursuing.

During the 1930s Europeans had been torn between communism and
fascism; now another binary choice was presented to them. At the end of the
war Albert Camus asked André Malraux whether it would be necessary to
choose between Russia and America. Malraux evasively replied that he chose
France, even though the either/or quandary did not give him that option.

The British had been thoroughly Americanized by the million troops stationed up and down the country before the Normandy landings, and now,
more or less gracefully, they accepted their relegation to a supporting role
in world affairs. Auden, having become an American citizen, enforced the
point with unnecessary crudity when he returned to London after the war

as a Bombing Research Analyst in the Morale Division of the United States Army. He informed his old friend John Lehmann that Britain was lucky to have survived and – now that the world belonged to 'two giants, the USA and the USSR' – it would have to get by without the subservience of its dominions; Lehmann nicknamed him Uncle Sam Auden.

For the French, America's eminence was a more sudden affront. They feared and therefore disliked the country on principle, even if they nurtured a weakness for certain of its delicacies. Camus, arriving in New York with a fluey fever in 1946, was disgusted by the garish neckties, the screeching jukeboxes, and the electric orgy of Times Square; nevertheless he lapped up American ice cream. The British could regard Americans as relatives, perhaps secretly envying them for having rejected the oppression of the family home in 1776, but Jean Renoir, who sailed to New York after France fell to the Nazis, saw Americans as outcasts not long-lost cousins. He called them 'European malcontents', and thought that their restless idealism kept them from feeling at home in the new country to which they had fled, though he preferred this grumbling disaffection to the 'national – that is to say, vertical outlook' that emerged in subsequent decades whenever the United States swaggered off to war. To Renoir, everything in America seemed groundless, flimsy and contingent. The avenues in New York were wind tunnels, conduits for tornadoes of grit and shredded paper, and the homes on suburban streets in Los Angeles looked like bathing huts. Sartre too abhorred the boxy shape of American houses, and their flat, unambitious roofs made him absurdly nostalgic for mansards. In 1944 he inspected a prefabricated pinewood village near one of the Tennessee Valley Authority's dams. Inside, the dwellings looked like ship's cabins; outdoors, the litter of inhabited crates reminded him of a 'caravan scrap yard'. The migratory place, he reported, was 'weightless': oddly enough, he did not recognize that this style of domestic architecture suited the lightness of our existential being.

Renoir watched in astonishment as facsimiles of French chateaux or Spanish haciendas were sawn into segments and driven off to a new site. Like matchboxes, these mansions were reputed to shiver in earthquakes, absorbing stress rather than being dismembered by it, but, unlike Maritain, he did not fancy living in a symbolic tent pitched in the desert or above a seismic fault. He found the same preparedness for rupture in human relationships. In Hollywood, his Brazilian companion Dido Freire was befriended by Paulette Goddard, who acted as her 'sponsor in the American way of life'. Goddard, then living with Charlie Chaplin, was scandalized to discover that her pupil had no expensive baubles: jewels, she advised, were essential for making a quick getaway when the relationship ended. Yet despite this hard-bitten, almost nihilistic wisdom, America's founding myth made it the homeland of happy endings. The MGM studio was next to a funeral parlour, which had a continuous traffic of mourners; the exasperated studio spent huge sums attempting to dislodge the business, as the presence of death blighted its blithe fantasies. In 1946 André Maurois overheard an inimitably American exchange at his local cinema in New York. An elderly lady wanted to be assured in advance that the week's offering contained no atrocities or crimes. The ticket seller gave her a guarantee: 'Nothing sad can happen. They're all dead right from the beginning.' The film was *Between Two Worlds*, about a shipload of migrants to the United States who turn out to be ghosts, killed in the London Blitz while awaiting their immigration permits. Adrift in the hereafter, the characters could presumably look forward to a resurrection when they reached New York.

Before Renoir could begin to work in Hollywood, he had, as he put it, to make peace with the redskins, meaning the studio moguls. They sent him to make his first American film in the Okefenokee Swamp that straddles Florida and Georgia, the lair of crocodiles, rattlesnakes, giant tortoises, brown bears and (reportedly) black panthers. In Renoir's *Swamp Water*, released in 1941, Okefenokee is an oblivion where fugitives from the law can hide, even though, as the old-timer played by Walter Brennan puts it, 'there's not a solid bit of ground to stand on', and a bog gobbles up an absconding murderer. The film begins with an image of a skull on a stick poking out of the marsh to warn the unwary: the entrance to America? Things are not much more secure in Renoir's later American films. In *The Southerner*, made in 1945, a Texas farmer moves his family to a tumbledown shed in a quagmire. A flood washes away his cotton crop; he has to shoot possums for food, and grabs catfish out of a stream with his bare hands because he has no hook. In a land of supposed abundance, this is a more precarious existence than that of any European peasant. Even on Long Island, where the 1947 film *The Woman on the Beach* is set, civilization is reduced to water-borne detritus. Robert Ryan is a naval lieutenant whose ship was torpedoed offshore by the Germans. Joan Bennett and her husband share a shingled cabin on the dunes; she uses the hulk of a wrecked boat as the equivalent of a motel room and arranges trysts with Ryan there, warming it with a fire made from the splintered rudder. In this littoral America, people are flotsam, like the washed-up relics among which they live. Renoir, however, eventually settled in Benedict Canyon in Los Angeles, on a property where he planted an olive grove: he made California tolerable by dressing it as Provence.

The French esteem what they call 'l'oeil américain' or 'les yeux américains', a survival skill possessed by the hawk-eyed characters of Fenimore Cooper's frontier romances. But increasingly the French decided that American eyes were glassy and insentient, focused on a distance that was empty. Sartre described New York as a city for sufferers from presbyopia, or long-sightedness, because its straight lines, speedily bound for a vanishing point like the endless avenues, left you unable to focus on the blurry human foreground. Georges Simenon – who escaped to Quebec after the war, having been accused of collaboration with the Germans, and lived in Florida, Arizona and Connecticut until 1955 – made a similar point in his 1965 novel *Three Rooms in Manhattan*. For Simenon's disconsolate wanderers, the streetlamps are 'luminous globes . . . angling off into infinity', like a remote constellation that does not support human life. Sartre pined for the rondure of European cities, constructed in circles that expand like rings in tree bark or like Parisian arrondissements from a central, ancient fortress. Medieval walls and arched gateways established limits and offered protection from the vacuity of open space; in America, by contrast, voids yawned in the urban fabric, even though they were usually only parking lots. Los Angeles reminded Sartre of an immense earthworm that reproduced itself scissiparously, so that you could chop it into twenty sections – the 'juxtaposed cities' of the conurbation – without, alas, killing it. Bunker Hill in downtown Los Angeles, a pile of rickety lodging houses perched above a tiled, asphalted tunnel for cars, combined mouldy putrescence with cool, immaculate engineering in a way that was inimitably American.

On a smaller scale, fittings and furniture alienated people from each other, or ejected them into chilly outer space. De Beauvoir's sleeping berth on the train from Chicago to Los Angeles ensured 'absolute solitude' in a corridor where passengers were stacked in curtained coffins as if in a catacomb. Crossing plains and deserts, she felt 'no longer bound to the earth . . . no longer anywhere in the universe'. She considered herself equally rootless whenever she ate in a diner, where swivel stools at the counter ruled out the gregariousness of the Paris café by making you stare ahead rather than sideways at the people next to you. In the 1950s Françoise Sagan despaired of finding a New York restaurant where she could have lunch in the light of day, rather than under the glare of too many tingling bulbs: Americans overdosed on electricity, which left them, according to Sagan's diagnosis, with sore eyes, frayed nerves, and hearts inclined to cardiac arrest.

Despite the dictatorship of machines, nature punished the humans who had strayed into this scorching or freezing continent. The summer heat in New York seemed 'atomic' to Sartre, as if the bomb had already exploded; then in winter the same curdling, molten streets were lakes of icy slush. In New Orleans, de Beauvoir witnessed a rainstorm that she called apocalyptic. The heavens roared with rage, and when the sun came out again it seared the city with 'the light at the end of the world'. No wonder Americans were so anxious to temper or filter out the stresses of nature. The potatoes and apples on French market stalls were individuals, warts and all, but the fruit and vegetables de Beauvoir saw in Ojai, California, had a 'false lustre', having been protected behind glass from weathering by sun and rain. Yet deep down, these pampered people had grisly regressive tastes. In Harlem, de Beauvoir ate pork cutlets grilled on a spit at what she called a 'Barbe-Q' restaurant; she explained that such crude fare was 'thought amusing in a land of electric cookers'.

Despite American pragmatism, de Beauvoir was puzzled, as she travelled around the country, to find that 'the word "Abstraction" is always on my lips'. The rhythms of jazz were formalistic, like words turned into meaningless babble by a scat singer, and even money was somehow notional, valued only as a token of success, not for the comforts it could purchase. She turned to Hegel for an explanation, and theorized that in America the subject's merger with the non-human, mechanical object led to 'the triumph of understanding over the spirit' and hence to 'the triumph of abstraction'. In a scalding review of de Beauvoir's chronicle of *America Day by Day*, published in 1948, Mary McCarthy supplied a better reason: America itself was an abstraction, an experiment in spreading wealth that inevitably erased differences and distinctions, the inequalities that democracy wished to level. McCarthy had recently been called upon to entertain a visiting existentialist – she implies in her review that it was de Beauvoir – who asked to be taken somewhere typically American. McCarthy realized that her options were a chop suey joint, a pizza parlour or an Irish pub. But what could be more American than these recreations of a remote, remembered prototype? And their second-hand nature demonstrated that America was based on ideas about liberty and equality, not on inherited customs or a compulsory architectural style or a common diet. If the country looked raw or bare to de Beauvoir, that was because its people were still nomads struggling against an arduous terrain. McCarthy praised the plucky virtues of those settlers – not the same thing as the hard-boiled machismo of the dime-store detective novels which highbrow subscribers to the 'Série noire' enjoyed. 'Life for the European is a career,' McCarthy said; 'for the American it is a hazard.' Twisting the dialectic, this made Americans the true exemplars of an existentialism that the French merely talked about. Sartre inadvertently proved McCarthy's point during a scenic flight at the Grand Canyon. He quailed as the little plane lunged into air pockets and came close to scraping the canyon's walls during its descent: he seemingly lacked the stomach or the nerves to look into the abyss.

Jean Cocteau's reactions to New York were less solemn than those of Sartre and de Beauvoir. During his visit he posed for a series of photographic portraits by Philippe Halsmann in which he exemplified play and anarchy – creative forces repressed, in his estimation, by workmanlike America. He wore his jacket back to front as doves perched on his bare feet, sat inside an ornate picture frame, and hung suspended in the air, defying gravity. Outdoors, he whimsically altered the angular, inorganic city, likening the skyscrapers to giraffes with multiple eyes. He also found evidence of a more atavistic life behind the steel facades: he was impressed by the sweaty musculature and mumbling primitivism of Marlon Brando in *A Streetcar Named Desire*, and by the trumpet of Louis Armstrong which, he said, ventilated the anguish of an entire race. He had his own joking version of the anticipated American apocalypse, and suggested that the detonation of the atomic bomb would probably sound like an outburst of heedless laughter. Although he called on America to rescue mankind, Cocteau remained a European decadent, not especially eager to be saved. He once told the director Jean-Pierre Melville that America was the country of the Old Testament, France that of the New. He probably meant that Americans had a strict and starchy Protestant or Jewish morality, whereas the French could sin with impunity because Catholicism pardons our frailties and even allows us, if a fee is paid, to indulge them. Cocteau was pleased to see that Americans were acquiring the vices they lacked, though after skimming the Kinsey Report he suspected the volunteers of fantasizing about the enterprising, athletic sexual acts they claimed to have performed. Back in Europe, his reaction to Americanization was less frivolous. In Germany in 1952 he commented in his diary on the social upheavals caused by an industrial recovery that was happening 'too rapidly': the French phrase is 'à l'américaine', which was not a compliment.

At least Cocteau and the others set foot in the country before passing judgement on it. The poet and musician Boris Vian did not think that necessary, and wrote several novels – pastiches of thrillers published in the 'Série noire', though lewder and nastier than anything by James M. Cain – about an entirely imaginary or delusional America. The first, *I Spit On Your Graves*, appeared in 1946. It is an ugly fable about racism, supposedly written by an African American called Jack Sullivan who brings to Paris a scandalous manuscript that no New York publisher will touch. Renaissance Europe dreamed of a new western continent, and sailed off to discover it;

now the dream or nightmare, embodied by black GIs, had returned to its place of origins, 'perhaps' – as James Baldwin put it – 'to drive Europe mad'. The bizarre plot of *I Spit On Your Graves* exploits these delicious terrors. The novel begins in the Deep South, where the brother of Vian's narrator is lynched by the family of a white girl he has seduced; the narrator flees, and settles in a northern town where he works in a bookstore located on Pearl Harbor Street. (The downbeat address seems unlikely, but there is such a street in Bridgeport, Connecticut.) Passing as white, he plans a salacious revenge for his brother's murder. He deflowers two teenage socialites, then horrifies them by revealing that he is black, after which he murders them. A mob strings him up, but his body has the last laugh: his protruding penis enjoys a post-mortem orgasm. Vian also wrote slangy music criticism, some-times using the pseudonym Andy Blackchic, in which he praised jazz for prosecuting a racial war. In an article published in the magazine *Combat* in 1948, he asked whether white jazz musicians like Benny Goodman and Artie Shaw should be bayoneted as punishment for their anaemic feebleness. Deciding against it, he hoped they would drop dead of their own volition.

Harold Flender's novel *Paris Blues*, published in 1957, is titillated by the permissiveness of Europe but at the same time wary. A black saxophon-ist has fled from 'the cultural desert of America' and its racial injustice to play in a Left Bank 'club privé'. The Parisians sympathize with his need to break free. At a party, an effete bohemian with Shirley Temple ringlets shrills that America rates zero in the 'two most important areas of life', which are 'food and fornication'. The assertion goes unchallenged: human life is indeed sustained by food and continued by fornication, and at the time the French were better cooks, but what grounds did they have for thinking they were better lovers? Americans, however, wanted to believe it, since out-sourcing sex and identifying it with French naughtiness preserved the purity of their own culture. Another expatriate, a trombone player, takes a maid-enly teacher visiting from back home on a deranging journey through the Parisian night. After a transvestite show in Pigalle, they make a detour to the Jardin de Luxembourg, passing a mysterious 'small cylindrical structure'. It is, the jazzman tells the disgusted schoolmarm, an open-air pissoir. Worst of all, they dine at a restaurant decorated with obscene coital murals, where the bread rolls are phallic in shape and the food is served in chamber pots – an establishment that surely existed only in the quaking American imagination.

Culture's most basic ingredients are what we eat and drink, and the French obdurately refused to acquire American tastes. When the composer Virgil Thomson returned to Paris from New York in 1945, his cook warned him against offering crackers smeared with peanut butter to guests at parties, as such nibbles were not for grown-ups. Luckily Thomson did not attempt to introduce the American delicacies indigestibly dreamed up by Vian in *I Spit On Your Graves*, in which a bar and grill reeks of 'doughnuts fried in onions' and teenagers rip open a can of chicken and utter Indian war whoops as they gorge on it, spotting their clothes with mayonnaise and rivulets of gravy. The French reserved their most solemn anathemas for soda pop. The political scientist Raymond Aron protested that Coca-Cola was ousting 'the noblest product of the human soil (I mean, of course, wine)', and the actor Louis Jouvet regretted that palates accustomed to Burgundy and Bordeaux would now have to adjust to Coke, which 'for a Frenchman . . . amounts to renouncing his citizenship'. Back in New York, Billy Rose avenged the insult to the national elixir by refusing for a while to serve champagne in his nightclub. In 1970 Henri Cartier-Bresson's television documentary *California Impressions* paused to study a sign saying 'Don't Eat Grapes', set up by Mexican workers who were concerned about pesticides; the logical consequence is that we see iced water not wine being drunk at a Thanksgiving dinner. On the soundtrack of Cartier-Bresson's film, a radio commercial for frankfurters recommends a way of outwitting Eurocentric snobs: if your family thinks that food is only tasty when it has an unpronounceable French name, the announcer suggests telling them the franks you're serving have been slathered with '"sauce américaine" – that's mustard, pickles and relish'.

Nothing amused the French more than the fondness of Americans for milk, which was evidence of their enduring childishness. In the 1961 film of *Paris Blues*, Sidney Poitier as the saxophonist orders milk in a jazz cavern where more sophisticated customers are buying sachets of cocaine. A xenophobic essay by Roland Barthes contrasted milk and wine, the opposed libations of puritanical propriety and sensuous pleasure. 'Milk,' he contended, 'remains an exotic substance; it is wine which is part of the [French] nation.' Exotic? – it sounds as if the French are not nursed in the same way as other mammals. Barthes claimed to have seen 'some American films', not named, in which cowboys swigged a glass of fortifying, calcifying milk before they reached for their guns, and he reported that Parisian gangsters, imitating American tough guys, had been seen slurping down a mixture of milk and pomegranate juice. He blamed milk for propagating a 'Parsifalian myth' about innocence: Parsifal, the redeeming hero of Wagner's last opera, is a holy fool, which makes him – in Barthes' assessment – an honorary American. The world had been won, apparently, by a race of overgrown but unweaned babies.

The Germans could not afford to be so supercilious, and in 1945 their wrecked country had to accept the moral authority of the victors. Occasionally they gulled the would-be reformers. Winifred Wagner – who managed the Bayreuth Festival after her husband Siegfried, the composer's son, died in 1930 – was infatuated by Hitler, welcomed him to her theatre each summer, and encouraged her children to address him as Uncle Wolf. A tribunal denazified her, but she continued to refer to Hitler, when in like-minded company, as 'unser seliger Adolf' – our blessed Adolf. Because post-war etiquette made him unmentionable, she shortened the phrase to USA. Every year she held a party to commemorate her lost leader's birthday, and sent out invitations inscribed with those coded initials, taking the name of Europe's saviour in vain. There is no point in pretending to regret the past if you are waiting for history to repeat itself, as in Europe it always does. Only in America can you start again, with your sins remitted as you move to a new and untainted frontier.

From one point of view, the continents had reversed their traditional roles, with elderly Europe reduced to helpless infancy: its history suspended, Germany had to relearn everything from its American tutors. Looked at differently, the relationship was not parental but treacherously erotic. The ancient continent with its wiles and charms resumed its role of tempter or

– since the innocents were always uniformed males – seasoned temptress. Americans wanted to be loved for themselves or for their ideals, not for the snacks and sweets in their pockets. In Samuel Fuller's film *Verboten!* an employee of the military government makes the mistake of marrying a German woman, for whom he is merely a 'chocolate Romeo'; their 'candy-bar romance' is her 'passport to food'. The hard-headed Fuller knew that sex and hunger were rudimentary urges that might be interchangeable. He also understood that donations to the needy could be made scornfully, continuing the war by other means. In *Verboten!* a GI nicknamed Meathead is confronted by a boy who remains loyal to the Nazis. As if hurling a grenade, the soldier tosses a Hershey's bar at him and says 'Chew yourself to death.'

Was Europe a seductive woman preparing to snare another victim, or a child needing to be adopted? On America's behalf, Montgomery Clift – twitchy and insecure, hardly a big brother and certainly not a father figure – tried out the custodial role in 1948 in Fred Zinnemann's *The Search*. A boxcar of ownerless, unidentified refugee children arrive in the rubble of Nuremberg. Aline MacMahon, as a United Nations relief worker, does her best to mother them, but they look like confused, fragile elders, not resilient beginners in life: the war has aged them with catastrophic speed, or sent them back to prehistory. Some, stuffing their mouths with their hands, have forgotten how to use a spoon and are no better than cave dwellers. They panic when crammed into an ambulance bound for a resettlement camp, although MacMahon instructs the translators to tell them they are being 'taken to some place where they'll be very happy' – Elysium, or America? A few break free and disperse into the pulverized city. Clift, a military engineer who specializes in building bridges, is lounging by his jeep when a runaway Czech boy called Malik creeps up, feral and mistrustful. Clift lures him with the bait of a half-eaten sandwich and then, astonishingly, takes him back to his lodgings. 'He may be a little wild now, but he'll tame down,' he assures a colleague: America's paradoxical task is to civilize Europe. The traumatized boy, who will not speak, is taught a language that will make him at home everywhere. 'Everybody knows what OK means,' says Clift. 'Even in England they understand English – well, sorta.'

A course in civics and popular culture follows, soon to be compulsory for everyone in an Americanized world. Clift shows this captive of totalitarianism what freedom means: he lets Malik run off, then waits for him to return voluntarily. The techniques used are those you would employ when housetraining a puppy or getting it to acknowledge who is master. Chocolate is doled out only if the boy will accept it by saying 'Yes'. The first milestone is reached when he identifies a photograph of a deer as 'Bambi'. Having been introduced to Walt Disney, who was to become synonymous with American childhood, he graduates to recognizing a portrait of Lincoln. Then, shown a panorama of New York, he says 'United States of America', his most complex utterance so far. As a reward he receives a baseball bat. Clift plans to take little Malik home to the United States, like a souvenir. Other GIs have their brides, and he sees no reason why he should not return with a ward. His friend warns about bureaucratic obstacles – 'We'd have all of Europe in America if we didn't have these rules' – and luckily the boy's mother turns up to reclaim him, which spares Clift the responsibility of parenthood and saves America from having to take in an entire generation of European waifs.

Reconciling the continents is more problematic in *The Big Lift*, an account of the 200,000 flights that ferried food and fuel into Berlin during the Russian blockade in 1948–49; the film was made on location soon after the ground routes reopened. Clift is again on duty, urgently reassigned from Hawaii – where he and his buddy Paul Douglas are happily watching a newsreel in which Miss America contestants frolic in the ocean at Atlantic City – to take part in the relay along a narrow aerial corridor into Tempelhof. This ought to have been the kind of angelic embassy that Henry Luce envisaged, and in July 1949 *Life* published a photograph by Walter Sanders in which the scene does look biblical: like the children of Israel in the desert, Berliners stand on a mound of crumbling bricks at the edge of the airfield, looking up as a plane miraculously descends from a frowning sky with a consignment of bread and coal as the heaven-sent manna of a new divinity. But the sacred fable warps when you get closer, which is why the pilots are advised not to leave the airport between flights. In a city that consists of unsteady, unsupported facades, with a few heroic statues still posturing among the butchered trees on the Siegesallee, these gruff but callow Americans will surely come to grief – as Douglas does after recognizing a prison guard who mistreated him when he was a captive of the Nazis. He tracks the man down and beats him without mercy, thus squandering his moral superiority. His errors are sorted out by a feisty German waitress, who studies the American constitution and the Bill of Rights and then accuses Douglas of betraying his country by bossing her about as if he were a stormtrooper. He congratulates her on her rebellion, improbably glad to be henpecked and harangued about his own political creed: 'That's democracy, now you got it!' Remorseful about his attack on the guard, he realizes that his mission is to exemplify a new and unauthoritarian way of living, which means that he needs to act towards the Germans like a good salesman, ingratiating not abrasive.

The woman Douglas dates comically castigates him; Clift's woman, a war widow with the ingrained cynicism of her continent, deceives him. She accepts his marriage proposal because that will get her to the United States, where a German lover awaits her. When the fraud is exposed, she looks around for another victim: those who live off charity soon lose any sense of shame. Her re-education of the tremulous, trusting Clift is crueller than the waitress's dispute with Douglas. During an expedition into the Russian zone, she dresses Clift in shabby clothes borrowed from a spy and tells the nosy police that he cannot talk because of a war wound. Disempowered, he is no better off than the catatonic child in *The Search*.

Billy Wilder left Berlin after the 1933 German election; he immediately found work in Hollywood and became a naturalized citizen in 1934, but he retained his sour European estimate of human nature and refused to believe that human beings underwent a rebirth when they reached the United States. In *Hold Back the Dawn*, released in 1941, he surveyed the plight of refugees from the Nazis who wait in Mexico to be allowed across the border into California. Some are deserving, others not. A Dutch professor feeds his family an Independence Day repast of donuts and Boston baked beans and recites a grace giving thanks to the land that they hope is about to receive them, not to the food they are about to receive. Meanwhile a Romanian gigolo jumps the long, slow queue by duping a mousy American schoolteacher into marriage.

The immigration officials who wave him through are hardly worthy of the country to which they control access: one of them, interviewing applicants about America's sacred texts, thinks that 'life, liberty and the pursuit of happiness' is the slogan inscribed on the Statue of Liberty. And how desirable is the world on the other side? A gang of boys who have travelled south from the town of Azusa – presumably representative, because its name boasts of containing everything from A to Z in the USA – reserve all their mischief-making for Independence Day and behave in Mexico like cowboys running riot. Late in life, Wilder remarked that whereas the French close ranks suspiciously when foreigners apply for citizenship, Americans tend to resent it if you do not want to be one of them: 'Aren't we good enough?' they implicitly ask. In *Hold Back the Dawn* that question receives an unwelcome answer.

Wilder returned to Germany in 1945 to work on *Death Mills*, a documentary about the concentration camps produced by the Psychological Warfare Department, to be shown to a civilian population that professed ignorance of Nazi atrocities. It begins with the prisoners behind barbed wire raising banners to welcome their American liberators, and ends with the entire population of Weimar marched out to witness the piles of putrid corpses at nearby Buchenwald. With its compilation of horrors – internees with gouged-out eyes or pustular wounds, discarded bodies of newborn babies, the tottering skeletons of those who survived – *Death Mills* was both punishment and aversion therapy. By 1948, when Wilder set *A Foreign Affair* in post-war Berlin, this lacerating indictment had lost its force. The Germans in the film are incorrigible, but the American victors are not much better. *A Foreign Affair* begins by joking about the defeat of the Third Reich: its first scene parodies the prelude to Leni Riefenstahl's *Triumph of the Will*, in which Hitler's plane slices through clouds as it descends towards Nuremberg before a party rally, bringing the Führer down from the sky as a saviour. Now the shadow of an American plane that carries a Congressional deputation skims along the ground through the remains of the Reich's millennial capital: a tundra of brick dust, interrupted by the stumps of trees chopped down for firewood. But despite the American victory, these delevitating politicians are no supermen. The airsick delegate from New Hampshire staggers off to vomit when his colleague from Texas says that the ruins remind him of a Roquefort cheese gnawed by rats, or 'chicken innards at frying time'. The cattleman thinks rebuilding the city a waste of time, and suggests sowing grass and moving in a herd of longhorns.

The politicians have come to report on conditions in the occupied city, though even before landing they agree that there is no point in being generous, because their motives will be misinterpreted. As one of them says, to give a loaf of bread to the starving is humanitarian, 'but if you leave the wrapper on, that's imperialism'. Wilder's sardonic scene is mild when set against the truth about such junkets. Margaret Bourke-White, photographing for *Life* in 1946, talked to a driver who had ferried two visiting Congressmen around Berlin. On arrival at Tempelhof, they asked to be taken directly to the black market, where one sold a pinstripe suit for $500, the other a pair of herringbone tweed trousers for $600. Only then did they proceed to their billets. A less censorious driver reasoned that the resale of cigarettes and candy compensated GIs 'for what they went through in the war'. So were they fighting not for freedom but for the right to profiteer? Bourke-White regretted that her countrymen had such limited comprehension 'of a world now shrunken to our doorstep'; she concluded that they were exporting capitalism but not establishing democracy, which – because it 'lives in its citizens, in the way they live with their fellow men' – is hard to transplant.

The military officials in *A Foreign Affair* are bewildered by their new commission: during the war they were expected to be destructive, now they are asked to be moderate and just. They have no idea how to deal with the recusant Germans. The officer played by John Lund has to discipline a boy who chalks swastikas everywhere – including on a desk in the Denazification Office – and a father who threatens the lad with Gestapo-like tortures; all he can do is prescribe membership in a youth club that will teach the young fanatic to play baseball. Whereas the Nazis planned wholesale slaughter, the exasperated Americans hope that the Germans might quietly do away with themselves. Briefing the politicians, one of Lund's colleagues says with evident satisfaction that on the day the US Army got the gasworks running again, there were 160 suicides in Berlin alone.

Lund conducts his foreign affair with a blonde witch played by Marlene Dietrich. Until recently the mistress of Goebbels, Dietrich's character says 'I have a new Führer now. Heil Johnny.' She claims to be apolitical and considers ideology to be a fashion, airily changeable like a spring hat that was decorated with a swastika last year and now sports ostrich feathers coloured red, white and blue. She sings at a nightclub called the Lorelei, though unlike the fatal mermaid she does not kill men but uses them to supply her with contraband goods. When Lund drags a second-hand mattress to her flat, she orders a pillow to go with it plus a consignment of soap and hairpins. Armour-plated in glamour, her face a mask of contempt, Dietrich descends in a slinky nightgown to the rubble-strewn street to confront a prudish Republican Congresswoman from Iowa, played by the squeaky-voiced Jean Arthur. 'You are an American woman?' she asks. In an aside that disparages both puritanism and domesticity, she likens Arthur's unpainted face to 'a scrubbed kitchen floor'. James Agee warned that Europeans would judge America, and Dietrich does so, not morally but aesthetically, by mocking Jean Arthur. She is herself judged at the end of the film when she is summarily sent to a labour camp, though it is hard to believe that she has been chastened. Wilder is still European enough to admire her effrontery, and to laugh at the priggishness of the Americans who condemn her.

In Germany, the right of judgement possessed by the occupying army was invested in military courts; Stanley Kramer and his writer Abby Mann treated this legal reckoning in *Judgement at Nuremberg*, which in 1961 looked back at the trials of war criminals held during the Berlin blockade. The sessions of the Nuremberg court begin with an aide declaring 'God bless the United States and this honourable tribunal.' But the defender of the accused Nazi jurists questions God's partiality for America, and claims that the country squandered whatever divine favour it once enjoyed when it bombed Hiroshima and Nagasaki. Enraged by this assault on national honour, one of the prosecutors, played by Richard Widmark, seeks vengeance not justice, and when drunk he complains – coinciding with Sartre's point in *Les Temps modernes* – that Americans have a national inferiority complex which makes them too forgiving. Because judges in Nuremberg were not required to consult a jury, the persona of the presiding official in the film had to vouch for the integrity of the process by exhibiting American humility and charitable goodwill. Hence the choice of Spencer Tracy to play Judge Haywood, a provincial from Maine who says he was jobbed in because no one better could be found. Tracy tells Marlene Dietrich – here cast as the sly, amoral widow of an executed Nazi general, wrapped in furs and stiffly permed – that he is lamed by his ignorance of Europe, which he has not visited since he served as a doughboy in the previous world war. Instinctively democratic, he offers to carry his own bags, prepares a sandwich for himself rather than giving orders to servants, and squeezes onto a crowded tram instead of using the car assigned to him, which comes with an embarrassingly servile driver. His very ordinariness, according to Kramer and Mann, is what authorizes this archetypal American to preside at a trial of crimes against humanity.

Reporting on Adolf Eichmann's prosecution in Jerusalem in 1961, Hannah Arendt said that the prisoner in the dock exhibited 'the banality of evil'; Tracy, grandfatherly and unintellectually taciturn, represents the banality of goodness, which gives credence to his punitive verdict at the end of the film, when he finds the accused lawyers guilty. But in a world that had been newly Americanized, right and wrong turn out to matter less than the projection of what advertisers had begun to call an 'image', a saleable veneer. The judge's decision dismays the court's military advisers, who argue for leniency because, with the Cold War underway in besieged Berlin, they need the support of German public opinion. America had given up expecting love, and forlornly hoped for popularity as a second best.

5 | Prosperity or Tragedy

Telling stories about Americans abroad, Henry James warned the wide-eyed innocents that they would probably have their pockets picked and their illusions dashed. Needing love, as Henry Wallace implied in his comment on the Marshall Plan, Americans were thin-skinned, easily hurt, and their wounds healed slowly. During the Korean War, the French journalist Jean Larteguy reported on the results of a study conducted in a Japanese hospital to which casualties were evacuated. Except for draftees from Puerto Rico, Americans took longer to recover than those of other nationalities. Larteguy attributed this to the over-sensitivity of the tough-talking GIs, who thought of their country as a nurturing mother and could not understand why it had not protected them from harm. Mediterranean men, Larteguy argued, were thicker-skinned, because they regarded the state as an enemy and knew how to look after themselves. The damage done to the Americans in Korea had been emotional not physical: the doctors were treating broken hearts.

After 1945, the nation braced for more distress. Russell Davenport in his *Fortune* essay described foreign policy in startlingly literary terms, calling it 'a tragic art'. The policy makers, he predicted, would have to grapple with the stark realities of the human condition, from which America had been spared by its isolation: the irrationality and ineradicability of conflict, the possibility that human beings might be innately bad or that laws might be unjust, the need to choose between greater and lesser evils – all the insoluble dilemmas that torment tragic characters from Antigone to Hamlet. The historian Crane Brinton hoped it was not too late for America to turn itself into a 'pessimistic democracy', although, since democracy relies on an optimistic assessment of human nature, that sounded like a contradiction in terms.

Pursuing happiness may be a sufficient aim in life for characters in comedy, but even politicians, accustomed to saying what the voters wanted to hear, recognized that this could no longer be America's only purpose. In August 1945, President Truman declared the United States to be 'the most powerful nation in the world – the most powerful nation, perhaps, in all history', then went on to recognize the cost of that power and its baleful consequences by admitting 'the tragic significance of the atomic bomb'. Adlai Stevenson, lecturing at Harvard in 1954, said that because 'we never came across a river we couldn't bridge, a depression we couldn't overcome, a war we couldn't win', the United States, unlike the knocked-about nations of Europe, had not been made wise by the experience of 'tragedy, frustration and defeat'. Henceforth the conduct of foreign policy would require 'a new attitude to the problems of life' – tragic stoicism or self-excoriation, not the glad-handing cheerfulness of comedy.

In Europe, a long tradition of commentary had derided Americans for being so irrepressibly happy. Spengler opined that American life 'evolves solely around its economy and lacks depth'; without having crossed the Atlantic, he presumed that the country was ignorant of 'true historical tragedy', of disasters like those that had 'educated the souls' of Europeans. That overlooked the Civil War, which thanks to Lincoln had surely educated the souls of Americans. And did Europe's latest tragedy, which began in 1933, further educate the continent's soul? Hitler planned for the ruin of the capital city he designed, and thought that, a thousand years hence, the monumental debris would vouch for his superhuman ambition; instead, after not much more than a decade, he had to commit suicide in a bunker as his capital was wrecked by the invaders. Still elated by the hubris of the Third Reich, some Europeans pitied the blunt-minded, better-fed victors, who would never experience this vertiginous plunge from exaltation to anguish. In 1948 the conductor Wilhelm Furtwängler, whose career stalled while he underwent denazification, pitied those who judged him. 'In America,' he wrote in his notebook, 'there is said to be no tragedy, but only prosperity and its opposite.' No self-respecting European, he implied, would want to be prosperous.

Sartre summarized the European prejudice in a neat, specious paradox: Americans, he said, are 'tragic for fear of being so'. Sartre made an exception for the New Yorkers who listened to jazz at Nick's Bar in Greenwich Village in 1947; the music jangled the nerves with the screech of a predatory bird, but he left the cavern in 'a kind of dejected calm', which is more or less what Aristotle meant by catharsis, the purgation that is the aftermath of tragedy. Roquentin in his novel *Nausea* derives the same strung-out elation from the melodious anguish of 'Some of these days/You'll miss me, honey'. Listening to the song on record, he guesses that the composer was a New York Jew, the singer a 'Negress', both belonging to races with a history of persecution (though he got this back to front: the composer was an African American, Shelton Brooks, and the performer was the Jewish Sophie Tucker). De Beauvoir agreed, and thought of jazz as 'the sole antidote to American conformity and boredom'.

The problem, as de Beauvoir repeated during her tour, was that Americans had no comprehension of evil. Hence, in her opinion, the fad of psychoanalysis, which unkinked the brain and dampened its static electricity. She travelled to the southern states in quest of 'squalor, weariness, hatred, cruelty and revolt' – not what tourists usually want to see. To her dismay, the bloodstains had been cleaned away before her arrival; even in Reno, with its quickie divorces, the misery of marital breakdown was balanced by resurgent hope as new couples paid for speeded-up ceremonies at the town's wedding chapels. De Beauvoir finally identified an atmosphere that was 'so tragic' in Chicago, to which she doubled back because of an affair with the novelist Nelson Algren, who took her on a pub crawl through the brawling downtown bars. She praised the city's sombre air – which had more to do with soot than with philosophical gloom – and imagined that the elevated trains in the Loop were groaning in pain as they clattered past above her head. She came closest to 'dark and murky deeds' at the Chicago stockyards. Her account of her travels ended here, as cowboys on horseback ushered their herds into what she called 'the concentration camp'. The stench of blood left her nauseated, afflicted by the philosophical malady of Sartre's Roquentin, who is sickened by the squashy, oozing infirmity of the physical world. There was a moral equivalence between the continents after all: de Beauvoir reacted as if she had located America's Auschwitz.

Accusations like this mattered so much that *Life* attempted a rebuttal in December 1948. Its editorial on 'Untragic America' is a rare case of literary theory attempting to boost national morale, or perhaps – since *Life*'s conclusion was that Americans needed to abandon their belief in unconditional freedom and inevitable progress – to puncture it. The essay began by dismissing the latest Eugene O'Neill play, *The Iceman Cometh*, as a 'cosmic bellyache', not a true tragedy; it then asked whether the drama's inadequacy betokened 'some deeper failure in the American character'. Democracy was in part to blame. It insisted on 'the dignity of the common man', the regular guy for whom Aaron Copland had written an orchestral fanfare in 1942; it failed to understand 'man's occasional greatness' and the littleness or meanness that went with it. Nor did the religion of progress recognize a higher power that might crush the industrious individual and smash his machinery.

Life did not identify that superior force, supposedly even more potent than mighty America. In the modern world it could not be a god angry at human infringements, as in Greek tragedy. Instead, catering to a culture of brisk self-help, the magazine immediately prescribed a remedy. In the interest of becoming 'a more civilized people', it told Americans that they must recover their 'awareness of evil, uncertainty and fear'. That sounded a little like a recommendation for an adult education course: could people somehow learn about evil while remaining at an unperturbed analytical distance? In fact, despite *Life*'s dissatisfaction, popular culture was already ministering to the dissatisfaction that tragedy was expected to address. In 1952 in *Partisan Review* Leslie Fiedler noticed that 'the most widely read fiction in America asks endlessly, "Whodunit? Where is the guilt?"' Contributing to the same issue of the magazine, Norman Mailer said that affluence was what made American happiness possible, but pointed out that it depended on military spending, which accounted for three-quarters of the national budget. All those smiling people in their plush homes relied on 'the production of the means of destruction', which perhaps explained the gnawing anxiety behind American contentment and conformity.

Life was calling for an experiment in self-destruction, a tragic 'humbling' of American conceit. This did not happen until the 1960s, when the agents of the humiliation were Vietnamese peasants; whether or not that lethal mess made Americans more civilized is an open question, but in 1963, early in a decade of assassinations, civil strife and military defeat, Mailer was able to refute Sartre's notion that Americans were existentially shallow. They did know about evil, Mailer said in his essay collection *The Presidential Papers*, along with 'the possible existence of Satan' – who might, as subsequent events suggest, be living in the suburbs or in a woodland cabin, waiting for the moment when he would strike down a man riding through a city in an open car, blow up an office building, or eliminate a few inoffensive nobodies at a school or in a movie theatre, just for the fun of it.

Happiness is surely not a reprehensible aim. Nevertheless, Americans now made conscientious efforts to be unhappy.

The hero of Lionel Trilling's novel *The Middle of the Journey*, published in 1947, cannot warm to the post-war creed of 'peace and brotherhood', which had its visible symbol in the United Nations. The very idea of the organization was American, and its name came from a phrase Roosevelt had used when referring to the alliance against Hitler. But Trilling's character prefers 'the world's imagination of strife', which 'allowed men their force and their selfhood as well as their evil', and he sees literature as the record of our conflicts, somehow more glorious than any reconciliation. In novels like Sloan Wilson's *The Man in the Gray Flannel Suit* and Richard Yates's *Revolutionary Road*, the average looking employees of Manhattan corporations conceal sordid secrets and are dismayed by the vacuity of their placid lives. The heroes of Arthur Miller's plays extricate themselves from the contented suburbs by committing nobly reckless gratuitous acts. Willy Loman in *Death of a Salesman* kills himself to ensure that his family has the benefit of his insurance policy, and Joe Keller in *All My Sons* does the same to make amends for the tainted source of his fortune. Unfortunately, the government did not understand that Miller's aim was to usher America into sober moral adulthood, and in 1954 the State Department refused him a passport because his case histories of failure and corruption maligned the country.

Trainees at the Actors' Studio, founded by Elia Kazan in 1947, had to take a vow of virtual martyrdom: in the school's oath of induction, Brando and the other aspiring tragedians swore 'I will admit rejection, admit pain,/ Admit frustration' and so on, volunteering to experience emotions inconsistent with the pursuit of happiness. Even painting became a stage for the enactment of a visceral drama, as the critic Harold Rosenberg implied when he urged contemporary artists to abandon small pictures, where the world could be neatly contained and organized, in favour of large canvases with space for the dialectical clash of opposites. Barnett Newman, Mark Rothko and Adolph Gottlieb wrote a letter to *The New York Times* in 1943 disparaging the regional folklore then popular in American art – Grant Wood's Gothic homesteaders, the eroded Dustbowl landscapes of Thomas Hart Benton – and arguing that the only valid subject matter was 'tragic and timeless', emotionally expressive despite its abstraction. In Newman's zip paintings, a vertical or horizontal line signalled an apocalyptic rupture or sketched a tightrope strung across a coloured chasm. These images, according to Newman, somehow prefigured 'the end of the capitalist system'; the painter shook his fist at fate as he made those self-dramatizing brushstrokes. In 1943 Rothko painted the omen of the eagles devouring a pregnant hare from *Agamemnon* by Aeschylus: the scene – invisible in the play, where it is merely described – was now a fable about the artist and his self-rending, self-tormenting creativity. When Rothko got to Europe after the war, he responded to the art of the past with a truly American originality, emphasizing chaos, carnage, gore. He thought the facade of Chartres Cathedral 'wild', and was astonished by the 'brutality' of Italian Renaissance painting with its scourgings, stigmata and tortuous martyrdoms. In the absence of tragedy, violence would do: in 1947 the critic Clement Greenberg commended Jackson Pollock for being 'American and rougher and more brutal' than French painters, who saw the world with such luminous hedonism.

James Baldwin said that living in France had demonstrated to him that life had limits, which went against American faith in an endlessly receding horizon of aspiration. In 1956 he imparted this tragic sense to the characters in his novel *Giovanni's Room*, about the affair between the expatriate David and a Paris barman. Giovanni the hapless European knows that David's compatriots don't believe in 'all the serious, dreadful things, like pain and death and love'. Another Frenchman regrets that the fate of the West has been entrusted to people who think 'the world is simple'. Clients at the American Express office near the Opéra look as if they had woken up that morning in Nebraska, and smell of the soap that is meant to keep them disinfected in wicked Europe. Such people have no capacity for love, which entails suffering: it is Giovanni – eventually guillotined after murdering his abusive employer – who offers himself to David as a sacrifice. Americans are the sadists, empowered by their insensitivity; Baldwin's version of the transatlantic psychodrama casts Europeans as the masochists, victimized by their emotional ardour. On the rebound, David retreats into conventionality by getting engaged to a woman from Minneapolis, who returns to the midwest when she finds him entwined with a clutch of randy sailors. 'Americans should never come to Europe, it means they can never be happy again,' she reflects. 'What's the good of an American who isn't happy? Happiness was all we had.'

Industrial society had made men rich, but its 'tragic consequence', according to the theologian Reinhold Niebuhr, was the psychological blight of isolation and alienation. Niebuhr criticized the quick fixes of America's therapeutic clinics for depriving life of its 'grandeur and misery', and preferred the 'note of tragedy' sounded by Karl Barth, who envisaged man walking 'on the narrow ledge at the side of the abyss of despair'. The metaphor soon became a recurrent American scenario, acted out by Private Roth in Mailer's *The Naked and the Dead*, who loses his nerve when required to leap over a four-foot wide gap on a ledge during the Philippines campaign and tumbles to his death, or by the insanely wilful heroine of Ayn Rand's *Atlas Shrugged*, who lives behind glass walls at the top of a skyscraper where she stands 'alone between sky and city'. The corporate conformist in *The Man in the Gray Flannel Suit* shudders as he recalls actual leaps of faith from a plane over Italy in wartime. At the window of his office high above Manhattan, he feels 'suspended motionless', as if 'his parachute had got stuck in midair': the building is an insecure perch on which he teeters. Auden virtually paraphrased Barth in *The Sea and the Mirror*, a meditation on *The Tempest*

written in New York during the war, when he imagined 'ourselves as we are
... swaying out on the ultimate wind-whipped cornice that overhangs the
unabiding void'. In 1949 George Tooker painted exactly that predicament
in *Cornice*. A figure with staring eyes hesitates on the few exiguous inches
of a ledge jutting from a cast-iron warehouse south of Canal Street in New
York. Everything in Tooker's painting is paralysed – the blue unfeeling sky,
the fuzzy but immobile clouds, the stiff, severe facade of the building – but
the hesitation of the insecurely balanced man can only be temporary. Will
he have the courage to jump?

The same question preoccupies much of New York in Henry Hathaway's
film *Fourteen Hours*, released in 1951. A man steps out of the window on
the fifteenth floor of a hotel near the Woolworth Building and stands on the
ledge, considering his position. Far above on the roof, a sculpted American
eagle grips a global ball with its claws: might it swoop down to catch him if
he decides to hurl himself into space? With wings spread, the bird is meant
to be a national emblem of protectiveness, though here it looks more like a
predator hovering before a kill. Spectators on the street below and helpers
or do-gooders in the room behind the man speculate about his motives, and
in doing so disclose their own. Two frumpy cleaners agree that he must be
taking part in an advertising stunt; a taxi driver sets up a betting pool and
invites guesses about when he will jump; a traffic cop says 'Maybe he was in
the army', as if all veterans had been damaged by their exposure to death;
a psychoanalyst suggests he is 'bigshotting it' and adduces the Oedipus
complex. The man on the ledge is the point where all these projections
cross, although none of them explains him. Perhaps because of his isolation, he sponsors a snuggling togetherness in others, who never want to find
themselves on that stark, windy precipice. Grace Kelly and her husband,
wrangling over the terms of their separation in a nearby lawyer's office,
decide after watching him to stay together; his divorced parents reunite
when they are summoned to the hotel. 'Out there, he's free,' says the psychoanalyst, 'he's got a choice.' But the abstract, anonymous figure remains
indecisive, perhaps because he now shoulders a national burden. The end
is involuntary. He stumbles and loses his balance, but clasps a net as he

lunges through the air and is hauled inside: society reclaims him and recovers its own sense of safety. A final announcement is inscribed across the screen, testifying that the New York Police Department's emergency rescue squad has 'techniques to deal with problems of this nature quietly, quickly and efficiently'. Tragedy has been averted, and – according to this promise – always will be.

Also in 1951, Billy Wilder directed a more sinister subterranean version of the same story in *Ace in the Hole*, about a man pinioned in a collapsed mineshaft in New Mexico. As he waits in the dark tunnel, gasping for air, a mob gathers to watch the man's rescue or the withdrawal of his body, and the disaster becomes an entertainment. Admission charges are levied at the parking lot outside the mine, and ice cream is sold to the over-heated spectators. Broadcasters exploit the victim's agony and make him briefly famous, but as soon as he dies, everyone drives off in quest of some new sensation. Walter Newman, Wilder's writer, said that hostile reviewers acted like officials of the State Department and worried about how foreigners would react to the film's account of the voyeurism of Americans and their vampiric mass media; *Ace in the Hole* was banned in Singapore to avoid offending the United States. Here there can be no tragic fall because the trapped man cannot move or make a choice. Instead Wilder watches society morally capsizing, caving in as the mine does.

Perhaps America had no need to kowtow to the elevated prestige of European tragedy. In *Partisan Review*'s 1952 symposium on America and its intellectuals, the critic Louis Kronenberger stood up for comedy as a 'cultural unifier' and questioned the highbrow preference for acid-tongued satirists like Mort Sahl and Lenny Bruce. The sitcoms that filled up the television schedules toyed with conflicts but pacified them within half an hour, using a laugh track to ensure that happiness was generally diffused; commercials did not so much interrupt these little domestic fables as confirm their optimism by recommending products that would make your house gleam and expel stains from the clothes you washed. Here was a model of what comedy could achieve, 'sparing nobody but including everybody' as

Kronenberger said: a democracy of mirth that humbled people, as the *Life* editorial required, without breaking them. In a society fathered by pilgrims, even secular pursuits have remnants of that religiosity, so the most archetypal American comedy is often divine, or supernatural in its preview of heaven. An angel watches over Bedford Falls in *It's a Wonderful Life*, and a good witch makes sure that Dorothy gets back from Oz to homely Kansas.

Lionel Trilling had no patience with this comic conditioning. 'For purposes of his salvation,' he said, 'it is best to think of the artist as crazy, foolish, inspired – as an unconditionable kind of man.' Examples were plentiful – Rothko and Jackson Pollock, William S. Burroughs and Trilling's student Allen Ginsberg – but this was another borrowing from Europe, where modern artists felt obliged to taunt the bourgeoisie. Although William Phillips, writing in *Horizon* in 1946, deplored the French enthusiasm for the 'slobbering he-men of Americana' in the novels of John Steinbeck and Erskine Caldwell, other critics were less snooty about a culture that for the first time in history was literally popular, catering to the uncountable masses. Philip Rahv allowed that there might be merit in 'some types of jazz and the folklore of sport', and William Barrett identified 'streamlined mass journalism' as one of America's great new inventions, destined for worldwide success. David Riesman satirized Babbitry in *The Lonely Crowd*, but had to admit that the ever-expanding American middle class avoided the twin extremes of 'upper-class insouciance and lower-class uninhibited aggression'. Even Trilling, so keen to radicalize the artist, knew that there were no longer any alternatives to cheery democratic America – certainly not the Workers' Fatherland, which duped left-wingers in the 1930s, and not the 'bright cosmopolis' of Paris, now less enticing than when aesthetes fled there in the 1920s. Like the rest of Europe, Paris was physically and morally besmirched. At the Ritz in 1945, Virgil Thomson kept his cache of American soap locked up, afraid that the staff would steal it. In 1948 Saul Bellow found the city grim not gay, and flinched from the foul medicinal odour of the Seine. The old world had lost its allure, and there were no spare continents on which new worlds could be created; America, it seemed, was history's consummation, the place where the pursuit had ended.

This became the country's gospel, a reprieve from tragedy like that promised by the early Christians as they spread their message of redemption. In 1947 the president of the Motion Picture Association, Eric Johnston, said that Hollywood should send abroad 'good pictures of American life – and show an unhappy world that democracy works'. Two years later the producer Walter Wanger added that 'Just a picture of well-dressed people walking down Fifth Avenue would show what Americanism can do.' The vision was selective: shabbily dressed people on Tenth Avenue would not have exemplified Americanism quite so appealingly. All the same, unhappiness could be waved away by surveying an average commercial strip, the locus of desire for Americans and of aspiration for others. In *The Best Years of Our Lives*, the veterans returning to Boone City, which is Cincinnati in all but name, watch from their car as a panoply of indispensable institutions and familiar brands slides by – a Woolworths, a shoeshine parlour, a hotdog stand, a used-car lot, a diner promising GOOD FOOD. Here is the home front they were defending.

In *The Thief*, released in 1952, Times Square turns on all its lights to dissuade a spy from betraying his country. Ray Milland plays a scientist with the Atomic Energy Commission in Washington, who photographs secret documents and passes them to couriers to be spirited abroad. These exchanges are conducted without words: this is a silent film, about a man who relies on signals and conspiratorial glances when making contact with others. One rendezvous takes place in the Library of Congress, where cellulated readers hunch in their noiseless cubicles; another, after Milland travels to New York, is on the observation deck of the Empire State Building, with the city below inaudible as the wind keens. His mission complete, Milland then walks to the pier where a freighter will take him to Cairo. But on the way he wanders through Times Square, and surveys its rowdy midnight blitz of neon. The camera takes note of Schrafft's, Sardi's, Lindy's and the Astor Bar, of Roseland and Playland, with effulgent announcements for Chop Suey, Ham 'n Eggs and Frankfurters. The Horn & Hardart Automat is included, with no suggestion of the steely inhumanity that repelled Sartre when he extracted a chilled pie from a glazed niche in the wall. Most stirringly patriotic of all is the sign that offers baseball tickets for sale.

Here, not in Washington with its bleached classical monuments, is the repository of national values. Milland remorsefully realizes that America means food and drink, fun and games, puerile enjoyments and shadier adult pleasures, all of which are on offer in this galactic forum, from which harsh tragic necessities and dizzy moral choices have been banished. Changing his mind, he gives himself up to the FBI.

6 | 'Master of the Earth'

Americans were reticent at first about their status as the new Romans, and when President Roosevelt dedicated the Hoover Dam in 1935 he revised Caesar's boast by complimenting the concrete arch that held back the Colorado River and generated hydroelectric power for the desert states of Arizona and Nevada. 'I came, I saw,' said Roosevelt, modestly marvelling, 'and I was conquered.' The imperial presidency, with all its pomp and paranoia, lay in the future.

A little later, Lloyd C. Douglas found the Roman analogy both inescapable and alarming. In 1942 he set *The Robe*, his novel about Christianity and its subversion of Roman power, 'in an age so very like ours', which also needed Christ to 'come again to renew his peace terms'; the saviour would re-emerge, Douglas predicted, from one of the 'wounded, weeping little countries' that were currently tormented by war. Douglas initially identified the Third Reich as a presumptuous modern Rome. In the novel, a patrician with liberal sympathies calls the roll of enslaved cultures – Persia, Egypt, Greece – and derides the legions that loot and murder 'to make Rome the capital of the world', while the seasoned or cynical politician Paulus acknowledges the rapacity with which Rome buys up 'the big men of a little country' and leaves the poor to look after themselves. The emperor Tiberius, ranting like Hitler, shouts 'Let the whole world hate us!', but Marcellus, a tribune who is converted to Christianity, warns that 'there will be no Roman Empire . . . when Jesus takes command'. Henry Luce's editorial in *Life* envisaged a rebirth of Rome not its extinction: the American century sought to reconcile empire and evangelism, training what Luce called 'the skilfull servants of mankind' and sending them out to 'establish ever-widening spheres of enterprise' and to better the common human lot.

In the 1953 film version of *The Robe*, a portentous narrator introduced Rome more bluntly as 'Master of the Earth'; by now, with the Third Reich obliterated, it was clear to which country the story referred. Another toga-clad epic, *Quo Vadis*, had already been filmed in Rome in 1951. Italian bystanders saw this expensive recreation of an earlier empire as a state-ment of intent by its successor, a sumptuary culture that valued glamour not grandeur. Alan Moorehead remembered local reaction to the fantastical display of abundance inside the Cinecittà studios: 'here was America, the cornucopia, in action'. Roland Barthes sniggered at American imperialism in a waspish essay on the coiffure of the Romans in MGM's 1953 version of Shakespeare's *Julius Caesar*. Faces suiting Chicago mobsters or Colorado sheriffs had been classicized by their fringes. As Caesar, Louis Calhern looks and sounds like a corporate lawyer; his hair is combed forward, which mini-mizes the forehead and – in Barthes' analysis – signals 'a specific mixture of self-righteousness, virtue, and conquest'. It remains unclear how a fringe can convey that American moral message: a crew cut would do the same, or a head shaved into the likeness of a cannonball. Without pausing to explain, Barthes added that Marlon Brando's Mark Antony sweated through his soliloquies, which he took to be proof that, for 'a nation of businessmen', thinking involved an almost costive strain.

Perspiration, however, was a minor symptom of the conquerors' inde-fatigable work ethic. It was the heat, toil and clamour of heavy industry that established American mastery, turning the tycoons who managed such pro-ductivity into emperors. In Ayn Rand's *Atlas Shrugged*, published in 1957, the mill owner Rearden drives past factories and power stations that embla-zon his surname in fiery letters across the nocturnal Pennsylvania sky. The scene is described by Rand as if it were a parade in ancient Rome, with 'the curves of blast furnaces standing like triumphal arches, the smokestacks rising like a solemn colonnade along an avenue of honour in an imperial city, the bridges hanging like garlands, the cranes saluting like lances, the smoke waving slowly like flags'. More than a coronation, this is an apothe-osis: buildings and inanimate machines honour their proprietor, and the militarism of the metaphors gives the ceremonial episode a brazenly fascist magnificence. Rome had set a dangerous precedent.

The ancient empire proverbially declined and fell, and this was the outcome foretold for America by Howard Fast in *Spartacus*, his novel about the uprising of Roman slaves in 73 BC. Fast began writing the book in 1950, and continued work on it after being imprisoned for his failure to cooperate with the McCarthy committee; introducing an extract in the journal *Masses & Mainstream* in 1952, he remembered that Spartacus had been used as a prototype for proletarian revolt by Rosa Luxemburg and her communist colleagues in Germany in 1915. The references to contemporary America in Fast's novel have a slangy, up-to-date insolence: despite their togas, his Romans are sleazy fixers and influence-peddlers who belong in smoke-filled rooms on what Washington, adopting Roman terminology, calls Capitol Hill. Batiatus, who owns the school of gladiators where Spartacus is trained, is described by Fast as a 'gangster', apprenticed in 'ward politics'. He doubles as a slum landlord, owning 'tenements' in Rome to which he adds rentable storeys until he has 'skyscrapers' of seven floors. Gracchus the professional politician cozens the citizens by telling them that they are the source of all power, which merely means that they have been wheedled into voting for the candidates the rulers choose, and at the baths he discusses a slew of problems very similar to those that preoccupied American senators in the 1950s and later: 'the trouble in Spain, the African situation, the necessity of Egyptian neutrality . . . and the eternal problem of what to do with the incessant Jewish provocation in Palestine'. Only Asia, so vexatious in the 1960s, is missing from the list.

Crassus, both a politician and an industrialist, employs the catchphrase of Truman and Eisenhower when he calls Rome 'the mightiest power the world ever knew'. 'We are not just any people,' he says, 'we are the Roman people'; he then declares that Romans are deservedly omnipotent because 'we are the first to understand fully the use of the slave', and he proves the point by taking guests to see the sweated labour in his perfumery at Capua. The Egyptians knew about distilling scents, but had not hit on the idea of mass production: 'It takes Rome to organize a thing,' Crassus says. Fast's contention is that the northern states did not abolish slavery after the Civil War but simply redefined it as factory work. Thanks to this underclass, Rome basks in what came to be known as affluence, 'a splendour of life and luxury and abundance never known in the world before'. Spartacus sends a challenge to the Senate, charging that Roman grandeur depends on the expropriation of foreign wealth, while 'your citizens live on the dole and spend their days in the circus and the arena' (or – since Fast encourages such anachronistic asides – at the movies?). Gracchus, penitent, says before his suicide 'We never talk about how empty our lives are. That is because we spend so much time filling our lives. All the natural acts of barbarians, eating and drinking and loving and laughing – all these things we have made a great ritual and fetish out of. . . . With us, amusement has taken the place of happiness.' As a Marxist analysis of American mass culture, which is the industrialization of enjoyment, this has a striking cogency.

Could mastery of the earth ever be more than a spasm of megalomania? In 1962 Robert Lowell was despatched to Buenos Aires by the Congress for Cultural Freedom. Encouraged by a succession of martinis, Lowell discarded the medicine that controlled his manic episodes, introduced himself to a crowd at the presidential palace as 'Caesar of Argentina', and solemnized his conquest of the country by clambering naked onto an equestrian statue. Otherwise the Roman analogy served mostly to warn about the temporariness of imperial power. Organizing opposition to the Vietnam War, Todd Gitlin urged radical students – honorary Spartacists, who saw the draft as a kind of enslavement – to think in the long term and make plans to stop the war after next. 'Rome,' he told the demonstrators, 'wasn't destroyed in a day.' And during the evacuation of the Saigon Embassy in 1975, the Chicago reporter Bob Tamarkin spotted a Marine hurriedly stuffing into his knapsack a paperback entitled *The Fall of Rome*: too symbolically convenient, perhaps, to be altogether believable.

Rome was a city that mastered the world because its roads reached into outlying provinces and transported back their riches. Britain was a small island, haphazardly aggrandized because its navy controlled the world's trade routes. Hitler's Germany, uncomfortably landlocked, sought extra room in the east. James A. Michener in his novel *Hawaii* laughed at 'the pathetic material base from which the Japanese' – crammed onto a rocky, infertile archipelago – 'had aspired to conquer the world'. If empires are a form of posturing over-compensation, then the United States had no need to bother. The country occupied a generous swathe of an intermittently empty continent; its land grabs happened long before the American century began, with the Louisiana Purchase, the realignment of the Mexican border, and the ceding of Cuba, Puerto Rico and the Philippines after the Spanish-American War. During the 1950s, Alaska and Hawaii were incorporated as states, but whatever political and commercial finagling went on out of sight, there was no question of conquest.

As American influence extended around the world, the process of empire-building was examined indirectly in stories about the consolidation of the United States. The first of the Rodgers and Hammerstein musicals, *Oklahoma!*, which opened on Broadway in 1943, is as much a product of the war as their *South Pacific*, located on the islands where American forces fought the Japanese. The source for *Oklahoma!* was a play by Lynn Riggs, *Green Grow the Lilacs*, staged in 1931; it is set before Oklahoma acquired statehood in 1907 and its characters still refer to 'the Territory', a reservation promised to the Choctaw tribe, who gave it a name that means 'land of the red people'. Those aboriginal occupants had to be dispossessed before Oklahoma could be Americanized, and this ethnic cleansing is hinted at in the way Riggs and then Hammerstein treat the rancorous ranch-hand Jeeter (who becomes Jud in the musical), a Caliban-like miscreant with 'a curious earth-coloured face and hairy hands', always 'dark and sullen', lurking in a smoke-house that is his smelly cave. Native Americans are absent, except for a song Riggs writes for an old man who remembers their assault on Custer's army. Jeeter or Jud is their token representative, and to clear the way for white settlement he is killed off by the cowboy Curly. Curly's arrest is postponed because the federal marshal has no jurisdiction in the Territory, and even if put on trial he seems certain – thanks to the higher law that governs American happy endings – to be exonerated.

Riggs's Curly prophesies that 'they gonna make a state outa this, they gonna put it in the Union!', and after his marriage to the farmer's daughter Laurey he indulges in a territorial reverie. Instead of singing about the bright golden haze on the meadow, as Curly does in the musical, he admires the moonlight on a crop of wheat and corn, then allows his gaze to cross 'the country all around it – all Indian Territory – plumb to the Rio Grande, and north to Kansas, and 'way over east to Arkansaw': what excites him is the fertile land, not his nubile bride. Laurey in her turn luxuriates in a daydream that depends on membership of the Union, and says she fancies living in the White House. The play ends with the matriarch Aunt Eller stubbornly asserting the autonomy of 'Territory folks' and resisting assimilation by 'them ole United Statesers', who in her opinion are citizens of 'a furrin country'. But the musical names the new state, equates it with the laconic and irresistibly American expression 'OK', and completes the christening with a jubilant exclamation mark. America is amassing its own internal empire.

In a similar spirit, the Texans in Edna Ferber's *Giant* rejoice at the wartime upheaval that rebalanced the continents and joke that there ought to be a new calendar, since the eras divided by 1945 are as different as BC and AD. Among the casualties of Europe's collapse are a deposed king and his consort, refugees from the imaginary country of Sargovia; the unemployed monarch, dressed in a discounted imitation of a Savile Row suit, has retreated to a pitifully small ranch – 'a few thousand acres' – in the Panhandle. Bick Benedict's property, by contrast, is 'practically a kingdom', where he is the 'ruler of an empire' with cattle as his compliant subjects. Ranches like his are self-sufficient and self-governing, so in league with the owners of similar spreads he sees Texas as a slightly smaller replica of the United States. His Virginian wife – who travels north with regal swank in a private railway car, provoking her sister to remark that she thought Texas was a republic or a democracy – asks why the cattlemen all have their own planes. 'That's just Texas making sure that they can't ever start another World War on us,' says Bick: with its private air force, the state could surely intimidate upstart nations like Germany or Japan. Not content to be monarch of all the grazing land he surveys, Bick at his cockiest behaves like the lord of creation, hybridizing cattle to produce a new breed and compensating for the over-grazed topsoil on the ranges by using cottonseed cake as feed because 'man hasn't got the trick of making earth – or perhaps he just hasn't got the time'.

The meaty Texan plutocracy upends the United States by refusing to respect the hegemony of the north-east: Ferber describes San Antonio as the antithesis of Boston, with faded gentility replaced by rude festive vigour. Bick's wife, whose Virginian ancestry has endowed her with an inherited memory of defeat, knows she has married into a dynasty, and wonders when the Benedicts will be deposed, like the sad Sargovian king. Sure enough, the end approaches when the cowhand Jett Rink strikes oil on his patch of ground. Enriched by the baptismal gusher, he builds a hotel called The Conquistador. The name sums up a history of brutal expropriation: earlier settlers, alarmed by the emptiness of this hot dry plain, 'set out to conquer it and the people whose land it was. And these, too, they must overcome and keep conquered.' Ferber sees in the six flags of Texas a memento of disputes that pre-date the United States and still rumble on beneath the dusty surface, so that a troublemaker on Bick's ranch is said to be 'another Mexican Indian coming back to Tejas'. The state's current potentates appreciated neither these hints of illegitimacy nor the novel's suggestion that the local 'mania for bigness' concealed a secret littleness. After the publication of *Giant*, Ferber was warned that if she revisited Texas she might be welcomed with a 'necktie party' – that is, a lynching.

In 1958 Ferber gave a similar account of Alaska in *Ice Palace* – mock-heroic in its treatment of the bluster and boosterism that preceded the territory's admission to the United States a year later, yet genuinely epic in its response to the region's amplitude and its wealth of minerals, forests, fish and fur. This white wasteland can absorb and efface the old continent, being 'bigger than a whole parcel of European countries put together'; it is even, as the wise crone Bridie Ballantyne declares, 'two times the size of that little bitty Texas' – Ferber's rejoinder to the ranchers who wanted to string her up. Her Alaska is 'this great empire of the north', and after the gold rush there is a scramble to set up 'basic industries to make an empire out of a wilderness'; Mount McKinley is likened to the Empire State Building, because it too jumps around to appear in the background of all vistas. The term that Americans find so problematic can be used with impunity because Alaska – bought from the Russians for $7 million in 1867 – already belonged to the

United States, though until 1959 it was treated as a military possession and had no representation in Washington. In the novel, statehood rescues the region from its demeaning colonial status, but at a price: the arctic landmass that once stretched into Asia is now, like everywhere else, Americanized. The members of Ferber's Guildenstern family take to eating steak rather than blubber, caribou and tundra greens, and complete their assimilation by reading *Life* and going to the movies; a boy dresses in cowboy regalia and is nicknamed Hopalong Askaluk. Thor Storm, the mystical backwoodsman who is the spirit of this frozen place, grumbles about these adopted fads and looks ahead to a time when monopolistic America will go under. He keeps a copy of Spengler's *Decline of the West* in his cabin, and he transfers its terminal gloom from debilitated Europe to juvenile America. The race, he predicts, will lose its virility, the frontier will close; eventually 'this America will be like India, like the barren over-populated countries of the East, like China'. He could not have been more wrong about India and China.

Ferber's friend Michener, another specialist in territorial epic, dealt with the American claim to Hawaii in the novel he published in 1959. As with Bick Benedict's genetic manipulation of his herd, the pedigree he traces extends back to a lusher, more tropical version of the unspoiled paradise that is regained in America. Michener's *Hawaii* celebrates the creation not of a single man and woman but of a new breed of 'Golden Men', the products of racial mixture in Polynesia. A Congressman sent to investigate Hawaii's fitness for statehood watches as Japanese, Koreans, Chinese and Filipinos – enemies when on home ground – matily commingle in a Honolulu street. Or is this an eclectic muddle, not a melting pot? A vacationing widow from the mainland who takes up with a beachboy analyses the constituents of the hula dance: the Filipino girl she studies is 'wearing a cellophane skirt from Tahiti, playing a ukulele from Portugal, backed up by a loud-speaker guitar from New York, singing a phony ballad from Hollywood' – which neatly unpicks the indigenous folklore of the islands.

In 1988 Michener's saga *Alaska* registered other doubts about American perpetuity. The novel advances from a time when Americans dismissed Alaska, which they saw as a blank on their flat maps, to the period after 1945 when military chiefs began to think globally, followed the curvature of the earth and realized that this frozen zone, purchased from Russia for two cents an acre in 1867, might be a bastion against 'anyone who comes at us from Asia'. Yet Michener undercuts such defensive schemes by pointing out that Alaska belongs less to human beings, whether Russian or American, than to the wild creatures for which it is truly a habitat: one of the novel's characters is a sockeye salmon from Lake Pleiades, supposedly called Nerka, whose life, loves and death are solicitously chronicled. And the political calculations of the generals in Washington are contested by geology, which has its own patient, implacable agenda. Michener's narrative begins 'about a billion years ago' when the continents had not yet separated, and the plot is interrupted by odd accidents – a tsunami that sweeps away one of Alaska's legal protectors during an antelope hunt on the ice, for instance – that are a reminder of ructions underground or underwater, where dyspeptic volcanoes or abrasive tectonic plates upset the timelines of human empires. The invasion from Asia that the politicians hoped to ward off turns out to be meteorological: bush pilots taking off from Anchorage to probe the interior have to battle 'whole continents of air rushing madly out of Siberia', which implies that winds are more of a menace than communist hordes.

Michener ends by noticing that a character who kennels huskies and mamalukes outside his cabin at Desolation Point – a geology major when he attended college in the Lower Forty-Eight – wears a T-shirt with the motto REUNITE GONDWANALAND. There is no way of undoing the schisms like those that split the southern supercontinent apart or splintered the land bridge across which the first humans trekked from Asia into America; instead the United States vaulted across the intervening seas when it annexed Hawaii and Alaska. All the same, Michener knew that its power was as unstable as the ground beneath our feet. In 1996 in *This Noble Land: My Vision for America*, he worried that his compatriots had become 'international parasites', shipping raw materials to Asia where 'brilliant minds' converted them into products that were then shipped back to America to be sold. How long could this continue? Until 2050, Michener guessed, thanks to the country's current momentum; this would complete the American century and add an extra decade for good measure. He died in 1997, four years before there was any reason to reduce his estimate.

'For one magnificent century,' says a vaunting capitalist in Rand's *Atlas Shrugged*, '[America] redeemed the world. It will have to do so again.' Rand's novel is set in the future, so the extra lease of life Michener awarded to his noble land has been almost used up, and a renewal of the covenant seems unlikely. America, once the home of individualism, precariously holds out in Rand's novel against a collectivized world of People's States, where nationalization has wrecked industries and the shiftless masses are kept alive by American aid. Rand never forgave the Russian Revolution for impoverishing her family, and she despised a foreign policy that wasted American food on 'the rotted cultures of the looters' continents'. Atlas – who bends under the weight of the world in the bronze sculpture by Lee Lawrie outside Rockefeller Center in New York – is here advised to shrug, casting off his burden.

Rand arrived in New York from Petrograd in early 1926, and wept when she saw the city's skyline, a graph of clamorous willpower. Moving to Hollywood, she worked as an extra on Cecil B. de Mille's Christian epic *King of Kings*, which confirmed her belief that to be in America was to be born again. In *Atlas Shrugged* she, like Ferber's Texans, saw in contemporary history a repetition of the millennial change that had occurred at the birth of Christ, when time was intersected by eternity. The redemption Rand had in mind was explicitly religious, although its blessing, traced in air at the end of her novel by the engineer John Galt, is not the sign of a cross that imprints its stab wounds on the believer's head and chest but the sign of the dollar – a financial emblem that sketches the superimposed initials of the United States, the parallel bars of a U stamped on and merged with an S. In *Atlas Shrugged* it serves as the monogram of a new faith, announcing the resurrection of an America where 'the highest type of human being' is the self-made, self-serving industrialist.

Christ gave proof of his divinity by performing magic acts that turned water into wine or multiplied loaves and fishes; Rand's Messiah exercises a pseudo-scientific wizardry. Galt harnesses a new source of power from static electricity, weaning the economy from its reliance on a limited store of fossils – a true miracle for a society that requires constant calorific infusions. To complement this feat, Rearden the steel magnate invents a new metal that weighs nothing but can heft anything, and another wonder-worker somehow extracts cheap oil from shale. The bonus guaranteed by this ignition will be 'an extra pack of cigarettes bought with the money saved from one's electric bill': for the over-excitable Rand, a Promethean fire flared up every time someone lit a Lucky Strike. But like Christ departing from an unworthy world, Galt and his apostles sabotage their own industries rather than capitulate to the demands of the labour unions that, in Rand's view, were wrecking America. The scientific magi retreat to the mountains while their mean-minded democratic country succumbs to entropy, slowed down by shortages of heating fuel during a series of bitter winters. Cinemas, nightclubs and bowling alleys close to conserve energy, and 'the world's motor which was New York' splutters, coughs and dies when its lights are switched off.

A less high-minded precursor of Rand's supermen hectors the world in Budd Schulberg's 'Your Arkansas Traveller', included in his collection of stories *Faces in the Crowd* in 1953. Lonesome Rhodes, an Arkansas drifter, talks his way into power on the radio, appears on the cover of *Life*, and is hailed as 'America's Uncle Lonesome, Big Brother to all the world'. He rails at the Chinese and recommends ending negotiations over Korea, questions the Good Neighbour Policy because the 'banana republics' down south all hate America anyway, and jeers at the pretensions of poverty-stricken Britain, even suggesting a second War of Independence to rupture sentimental ties. His harangues appeal to a constituency of 'rednecks, crackers, hillbillies, hausfraus, shut-ins, pea-pickers' whom he goads to a xenophobic fury, and when he brags that GIs will break ranks to follow him and his volunteer militias, his producer fears that he might indeed provoke another war. The Roman analogy recurs: Rhodes is 'a gum-chewing Nero . . . easing into the commercials while civilization burned'. He is also Joseph McCarthy, whose committee interrogated Schulberg in 1951. As it happened, the media were McCarthy's undoing – the televised hearings in 1954 exposed his thuggish methods – but Schulberg's story worries that America is a 'hopped-up kind of free society', a 'screwball country' where rabble-rousers with access to the airwaves can coax a nationwide mob into hysteria. In 1957 Elia Kazan directed a film version of Schulberg's story, entitled *A Face in the Crowd*. Here Rhodes graduates from radio to television, and on his programme touts a spurious pep pill called Vitajex – his equivalent to the 'new kind of energy' that Galt has synthesized in *Atlas Shrugged*. In the story he is a fascist, killed off in order to preserve the republic; in the film he is merely a fraud, who suffers disgrace not death when an open microphone eavesdrops on his cynical mockery of his fans.

François Truffaut, reviewing *A Face in the Crowd* when it was released in France, reflected with dread on its account of a culture in which 'politics always overlaps show business, as show business overlaps advertising'. His comment was truer than he knew: Ronald Reagan, employed by General Electric in 1954 to expound its creed of economic progress on television, was a less vitriolic specimen of the type, and in the 1980s he went on to become the spokesman for a rebranded America. Truffaut saw demagoguery as an American phenomenon because of its euphoria – hence the pep pill and its vitalizing potency – and its good-guy amiability, but he acknowledged that it had already spread to France, where 'the media are more and more inspired by American methods'. Here was a disturbing redefinition of the democracy that America prescribed as a remedy for the world's ailments: the liberators had rescued Europe from one kind of totalitarianism only to impose another, with Hitler's apoplectic rants replaced by a friendlier, more insinuating form of thought control, composed of folksy homilies and maddeningly memorable commercial jingles. At the end of Kazan's film, as Rhodes drives away from the television studio on the Upper West Side in New York, a Coca-Cola sign in Columbus Circle advertises the virtues of effervescence, and another gleaming neon logo silently shouts the word EMPIRE – the name of a hotel that still stands on West 63rd Street. Rhodes fails, but the imperial agenda remains, perhaps freshly invigorated by a swig of Coke.

7 | American Girls in Italy and Elsewhere

Time, *Life* and *Fortune* functioned, according to William S. Burroughs, as 'control mechanisms', adjusting the minds of Americans and persuading the rest of the world to accept the dominance of this new power. Less strident than Luce's magazines, *Saturday Evening Post* popularized a vision of America that was nostalgic not prophetic. Norman Rockwell's covers looked back towards a place of Edenic origins, not ahead to the grand finale of human history. In a small New England town, elders somnolently rock on the porch or reminisce in the barber's shop while mothers cook up sacramental feasts of fat white turkey, fathers tinker with their cars, and children romp with non-pedigree dogs. This was paradise preserved, with serpents debarred; the ultimate gated community. Because America is where dreams materialize, Rockwell's ideal types have been willed into existence. The billionaire Ross Perot once said that he imagined the young Steve Jobs playing with computer chips in his garage, supervised by 'his dad, who looks like a character out of a Norman Rockwell painting'. Jobs's adoptive father came from Armenia, and the adolescent Steve, whose actual father was a Syrian Muslim, had distinctly Middle Eastern features; neither resembled Rockwell's WASPS. But Perot's scenario naturalized them, tamely suburbanized the geeky oddity of cybernetics, and brought what Rockwell called his 'best-possible world' up to date.

For Rockwell's people, expulsion from this idyll was like the fall of man, except that they had committed no sin to justify being cast out. In magazine covers he painted in 1917–18, American soldiers in Europe gawkily insist on their harmlessness. One of them softens the heart of a French matron by showing her a picture of his own mother; another lanky uniformed lad bends down to converse in pidgin with a peasant girl who wears wooden clogs. Despite their armaments, Rockwell's Americans abroad are lost children. The next war, however, hustles them into maturity. An airman on a

1945 *Post* cover tries on his civvies when he returns home and finds he has grown several inches while fighting the Luftwaffe: is he sadder and wiser as well as taller? A Marine on another cover sits in the garage where he worked before the war, holding a torn, limp Japanese flag. His former cronies cluster round, but he is pale, haunted, unable to invent the tales of derring-do they expect to hear.

In 1955 Pan American World Airways – which changed its name from Pan American Airways in 1943, to keep pace with the ever more panoramic interests and influence of the United States – engaged Rockwell to sketch the destinations in Europe, Asia and the Middle East to which its clippers now flew. He called the airline his 'magic carpet', and drew one of its pilots with such a clear, stern, weather-wise gaze under the brim of his pseudo-military cap that the advertisement was headlined 'Eyes that see around the world'. This, surely, was what Luce's aeronautical angels should look like. 'Uncle Sam's your Skipper,' Pan Am told its passengers, and in another of its magazine ads a captain doubling as paterfamilias leaves his cockpit to tuck a mother and daughter into their sleeperette as they are wafted towards Europe. The little girl clutches her teddy bear, with her Pan Am flight bag also comfortingly within reach.

Homely American cosiness prevailed on the airline's double-decker Stratocruiser, but when the plane landed, passengers disembarked in a world that was worryingly foreign. Europe offered no particular threat. Rockwell sketched a spry American woman attempting to distract an immobile guard at the Tower of London, and in Gay Paree her husband photographs the risqué high kicks of the can-can dancers. In Rome, the same man holds up a miniature replica of a classical statue, with an emperor raising his arm in a salute: the ancient empire's colossi have shrunk to toys, ready to be bought up by the new Romans. As the journey continued, however, Rockwell and his minder from the New York advertising agency grew increasingly uneasy. Arabs confused their sense of decorum by wearing bed sheets outdoors. In India, poverty was picturesque not drab, but it smelled bad. The country's temples could have done with a good clean by the ladies of the Women's Auxiliary, and those in which sculpted deities copulated were downright shocking. After completing his circuit of the world, Rockwell brought back to New York a portfolio of matadors, snake charmers, monkey tamers, geishas, Hawaiian canoeists, and a bustling sketch of 'a camel-elephant-water buffalo-bicycle-and-beggar-thronged street in Karachi'. That hyphenated chaos was too much for Pan Am's copywriters, who declared his work unusable. The 'strange lands and people' frightened them; what they wanted were views of 'smart-looking tourists sunning on smart beaches in front of smart hotels'. Florida was as exotic as they cared to get.

In rejecting Rockwell's submission, the airline and the agency overlooked the intrepidity of individual Americans, less brittly sophisticated than the members of the itinerant 'smart set' in the 1930s, who now had the chance to explore a wider world. But tourism did not come naturally or easily to them, as they had to battle against a residual guilt. Other countries were surely less serious than the industrious United States, more given to the lazy delectation of life; to travel abroad was a mark of dilettantism, or worse. As Virgil Thomson said, people assumed that 'unless one was in Europe for study or business, one was there for the fleshpots'.

In Patricia Highsmith's novel *The Talented Mr Ripley*, published in 1955, a New York boat-builder with the blatantly allegorical name of Greenleaf hires Tom Ripley to bring his son Dickie back from Italy, where – to his father's consternation – the young man has the cheek to be enjoying himself. 'He has responsibilities here,' grumbles Mr Greenleaf, equating Italy with irresponsibility. Tom's friend Cleo, amused by the dour commission, says 'You're the only person I know who ever went to Europe for a *reason*' – that is, to do a job, rather than to behave irrationally, like the shiftless Dickie. In American usage, holidays refer strictly to holy days, which extend from Thanksgiving to Christmas and resume at Easter; the word does not mean a relief from work. For that purpose, the proper term is vacation, which suggests vacancy. Is free time a dereliction of duty? This certainly is how Dickie's father regards his extended absence.

At the time of Ripley's expedition, mass tourism was yet to begin; Americans in Europe counted as exiles like James Baldwin, or – giving them the benefit of the doubt – as adventurers, who had chosen to risk themselves in a cultured wilderness. In 1951 Ruth Orkin photographed 'An American Girl in Italy', in which her friend Ninalee Craig strides through the Piazza della Repubblica in Florence while fifteen Italian men, carefully choreographed by Orkin, ogle her and whistle appreciatively. One of them, whose gesture was censored when the image was cropped, even clutches his groin in tribute as she passes. As a group, they rowdily exemplify a Latin habit of treating the street as a stage, not a thoroughfare for businesslike traffic: in Highsmith's novel, Dickie tells Tom while they lounge in the Galleria in Naples that 'the Anglo-Saxons make a great mistake not staring at people from a sidewalk table'. The staring in Orkin's photograph is a form of sexual solicitation, but though this may look like a tableau of besieged innocence, the young American woman has little to fear from the Italian wolf pack. The lecherous chorus offers her an ovation; cowed despite their lecherous bravado, the men clear a path for her, and marvel at her independence – an American characteristic, lacking in her Italian counterparts, who would not have undertaken this promenade (and who also lacked the financial means to cross an ocean). The folder she carries, a mark of her studious and artistic nature, announces that she is there to take stock of a culture of which these unemployed idlers are no longer worthy. Her averted eyes signal avoidance not alarm, and Craig thought of herself as Dante's Beatrice, a celestial spirit floating through the earthy streets. Writing in the magazine *Holiday* in 1955, Sean O'Faolain told a comparable story about a Neapolitan acquaintance who had set about seducing a young American. He softened her up, but then as he moved in to complete his conquest she remarked 'I must go to the Museum of the History of Science tomorrow morning at nine.' The randy Italian instantly wilted, unmanned by this evidence that she had her own mind and timetable and an interest in life beyond satisfying him, and decided that American women were frigid. The high-minded preoccupation of such female pilgrims made them, in their own way, as impregnable as their militarized menfolk.

The other photographs in Orkin's sequence suggest that Europe is this young American's sentimental and perhaps sexual induction. In the Piazza della Signoria in Florence, Craig grips her guidebook as she gapes at a statue of two naked musclemen grappling: here she learns about the carnality of art, not its spirituality. Elsewhere she makes smart use of the allure that, thanks to those appreciative bystanders, she knows she possesses. She rides pillion on the motor scooter of the young man who smirks at her in the Piazza della Repubblica, dons goggles and a bathing cap for a jauntier outing in an MG, and when she gets to Paris is admiringly saluted by a gendarme outside Saint-Germain-des-Prés. Henry James's model of the American girl in peril abroad – Isabel Archer in *The Portrait of a Lady* pursued by fortune hunters, Daisy Miller killed by a 'Roman fever' after a nocturnal tryst in the Colosseum – has been revised. Craig can create a stir without being an heiress, and does not have to die as the penalty for her effrontery in venturing out alone among the predatory Italians. Orkin herself was even less bashful than her friend. In her travel diary, she mentions hiking up to an outlook in Fiesole, where the view of Florence made her want to emit 'a Tarzan yell'. Although she was too well behaved to let loose that ululation, this American woman felt she was queen of the European jungle.

Orkin's girl is striding or romping through the American century, reducing Europeans to gaping amazement. Her courage and confidence were atypical: a cycle of films made over the next few years upheld a wary moral isolationism, telling different versions of an admonitory tale about American women ensnared by Italian men (or by the same generic man, since the wooer in three instances is played by Rosanno Brazzi). The first, released in 1953, was Vittorio De Sica's *Indiscretion of an American Wife*, in which Jennifer Jones is arrested during a rendezvous with Montgomery Clift – who gesticulates like a windmill to establish that he is Italian – in a shadowy railway carriage parked on a remote track at the station in Rome. In 1954 in Jean Negulesco's *Three Coins in the Fountain*, a trio of imported secretaries ignore warnings about Latin lechers. Here Brazzi is a chivalrous translator who rescues his foreign colleagues when they are pinched and fondled by some cocky men. 'Things can happen that American girls don't understand,' he says as he shepherds them away. In 1955 in David Lean's *Summertime*, a less scrupulous Brazzi, now cast as a married Venetian, returns to seduce

Katharine Hepburn. In Douglas Sirk's *Interlude*, released in 1957, June Allyson – who says she is 'a nice quiet uncomplicated optimist', which is another way of identifying herself as an American – has her misadventure in Munich, but the orchestral conductor who leads her astray (Brazzi again) is half-Italian. Like the American wife in *Indiscretion*, Allyson's character comes from Philadelphia: both women find themselves in a city of love, but not of the brotherly variety. The series ends with the very different case of Tennessee Williams' middle-aged widow in *The Roman Spring of Mrs Stone*, filmed in 1961 with Vivien Leigh. Hardly a neophyte, she shares Williams's own delight in Italian flagrancy – visiting Rome in 1947 he noted that young men wandered down the Via Veneto with their hands in their pockets 'caressing their genitals quite unconsciously' so they could display 'a slight erection' – and pays the gigolos on the Spanish Steps for their services.

The recurrent situation has some intriguing variants. In 1953 in William Wyler's *Roman Holiday*, the nationalities are reversed: Audrey Hepburn plays a fugitive European princess who shelters in Gregory Peck's apartment, and gets through the night without being Americanized. In 1960 *It Started in Naples* switched the genders: Clark Gable, a Philadelphia lawyer, is vanquished by the rampantly sensual Sophia Loren. In 1963 in *A New Kind of Love* the European libertine is again a woman. Eva Gabor tries to educate Joanne Woodward, a timid, dowdy buyer for a discount clothes emporium who at first is scandalized by flighty Paris. 'Most Americans don't know how to enjoy themselves,' purrs the promiscuous Gabor. 'In Europe we learned to let ourselves go. That's why most wars begin here.' Woodward's revelation occurs on St Catherine's Day, when she tipsily joins the revelling procession of spinsters who bedizen themselves with showy hats and set out to look for mates. (The parade of Catherinettes still happens in New Orleans, probably without the expectation that the participants will be maidens.) Woodward consults a statue of St Catherine on a street-corner shrine, and a supernatural voice directs her to Elizabeth Arden in the Place Vendôme. 'Go in and stay all day,' murmurs the sybaritic saint, who prescribes a cosmetic makeover not a spiritual conversion.

The story was retold so often because it was not just about holiday flirtations; it examined the risks of America's new relationship with the rest of the world. George Washington in his farewell address in 1796 encouraged 'liberal intercourse with all nations', but warned against the 'humour or caprice' of Europeans, who possessed 'insidious wiles' and practised 'the arts of seduction'. He therefore advised Americans to adopt a 'respectable defensive posture'. He was talking about commerce and diplomacy, but he used suggestively erotic language. If personified as a man, America is strong, dominant, fearless, like Rockwell's version of a Pan Am pilot. But the national persona can also be female, or perhaps feminine – vulnerable or even virginal, idealistic and therefore endangered by mercenary cynics.

The secretaries in *Three Coins in the Fountain* work for something called the United States Distribution Agency, where a sign on a grey marble wall enjoins them to 'Defend America'. Is the agency distributing largesse or maintaining the clenched, guarded posture that Washington recommended? The Trevi fountain spurts and splashes in vain: an almost racist regulation forbids the young women to date 'local employees', and warnings circulate about a rakish aristocrat played by Louis Jourdan – if you accept his invitation to Venice, you'll have to slink back to America, dishonoured. Impoverished Europe is still wicked, lust being the revenge of the vanquished natives. In *Interlude*, Allyson is employed by the Information Service at Amerika Haus in Munich. When she arrives, someone asks whether this is her first trip to a foreign country. 'Yes,' she replies, 'except for Montreal once.' She then adds 'Canada', registering her sudden awareness that even in North America there are places that have to be classified as foreign. She meets Brazzi at a rehearsal for a concert sponsored by Amerika Haus. The event aims to befriend the Germans, but Allyson's bossy supervisor says that she has reserved her block of seats 'to let them know we're holding onto our beachhead', as if the performance were a re-enactment of the Normandy landings.

Brazzi overwhelms Allyson by conducting the orgiastic Venusberg music from Wagner's *Tannhäuser*; later a downpour forces them to spend the night in his summer cottage. Next morning he makes coffee. 'Without cream or sugar?' she asks, aghast, when he hands her a cup. She demands four lumps, perhaps hoping to reassert her sweetness and immaculate good nature. At the time, espresso coffee counted as one of Europe's toughest challenges. Gable gamely learns to drink the stuff in *It Started in Naples*, but as late as 1972 in Billy Wilder's *Avanti!* Jack Lemmon, a nerdy organization man visiting Ischia, declines the offer of a mud bath and says with a shudder that he already had one on the train from Rome: they called it an espresso. In *Interlude*, a dreary American doctor proposes marriage to Allyson and takes her back to Philadelphia, where the coffee presumably is whiter.

Although the heroine of *Summertime* is from Akron, Ohio, Hepburn plays her as a starchy New Englander, an earnest cultural pilgrim. She acknowledges her own immaturity when she tells a story about a girl she met on the Atlantic crossing, who hoped that she would have a miraculous experience in Europe: wincing, Hepburn reflects that 'in America every female under fifty calls herself a girl'. By contrast, in Europe even children, having been seasoned by war, behave like elderly roués, and the Venetian urchin who attaches himself to Hepburn begs for cigarettes and sells dirty postcards on the side. Strays like this had turned Italy into a bordello for the benefit of visiting Americans. When Truman Capote arrived in Venice in the late 1940s, he was pursued by an adolescent termagant called Lucia. Capote's companion tried to buy her off with a packet of Chesterfields; she caused a scandal in their fancy hotel by sneaking upstairs to offer repayment in kind. Capote delightedly adhered to the old-fashioned American notion that Europe was wicked, though he preferred to think of the city as a dietary binge, with calories as a substitute for sin. Venice, he said, was 'like eating an entire box of chocolate liqueurs in one go'.

Arriving at her Venetian pensione in *Summertime*, Hepburn unpacks a bottle of bourbon, and gallantly announces that she is determined to learn to drink it without ice, which in Europe is less easy to come by. But ice, which functions as a preservative, is essential to her moral economy, just as sugar was to Allyson's in *Interlude*. Hepburn finds herself in a place where virtue is likely to liquefy, and morality is no longer a choice between black and white. The colour of Lean's film is literally ravishing, and therefore a threat: the golden haze of the Grand Canal, a row of painted houses like a fallen rainbow on one of the outer islands, the inflamed crimson goblet Brazzi sells Hepburn, the firework display that accompanies her overdue sexual initiation. Hepburn herself had reason to think that Venice, for all its beauty, was toxic. For one scene, Lean directed her to walk backwards while filming with her movie camera – an American scruple, since she is storing memories rather than permitting herself to have sensations. Misjudging her step, she tumbles into a canal; the dip in the foul water left Hepburn with an eye infection that gave her trouble for the rest of her life.

The most complex of these encounters is in *Indiscretion of an American Wife*, which has a sharper critical edge because its director was European – though De Sica's work was sabotaged by the producer David O. Selznick, Jennifer Jones's husband. Selznick made slashing cuts, then by way of compensation added a prologue in which Patti Page sings 'Autumn in Rome' as she wanders round an expensive duplex with a view of the Empire State Building: although the singer is in New York not Philadelphia, the irrelevant overture vouches for the heroine's safe repatriation. De Sica called his own, longer version of the film *Stazione Termini*, which implied that it was as much about the station and the crowds in transit through it – commuters, migrants, urban drifters, even a quartet of dumpy provincial American priests who speak no Italian and order tea, not over-stimulating espresso, in the restaurant – as about the erotic tribulations of the imported stars. The subsidiary cast of anonymous Romans alarmed Selznick, who asked the American Embassy to ferret out any communists in De Sica's team of writers; he re-established American cinematic values by hiring another cameraman to make glamourized close-ups of Jones and Clift, inserted to ensure that they did not merge with the masses.

The relationship between the American wife and her needy Italian admirer allowed De Sica to measure the economic disparity between the continents. Jones, intending to run away, arranges for her mink coat to be brought to the station; Clift warns her that if they cohabit in Pisa, she will have to help pump water from the well and sit in darkness when it rains because the electrical supply is unreliable. Objecting to her habit of giving him orders, he complains about Europe's emasculation, exemplified by Cary Grant in his horsehair wig in *I Was a Male War Bride*. 'In this country it's the men who count,' Clift says. 'You American women are much too emancipated.' Jones softens when she takes pity on a penniless migrant family in the third-class waiting room and buys a supply of chocolate bars – the wartime currency of American munificence – to feed the three hungry children. But De Sica did not mean to commend her for assuming the proper maternal role; his point was that Italians belong to clans or classes from which they cannot escape, whereas Americans are free to pursue a personal happiness, like Jones incongruously sorting out a private dilemma in this most public of places.

Like the young woman in Orkin's photograph, Jones is greeted salaciously or stalked as she walks through the station. The banter is harmless enough, and Italian audiences found the American wife's shamed prudery absurd. They also laughed when she and Clift are marched away by the police for huddling in the parked carriage: even if they had been making love, was that a crime? The commissioner's consummately European response is to pardon weakness and maintain conventional hypocrisy, so he rips up the charge. Discretion is a European notion, implying a need for concealment; from the American point of view, an indiscretion is a more grievous lapse. Jones therefore vows to tell her husband about her dalliance when she returns to Philadelphia, even though it will hurt him. As a puritan, she needs to punish herself, whether or not this involves collateral damage to others.

Clift accosts Jones on the Spanish Steps, which is where the gigolos display themselves to potential customers in *The Roman Spring of Mrs Stone*. Tennessee Williams's widowed actress does not pretend to be shocked by the impudence of the hustlers. Ripe and worldly-wise, unlike Jones in *Indiscretion of an American Wife* or Allyson in *Interlude*, Mrs Stone warms to the demoralization or amorality of Europe. Her tutor is a female friend called Meg, a journalist who has covered cataclysms from the Spanish Civil War to the present guerrilla fighting in Greece: Williams's novel was published in 1950, not long after the British government appealed to the United States to pay the cost of defending Greece against the communism that had claimed Albania, Bulgaria and Yugoslavia. Meg's political philosophy is a conservative fatalism, and to her the 'golden antiquity' of Rome is a symptom of 'the evil . . . latent in all modern history'. Europe, she says, is populated by 'stately witches and epicene dandies'. That could be the cast of any Tennessee Williams play, so Mrs Stone is not deterred. Paolo, the impoverished aristocrat who becomes her kept boy, has a cynical mentor of his own, an elderly bawd who operates as his pimp. In the 1961 film, this role was played by Lotte Lenya, for whom a pan-European identity was invented. Her character is called Countess Magda Terribili-Gonzalez, with each word giving her a stake in a different country and the sum total adding up into a survey of Europe and its grotesquely titillating terrors. An acid-tongued snob, the countess disabuses Paolo of his respect for the woman he has battened on: 'There's no such thing as a great American lady. Great ladies do not occur in a country that is less than two hundred years old'. She expresses a nastier and more intimate resentment in a later film version written by Martin Sherman, an American dramatist resident in London. Sherman's countess sneers that Mrs Stone, here played by Helen Mirren, is 'a victorious American – she has better toilet paper'.

That victory is unforgiven, and sex in *Roman Spring* counts as reparation: the Americanization of Emily is balanced by the degrading Europeanization of Mrs Stone. Warren Beatty as Paolo tells Vivien Leigh that 'rich Americans' are not 'the new conquerors of Rome', because the city is eternal and will wear down all who imagine they have power over it. He fabricates a tale about a friend defrauded when he invested in a black-market scheme to resell whisky obtained from a discount store on the American base in Naples; an Italian squandered the friend's funds, but for Paolo the tempt-ingly affluent Americans are the ultimate corrupters. He adds that the only person he ever loved was a cousin who was 'raped by your soldiers and spent the rest of her life in a convent'. At the end, rather than returning to America, Mrs Stone replaces Paolo with a scruffier loiterer from the Spanish Steps. Letting an unkempt stranger into her apartment, is she inviting him to kill her? Or is she undertaking to suffer in expiation for the wrong done to Paolo's probably imaginary cousin? No, her unrepentant decision shows off her purchasing power and demonstrates that women have as much right to debauch themselves as men. For Tennessee Williams, wickedness was one of Europe's selling points, the prerogative of a civilization that had been lengthily marinaded in vice.

Quietly wistful rather than vindictive like *Roman Spring*, *Roman Holiday* despairs of America's capacity to save Europe from itself. Audrey Hepburn, a princess from an anonymous Ruritanian country, slips out of her embassy during a stuffy official visit to Rome, and after wandering happily through the city falls asleep on a wall above the ruins of the Forum. It is here that Gregory Peck, a newspaperman whose bureau is next to Trajan's Column, discovers her after he leaves an all-night poker game. The landmarks comment on the situation: the Forum recalls the cycle of crumbling empires, and the Column, with its wrap-around comic strip chronicling Roman victories, suggests that the techniques of American journalism are not so very new. Hepburn thinks she is incognito; Peck knows who she is but plays along, hoping to be paid a premium for an illustrated story about her day on the run. When he questions her about her father's job, her reply inadvertently equates old and new regimes. She can hardly admit that he is a king, so she says, accurately enough, that his work is 'mostly public relations', which cites a profession invented by America as part of its project to befriend the world and please its customers or clients.

Peck thinks better of his plan to exploit Hepburn for journalistic profit. Instead, *Roman Holiday* envisions a comic Utopia where hereditary rank is irrelevant and legal strictures are waived: the police release Peck and Hepburn after their rampage through Rome on his motor scooter, despite the damage they have done. But this playful anarchism is a mere dream, and after sampling freedom for a day, Hepburn decides against a liberated American future and retreats into her half-alive ceremonial role. The script was written by Dalton Trumbo, who received proper credit only in 2011; he had to use an alias because he was blacklisted as a former member of the Communist Party, and like Howard Fast had been imprisoned for refusing to testify before McCarthy's Un-American Activities Committee. All the same, Trumbo's conclusion is staunchly patriotic. Like *The Americanization of Emily*, *Roman Holiday* expresses American frustration with Europeans whose reverence for tradition keeps them from engaging in the Vespa-powered pursuit of happiness.

It Started in Naples ingeniously brokers an accommodation between the continents. Here Clark Gable returns to Italy, long after landing with the Fifth Army in 1944, to sort out the estate of his brother, who has died in Capri, leaving behind a child from an extramarital affair. The result – as he tangles with Sophia Loren, the illegitimate nephew's guardian – is an imbroglio that makes Gable exclaim 'The whole Roman empire's falling on me.' Despite his middle-aged masculinity, he is as discomfited by the manners and morals of the natives as Jones in Rome or Hepburn in Venice. His eight-year-old nephew Nando, whom he intends to rescue, is another decadent European stripling: he swigs Chianti, and at night is a tout for a basement club where Loren raunchily performs the song that is the film's anthem, Renato Carosone's 'Tu Vuo' Fa l'Americano', which mocks a Neapolitan pretender who puffs on Camels, drinks whisky and soda and plays baseball, hoping to pass for a Yank. Gable initiates his battle for hearts and minds by offering Nando a chocolate sundae. The boy winces and demands an espresso instead, leaving Gable to finish the sundae. Like Hepburn's waif in *Summertime*, Nando trades in dirty postcards; shocked, Gable orders him home to bed to dream of Indians, specifically 'men Indians!' America is so impeccably wholesome that its tales of genocide on the frontier are thought to be suitable for children.

Loren treats the adoption of Nando as a kidnapping, a small example of America's geopolitical piracy, and her neighbours heckle Gable from their balconies: 'Why don't you get out of the Middle East? All you want is oil, oil, oil!' Jack Lemmon is similarly castigated in Wilder's *Avanti!* He too, like Gable, has a relative who escaped from America to enjoy himself illicitly: he is in Ischia to claim the dead body of his father, who died on holiday with his mistress. But before the corpse is handed over, he has to endure a lecture about contemporary carpetbaggers who buy up Europe's relics and set down London Bridge in the Arizona desert or anchor the *Queen Mary* off Long Beach as a nautical cafeteria. In *It Started in Naples*, Loren eventually agrees to let Nando go, despite her contempt for a country where spaghetti comes in cans. Her surrender appeases Gable, and prompts him to reconsider his mission. Disgusted by the crass bragging of some compatriots on the train that is taking him to the airport in Rome, he jumps off and returns to Capri. Happy endings are mandatory, at least on film: foreign policy is here not tragic, as *Fortune* warned it would be, but a comic compromise that satisfies all parties.

Under cover of disseminating happiness, Americans may have been exporting an affliction. In *A New Kind of Love*, the Jewish comedian George Tobias glumly swallows an aspirin in a café. When Paul Newman tells him that no one is allowed to be unhappy in Paris, he growls 'I'm an American citizen. I got a right to be miserable any place in the world.' In Harold Flender's *Paris Blues*, Eddie the saxophonist ruefully notes a consequence of American universality. At home, the kids are all crazy, turning into juvenile delinquents; now one of his colleagues in the band is 'the first Frenchman I know who's had a nervous breakdown'. Mental illness, he adds, is known locally as 'the American's disease'.

Or was Europe the disease? Some late stories by John Updike sympathetically examine the American dread of being infected or engulfed by a continent with too much history. At best, in 'The Afterlife', it offers the delights of a second childhood. For two retired New Yorkers, the English countryside is tidy, quaint, like illustrations in the books they read in the nursery, a relief from the businesslike rigours and pressures of Manhattan. England may be a literal afterlife, because Updike's protagonist stumbles in the dark on a crooked staircase, falls and almost – or perhaps actually – kills himself. Other characters find Europe to be a post-mortem underworld. In 'Cruise', two temporary shipboard lovers on an educational voyage through the Greek islands helplessly re-enact classical myths. The sites they visit are primordial, abysmal. In a cavern that was supposedly the mouth of Hades, 'the stones smelled of all those past lives, stumbling from birth to death by the flickering light of illusion'. Europe has spoiled their American faith in novelty and the prospect of endless rebirths, and that sepulchral realization puts an end to their affair. Another mismatched couple – an older man with many divorces behind him, an opinionated feminist twenty years younger – find that their relationship frays in Italy and again in Ireland. At Fiume, Vivian is enraged by the sarcophagi that the poet and warrior Gabriele d'Annunzio designed for himself and his comrades: Europe, she complains, is a mausoleum glorifying dead white males. When they reach Ireland, it is George who is downcast. The terrain in Texas is empty because unmarked by a human presence; here the vacancy tells of a 'Becketty nothingness', of poor, brief lives commemorated only by abandoned cottages with dirt floors. Vivian proposes a hike, though George warns her that 'Americans have lost all sense of how long a mile is. They think it's a minute of sitting in a car.' Soon enough, her back hurts from the concussion of the rocks and she can't continue. To be an Irish peasant required a mental and physical fortitude these cushioned Americans do not possess.

Travelling to America, you are projected into the future. Returning to Europe, you live backwards, drowning in time not outpacing it. When Thoreau set out from his cabin at Walden Pond he always walked westwards, following the sun (and the course of empire, as Bishop Berkeley predicted in 1726 in his 'Verses on the Prospect of Planting Arts and Learning in America'); if he had headed east, he might have been obliterated by the oncoming night. The confrontation Updike describes is no longer between innocence and experience, as it was in Henry James's novels about heiresses or in those films from the 1950s with their impregnably virtuous heroines. In these stories, Europe is a psychological and physical ordeal because it involves the acceptance of defeat – a premonition of death and, since history runs in circles rather than proceeding forever onwards and upwards, of America's eventual demise.

8 | Free-Enterprise Art

Despite the westward shift of political and economic power, an imbalance remained. Clement Greenberg, contributing to the American issue of *Horizon* in 1946, regretted that his countrymen still thought of culture as a foreign import, like French wine or British tweed. Soon enough, America's wholesale export of images, sounds and words was to leave every other country in its debt; Greenberg, however, pointed out that 'culture means cultivation', and although the American masses had acquired technical skills – the ability to drive a car or operate a flush toilet made them, he crustily remarked, cultured in the Soviet sense – he expected them to take longer to understand the value of art and the need for it to be home-grown.

Meanwhile he took heart from the work of two uniquely American artists, one of whom showed how the individual could register a protest against a standardized society, while the other put industrial materials and procedures to aesthetic use. The first was Jackson Pollock, who inhabited what Greenberg called a 'lonely jungle of immediate sensations' but in his paintings made an effort 'to cope with urban life'. The second was the sculptor David Smith, a blacksmith's son, who welded iron and stainless steel with a blowtorch or stippled the metal with a grinder, bending and making it fluent. Pollock tacked canvases to the wall or spread them on the floor, then spattered or dribbled colour and worked it in with sticks, trowels or knives until the picture plane, replete with lakes, thickets and ridges of pigment, was like a sample of American terrain seen from above. Smith likewise made sculptures that seemed to unfurl into open space rather than staying fixed on their pedestals. His *Hudson River Landscape* alluded to the views he saw from the train on his way through the Adirondacks: as if travelling on tracks, the steel takes a looping detour along valleys and up hills, surmounting locked gates and gathering up a succession of agricultural implements along the way before it completes its all-embracing circuit. For work like that of Smith and Pollock, artisanal in execution yet epic in scope, there was no European precedent, which gave Greenberg hope.

American artists themselves saw the end of the war as an opportunity to interrupt and renew the staid, fixed history of art. As Mark Rothko said on behalf of his colleagues, 'We've got to forget what the Old Masters did' – or what they once did had to be swept away with the rest of the European detritus. On his first trip abroad in 1950, Rothko declared Paris to be ugly, of visual interest only because 'crumbling plaster and dangling window shutters form a continuous pastiche of textures'. Italian museums, he discovered, contained art that was merely decorative: Botticelli's Madonnas knew nothing about the bloody, milky business of motherhood. Returning in 1958, Rothko visited the ruins at Pompeii and Paestum and remarked 'I have been painting Greek temples all my life without knowing it'; at least, in his crimson, purple and black abstractions, he had been painting the sacrifices made on gory altars inside such temples. 'Free from the weight of European tradition,' as Barnett Newman announced, Americans were redefining the sublime, which in its attempt to grasp infinitude challenged art to compete with religion. Although Newman did not expect his fellow painters to make 'cathedrals out of *Christ*, man, or "life"', they found new ways of sanctifying space. Commissioned to design an ecumenical chapel for a Catholic university in Houston, Rothko pondered the examples of Michelangelo's Medici library with its blind windows and the monastic cells painted by Fra Angelico at San Marco in Florence. The enclosure he designed, walled with non-representational canvases, is a gallery where contemplation is meant to lead on to revelation: the viewer who sits for long enough and looks hard enough may at last see into the layered depths of those hypnotic panels.

The pronouncements made by this generation of artists were a second declaration of independence. In a new land, Rothko insisted, 'we start anew'. In 1943 Newman had called for an art that abandoned bucolic anecdotes and instead reflected 'the new America', soon to be 'the cultural center of the world'. Clyfford Still portentously described a single brushstroke marking a blank canvas as 'one of the few truly liberating concepts man has ever known'. Such rhetoric appealed to the proponents of the American century, and in 1946 Nelson Rockefeller – the son of Abby Aldrich Rockefeller, one of three so-called 'adamantine ladies' who established the Museum of Modern Art – took to Brazil a collection of paintings by young Americans, supplemented by the work of Europeans like Chagall, Léger and Grosz who now lived in New York. As Coordinator of Inter-American Affairs, Rockefeller had worked during the war to combat German influence in South America, and after 1945 he established philanthropic agencies that paid for model farms in Venezuela (whose reserves of oil he channelled north as chairman of Creole Petroleum) as well as in Ecuador and Brazil. Art supplemented political persuasion by advertising the creative bonus of liberty. In 1949, trying to close the gap between Pollock's 'lonely jungle' and his own sleek, exclusive corporate boardrooms, Rockefeller described Abstract Expressionism as 'free-enterprise painting'. That persuaded Henry Luce to commission a pictorial essay about Pollock, which began by asking 'Is he the greatest living painter in the United States?' The photographs taken for *Life* by Martha Holmes made it clear that Pollock was no European aesthete: he dries dishes in his farmhouse kitchen, buys supplies at the general store, squats beside a neighbour's tractor, and mixes dry pigment outdoors on a rude palette of corrugated iron. Whether or not the gestural bravado with which he applied paint had anything in common with go-getting capitalism remained a matter of opinion.

The gallery owner Betty Parsons thought of Europe as a 'walled city', besieged and breached by these iconoclastic Americans. The French, having already been occupied by the Nazis, did not welcome this fresh assault on their citadel. In 1947 in the magazine *Carrefour*, Frank Elgar – a pseudonym used by the art historian Roger Lesbats – explained the abstraction of 'our American friends' by arguing that, in establishing technological dominion over the material world, they had lost contact with sensuous reality. As a result they lacked the 'plastic sense' required by visual artists; nature had punished them by depriving them of tactile, palpable contact with appearances, and their blank, featureless paintings could have been made by blind men. It was like the purported opposition between wine and Coca-Cola: the fruit of the human soil against a synthetic concoction brewed in a laboratory. French resistance was even more intemperate when the Museum of Modern Art's touring exhibition of American painting with what were called 'advanced tendencies' reached Paris in 1958. The critic of *Le Monde* railed against 'these contagious heresies' – although contagion assumed that the American fad would go on spreading, and heresy appealed in vain to a canonical orthodoxy that was overturned by the first modernists.

The French received a sly warning of their relegation in Vincente Minnelli's musical *An American in Paris*. The film is based on the symphonic poem George Gershwin composed in 1928, when Paris was synonymous with bohemian experimentation in life and art, the home of music that was modern because impudently mundane – hence the taxi horns, brought back to New York as souvenirs, that Gershwin added to his orchestra – as well as being the favoured resort of American writers like Gertrude Stein and Hemingway, whose originality was unwelcome at home. In a narration that introduces the film, Gene Kelly explains that he stayed on in Paris after the army discharged him in 1945 because he wanted to paint, and 'if you can't paint in Paris you'd better give up and marry the boss's daughter'. But by 1951, when the film was released, the capital of modern art had transferred from Montparnasse to downtown Manhattan, and Kelly's amateurish urban views suggest that he should have settled for the boss's daughter. He still behaves like an open-handed GI, distributing bubblegum to Left Bank gamins and offering Leslie Caron a candy bar as they stroll beside the Seine. But he is behind the times and out of place, washed up here like Winston Churchill who, after being rejected by ungrateful Labour voters, is glimpsed daubing a canvas in Montmartre. Minnelli's Paris is not the tatty, damaged place that Rothko and Saul Bellow discovered after the war. Horse-drawn carts still plod through the cobbled Left Bank streets, which are swept by a man with a birch broom; a concierge on her knees scrubs the steps of her lodging house. Modernity here is relative: when Leslie Caron is described as 'vivacious and modern', we see her dressed as a flapper dancing the Charleston, a throwback to Gershwin's racier 1920s.

Despite this homage to a lost paradise, *An American in Paris* takes tough-minded cognizance of a change in circumstances. Kelly's would-be patron is a kind of Mrs Stone, an heiress from Baltimore who wants to rescue him from bohemianism, and Caron, employed in a perfume shop, has to truckle to a fat customer from Milwaukee who is in Europe to spend her husband's money. An impresario implores the music-hall singer played by Georges Guétary to 'come to America and give us Yanks a break'. A break from what? In 1951 America was sending jazz musicians to Europe, not importing top-hatted boulevardiers. Guétary accepts the contract and smarmily tells Caron 'You'll love the Americans,' although Sartre and his intellectual comrades were warning against them. Oscar Levant, cast as a work-shy concert pianist, retaliates by demonstrating how Coca-Colonization works. He ceremoniously sits at a café table, swathes a Coke bottle in a starched napkin, embeds it in an ice bucket, then levers off the cap with an explosive flourish as if he were uncorking a magnum of champagne.

America asserts its primacy in the final ballet, which choreographs Gershwin's symphonic poem. Here Kelly, Caron and a team of demobbed GIs in tap shoes whirl through a succession of sets that jolt the paintings in French museums out of their immobility and bestow on them an American dynamism: the Place de la Concorde as Dufy might have seen it, with skipping gendarmes in tricolour uniforms and a fountain that spouts tinted smoke, a flower market of nubile Renoir blooms, a park that shades into an uncanny Rousseau jungle, the foyer of the Palais Garnier made molten and inflammatory by the palette of van Gogh, a Toulouse-Lautrec dance hall. There is an epilogue to this in 1964 in Godard's *Bande à part*, when three pranksters set themselves to beat the record set by an American tourist who sprinted through the Louvre in under ten minutes. Using the galleries as a race track, Godard's characters leave David's Horatii transfixed in their statuesque poses, skid down the staircase where the winged Victory of Samothrace is grounded, and shave a few seconds off the American's time. All the same, the feat cannot re-establish French pre-eminence. The paintings are smeared or blurred by motion: cinema is kinesis, which makes it intrinsically American.

Having shown how the seventh art combines all the others, *An American in Paris* ends with a survey of the twinkling painted city seen supposedly from the heights of Montmartre. Across the view is imprinted the self-congratulatory announcement 'Made in Hollywood, U.S.A.': Europe has been at once recreated and superseded.

The year after the release of *An American in Paris*, an opera written by two Americans in Paris at around the time that Gershwin was composing his symphonic poem received its first performance in the city. Virgil Thomson's *Four Saints in Three Acts*, set to a stammering but mesmerically monotonous text by Gertrude Stein, was presented as part of a Twentieth Century Festival, organized by the Congress for Cultural Freedom with funds from the State Department and the CIA. Opera, like painting, was required to advertise the advantages of a life spent in liberty: after all, song is a gloriously unnecessary mode of expression, abstracted from or raised far above spoken communication, and as W. H. Auden once said, 'every high C accurately struck demolishes the theory that we are the irrepressible puppets of fate or chance' – or, for that matter, that we are the mute and obedient creatures of a monopolistic state.

The collaboration between Thomson and Stein began on the Left Bank in 1927, although their opera was not staged until 1934 in Hartford, Connecticut, at the Wadsworth Atheneum, where St Teresa of Avila and St Ignatius Loyola babbled about theological mysteries in a sky of shiny cellophane as the orchestra played snatches of dance-hall tunes, hymns and popular ditties that floated up to heaven from the rustic midwest. Thomson had uprooted himself from Kansas City and sailed to Paris in 1925 in order to be rootlessly modern, yet in *Four Saints* he made a determined effort to align the baroque supernature of Catholic mysticism with the more humdrum landscape he had left behind. Gershwin's American in Paris is briefly homesick: on his strutting perambulation of the boulevards he is stopped short by a tinkling celesta, and in depressed recollection he hears a trumpet playing the blues on the other side of the ocean. Thomson assuaged such longings by finding replicas or precursors of America in Europe. Travelling south on a research trip for the opera, he hiked across the border between France and Spain to visit a chapel dedicated to St Ignatius. The meridional light reminded him of

Texas, and he thought that 'the Spaniards are all enclosed like Americans', externally tough but tender underneath.

Thomson returned to America late in the 1930s, but was back in Paris at the outbreak of war. The theatrical producer John Houseman ordered him to abandon what he called the 'moribund continent' as the Germans advanced; Thomson promptly came home and until 1954 worked as a music critic for the *New York Herald Tribune*. When the war ended, his columns immediately asserted America's new cultural primacy. In January 1946, he attempted to define musical Americanism, and said that one distinctive national habit was the steady crescendo – a sonic equivalent to irresistible progress? He admitted that a good deal of American music was composed by refugees from Europe, but this lent credence to his claim that 'we are producing very nearly the best music in the world'. In January 1950 he described New York as the art's international stock exchange, where fees were set and reputations made, now that 'the world's center of music distribution' had shifted away from Europe.

The young Thomson had deferred to the French avant-garde: he admired Erik Satie's so-called 'furniture music', which wanted to be practical and useful not foggily emotive, and he was intrigued by George Antheil's alliance between music and machinery. By 1952 he had no need to apologize for American music, and at the festival *Four Saints* was somewhat over-generously ranked with Alban Berg's *Wozzeck* and Benjamin Britten's *Billy Budd*, also being given their first performances in Paris, as one of the 'Masterpieces of the 20th Century'. The organizers, intent on asserting liberal principles, decreed that 'for psychological reasons the entire cast [of *Four Saints*] . . . should be American Negro'. The psychological reasons had to do with America's reputation in Europe: the aim was to allay criticism of what Gunnar Myrdal – a Swedish economist who spent the war years preparing a report on race relations for the Carnegie Foundation – called 'an American dilemma'. How, Myrdal asked, could a society founded on the love of liberty tolerate an ethnic underclass? Opera at least was a career open to those with talent, irrespective of colour. Missing the point, the Paris critics – as Thomson remembered – regretted the lack of 'Negro sex display' in *Four Saints*, and pined for Josephine Baker with her skimpy skirt of jiggling bananas.

Thomson and Stein intended the babbled colloquies of *Four Saints* as an ideal representation of their own unworldly lives as what the composer called 'consecrated artists', necessarily at odds with lowbrow, utilitarian America. What mattered to the opera's political sponsors in 1952 was its homespun sociability, not its louche sophistication or high-flown vocational rhapsodies. In fact the saints, as Thomson said, sound more like residents of Kansas City than mystical mentors looking down from the clouds. The St Teresa of the opera has outlived the erotic raptures of the febrile nun from Avila, and St Ignatius has softened the dictatorial dogmatism he bequeathed to the Jesuits; they share a picnic with their celestial colleagues and take photographs of each other, like a provincial glee club on a rural outing. At one point the gospel songs, ballads and jaunty marches are interrupted by a patriotic outburst from the chorus, which for sheer joy chants 'My country 'tis of thee, sweet land of liberty'. Stein indirectly explained the quote from the anthem when she remarked that In American religion 'there is no Heaven, because there is only "up"'. America already is heaven, sanctified by its virgin terrain and its unimpeded social mobility. What else is there to pray for? The Congress for Cultural Freedom could not have asked for more.

Music also beat the drum for American values in an international tour of *Porgy and Bess*, which travelled throughout Europe and the Middle East in 1954, then covered Central and South America in 1955. Again the cast was African American; the great soprano Leontyne Price appeared in both *Porgy* and *Four Saints*. Audiences everywhere enjoyed Gershwin's tunes, but when *Porgy* reached Russia late in 1955 its message was muddled by Cold War preconceptions. Foreign relations suffered an extra setback when Ira Gershwin's wife Leonore promenaded in a mink coat, bedizened with so many jewels – capitalist trophies – that she seemed to be walking through a blitz of flashbulbs. Mrs Gershwin also complained about the food at receptions and wondered whether all the caviar had been shipped to Beverly Hills, where, as she informed her hosts, it cost $35 a pound.

Truman Capote travelled with the company, and reported on the comedy of mutual incomprehension for *The New Yorker*. Despite their animosity, Capote saw the two empires as duplicates, alike in their boring obsession with industrial productivity. A Norwegian businessman he met in Leningrad agreed about the affinity. The USA and the USSR, he told Capote, were both isolated by their immensity; snubbed by Europe, they felt inferior, and though they begged for affection and acceptance they sometimes preferred to be feared. In addition, Poland in winter reminded Capote of Wyoming, and the spindly wooden guard-towers at the Russian border resembled those around convict farms in Alabama. Other analogies were more approximate, as when Capote was told that he looked like Dmitri Shostakovich: both had baby faces, but one belonged to a decadent cherub, the other – a mask that could not hide the composer's terror – to the demoralized victim of a regime that hounded, imprisoned and sometimes slaughtered refractory artists. Capote expressed no opinion of communism, but came to dread the bear-like brawn of his hosts. A Ministry of Culture official greeted him, he recalled, with a crushing 'handshake like a nutcracker'. The wooden figurine that struts through Tchaikovsky's ballet was not so harmless after all.

Porgy and Bess did little to convince the Russians that free enterprise was superior to a state-managed economy. The audience in Leningrad was shocked by the raw carnality of the duet between trollopy Bess and her brutish paramour Crown. The God-fearing piety of the characters seemed merely pitiful, since the Soviet regime had done away with religion; nobody understood the crap game because gambling was illegal. No synopsis of the action was available, and during the saucer burial, when neighbours making donations for funeral expenses cluster around the corpse of Robbins as his widow keens, Capote claimed that he overheard a Soviet dignitary whisper to a journalist 'Ah, now I see! They are going to *eat* him.' For the prudish Russians, the opera was a regression – as the Nazis said of jazz, which they vilified as 'Negermusik' – to tribal barbarity.

Elsewhere in Europe, especially during a season in Berlin, the touring production of *Porgy and Bess* triumphantly outfaced that racial slur. Jazz was now the voice of America, exemplifying the laid-back, liberty-taking inventiveness of the national spirit. Even Boris Vian admitted that its 'impro-visational soul' proved that not all Americans were dour, angular, inflexible machines. Jack Kerouac mimicked jazzy mannerisms in the riffs of his prose: 'We writhe and twist and blow,' he said of the Beat writers, who were experimenting with newly elastic uses of language. The same metaphor is used by Marlon Brando to explain the purpose of his motorcycle gang in *The Wild One*: 'The idea is to wail, to make some jive.' To rev up a bike is like tuning an instrument, and speed, as much as scat singing or trumpet playing, is a form of virtuosity. At home, this music could sound angry, as when Montgomery Clift demilitarizes his bugle in a Honolulu bar in *From Here to Eternity*: bent almost double, he puffs all his wind through the tube and releases a screech of fury that is a protest against war. But in Europe, the spontaneity of jazz, like the stratospheric high Cs in Auden's remark about opera, seemed to offer a blessed relief from history and destiny.

In 1957 Miles Davis improvised a score for Louis Malle's grimly determin-istic *Ascenseur pour l'échafaud*, in which Jeanne Moreau's lover murders her husband and is then trapped in an elevator when the power shuts off during his escape; he gets away with this crime but is found guilty of another that he did not commit. Waiting for him, Moreau calms her nerves by wandering along the wet, nocturnal Champs Elysées, accompanied by the solos Davis devised in response to the film during a midnight session in a rented studio. Although the story is about enclosure and fatality, Davis scoffed at the doomy mood of Paris, and when someone warned him that the singer Juliette Greco was an existentialist, he replied 'Man, fuck all that kind of shit.' What he composed as he watched Moreau wander, staring vacantly into shop windows and studying other passers-by, was the kind of 'pedestrian music' that Satie and Cocteau theorized about during Virgil Thomson's early days in Paris. His trumpet goes for a stroll; it lives in the present, and for a while can shut out remorse about the past and dread of the future.

After some decorous adjustments, jazz provided officialdom with a Cold War manifesto. Louis Armstrong believed that Khrushchev should be made to listen to music that was 'the swingin' sound of freedom'. Nicknamed Ambassador Satch, the jolly, avuncular Armstrong exemplified what the journalist Nat Hentoff called the 'power of jazz-as-diplomacy'. In London in 1955 he demotically enticed the stiff-backed Princess Margaret to stomp, and in Switzerland he compensated for the inequity of international trade: a critic said that his performances made up for the punitive American tariff on Swiss watches. Another commentator, Felix Belair, thought that Armstrong should have been invited to the Geneva summit conference, where he might have charmed Nikolai Bulganin and the Soviet delegation into an agreement not to stockpile nuclear warheads. The broadcaster Ed Murrow, describing the same tour, emphasized power rather than the affability of Armstrong's persona: Murrow likened him to Hannibal crossing the Alps, with a trumpet and five band members instead a baggage train of elephants. Adding extra heft to the metaphor, Murrow remarked that 'America's old-fashioned weapon was a blue note in a minor key.' On the Gold Coast in 1956, Armstrong played 'Black and Blue' for Prime Minister Kwame Nkrumah, who was soon to declare Ghana's independence from Britain. This, for Murrow, counted as diplomatic recognition by the 'great free nation across the seas where both the blues and the coloured people had their first awakening'.

Duke Ellington joined Armstrong in promoting the notion of music as a universal language – or of jazz as an American slang that could be adapted for international use. Ellington's tours took him to the Soviet bloc, the Middle East, India, Pakistan, Afghanistan, Japan, Southeast Asia and of course to Latin America; these travels exposed him to a range of musical styles that might, he thought, eventually coalesce in a wordless Esperanto. In 1970 he composed a suite entitled *The Afro-Eurasian Eclipse*, suggested by Marshall McLuhan's claim that 'the whole world is going oriental'. It included a blast of Teutonized rock and a brassily wayward version of Australia's 'Waltzing Matilda', along with solos for Chinese gongs, African drums and even the didgeridoo, represented in Ellington's band by a snorting saxophone – homages, or acts of co-optation? The State Department, which sent Ellington on these expeditions, was gratified to receive a report from Costa Rica testifying that his band's performance outdid 'the tremendous public furore over the establishment of a Russian embassy'. Challenged at press conferences in enemy territory, Ellington responded as suavely as a professional politician.

If asked, as he was in Russia, why the United States did not subsidize culture, he would say that American artists and scientists were so competitive that they spurned a helping hand. Needled about race relations, he usually cited the freedom of the American press, which stoked up indignation by openly reporting incidents of injustice that other countries would conceal. In most cities he found time to give a lecture explaining that what he played should not be called 'jazz' – an inexact term with a smutty pedigree, since it doubled as a synonym for having sex. 'We stopped using the word in 1943,' Ellington recalled; he preferred to call it 'the American Idiom, or the Music of Freedom of Expression'. Thus dignified, jazz earned constitutional protection.

A concert given by Ella Fitzgerald in West Berlin in February 1960 showed off the American idiom at its most freely expressive. The setting was the Deutschlandhalle, built in the blockish fascist style for the 1936 Olympic Games and inaugurated by Hitler. Fitzgerald free-associated through songs like 'The Lady is a Tramp' – into which she interpolated a compliment to the food at the Kempinski Hotel, where she was staying – and 'Summertime' from *Porgy and Bess*, before arriving at the finale, her first performance of 'Mack the Knife'. This song about a shark-like gangster and the duped women or defrauded men he kills introduced *The Threepenny Opera* by Kurt Weill and Bertolt Brecht, first staged in Berlin in 1928. Its acerbic, curdled tone was meant to denounce a corrupt and murderous society, but it had recently been Americanized. Armstrong, who often performed it, smoothed away its cynicism by remarking that in New Orleans he had often played at the funerals of rogues like Mack, who were harmless tomcats with harems of prostitutes – an opinion that brings to mind European complaints about America's incomprehension of evil.

Fitzgerald too overlooked Mack's crimes. Brecht's rasping words did not bother her, because she promptly forgot them. Always in tune and in rhythm, conscientiously inserting new rhymes, she paraphrased the original text – 'something 'bout cash?' she wondered, not quite sure – or filled the gaps with a take-off of Armstrong's catarrhal vocal style and a summary of the song's history up to this moment of unembarrassed panic:

> Bobby Darin and Louis Armstrong made a rec-ord,
> Now Ella and her fellas
> Are making a wreck
> Of 'Mack the Knife'.

She ended, still true to a melody that now sounded cheery not baleful, by joking about her own irrepressible creativity:

> Yes, we swung it,
> You won't recognize it,
> It's a surprise hit.

The absurd hilarity of her performance lightened the satirical odium of the Weimar Republic, and humanized the monumental arena where wrestlers and weightlifters Teutonically tussled and grunted during the Third Reich. Here was a precious specimen of what might be called free-enterprise singing.

'Poor Americans!' sighed James Morris, smiling at their crude rural pageantry after his cross-country trip in 1955–6. Morris pitied them because they had 'only a flag to honour', but he was concerned that they were beginning to flaunt it.

Luce declared in his editorial about the American century that the Stars and Stripes was 'the most exciting flag of all the world' – exciting, presumably, because it so boldly chronicled the nation's political history, with stripes representing the tearaway British colonies as they charged into combat and stars awarded like medallions to the states that subsequently joined the Union. During the Cold War, the flag once more became a battle standard. In 1953 the pickpocket in Samuel Fuller's *Pickup on South Street* accidentally steals a roll of microfilm containing national secrets, and is warned by the police that if he does not cooperate he will be as guilty as the traitors who gave the A-bomb to Stalin. The reply the script initially assigned to the pickpocket was 'Don't wave the goddam flag at me!' The FBI Director

J. Edgar Hoover objected to the line, and Fuller, assuming the problem was blasphemy, downgraded it to 'damn flag'. Hoover still disapproved: it was unthinkable, he said, that any American, crooked or not, should speak out against the waving of the flag.

Foreigners did not always share Luce's excitement, and Robert Frank's photographs in *The Americans* showed Old Glory looking dejected or thread-bare, which antagonized critics when his book appeared in 1958. Strung outside a window on a dingy building in Hoboken, the flag obscures the face of a woman who seems to be snacking as she watches a patriotic parade. Worn so thin that it is almost transparent, it droops over an Independence Day picnic in upstate New York, with no breeze to bestir it. In an overgrown backyard in Venice, California, it serves as a tent for the owner of a tumble-down house. At a political rally in Chicago it is ruffled into bunting, while its message is puffed out by a tuba with a mouthpiece that covers the head of the man who is playing it: the silent sound the photograph makes is a vulgar blare of militant brass. On his American travels, Henri Cartier-Bresson photographed an ancient, scrawny New England woman who is literally wrapped in the flag or, since she has looped it around her neck, is using it as a bib. Flags are raucously waved by women in Harlem in another photograph Cartier-Bresson took in 1960, but they are not the Stars and Stripes: the rally was held to welcome Fidel Castro to his hotel during a visit in which he hectored the United Nations, and the loyalists penned behind a police barricade are flapping Cuban flags.

In a series of paintings that he began in 1954, Jasper Johns disarmed the national banner. The idea came from a dream in which he saw himself painting the flag, and – like Betsy Ross allegedly tearing her petticoat to make the very first flag – he used a sheet from his bed as a canvas for his first version. Removed from the public arena, the flag became a private plaything. Newsprint collaged onto the fabric marked it as temporal not eternal, journalism not history, which may be why it requires daily pledges of allegiance. If you get close enough, you can glimpse the words 'Pipe Dream' – the title of a new Rodgers and Hammerstein musical set in Monterey, with locations including a flophouse and the Bear Flag Café, a brothel that is proudly named after the grizzly bear on the official ensign of California. Johns may have been suggesting that America too is a fantasy, a shared delusion. Sometimes he bled the flag, bleaching its excitable primary colours. On another occasion he replaced the red and blue with green, orange and black, a different symbolic spectrum. In his lithograph *Two Flags* the stripes relax into messy squiggles instead of charging straight ahead. A pencil drawing gives the flag a total of sixty-four stars, though Johns had no imperial expansion in view. He stencilled 'United States' in the corner that contains the stars, no longer trusting the symbol to be self-explanatory, but knocked the capital U sideways to sabotage the unity it stood for. Johns gave some specimens a plyboard backing or a stiff crust of encaustic and hardened beeswax, while he impressed another on a slab of lead. Immobilized, the flag cannot wave and is deprived of its traditional function, which was to identify the army above which it was raised. For Johns the flag is omnipresent, but always different. Not representing a consensus, it is a surface with no single idea behind it. At the funerals of presidents or fallen soldiers, the flag that shrouds the coffin is ritualistically folded until it is almost the size of a handkerchief; with its moral and emotional force compressed inside, it can be presented to the chief mourner as a token of national gratitude. This involution is contradicted by Johns, who opened the flag out or unstitched its bricolage of ribbons and asterisks.

A flag by Johns is a literal patchwork, like the federation for which it stands. In the maps he painted between 1961 and 1963, the slab of the continent occupied by the United States has the same instability. The seas here do not shine, contradicting the description in 'America the Beautiful'. The Pacific overflows and smears California and Arizona, as if the San Andreas Fault had opened, and the texture of the paint – a storm of brushstrokes for the inundated west coast, bulges and ridges that suggest some kind of geological upheaval in the north-east – mimes continuing disruptions. On the east coast the label ATLANT, its final syllable lopped off or perhaps located outside the frame, implies that oceans connect continents rather than separating them. Johns also stencilled in the names of British Columbia, Quebec and the Yucatan Peninsula, refusing the United States a monopoly of the landmass it shares with its occasionally resentful neighbours. Within national borders, he recognized the inconsistency of a country that adheres loosely and is neither unified nor uniform: some state names are spelled out (Colorado, Kansas) while others are abbreviated (N.D., Neb.), so that they all seem to be talking at once with different accents.

A nation defined by symbols has to guard them against misinterpretation or misuse. The American anthem relies on the symbol's immutability, proudly announcing that after a nervous night 'our flag was still there'. Stravinsky, a grateful immigrant, got into trouble when he re-orchestrated 'The Stars and Stripes' for a Fourth of July concert in 1941; the police in Boston confiscated the pages of his score because it was unlawful to tamper with national property. In 1989 the constitution was amended to protect the flag from desecration – a crime committed by wartime protestors who burned it, and probably by the Yippie leader Abbie Hoffman, who provoked a scandal when he used it as a shirt on a television talk show (though there was no protest when Roy Rogers wore a similar garment: a singing cowboy could hardly be accused of dressing ironically or seditiously). The ban on defaming the symbol might have been extended to the artisanal flags made from frayed cardboard or from Cape Cod driftwood and chunks of gooey plaster by Claes Oldenburg, or to the Old Glory dog blanket in which William Wegman wrapped his pet Weimaraner; and it would surely have censured the girls in the Tunis brothel in Samuel Fuller's film *The Big Red One*, who have 'patriotic pussies' and wear panties stitched from captured American flags when they entertain GIs who are on their way to liberate Italy. But in 1990 the Supreme Court ruled that comments on the flag should be considered speech, which entitled the speakers to protection under the First Amendment. The language of signs is as polyphonic as Babel, with endless variants and no single authorized version – like America, a literal free-for-all.

9 | Americanophilia

After American troops withdrew from the Pacific in 1945, Melanesians used magic to summon back those god-like men and the stacks of goods they brought with them. The islanders cleared landing strips no plane would ever use, and built boxy likenesses of radios that were empty inside. Some still await this second coming: in Vanuatu, formerly called the New Hebrides, 15 February is celebrated as the date when the legendary figure of John Frum – whose name probably means 'John from (America)' – will reappear overhead.

Post-war Europe had its own equivalent of these cargo cults. In France, the absent deities were movie stars; Hollywood films were banned during the Nazi occupation, so peace meant renewed access to their grandiose fantasies and charismatic actors. Paris intellectuals were especially keen for the return of Humphrey Bogart. Often cast as a convict or a hoodlum earlier in his career, Bogart had turned into a standard-bearer for liberation, like Byron glamorously joining the Greeks in their war of independence. As Rick in *Casablanca* and as Hemingway's Harry Morgan in *To Have and Have Not*, Bogart begins as a morally neutral isolationist. Yet eventually these loners recognize that they must take sides and, while maintaining their pretence of hard-bitten detachment, they lend a hand to Free French partisans in Morocco and Martinique. Bogart, profiting from the decisions of those fictional characters, became a conscience for the humiliated French and a boost to morale. Jean Gabin, fighting with the Allies in North Africa, happened to be in a naval convoy that was bombed; he lost his nerve and cowered against the ship's rails, shuddering. Then he remembered Bogart's tight-lipped composure when playing a similar scene on screen, which restored his self-control.

American films, like America itself, possessed a talismanic power. In Jean-Pierre Melville's *L'Armée des ombres*, some Resistance fighters travel to London to receive medals from the exiled General de Gaulle, after which they relax at a matinee of *Gone with the Wind*. 'For the French,' says one of the partisans when they emerge from the cinema, 'the war will be over when they can see that great film!' It was not enough merely to look. At their most idolatrous, the French had to get their hands on a particle of these entrancing ribbons of illusion. When *Citizen Kane* was belatedly released in Paris, François Truffaut was so desperate to own a scrap of Welles's box of tricks that he purloined some lobby cards from a display outside the cinema. In Godard's *À Bout de souffle*, Jean-Paul Belmondo, who mimics a hero he fondly calls 'Bogey', is larcenous on a more ambitious scale. He steals cars, which must be American to be worth the risk. He begins with a boxy Plymouth Valiant that belongs to the US Army, then graduates to sportier models – an Oldsmobile, a Ford Thunderbird, a Cadillac Eldorado. His 'New-Yorkaise' girlfriend Jean Seberg is interchangeable with these cars, and when he offers 'une américaine' to a shady dealer on the telephone she wonders if he means her. No, he explains, he was referring to 'une voiture américaine'. But car and girl are alike in being what linguistic theorists call a vehicle: the conveyance for an idea, a metaphorical token that will Americanize Belmondo by association.

The coveted objects promised transformation and, better yet, transportation. In Jacques Demy's *Lola*, a cabaret dancer in Nantes hopes that her aigrette will make her look like Marilyn Monroe in *Gentlemen Prefer Blondes*; she dates an American sailor called Frankie, perhaps because he reminds her of Gene Kelly and his nautical buddies who sing and dance through New York on shore leave in *On the Town*, and with her eyes closed she imagines that, as in a movie, he will whisk her away across the ocean. A teenage girl, equally besotted, confers an exotic aura on Frankie's home state of Illinois by gallically pronouncing it as Illinouwa. Lola's friend Roland studies a map of the United States and in a yearning reverie whispers 'Kansas City, Salt Lake City' as if invoking fabled destinations like Samarkand or Shangri-La; he would probably have found the actual places an anticlimax. To Truffaut, Demy and their fellow acolytes, the very process of film-making felt like a journey through America, even if they never left a studio in France.

Playing a harried director in *La Nuit américaine*, Truffaut remarks that the accident-prone business resembles a trip by stagecoach in the Old West: you begin by hoping to enjoy yourself, and end – like the characters in John Ford's *Stagecoach* when the Indians attack – by praying that you will just reach your destination alive.

Films were shop windows for a way of life that was now tantalizingly within reach. New American tastes changed the bodies of young Europeans from the inside out, while American clothes did the same from the outside in. The riotous carrot-haired child in Raymond Queneau's novel *Zazie dans le Métro* drinks only what she calls 'cacocalo' – her juggled vowels are no odder than the original brand name, with its compact allusions to cocoa, cocaine and coldness – and develops such a lust for a pair of 'blewgenes' on sale at a Paris flea market that, like Truffaut making off with the *Kane* memorabilia and Belmondo hot-wiring those cars, she steals them. The word 'denim' comes from Nimes and 'jeans' is a garbled reminiscence of Genoa, where cotton corduroy was first made up into clothes for artisans, but Zazie ignores this European provenance. What matters to her is that the jeans are US Army surplus, which will make her American from the waist down. Her partiality is shared by Yves, the young lover of the expatriate Eric in James Baldwin's *Another Country*, who squeezes into his partner's blue jeans even though they are too short. Exemplifying French double standards, Yves is 'not very fond of Americans, but he liked their clothes'. The sartorial fads spread rapidly around the world: in 1957 *The New York Times* reported that young Indonesians in Bandung had outraged their elders by replacing traditional dress with an approximation of the blue jeans and red bomber jacket worn by James Dean in *Rebel Without a Cause*.

Louis Malle filmed Queneau's *Zazie* in 1960, helped by the expatriate photographer William Klein. Malle admired Klein's book of New York photographs, published in 1956 in France but not in America, where editors disliked the grit and grain of the images, their jumbled composition, and the seediness of the street life they documented. Klein's appraisal of New York coincided with that of Le Corbusier, who described the city as 'une catastrophe féerique', an enchanted disaster. His book's title, *Life Is Good & Good*

For You In New York: Trance Witness Reveals, is a rowdy collage of tabloid headlines; it begins with a series of rambunctious parades, followed by visits to a burlesque show and a working-class wedding, after which it dispassionately surveys the garbage this ravenous society regurgitates. Sewn into the volume by a little cord is a tourist brochure shaped like a Michelin guide, illustrated with jabbering ads for a Chinese Rathskeller and a can of Franco-American spaghetti, Maidenform bras and Mercury cars, along with samples of magazines like *Ebony* and *Mad*. By 1960 America was exporting zaniness, and a copy of *Mad* appears on a café table in Malle's film, with the goofily grinning redhead Alfred E. Neuman on its cover – America's latest specimen of modernism's new man, as impishly scornful of adult propriety as Zazie.

At Malle's request, Klein transformed the Paris streets into a Pop Art circus, painting a coloured storm of noisily meaningless signage onto flimsy, portable false walls that blocked off any more sober backgrounds that the camera wanted to exclude. Malle adopted the short-focus lens with which Klein flattened faces and warped perspectives in his New York photographs, and even enlisted him as a co-director: Klein probably shot an episode that treats Pigalle at night as if it were Times Square, with Zazie hurtling through a crowd to get to the cabaret where her uncle is performing. Filmed in close-up by a 12-mm camera, people collide or are crushed together; the temperature is raised by the pulsation of neon tubes, bent and twisted by their reflections on the hoods of parked cars; jazz sets a skittering tempo. During Zazie's day of escapades, Malle chose to see Paris through American eyes.

To adopt an American point of view, like trying on a pair of distorting spectacles, was only the first step. Why not assume an American identity?

The Italians who directed and acted in spaghetti Westerns made their imposture more credible by adopting aliases. Early in his career, Sergio Leone tautologously passed himself off as Bob Robertson, and an obscure colleague who made a film about Buffalo Bill claimed kinship with the greatest of Western directors by taking the name John W. Fordson. Preparing to play cowboys, Mario Girotti from Venice and Carlo Pedersoli from Naples became Terence Hill and Bud Spencer. In France, Cartier-Bresson affected the joking pseudonym Hank Carter, suitable for a case-hardened private eye. René Lodge Brabazon Raymond, born in London but resident in Switzerland, wrote eighty thrillers about American gangsters, filling in the topographical details – since he made only a few brief visits to the United States – from maps and encyclopaedias. His books had gruff, slangy titles like *The Fast Buck* and *Just Another Sucker*, and he published them under the pseudonym James Hadley Chase, which in the absence of a hyphen must have sounded to him as redoubtably American as Erle Stanley Gardner or John Dickson Carr.

When Jean-Pierre Grumbach enlisted in the Resistance, he had to choose a 'nom de guerre' that would protect his family if he were captured. He elected to call himself Melville, which sounded idiomatic because it rhymed with the Paris district of Belleville, although he had in mind the author of *Moby Dick*. He retained the surname after the war when directing films, and justified his decision by claiming that in America people changed names as easily as they changed shirts. Besides, it suited him better than the surname he was born with. Ever since adolescence, he said in 1973, he had been enthralled by 'le grand Melville', the writer who best understood the deathly idealism of Americans like Captain Ahab, and he could only break the hold of this adoptive ancestor by nominating another American avatar. He therefore claimed that in middle age he was turning into Jack London, one of whose predatory lone wolves he transported from the frozen Yukon to the Paris underworld in *Le Samouraï*, with Alain Delon as an icily affectless hit man.

Melville took the imaginative identification to extremes by living inside his custom-made America. He owned the small studio just off the Place Louis-Armstrong on the Left Bank where he made his films, and he slept on the premises; his apartment was a set, with shaky prop screens like those Klein designed for Malle and a scenic window that had a photographic panorama of New York skyscrapers outside it. The view from Delon's bare room in *Le Samouraï* consists of zigzagging metal fire escapes that exist nowhere in Paris: it is a faded, monochrome snapshot, an excerpt from an American dream. At work, Melville habitually wore a white Stetson, as if he were a cowboy or one of John Ford's cavalrymen unhorsed in motorized Paris. His characters are equally choosy about their accessories. The hero of *Bob le flambeur* sports a trench coat and fedora in homage to Bogart, and drives a finned Plymouth Belvedere convertible through the narrow Montmartre streets. Scouting for locations, Melville selected rundown areas that might have been in the outer boroughs of New York, like the pedestrian tunnel under a railway bridge where *Le Doulos* begins. Sacré Coeur is visible in the distance; ignoring the landmark, Melville preferred this wasteland with its mounds of gravel and withered trees. Indoors he was equally precise, and one set in *Le Doulos* exactly duplicates a gangster's lair he had seen in Rouben Mamoulian's *City Streets*. Though Melville often groused about America's 'impérialisme de civilisation', it was his choice to be colonized.

His characters, however, sometimes have difficulty living up to their models. The hero-worshipping Paolo in *Bob le flambeur* asks a crony whether it's true that Bob introduced the Montmartre gangs to American methods. He is referring to the use of guns: American crime, in the French view, was as methodical as everything else in that semi-automatic country. Bob, however, does not deserve his reputation for brutal efficiency. He is old, weary, and has come to disapprove of fast transatlantic habits, which is why he rebukes a girl he has seen at dawn accepting a lift on a motor scooter from an unknown American sailor. Despite the allure of the movies, European gentility was not easy to discard.

In 1958 Melville had the chance to compare his fantastical America with the reality when he travelled to New York to direct *Deux Hommes en Manhattan*, in which he also appears as Moreau, a reporter who teams up with a photographer called Delmas to investigate the disappearance of a French delegate to the United Nations. The film begins in the galactic blaze of Times Square, with the Camel man puffing smoke rings from a billboard, Mr Peanut bouncing in the air, and a flashing headline from *Time* that announces a story about messages beamed from outer space – which is what, to Melville, these signs might just as well be. He was equally awestruck by the United Nations, first seen at dusk as the lights go on in the Secretariat. A luminous ladder climbs the sky, turning the building, as Melville's narration says, into a 'maison de verre'. He was probably recalling the actual Maison de Verre just off the Boulevard Saint-Germain, built in the 1920s for a doctor who believed that glass architecture discouraged skulking secrecy and could bring about the redemption of mankind; the United Nations achieved no such feat. The narrator notices three children playing around the base of a street lamp nearby, identifies them as Italian, Irish and Jewish, and says that their game exemplifies the cooperative mission of the building. The cheery parable does not explain why these ethnically assorted boys are out unsupervised at nightfall.

Away from the blaze of Broadway, Melville was surprised by how inky New York was, but his film exorcizes that darkness. The dives visited by the two journalists hold no terrors. In a greasy Brooklyn diner, an elderly bearded rabbi eats at the counter and chats to the grizzled cook in Yiddish. A man on an adjacent stool has a holstered gun and a club tethered to his belt; he looks dangerous until he puts on his jacket and is revealed to be a kindly cop, who helps a reeling drunkard to stay upright and gently admonishes an underage smoker. Another stop takes the Frenchmen to a brothel. Moreau remarks aphoristically 'On mesure une civilisation à sa prostitution.' If so, America handles such matters impeccably. 'Isn't it like France here?' purrs the blonde madam, proud of the Belle Époque furniture in her waiting room. The striptease dancers in a burlesque joint chuckle 'L'amour, toujours l'amour' when interrogated; on the way out, Delmas calls them sluts and laughs at Moreau's concern for their welfare. He likens his colleague to the Salvation Army revivalists who bang drums and rattle tambourines in Rockefeller Center, where Father Christmas is seen ho-ho-hoing while a trombonist wheezes through some carols. It might be Melville's self-accusation: in his infatuation with America, had he, a European pessimist, been led astray by its born-again creed?

Delmas, mimicking the tough guys played by Bogart or James Cagney, is less susceptible. Hoping to sell scandalous photographs to the tabloids, he gatecrashes the hospital room of the missing UN delegate's mistress after she attempts suicide, steals her keys, and in her apartment – where the missing man has died of a heart attack while sitting placidly on the sofa – drags the corpse into her bed to make the posed snapshot more profitably sensational. He then helps himself to the whisky in the dead man's glass, complains that it's warm, and pockets his wallet. After these outrages, he staggers into a waterfront bar on Pike Street and is knocked to the floor by the disgusted Moreau. A jazz musician detaches himself from his combo, which is still playing at dawn, and bends over him to improvise a lament: it is as if Melville were giving us a glimpse of Miles Davis, who remains out of sight on the soundtrack of *Ascenseur pour l'échafaud* as Jeanne Moreau mopes through Paris. Here the music acts as a reveille, rousing the conscience of the unconscious Delmas. He gets up, stumbles outside, drops his valuable roll of film into a grate in the gutter, then walks off towards the downtown skyscrapers, laughing as he goes – contemptuous of the quixotic sacrifice he has made, or light-heartedly relieved of guilt? In America, the hardest-boiled can suddenly go soft.

The sudden repentance of Delmas exposes a scruple that is characteristic of Melville and his colleagues. French civility repressed aggression, although Melville assumed this was how quarrels were settled on the other continent, which appeared to be a moral and legal vacuum. Before moving to America in the late 1970s, Malle saw the country as a rude challenge to Europeans who have been enfeebled or sickened by civilization. In 1963 in *Le Feu follet*, an alcoholic French writer who has attempted suicide is advised to place himself in the care of his American wife. 'American women,' his doctor says, 'are strong and healthy', which may imply that they are callous and insensitive. The wife pays for his treatment in a Versailles clinic, where he keeps a copy of Scott Fitzgerald's *The Crack-Up* in his room, along with some photographs of Marilyn Monroe. But when he recommends a visit to New York to a fellow patient, she shrills that the Americans would probably kill her and clutches her throat in terror. Later a friend describes New York as a crazed vortex that is 'no place for us'.

Behind the fear, of course, lurked a compelling, alarming attraction. The educated Frenchmen who fell in love with American movies after the war secretly envied the purgative rush with which those urban gangsters and Western gunslingers discharged pent-up energy. Eric Rohmer said that the violence in Nicholas Ray's films – the shoot-out between the women in *Johnny Guitar*, Bogart's possibly homicidal temper in *In a Lonely Place*, the knife fight in *Rebel Without a Cause* – was 'exhilarating and beautiful'. Ray, according to Rohmer, 'restored grandeur to the human gesture', like the conductor Wilhelm Furtwängler giving a downbeat or cueing an orchestral crescendo: an odd comparison, since Furtwängler was gesticulating with a baton, not brandishing a pistol or slashing the air with a blade. Another *Cahiers du cinéma* critic, Jacques Rivette, marvelled at the 'bouts of ordered madness' in the films of Howard Hawks when Bogart beat up uncoopera-tive informants in *The Big Sleep* or John Wayne and Montgomery Clift threw punches in *Red River*. Along with the covert worship of force, these refined intellectuals thrilled to the machismo of those who conducted their debates with fists or guns. Rivette praised the heroes of Richard Brooks for being 'real men', and in 1960 Michel Mouret rapturously described Charlton Heston as 'a god imprisoned, quivering with muted rage', and longed for the moment when he would unleash 'the stupendous strength of his torso'. Heston did so in due course by lending his authority to the National Rifle Association.

Others were more squeamish about such connections between vio-lence, virility and art. Claude Chabrol commended Robert Aldrich's *Kiss Me Deadly* – which ends with a nuclear bomb exploding in a suitcase at a Malibu beach-house – but had to admit that its 'overpowering sunlights' were the 'nauseous product' of a putrid story by Mickey Spillane, whose private eye Mike Hammer is less a human being than a blunt instrument, tooled to kill communists and manhandle trampy women. By contrast, in his obituary for Bogart, André Bazin daintily described the gun carried by Sam Spade or Philip Marlowe as a teaching tool, 'an almost intellectual weapon, the argument that dumbfounds'. Intent on the dialectic, Bazin did not notice that Bogart usually fires first and utters a mordant wisecrack later. Misgivings like this may have made Godard break the link between cause and effect at the start of *À Bout de souffle*, when Belmondo kills a cop who chases him – or rather when an ownerless finger presses a trigger in close-up, after which the cop tumbles backwards into the bushes: Godard's jump cut tactfully omitted the money shot.

The outsiders in *Bande à part* – based on an American novel which Godard transposed to Paris – are pardoned by their infantile frivolity. Crime for them is a game played in an imaginary America. In a Paris street, Sami Frey and Claude Brasseur re-enact Pat Garrett's shooting of Billy the Kid; the funds from a muddled heist will subsidize their escape to 'Jack London country', which of course no longer existed, except in the imagination of Jean-Pierre Melville. Sergio Leone excused the New York gangsters in *Once Upon a Time in America* by ageing them, not by treating them as unsocialized children. They rob and kill when young, then spend the subsequent decades in morose, penitent recollection. When a stooped, wrinkled Robert de Niro reappears after an absence of thirty years, he is asked what he did during that lost time. 'I went to bed early,' he replies, fortuitously quoting the first sentence of Proust's mnemonic novel. For Paul Muni's Scarface or Edward G. Robinson's Little Caesar, crime was a means of getting rich quickly; de Niro and James Woods in *Once Upon a Time in America* are slower and graver, like Europeans encumbered by a history that is at once personal and political.

Rivette in a 1955 essay on his favourite American directors said that fisticuffs and bullets established 'a void, a state of grace', so that violence was 'justified by meditation'. It is hard to think of any such beatific aftermath in American films, but Rivette's point is illustrated in the first scene of *Le Samouraï*. Delon lies on his bed in an empty room, smoking as he listens to the chirp of his pet bird; a blue cloud from his cigarette curls above his head. He is thinking. This is what he does between homicidal assignments, which for him are like swift, clinically precise surgery. He even dons white gloves before taking up his gun, and at the end, treating murder as a conceptual art, he removes the bullets before a hit. An American killer acts, pummelling or puncturing his victim. His European equivalent spends the time contemplatively, so the actual slaying can be treated as a theoretical elimination.

Perhaps the French version of America flattered the reality, which could be sordid, mean, and sometimes even boring. A Hollywood contract gave

Jacques Demy the opportunity to actualize his fantasy, and on arrival in Los-Angeles he celebrated by buying a white convertible like the one driven through Nantes by the heroine's Americanized lover in *Lola* – another metaphor on wheels, recalling the vehicles to which Belmondo helps himself in *À Bout de souffle*. Demy brought Anouk Aimée's character Lola with him, and invented a transatlantic afterlife for her in *Model Shop*, released in 1969. This epilogue is a dejected decline, not the fulfilment of an American dream. The lover with the glamorous car has taken her as far as New York, then dumped her; the sailor Frankie is unavailable as second best, having been killed in Vietnam. Now, after drifting to the west coast, Lola is reduced to modelling for prurient snapshots taken by strangers in a shop on Santa Monica Boulevard. Homesick, she passes the time between appointments by driving around at random, which allows Demy to take a rambling inventory of Los Angeles – the sluggish surf and the derricks that pump oil on the beach at Venice, the floppy palms, the telephone wires that web the sky, the white haze of the lowlands seen from Mulholland Drive. At one point a character enters a pool hall, buys cigarettes from a vending machine, puts a coin in the jukebox to play a record, orders a burger at the counter, and while waiting samples the free pickles in a jar. The scene is a sociological report: this, to Demy's evident amazement, is how Americans live.

Lola is stalked by a Vietnam draftee, who on Demy's behalf compliments the city's 'baroque harmony', which does not sound like something an Angeleno would say: to those who live there, the place blurs into invisibility as it slides by outside their car windows. When her shy, dogged pursuer blurts out his feelings to Lola, she replies 'You're a child', meaning that he is an American. But she sleeps with him in exchange for the money he has borrowed to make an overdue car payment; she uses her fee to buy an airline ticket and returns immediately to France. Demy's American affair was equally one-sided, and after nicknaming his ill-fated film *Model Flop* he followed Lola home.

Movies were mirrors in which young Europeans adjusted their dress and their sense of identity. Those who sat in the dark irresistibly projected themselves onto the screen; if they had the gumption, they recreated the mannerisms of their favourites when they emerged into the daylight. The simple act of tugging a hat brim down, as Truffaut noted, could turn you into Bogart: a floppy beret became a helmet, outfacing whatever hostility you confronted. Or you could run your thumbnail along your upper lip – a symptom of pensiveness for Bogart, although when Belmondo does it in *À Bout de souffle* the gesture is more sensual and narcissistic, tracing the outline of his ripe facial features.

The cult of James Dean required more of its adherents than such minimal semaphoring. The way Dean acted – physically lithe but verbally incoherent, agitated by inconsistent moods, befuddled by his groping near-sightedness – changed the behaviour of a generation which was the first to dramatize the stresses of teenage, a new and uniquely American time of life. When Dean died in a car crash in 1955, Truffaut said that he embodied the spirit of 'today's young people' with their 'simultaneous desire and refusal to be integrated into society'. Truffaut called him Baudelairean, brooding and accursed; Alain Bosquet referred to him as 'leur Rimbaud', America's equivalent to the poet who gave up writing when he reached the anticlimactic age of twenty. But despite this possessive French affection, the origins of Dean's persona were specifically American, deriving from social and psychological conditions that existed nowhere else. European rebels had causes, which were mostly political; Dean, playing Jim in *Rebel Without a Cause*, was a neurotic not a revolutionary. A child of affluence, he drives to high school in his own car and has a father who asks 'Don't I buy you everything you want?' This superfluity leaves Dean unsatisfied, but if asked what he was rebelling against he might have replied, like Brando in *The Wild One*, 'Whaddaya got?' Before the 'chickie run', when he and his rival Buzz race their cars towards the edge of a cliff, Jim wonders 'Why do we do this?' Buzz, who within minutes will be dead, says 'I dunno, we gotta do something.'

Rebel Without a Cause started as a catchy title with no film attached. The studio bought the rights to the phrase from Robert M. Lindner, who in 1944 affixed it to the account of his hypnoanalysis of a criminal psychopath called Harold, 'a religious dis-obeyer of prevailing codes and standards'. Lindner identified his patient with America's current enemy: he was an 'embryonic Storm-Trooper', and because he came from Polish-German immigrant stock his problem could be treated as a European import. Concluding the narrative of his cure, Lindner equated Harold with the deranged world that was to be put right during the American century. 'History,' he said, 'has assigned to this country and her allies the task of cleansing civilization of the predatory creature whose typical history is presented in this volume'; if the malefactor wished to survive, he must become 'a good citizen in a new world'. By the time Nicholas Ray made his film in 1955, that new world, pacified by plenty, had come into being, though the rebellious Jim rejects it. This does not make him a radical: he even wants to give himself up to the police after the chickie run. Lindner's patient only disclosed his Oedipal trauma under hypnosis or in his dreams, but Jim has no need to dream because his waking life is the enactment of his fantasies. Hence his surreal pantomiming as he acts out his hang-ups: he curls his body into a foetal shape or rubs his forehead with a bottle of milk or attempts to strangle his feminized, apron-wearing father.

On a visit to the planetarium in Griffith Park, Jim's school class learns about the decay of the universe, which in its last throes will fire off asteroids. The lecturer describes the appearance in the night sky of 'a star, increasingly bright and increasingly near'. This is Dean's cue: at that moment Jim slouches into the auditorium. Has this nova arrived in suburban Los Angeles from the future, or from outer space? As our planet fizzles out in an exhalation of gas and a burst of fire, the lecturer at the planetarium concludes that 'the problems of man' are 'naïve and trivial'. This nihilism releases Jim from Lindner's punitive moralizing and from the responsibilities of adulthood, and encourages him to behave absurdly. The tantrums of Jim's friend Judy (Natalie Wood) are similarly blamed by her mother on 'the age'; her little brother fires his ray gun and confirms the diagnosis by excitedly yelping 'The atomic age!' A cop who quietens Jim uses an equally contemporary technological image. 'That's enough static out of you,' he says, which treats Jim's ravings as so many radio waves atonally crackling in the ether. Buzz pays Jim a bewildered compliment by calling him 'real abstract': like Pollock or Rothko, he is abstractly expressive, convulsed by emotions that have no discernible motive. He imitates the siren of a police car and hums a snatch of Wagner, batters furniture or dives into an empty pool to swim on the dry concrete, and simultaneously laughs and cries at the mismatched socks of his friend Plato. Ray is not diagnosing a social problem but celebrating, in the performance he elicited from Dean, a new, histrionic, self-indulgently American mode of being.

Truffaut paid tribute to Dean's flailing rebellion in 1959 in his autobiographical film *Les Quatre Cents Coups*, though in doing so he acknowledged the gap between America and post-war Europe. Truffaut's young alter ego Antoine, played by Jean-Pierre Léaud, has more reason for his rages than Jim. Not pampered like an American teenager, he lives in a cramped apartment at the top of a squalid house in Pigalle. Lacking bed sheets, he spends his nights in a sleeping bag. His parents beat him, and threaten to send him away to be straightened out by the Jesuits or disciplined at a military academy. The situation recalls Truffaut's own turbulent childhood: in 1947, aged fifteen, he was arrested for vagrancy and – because the penal institutions for children were all full, a symptom of social breakdown after the war – he found himself caged with prostitutes and locked up in a police cell. Jim in *Rebel* is a nuisance but not a menace, and far from manhandling him, the police are as solicitous as therapists. Jim and Buzz stage the chickie run as an existential experiment, reacting against a life that is too safe and shockproof, but Antoine and his schoolmates in *Les Quatre Cents Coups* are criminals in embryo, smart young ruffians who steal from their elders and from one another.

Plato in *Rebel*, played by Sal Mineo, pretends that his father died heroically in the Pacific war, though he is actually alive, well, and earning a fortune in New York. Plato is elaborating a myth for himself, dramatizing his history in a way that is characteristic of his American generation, for which life has to be a self-aggrandizing performance. Antoine tells the same lie when he excuses himself from school by claiming that his mother has just died, but his motives are different. His disposal of an unloved parent is a just revenge: he knows that she only grudgingly permitted him to be born and had to be persuaded not to have an abortion. Tolerant to a fault, American

society makes room for misfits, and honours its founding pledge by allowing for alternative ways of living. Jim, Plato and Judy therefore take over an
abandoned mansion in the Hollywood hills and treat it as their castle, which
they pretend to be renting for $3 million a month. No such luxurious liberty
is possible for Antoine, who is sentenced to a reformatory. He manages to
escape, but is brought up short by the Atlantic, a barrier that abruptly ter-
minates his adventure as *Les Quatre Cents Coups* ends with a frozen frame.
Only in America does the horizon indefinitely recede ahead of you.

The source for Truffaut's next film, *Tirez sur le pianiste*, was David
Goodis's novel *Down There*, about the moral and professional collapse of
a classical pianist. Unmanned by a fickle wife, hollowed out by his wartime
experience as a uniformed killer, he abandons his highbrow career and
takes a job in a honky-tonky dive in Philadelphia. Truffaut transposed the
story to Paris and rather than emphasizing the pianist's descent to the lower
depths chose a new title, quoting a legendary sign in a Colorado saloon that
asked the miners not to shoot the piano player because he was doing his
best. He omitted the negative because although the pianist deserves the
reprieve – Charles Aznavour, as the slumming virtuoso, performs jazz in a
bistro with dedication and genuine flair – he is targeted by gangsters who
have non-musical reasons for wanting him dead.

Down There pleased Truffaut because it offered him a way of not
being French: unlike Antoine at the end of *Les Quatre Cents Coups*, he had
managed to project himself across the ocean. The clunky plot allowed him
to direct fights, chases and shoot-outs, all of which were so remote from his
own experience that they seemed fanciful not grubby, like excerpts from
the fairy tales of Cocteau. He hoped that the stilted dialogue would have
the charmed strangeness of a dubbed film – something Americans could
never understand, given the monoglot empire they had created. Even after
Truffaut learned English, he preferred to watch dubbed versions of American
films; he especially loved hearing Joan Crawford and Sterling Hayden in
Johnny Guitar address each another in French with the courtly formality
of aristocrats in a neoclassical tragedy. For those who were more irritably
envious of America, the reliance on dubbing was a mark of marginality

or inferiority, and in 1986 Jean Baudrillard used a cinematic metaphor to establish the backwardness of France. 'America is the original version of modernity,' he claimed. 'We are the dubbed or subtitled version.' That is literally true in Godard's *Made in USA*, where French faces and places are randomly assigned American names. One character is called David Goodis, others are surnamed Aldrich and Siegel in homage to Godard's favourite directors, and the action straggles through an Atlantic City that is only too obviously Paris. The dislocation is intentional: the French, Godard thought, had become ersatz Americans, so why not complete their abject surrender of identity? His annoyance was self-spiting, since the sources of his own art were primarily American, and *Made in USA* is dedicated to Nick and Samuel, respectively Ray and Fuller, his elective godfathers.

Truffaut's aim was more benevolent. He rescued the characters of *Down There* from the degradation to which they are subjected in the novel. The film's pianist does not disgrace himself by quitting Carnegie Hall. Like the Americanophiles of the 1950s, he discovers a popular culture that must be treated with respect, and although Aznavour is seen studying the score of a Prokofiev concerto, he also praises Erroll Garner and Art Tatum, the models for his displays in the bistro. Truffaut cast Aznavour because he looked so un-French, and since the actor's family came from Armenia, the character's surname was changed from Lynn to Saroyan – an incidental compliment to the Armenian-American William Saroyan, whose novels Truffaut admired for their 'warmth and beauty'. Growing up in rough Pigalle, Truffaut knew hoodlums like those who persecute the pianist. He detested them, he said; social outlaws were endearing if solitary, like Dean in *Rebel Without a Cause*, but not when they formed packs to terrorize law-abiding citizens. He therefore humanized the ruffian who kidnaps Aznavour's young brother by having him show off an American trinket. He tries to impress the boy by flashing his new Sheaffer Snorkel pen, with automatic refill and retractable nib; it is hard to imagine him writing, but his naive consumerism vouches for his good nature. At worst, Truffaut teased America. A prostitute tells Aznavour that she has just seen a spurious John Wayne film called *Torpedoes in Alaska*, whose message to the world is that the Americans only want peace, despite their bristling preparedness for war. Aznavour ignores her sarcasm and replies that the Yanks – he uses the colloquialism 'amerloques'– are just like him: all he wants is a quiet life. The American censors cut these lines, on puritanical not patriotic grounds: the joke about the Cold War was passable, but the prostitute's bare breasts happened to be on show during the exchange.

In 1954 Truffaut declared that 'European cinema . . . treated the decadence of man, whereas American cinema . . . exalted that same man.' In this high-minded view, even decadence could be ennobling if it overtook an American idol, and when Bogart died in 1957, Bazin said that his stoical conduct during his last illness exhibited 'the dignity and eminence of our decay'. Truffaut concluded his eulogy by declaring that 'The whole history of Hollywood equals a long flirtation with heroism.' He wanted to believe that America could function, both artistically and morally, as an influence for the good, enjoining downcast Europeans to lift up their heads, just as the memory of Bogart had once given courage to Gabin. He made it true, for himself at least, by awarding the American characters of *Down There* a sentimental re-education in Europe.

In *À Bout de souffle* Godard saw the transatlantic relationship as a lovers' quarrel. He treated the characters played by Belmondo and Seberg as representatives of their continents, respectively doom-laden and callowly optimistic: 'He thinks about death all the time, and she never gives it a thought.' Belmondo hustles Seberg into bed in the hope of achieving Franco-American rapprochement beneath the sheets, but despite their erotic attraction, they remain incompatible. The problem was Godard's own: disapproving of America, how could he forgive his own treasonous taste for its cultural products?

Paris in the film has been thoroughly Americanized, and an avenue the French call Elysian is an extension of Main Street. Seberg trails along it selling copies of the internationalized *Herald Tribune* to American tourists; she dodges into a café that pretends to be a drugstore, and passes cinemas showing a Robert Aldrich film about bomb disposal in post-war Berlin and a Western directed by Budd Boetticher. Around the corner, Belmondo visits a friend at a travel agency called Inter-American, with posters advertising flights to the United States. As he and Seberg wander on the pavement, de Gaulle and Eisenhower are glimpsed on their way to lay a wreath on the tomb of the Unknown Soldier at the Étoile. It is right that the heads of state are relegated to the background: soon after the next American presidential election, Larry Rivers finished his painting *The Friendship of America and France (Kennedy and de Gaulle)*, in which the current presidents are dim figureheads presiding over a patchwork of cigarette packets – Camel, Lucky Strike and Marlboro versus Gauloises and Gitanes – that establish the true state of relations between their countries. Lucky Strike has its red bullseye, Marlboro its rearing horse. Next to these images of power, the languid, expiring plume of smoke from the Gitanes looks effete, and the winged helmet that identifies the Gauloises is a curio, unfit for modern battle. Friendship matters less than market penetration, in which American brands have the advantage, and fashion bypasses the clumsier efforts of political negotiators, as President Kennedy admitted in 1961 when he remarked that he had merely accompanied his immaculately outfitted wife Jacqueline to Paris.

The mismatched lovers in *À Bout de souffle* are, as the therapists say, co-dependent. Belmondo is a criminal who has learned the tricks of his trade from American films, Seberg a student who has come to France to gobble up European culture. She has posters and postcards of Renoir, Klee and Picasso on the walls of her bedroom, with gramophone records of Mozart and Chopin within reach: she too is a kind of thief, helping herself to a foreign heritage like Belmondo stealing those cars. Indifferent to her highbrow trophies, he remarks that Americans must be dumb because they dote on Frenchmen like Lafayette and Maurice Chevalier. Lafayette is venerated in America because he led troops against the British; in France he is less highly regarded, as he fired on demonstrators during the revolution. Chevalier represents France slickly merchandized for export, a debonair caricature with an affectedly thick accent. Seberg might have replied that Belmondo's taste in Americana is equally faulty. He is an amateur who refuses the gun he is offered before the cops arrive to arrest him in Montparnasse – more romantic than his trigger-happy cinematic heroes, and therefore a loser.

As they exchange post-coital insults, Belmondo studies Seberg's blank face and androgynous haircut and tells her that up close she looks like a Martian: he is voicing the customary complaint about Europe's occupation by a master race of extra-terrestrials. A comment made by Jean-Pierre Melville, who appears briefly in the film as a novelist interviewed by Seberg, connects international relations with sexual politics. Asked about the difference between French and American women, Melville replies that the Americans are more domineering; the old continent has been unmanned. Belmondo is henpecked by Seberg, who toys with him, betrays him, and is protected from his dying curse because she cannot understand the word he uses when he says he is disgusted by her. The critic Arlene Croce, anticipating Baudrillard's remark about subtitles, said that '*Sebergisme* is the logical destruction of *Belmondisme*. . . . She is the triumphant actual artefact of which he, in his delusion, is the copy, the dupe.' Croce's pun is harshly accurate: Belmondo is a duplicate, a pale copy of a Bogart character, but he is also duped by his imaginary America. Croce added, only half in jest, that if the United States truly cared about its reputation abroad, the American Legion would have picketed cinemas wherever *À Bout de souffle* was shown.

Belmondo here ineffectually apes Bogart the gangster. In later films, Godard went on to re-imagine Bogart the private eye. Anna Karina plays the role in *Made in USA*; the plot concerns a political assassination, but rather than locating a single culprit it incriminates America, deriding its politicians and besmirching its most popular artist. A juvenile thug identifies himself as Richard Nixon, and Karina classifies the dazzlingly bright, generically garbled film as 'Walt Disney with blood' – fantasy spattered with gore. Investigating a cultural malaise not a murder, she shakes her head over Europe's cosmic marginality. 'We are living,' she remarks, 'in an old part of the universe where nothing happens, whereas somewhere other galaxies are still being created by explosions.' America can be relied upon to continue producing starbursts, like James Dean's incendiary entrance at the planetarium. In *Alphaville*, Eddie Constantine is cast as the detective or secret agent, who takes his copy of Raymond Chandler's *The Big Sleep* with him when he travels from Nueva York to a futuristic city that is another version of Americanized Paris. Alphaville is ruled by a Los Alamos physicist called von Braun who has invented a death ray, and it is populated by sleepwalkers fed on tranquillizers that they store in boxes of Kellogg's cereal. Whereas Karina in *Made in USA* listens for echoes of the big bangs that occur across the Atlantic, in *Alphaville* those creative blasts are more remote, and America brings history to a numb, zombified end.

Godard continued to grumble about what he called 'the Americanization of French life', though the term was inaccurate. In 1960 in *Esquire* James Baldwin reported on the same complaint from Stockholm. The epithet, Baldwin argued, referred to social tensions caused by migration from country villages to the city; apart from a few jukeboxes, he saw little that was American in dour Sweden. Nevertheless America took the blame for Europe's motorized advance into modernity, and in *Weekend*, released in 1967, Godard shows France mimicking and foreshortening the larger, emptier continent's history of exploration. When his suburban characters drive out to the country, they find no elastic frontier. Instead a travelling shot spends ten minutes tracking down a rural byway past immobilized cars and fuming, squabbling drivers, at last reaching the fiery wreck that caused the blockage. In America, as *The Brooklyn Eagle* declared in 1910, 'automobiling' still answered 'the call of the wild'. Godard's compendious traffic jam halts the wagon trains that trundle progressively across the plains and valiantly clamber over mountains in the Westerns of Ford and Hawks. Sergio Leone, growing up on the thin Italian peninsula, liked to dream about American roads that 'begin nowhere, and end nowhere'. But in *Once Upon a Time in the West* he made a comment as sarcastic as Godard's about the territorial fantasies of Americans. A crippled railway tycoon – a mechanomorph held together by crutches and calipers – goads himself to reach the Pacific by staring at a painting of waves that never break, hung in a carriage of a private train that stands becalmed in the desert; he dies crawling towards a puddle that mockingly does duty for the ocean he will never see.

Going nowhere, the frustrated trippers in *Weekend* have to endure an anthropological diatribe delivered by a black garbage man. He learnedly expounds a theory derived from Lewis H. Morgan, a lawyer and director of a railway company who went native in the 1840s and formed a New Order of the Iroquois. Morgan summarized American history as an advance from hunting to agriculture, then to what is known as civilization (which nowadays means that everyone has a house stuffed with mod cons and a car parked outside); the Iroquois made the first transition, but were supplanted by European settlers before they could complete the evolution. In Godard's film the three stages unravel in reverse. Civilized bourgeois drivers blunder into agricultural terrain, where they are hunted by hippie guerrillas – a gallic Vietcong, and a forewarning of the Manson gang – who drag them into the woods to be killed and cannibalized. Like the showdown near a cabin in snowy Grenoble in *Tirez sur le pianiste*, the final shootout on a deserted farm is a Western scene staged in a French landscape, and Godard's rustic warriors use the titles of classic films – *Johnny Guitar* or *La Prisonnière du desert*, which is how the French translated Ford's *The Searchers* – as code names when sending radio transmissions. The pseudonym Melville was Grumbach's shield, which fortified him by association with an American hero; the ciphers employed by the guerrillas enable them to get away with murder.

That, Godard suspected, was always the purpose of American films, which existed to serve the country's commercial interests and to justify its military exploits. He outrageously claimed that Nixon's trade deal with China gave priority to movies, and added 'Cheese, aeroplanes – that comes later': a wacky assertion, since the Chinese had no appetite for American dairy products. At the time of the Iran hostage crisis, Godard told an interviewer that 'the American generals make bad Hitchcock films in the Tabas desert', apparently referring to the Pentagon's use of cameras mounted in satellites to identify the targets they attacked. Later he turned on Steven Spielberg, whom he saw as a crony for the warmongers. Spielberg chose Truffaut to play the scientist who talks the spacecraft down to earth in *Close Encounters of the Third Kind*, and explained his choice by calling Truffaut 'a man with the soul of a child', an earthling whom the visitors from another planet could trust: a rare case of an American finding a European to be dewy-eyed. Scornful of such camaraderie, Godard described Spielberg's *Saving Private Ryan* as the beachhead of another Normandy landing, and accused the director of a 'totalitarian' ambition to commandeer all markets.

Yet while railing against monopoly capitalism, Godard paid America a breathtakingly generous compliment, and for an unexpected reason. 'If the US dominates the world,' he said in the interview containing the aside about Iran, 'it's because it's the country that comes closest to being a democracy.' It succeeded, he explained, because of its visual culture, which bypasses language and is accessible to all, at home or abroad. Truffaut, with fewer political grudges, made a similar point when describing a scene from *Written on the Wind*, Douglas Sirk's delirious melodrama about the psychological kinks of a Texan oil dynasty. As Truffaut remembered it, Robert Stack rushes out of a blue bedroom, sprints down a red corridor, jumps into a yellow taxi, then boards a steel-grey aeroplane; his excited summary missed out the bright green dress of the receptionist Stack quizzes on his way out of the New York hotel. Sirk's saturated palette delighted Truffaut: these were 'the colours of America, the colours of a luxury civilization' that was the headquarters of 'the age of plastics', all the more enticing because of their synthetic glare. Truffaut was dazzled by the display, as Stack expects Lauren Bacall to be when he entices her away from her job on Madison Avenue and flies her in his Skyrama plane to another hotel suite in Miami Beach, which is stocked in advance with closets full of sequined gowns and boxes of scintillating baubles. She refuses the bribe, but her eyes, all the same, are wide with amazement. No matter how many words the polemicists expended, it was images of America – electrically luminous, kinetic, as vibrant as rainbows – that won the world.

10 | On the Roads

The rest of the world at first knew relatively little about the vast, remote country that took a determining role in its affairs in 1945. Exploration became easier after 1956, when the federal government laid out a network of National Interstate and Defense Highways covering forty thousand miles. Ironing out topography and snubbing scenic views, these high-speed roads were a kind of abstraction, and in a 1957 cover story *Time* called road-building 'America's art', an engineered revision of nature. Like NASA's forays into the stratosphere in the next decade, this was a Cold War scheme, partly financed from the military budget: Hitler built autobahns to accelerate the movement of troops, and Eisenhower believed that the road network would speed the evacuation of cities that might be targets of an atomic attack.

Until that happened, the highways were put to recreational uses. During the 1930s Jacques Maritain had been overjoyed to find that Americans were not victims of the onerous necessity that Marxism imposed on Europeans: they felt free and they proved it by walking, like Thoreau who undertook his daily rambles 'in the spirit of undying adventure'. Now they proved it all over again by driving. Destination mattered less than the manifest destiny of aiming at the horizon. In *The Wild One*, Brando is asked where he and his motorcycle gang are headed. 'Goin' somewhere is for squares,' he snorts. 'We just *go*.' For sedater Americans, the Winnebago replaced the covered wagon, and every summer suburban families recapitulated in comfort the arduous trek of westward exploration.

In 1949 William S. Burroughs drove from New York to San Francisco, then made the return trip three days later; on the way he remembered 'the mass migrations of the Mayans' – a restlessness now confined to a few chosen, dissatisfied spirits. Burroughs recommended Buddhism to Kerouac as an antidote to the striving American will, but he admitted that modern man had trouble being static. Kerouac did not even try: he declared in *On the Road* that the 'one and noble function' acknowledged by his generation was '*move. And we moved!*' His friend Sebastian Sampas had dosed him with Spengler's credo of Faustian yearning, summed up by the 'prime symbol' of 'the "plane without limit"'; in America, that symbol took the form of a highway running straight ahead, if possible forever. Kerouac at first planned to hitchhike from the east coast to the west, like a dilatory hobo left over from the Depression; he recharted his course when he noticed that Route 6 led directly from the tip of Cape Cod to Ely, Nevada, after which it veered towards the coast and ended at Long Beach. He never learned to drive, but was content to occupy the passenger seat, especially when his travelling companion Neal Cassady urged a Cadillac across the plains at 110 miles an hour. Backtracking east, Kerouac completed a victory lap by venturing out to the tip of Long Island, touching another of the points where the continent broke off.

Despite this shuttling to and fro, Kerouac regretted the interstate system because it prohibited digressive meandering: in the future, he said, no one would moon over the melancholy sound of distant train whistles, or pause to ponder 'dew on fences at dawn in Mississippi'. The photographer Berenice Abbott also dreaded the placeless uniformity fostered by the new highways, and in the summer of 1954 she travelled on Route 1 from New York to Key West and then back up to Fort Kent in Maine, anxious to document regional differences that were being erased. She went out of her way to photograph a woman scrubbing the marble blocks of her front stoop in Baltimore, just because it was a sight that existed nowhere else; she was amused by anything that slowed down the relentless drive towards the future, like a stationary row of disused buses being used as cabins by tourists in St Augustine, Florida.

Eisenhower, remembering the Army's first transcontinental motor convoy in 1919, described it as a trek 'through darkest America with truck and tank' – a reprise of earlier journeys west, with vehicles bogged down in mud or held up by overloaded, insecure bridges. Now space could be conquered with dreamy ease not lumbering effort, and roads catered to the revved-up impatience of desire. In Nabokov's *Lolita*, a European seducer on the run with an American nymphet views the highways as obliging panders.

On 'smooth amiable roads', Humbert Humbert speeds Lolita across state borders in defiance of the Mann Act against white-slaving, while everything along the way is eroticized by his incredulous foreign eyes. Scanning the map, he describes the coloured pattern of the forty-eight states as a 'crazy quilt' stretched on a bed. Garages dispensing slippery fluids send out lewd messages: one murmurs 'genuflexion lubricity', then as Humbert blinks corrects itself to 'Gulflex Lubrication', which is not much less suggestive. Other appetites are not forgotten. Drivers like to imagine that they are eating up the miles that pass beneath their cars, and Humbert squeezes extra value from the metaphor, remarking that 'voraciously we consumed those long highways'. Roadside motels, pretending to be made of pine logs, remind Lolita of the golden-brown glaze on fried chicken. Humbert regrets that the American landscape discourages al fresco sex: poison ivy, pine needles, insects and slithery reptiles make it inadvisable to bed down on the grass. The national parks, however, taunt him with their cavities and spouts, and he views the Yellowstone geysers as 'symbols of my passion'. Titillated by motion, tantalized by America's supine availability, he fancies that somewhere in the exotic hinterland there must be a town called Climax, a hedonistic resort which with luck will live up to its name. Nabokov's fellow émigré Billy Wilder took that as a challenge, and set his comedy *Kiss Me, Stupid* in just that town, conveniently located outside Las Vegas. It is here that Kim Novak, sexually famished, lies in wait for Dean Martin when he wanders off the main road.

The new highways replaced scenery with a montage of billboards to entertain travellers in their speeding cars. With her craving for candy or ice-cold drinks, Lolita is 'the ideal consumer, the subject and object of every foul poster' beside the road. A car crash is one more incitement to shopping, as she eyes a victim's stylish moccasins, catapulted into a ditch. Humbert – born in Paris, with a Swiss father of French and Austrian descent and an English mother – regards all this with disdain, and makes American scenery tolerable by recalling illustrations in imported art books. Some fluffy clouds could have been painted by Claude Lorrain, an inky sunset sky is an imitation El Greco. Nabokov dismissed two opposed readings of *Lolita*, which saw it either as a fable about 'Old Europe debauching young America' or

'Young America debauching old Europe'. In fact, like *À Bout de souffle*, it is both at once. The European brings with him a learned depravity, exhibited in his slip about the Gulf station; the 'disgustingly conventional' American with whom he becomes obsessed laughs at his superciliousness and demonstrates the potency of a culture that is cheap but truly popular.

Although Humbert is unimpressed by the mountains in the south-eastern states, 'altitudinal failures as alps go', he adores the coincidental linguistic quirks of this new world, as when he leaves Ohio to drive across 'the three states beginning with "I"': geography for him is a form of Scrabble. The map is also a geometrical diagram, since many state lines were drawn with a ruler, as Humbert notices when he mentions a visit to 'the world's largest stalagmite', located near the point where three states separated by right-angled borders 'have a family reunion'. He is referring to Carlsbad Caverns and the Four Corners, where Colorado, New Mexico, Arizona and Utah touch. America – a blank slate, or a kit of parts – allows Humbert to rewrite or redesign it as he pleases.

Claustrophobic Europe had no room for such lexical and spatial games. In 1956, writing about the muddled cross-country tour of Dean Martin and Jerry Lewis in *Hollywood or Bust*, Godard suggested that the trip from New York to Los Angeles corresponded to that from Paris to the Côte d'Azur. But the journey south was brief and scenically uneventful in comparison with a drive through the American west, and Godard had to concede that it was impossible to make a road movie in Europe; the result, as *Weekend* demonstrates, would be gridlock. Besides which, Europeans were fixed to their traditional patches of ground, unlike deracinated Americans. 'The theme of migration came to us from America,' Godard said, and migration made possible a kind of transmigration: shedding the past or an inconvenient identity, the onwardly mobile American can become someone else somewhere else. No other country ever offered such an ample refuge to the discontented, or invited those who were still dissatisfied after arrival to try their luck further west. Nor did the aspirational journey have to stop at the coast. In 1964 Ken Kesey went on a druggy ramble from California to New York in a decommissioned school bus he nicknamed 'Furthur'.

But would there always be a further frontier? James Baldwin warned that America created expectations that could never be satisfied, encouraging people to expect endless progress, automatic growth, galloping enrichment. The pursuit of happiness, Baldwin predicted, would expire in 'a furious, bewildered rage'. Accepting limits, European versions of the American road trip tend to go round in a circle, with death at the point of arrival. The student rebel in Michelangelo Antonioni's *Zabriskie Point* steals a plane at a suburban Los Angeles airport, flies it to freedom in the Mojave Desert, but feels inexplicably obliged to return it; the police are waiting, and shoot him as he lands. More tightly trapped, the producer in Wim Wenders' *The State of Things* – a fugitive from Europe, where he is making a film on a wintry Portuguese beach at the westernmost point of the continent – drives aimlessly to and fro along Sunset Boulevard in that most oxymoronic of American inventions, a mobile home, and when he emerges from it he is gunned down by his creditors in a parking lot.

European photographers, able to explore the far reaches of America in the 1950s and to look more closely at the country than ever before, cast doubt on its claims to beatitude. The American section in *The World of Henri Cartier-Bresson* is book-ended by religious slogans. The first is GOD BLESS AMERICA, carved on the pedestal of a statuette with a stone eagle rearing above it, now discarded in a littered yard behind a Chicago tenement; the second is JESUS IS COMING SOON, painted on a cross driven into the dry earth beside a cabin on an eroded Tennessee hillside. Only a few pages separate the benediction from the prophecy of impending retribution. And does the migrant really experience a resurrection or a heavenly afterlife after arriving? At Ellis Island, Cartier-Bresson photographed an elderly bearded Jew with a battered briefcase who cannot read the sign that points WAY TO TENDER and trudges wearily off in the wrong direction. Another man whose dream has not come true squats on a kerb in a Manhattan alley, scrutinized by a cat that is better able to cope with homelessness.

The patriotic hymn vouched for 'America the Beautiful' by itemizing its landscapes: spacious skies, fruited plains, purple mountain majesties. But how beautiful were the ordinary Americans the photographers now examined? America for Robert Frank was an elective affinity, a nationality you could choose, and he valued the chance to live anonymously in New York: as he told his parents back in Switzerland, no one asked him to show an ID card. Liberty, however, had as its underside an aching solitude, and the view from a bus on Fifth Avenue exhibited to Frank the 'desperation and endurance' of New Yorkers. Their faces scarred by unintelligible pains, the people he photographed loiter in doorways to ponder some private dilemma or drag emaciated shadowy selves behind them in the late-afternoon summer sun; whatever their misery, they are soon left to their fates as the bus meanders indifferently on.

Applying for a Guggenheim grant in 1955, Frank said that he wanted to document a rootless, impersonal way of life that was developing in America and would, he predicted, spread elsewhere. It was a tendentious notion, prompted by European fear of the country's automotive haste. The Guggenheim Foundation supported his project, but at the same time gave a grant to an American photographer, Todd Webb, who planned to cross the country on foot. During the Depression, Webb had panned for gold in California; now he set out to retrace the routes the pioneers took to the mines. Webb first walked from New York to Pittsburgh along the old stage-coach roads, then travelled to Missouri by river in a skiff with an outboard motor, which was his replacement for the steamboat the gold-diggers would have taken. He weakened in Kansas, and as the towns got further apart and the heat increased he transferred to a bicycle. In Santa Fe he cheated again when he bought a Vespa motor scooter. Despite these lapses, Webb believed that only as a pedestrian could he share the experience of the forebears whose tracks he followed. Frank, by contrast, drove at speed through a society he considered hostile, glad to be insulated by his car.

In the hinterland, the mere act of observation made Frank suspect. A gang of teenage boys in Mississippi demanded to know why he was taking pictures, and when he said that his aim was 'Just to see' they accused him of being a communist and told him to go across town 'and watch the niggers play'. In Arkansas he was arrested, the evidence against him being his photographic equipment. On the police report he was made to sign his name under the designation 'criminal'. The fact that he was Jewish added extra demerits, as did the 'foreign names' of his children, Pablo and Andrea, and the 'foreign whiskey' and 'foreign candy' he carried in the car. Even the mention of Guggenheim, his sponsor, incited a xenophobic or anti-Semitic scare. He was soon released, but the incident warned him that he was in enemy territory. James Morris mistrusted the 'veneer of standard charm' he encountered on his travels, and in Hawaii decided that the 'smiles and friendliness' of the islanders were 'of the mercenary kind'. The subjects in Frank's *The Americans* – who glare at his camera, or threateningly rear up in protest, like the black man photographed on the grass with his girlfriend in a San Francisco park – make no effort to ingratiate, and every image crackles with the danger of direct confrontation.

For Frank, the open road had no romance. His Americans use their cars as weapons, daring each other to combat like the teenagers at the chickie run in *Rebel Without a Cause*, or seeking extinction at high speed, like Dean himself who was killed in his Porsche Speedster on his way to a racing event in September 1955. The visual narrative of *The Americans* is punctuated with memorials of crashes, like the Golgotha of three crosses beside a highway in Idaho. At the Ford Motor Company's plant near Detroit, where iron ore was shipped in at one end and a car emerged every forty-nine seconds at the other, Frank joked that he had come to visit 'God's factory'. That was how the place looked to Charles Sheeler in 1927; the ladles that scooped up hot metal resembled prehistoric ogres at a watering trough – the monster, Sheeler said, 'has a Diesel engine for a heart and prefers crude oil for its diet' – but his photographs and paintings gave the immense sheds the geometrical severity of Greek temples, with the blast furnaces as altars exuding enlightenment, not heat or grime. Frank's opinion of the Ford plant was less reverent: 'I am sure that the devil gave him a helping hand,' he said of the tycoon's seething inferno.

The gas station that pandered to Humbert's drowsy erotic reverie in *Lolita* murmured something different to Frank. Driving through Maryland on the way to Florida, he noticed a GULF placard. Kerouac, who was his passenger on this occasion, remarked that 'the big sign' invited Frank to plunge into 'the gulf of time'; it evoked the abyss not, as for Humbert, a sexual orifice. At the Hoover Dam, Frank photographed three postcards, stacked on a rack in a vertical triptych that reviews the three ages of the American earth. On top is the Grand Canyon, underneath it the dam, on the bottom a nuclear test in the desert near Los Alamos. The canyon is a tribute to the stealth and patience of American nature, visibly at war with itself: the Colorado River spent millions of years scything this channel through the rock. The dam challenges that inexorable process. A membrane of reinforced concrete holds a lake that is an arrested river, and engineering wins a victory over the natural forces whose conflict formed the canyon. Why shouldn't science go on to restage the moment of creation, even if that blinding instant unleashes destruction? The detonation of the bomb – a release of the energy that the country worships, hungrily consumes, and expends with such recklessness – is an inevitable consummation. Old Glory, fluttering from a flagpole on the road over the top of the dam, is exactly aligned with the bomb's bursting cloud on the card below.

The Swiss photojournalist Gotthard Schuh asked Frank why his traversal of the continent ignored any sign of natural or human beauty. Collectivized, the people in his survey seemed to form a dour, sullen mass: did they never laugh? 'Ich kenne Amerika nicht,' Schuh told Frank, evidently without regret. When *The Americans* was published in New York in 1959, Kerouac contributed an introduction implausibly allying Frank with the immensities of 'impossible-to-believe America'. For Kerouac, America's dense, over-stimulating cities had the same romantic excitement as 'the great open spaces' and 'the uncrowded places'. He and Allen Ginsberg were fond of greeting the hubbub of Times Square with a tag from *As You Like It*: 'Well, this is the Forest of Arden,' they would say, meaning that the genial muddle of 'God's creation' was here on view. This, Kerouac once added in a moment of Cold War bombast, proved that America was 'much further advanced than Sovietism'. In his commendation of *The Americans*, he claimed that Frank, with a 'milk of humankind-ness' that was Shakespearean, embraced the 'EVERYTHING-ness' of the country. Unfortunately this rhapsodic riff did not correspond to the mood of the photographs. They include portraits of an unhorsed cowboy in New York for the rodeo who leans against a trash can on a dirty sidewalk, a doubled-up shoeshiner at work among the urinals in the Memphis railway station, a derelict stretched on the dirt in a Cleveland park, and a grizzled Jehovah's Witness waiting for the world to end in downtown Los Angeles.

The French edition of Frank's book, which had appeared in 1958, came with an anthology of texts that corresponded more closely to his vision. The extracts were assembled by Alain Bosquet, a poet born in Odessa who, after fighting in the Belgian and French armies, sought refuge in Manhattan in 1942 and later became an American citizen. Bosquet's choices did not flatter the country that had taken him in. As a comment on Frank's recurrent flags, he quoted Henry Miller's belief that the Civil War had never ended: southern states still brandish the Confederate flag because they begrudge the north its power and prosperity, like Ireland nurturing its resentment of the United Kingdom. Frank's omnipresent cars are explained by a quip from William Faulkner, who said that the American's one true love was his automobile. Bosquet concluded by alleging that Americans had confused happiness with technological progress, which might lead them to casually exterminate us all by pressing a button.

Perhaps the annihilation had already occurred, with a muffled bang. In their 1959 'picture tour', Bernhard Moosbrugger and Gladys Weigner reported on a society in which machines had apparently remade nature and done away with human beings. Their book *USA – Europa sieht Amerika* included photographs of prairies sectioned for strip farming, Texas oilfields with forests of derricks instead of trees, earth-movers levelling mountains to build highways, combine harvesters rumbling through the corn like mutant insects, and looped Los Angeles freeways precariously stacked on stilts. Vehicles outnumber people, and have frisky, pseudo-human whims: in San Francisco, the authors heard tales about 'runaway, driverless cars', not parked at the correct angle, that slither down the steep hills and crash. At the University of California, they photographed a cyclotron accelerating particles: perhaps Americans were staging an assault on the very structure of matter. On the streets, Moosbrugger and Weigner saw 'stereotyped people all dressed alike, all with identical made-up, mask-like faces, all moving and speaking in the same manner', conditioned by tranquillizers and rebuked by the advertising industry if they did not do their allotted share of shopping. Wasn't it the Swiss visitors who applied the stereotype (which after all is a printing plate used by nineteenth-century photographers when reproducing their images)?

In *L'Amérique lunaire*, a short film made in 1962 on Route 66, François Reichenbach documented an America that looked more like Mars than the moon. Derricks puncture the earth and chew it up, foraging for oil. Cars wheeze, stall, die and are junked in graveyards where they wait for bulldozers to mash and pulp them: the machines in this red, rusted waste have cannibal appetites. Reichenbach's longer documentary *L'Amérique insolite* is introduced by a testimonial from Jean Cocteau, who claims that, despite America's robotism and the deathly symmetry of its corporate architecture, its society still exhibits the surrealist virtues of surprise, excess and anarchy. Yet Reichenbach's America has not safeguarded human dignity, as Cocteau appealed for it to do in the letter he wrote during his return flight to Europe in 1949; it is populated by humanoids, no longer frightening but merely weird. Gamblers in Las Vegas shake hands with the metal bandits that swallow up their coins, and two suburban old timers at a Ghost Town theme park creakily flirt with saloon-bar floozies who are actually effigies carved in wood. In the Indian village at Disneyland, animatronic figures huddled around a campfire that does not burn wave to the paying customers, who return the greeting. At a prenatal class in New York, prospective parents bathe plastic babies in enamel dishes, feed them from empty bottles, then encourage them to release inaudible burps. Reichenbach remarks that Americans travel through outer space but have to be taught such rudimentary biological routines: they possess technical know-how but lack mother wit. When an actual birth occurs, a father bonds with his offspring on closed-circuit television in a hospital waiting room. At first television watches over the baby, and Reichenbach shows excerpts from cartoons screened for infants in cribs. The mass medium serves as a pacifier for an entire society, whatever the age of its audience; it also standardizes American minds. This is a democracy in which people want to be the same, not merely equal, so that – as Reichenbach airily asserts – the country turns out more than the average quantity of twins. Rarer monsters are also rounded up: a set of triplets who suck Coke through straws while someone squirts sauce from a plump plastic tomato onto their mass-produced hamburgers, or a reveller at the Mardi Gras in New Orleans who sports three identical heads, two of them mercifully made of papier mâché.

Another prize specimen in Reichenbach's film is a chicken with expertly conditioned reflexes that has learned to play ten-pin bowls and knocks over skittles to ensure that its supply of grain continues – the perfection of behaviourism, which for Freud was the philosophy best suited to America. This anecdote is followed, thanks to the sneaky logic of montage, by a line-up of cheerleaders brandishing pompoms as they execute their choreographed drill, a brass brand strutting with 'military precision' at a college football game, a roaring battalion of Hell's Angels, and a succession of fighter jets taking off from an aircraft carrier in the Pacific. In an evolution that is made to look inevitable, we are hustled from the farmyard to the playground to the sports field and on to a potential theatre of war. All these activities, along with demolition derbies, roller coasters and the ecstatic epilepsy of the Holy Rollers, are meant to demonstrate the American obsession with 'mechanical violence'. Fortunately that violence is for the most part erotic or messily absurd. A trainee at a striptease academy in Los Angeles places protective rubber caps over her nipples, which give them the look of armoured missiles. There is no need to fear the detonation of a bomb like the one on Frank's postcard. Instead a succession of teenage girls blow up pink sacs of bubble gum that pop and splatter across their giggling faces.

Whereas Frank's subjects resent being spied on by his camera, Reichenbach's Americans have no such paranoia. 'In every American there's a photographer,' he says in his commentary, 'and in every photographer there's a tourist.' Or a performer: if you possess a camera you can star in the movie of your own life. The people in *L'Amérique insolite* know that they are on set, and feel at home in what Reichenbach calls the country's 'thousand little artificial worlds', like Disneyland, the reclaimed swamp of Cypress Gardens in Florida, or the Ghost Town outside Los Angeles where office workers pile onto a steam train in order to be thrillingly robbed by masked ruffians armed with plastic guns. We are warned against being deceived by a man and woman who romp in the surf at Santa Monica. They are models, hired out by their agency to a photographer at an hourly rate; their frolics are intended to advertise some unknown product that will make you as glad or as good-looking as they are. Reichenbach defines America as a department store that promises to have in stock whatever you want, even if you do not yet know that you want it.

His survey begins by abridging the coasts, with traffic on the Golden Gate or Bay Bridges in San Francisco and on the New Jersey turnpike approaching New York. Those cars, Reichenbach says, are aimed at 'all possible Americas, and all Americas are possible'. He is paraphrasing Dostoevsky's supposition that if God is dead, everything is possible – except that these vehicles are travelling in one compulsory direction, few of the harried drivers are elated by what lies ahead, and the range of possible Americas is narrower than Reichenbach fancied. A character in Don DeLillo's novel *White Noise* neatly summarizes the indiscriminate succession of diners, gas stations and public toilets that obstruct the view on roads that are no longer so invitingly open: 'The great western skies. The Best Western motels.'

In *Americana*, another DeLillo hero leaves his job at a New York advertising agency to take a road trip that is meant to be 'a religious journey'. He vows to drive, explaining that 'planes aren't religious yet. Cars are religious.' You can hardly undertake a quest or search if a pilot plots your course. Planes are an unearthly, almost post-mortem mode of transport; a car is more suitable for a pilgrim, especially if it bumps along back roads. But the sacred source is nowhere to be found. A Sioux mystic describes the triumph of Megamerica, the superstate that on its long march has flattened inconvenient terrain, suppressed any sense of locality, and synthetically recreated the world in 'neon, fiber glass, Plexiglass, polyurethane, Mylar, Acrylite'. The journey becomes an act of penance for the country's crimes against nature and its political or military transgressions: *Americana* was published in 1971, near the end of the Vietnam War, which is why DeLillo's disillusioned seeker refers to 'guiltless Canada'. But he will not allow himself to flee from a share of that national guilt by slipping across the northern border. At the end of the novel, he quits the hippie commune in which he has taken refuge and drives into Dallas, where he recapitulates the route President Kennedy took – past the Book Depository, around the grassy knoll – as a way of slipping back into America's inexorable history. From there he continues to the airport, returns his rental car, and buys a seat on the first flight back to New York.

An American road trip has become the modern equivalent of the Grand Tour taken by eighteenth-century gentlemen, who crossed the Alps to inspect the classical origins of their culture. Or perhaps it is the reverse of a Grand Tour, venturing beyond the limits of culture. At Yellowstone with its bubbling lakes the traveller finds nature still in ferment; Yosemite shows off the wounds of geological upheavals that might have occurred yesterday. Here is the earth in its raw state, as unfinished as America.

In Italy, Grand Tourists worked through a checklist of galleries and churches. In America, nature took the place of both art and religion. Olivier Messiaen, commissioned to compose a symphonic celebration for the American bicentennial in 1976, went on an almost sidereal journey to Utah, where the landscape seemed to be a preview of other planets that we might visit after death. In *Des Canyons aux étoiles*, Messiaen treats the amphitheatre of Cedar Breaks as an education in awe, a terrifying confrontation with divine power. Bryce Canyon, with its spindly Gothic spires and buttresses of striped red and orange rock, emits sound in jubilant volleys like draughts of energy; a piano dizzily skitters up and down the pinnacles while percussive rumblings and thunderclaps of brass serve notice that this is holy ground. In Zion Park, orchestral chorales carve clefts through the sandstone, and make room for birds whose song announces that this is the celestial city. Berenice Abbott had noticed the dire predictions that threatened drivers on Route 1: one roadside sign warned that 'BEFORE U REACH FLORIDA YOU MAY BE IN ETERNITY'. Here was American religion at its grimmest, with a hint of where the society's death-driven urgency was leading. In Utah, Messiaen deprived the announcement of its terror. Americans were living in eternity already.

Thanks to the ease of travel, the country's wonders soon became over-exposed, so foreigners had to work harder and travel further to find sites of revelation. In 1967 Hiroshi Hamaya made an exhausting trip through thirty states to prepare a photographic book entitled *American America*. The title is ironically inaccurate: this was a Japanese appraisal of America, deliberately peripheral in its vision. Hamaya clung to the coasts, except for a drive in a straight line from Chicago to Lincoln, Nebraska, and on to the Great Salt Lake, but he made a point of documenting the places where the mainland United States either runs out into the ocean, as at Key West and again at Cape Flattery in Washington State, or comes up against another country, which it does at Millinocket in Maine and Big Bend in Texas. Those termini were a relief: America after all was not infinite. Otherwise Hamaya found it full of emptiness, unlike over-populated Japan. He photographed a white waste of snow in Maine and another of scorching sand in the Mojave Desert, as well as Cape Cod out of season with icy puddles and dead grass lashed by a gale, a hotel at Yankeetown abandoned to the encroaching Florida jungle, and a deserted settlement beside an exhausted mine in Drytown, California. Clumps of prickly tumbleweed in Fabens, Texas, are like cocoons that contain no life, and Afton, Wyoming, boasts 'the world's largest elkhorn arch' – a raised portcullis of antlers, as forbidding as barbed wire, that extends above the main and only street of the town, perhaps to discourage visitors. After Robert Frank, the definition of the picturesque had changed: for Hamaya, the things in America worth photographing are those that Americans might prefer you not to notice.

Frank explained his departure from Zurich, where he grew up, by asking an unregretful rhetorical question: 'How can one be Swiss?' Travelling through America in the 1980s, Jean Baudrillard asked a more generalized version of Frank's question. With his preconceptions about culture shattered by speedways and Safeways, skylines and theme parks, he wondered 'How can anyone be European?' Baudrillard's post-modern itinerary wasted little time on New York and Washington, which were not American enough for his purposes. Instead he began his account of the country among the whittled buttes and fractal bluffs of Monument Valley and on the leaden flatness of the Great Salt Lake. Here, in 'astral America', he had his own equivalent of Messiaen's mystical insight, although he glimpsed no heaven and expected no redemptive afterlife. Baudrillard saw the canyons visited by Messiaen as the setting for a millennially slow but implacable catastrophe: they were portents of a time when man, ground into dust, 'will have no significance' – the same post-human premonition sonorously intoned by the lecturer at the planetarium in *Rebel Without a Cause*. By contrast with this furnace of rock and crumbling sand, European society was a theatrical facade, the backdrop for a comedy that relied on an 'aesthetic and rhetorical system' of gesture and pretence, 'ridiculous in its hereditary culturality'. Frank's rhetorical question had become an existential accusation: America made Baudrillard ask, in effect, how one can be human, or why one should bother.

The land was a racetrack or a launching pad, and Baudrillard watched America dematerializing as it took off into the future. The 'absolute horizontality' of Salt Lake, he said, prompted the invention of the supersonic cars that were tested there, like Craig Breedlove's aptly named Spirit of America, fitted in 1963 with a turbojet engine that was taken from a fighter plane deployed in the Korean War. Even joggers were drivers anxious to wear out their vehicles of flesh and blood, panting towards collapse or cardiac arrest; the sedentary Baudrillard called these faddists 'the protagonists of an easy-does-it Apocalypse' and described the finishing line of the New York Marathon as 'the end-of-the-world show'. Speed for Baudrillard was 'the rite that initiates us into emptiness', and driving induced 'a spectacular form of amnesia'. As he travelled through Los Angeles, the city became a movie, consisting of 'nothing but long tracking shots of signals' with intermittent orders saying 'Must exit', which might have been a sentence of death. Nothing remained of the delight in 'this morning world' that Kerouac felt when, with Cassady at the wheel, he crossed the salt flats of Nuevo León in Mexico.

In late 1987 and early 1988 the film-maker Robert Kramer made a road trip that studied America with the disenchanted eyes of an expatriate. Kramer began his career in the 1960s by documenting student protests for the New York Newsreel Film Collective; he went on to direct *The Edge*, in which an American president is assassinated as payback for Vietnam, and *Ice*, about squads of urban guerrillas who terrorize the United States during an imagined war with Mexico. Predictably, these vengeful fictions did not appeal to the domestic market, so Kramer moved to France where he concentrated on European political problems – neo-Nazi cells in Germany, class war in Portugal after the 1974 military coup. When he came home to investigate the state of his own nation, he chose to travel the entire length of the east coast on Route 1, as Berenice Abbott had done thirty years before. It was an old-fashioned plan: the Atlantic Highway had been bypassed by Interstate 95, which took a shorter inland route through Maine and in Florida drove straight across swamps that the previous road had to circumnavigate. But the wayward itinerary suited Kramer, and in his four-hour-long film *Route One/ USA*, speed matters less than the sober, systematic anatomizing of America.

Kramer's alter ego in front of the camera is his friend Paul McIsaac, who plays a character nicknamed Doc, 'a doctor without a clinic'. Doc begins his journey by baptismally immersing himself in a mountain stream in Maine, after which he declaims Whitman's 'Song of the Open Road'; cancelling the poem's vista of a 'long brown path before me leading wherever I choose', Kramer immediately cuts to bulldozers chewing up pine forests for paper pulp. En route, Doc seeks out Whitman's house in Camden, New Jersey, but finds it closed, which he takes as evidence that it is no longer possible to 'inhale great draughts of space' as Whitman did when he decided that everyone he met on the road 'must be happy'. He also visits a facsimile of Thoreau's cabin at Walden Pond, where the sage went 'to live deliberately', not distractedly like modern Americans. Others scrutinize America for anticipations of the future, but Doc finds everywhere a helpless re-enactment of the past. 'The civil wars are still going on,' he says as he notices the friction of races, classes, regions. At Fort Kent on the Canadian border, where a monument celebrates the beginning of Route 1 by marking 'America's first mile', a female cop frisks him: despite his passport, he is an honorary alien, estranged from America by his morose pensiveness.

Doc's father, he recalls, had been sent on a post-war mission to study the medical effects of atomic radiation in Japan. A generation later, Doc undertakes to diagnose America's ailments. He goes to see the Vermont Yankee nuclear reactor, shut down by protestors who were alarmed by the prospect of birth defects, and in a disadvantaged district of Brooklyn he gives lessons in first aid to neighbourhood kids, who are sure to encounter broken, bleeding bodies on the streets where they play. Reaching Miami, he signs on at a hospital, but when he treats Haitian patients he is told that he must respect the contrary prescriptions of voodoo priests. Does America need exorcism rather than medicine?

An elderly, skeletal New Englander, her fingers twitching as she wipes dust from the telephone exchange over which she presides, tells Doc 'We're living in the last days' and makes preparations for the imminent reappearance of Christ. Nature dies as he trudges on through the autumn weather; in Boston he finds people transforming themselves into corpses for Halloween, and a coven of witches tell him about their plans to quit the doomed planet. 'I am the face of Death,' Doc whispers as he takes stock of the Gothic designs available in a tattoo parlour. In thick, mortifying snow, he stops in Washington to tally the names of the dead on the Vietnam memorial. By the time he reaches Fort Bragg in North Carolina (where McIsaac himself was stationed during his military service), Doc has become a revenant. 'I thought you were dead,' says an old friend who is startled to see him; the friend also looks moribund, having been shot through the mouth and lost half his esophagus. A fellow Vietnam veteran, building a secluded house in the woods, says he is slowly returning to life, unfreezing emotionally – a difficult process, since the war robbed him of his humanity. In Georgia, a grizzled old timer who keeps rattlesnakes picks up a reptile and prises open its mouth to show Doc its pinkish gullet and curved white fangs: a glimpse of America's primordial savagery. Further south, he pauses at a ghoulish roadside museum whose treasures include the car in which Jayne Mansfield died when its top was sheared off beneath a trailer, and the ambulance that took Lee Harvey Oswald to hospital after Jack Ruby shot him. The creepy curator tells Doc he is 'looking fer more tragedies, y'know'.

After Miami, the eschatological highway straggles on to Key West and halts at a sign that tersely says 'End of the Rainbow'. The destination is unidyllic: on the lawn outside the Monroe County courthouse a caretaker spears waste paper. The last shot in *Route One/USA* is of a coral reef just off the Keys, where the continent's frayed fringe dissolves into a catacomb of insects. It may be some consolation to remember that Europe too is crumbling, and perhaps has already gone under. A character on a road trip in DeLillo's *Americana* hears a radio newsflash that announces the inundation of the old continent, which has sunk like Atlantis, capsized by the weight of its history and its mountains of antiques. All that remains, according to the report, is some Louis XIV flotsam bobbing in the ocean off Greenland.

11 | 'Americanize Yourselves!'

Both the USA and the USSR were revolutionary experiments, alternative versions of an undifferentiated mass society. In principle there was a clash between self-help and state management, individualism and collectivity, but the two systems functioned in parallel ways. In Russia a central bureaucracy managed everything; in America, although the government kept its distance, the media and the advertising industry manipulated minds and tastes to create a market for whatever the corporations needed to sell. Lenin's last order to his successors is supposed to have been 'Americanize yourselves!' Or had the Americans already bolshevized themselves? Alexandre Kojève – a political philosopher who was born in Russia but lived in France where, while allegedly spying for the KGB, he helped plan the European Common Market – commented that if Marx was God, Henry Ford was his prophet: Kojève called the manufacturer of the Model T 'the one great authentic Marxist of the twentieth century'.

'As for wars,' the sociologist C. Wright Mills wrote in 1951, 'the United States has been lucky to a degree that is unimaginable to most Europeans', with World War II as the consummation of its military and economic good fortune. The Cold War, then getting underway, was equally beneficial. The weapons stockpiled by each side were meant to provoke envy not dread; the conflict was actually a competition, and the opponents fired off ideological salvoes rather than missiles. Sidney Lumet's film *Fail-Safe*, released in 1964, deals with an American nuclear strike on Moscow, triggered by a mechanical error. The American President and the Russian Chairman confer, anxiously but without recriminations, as they attempt to recall the bombers or shoot them down, while the generals in Omaha and Moscow reminisce for a moment about the time they each spent in London during the last war. Their political doctrines, supposedly so inimical, are never mentioned. The President, played by Henry Fonda, agrees to sacrifice Manhattan to make up for the destruction of Moscow, with the Empire State Building as the target for the Strategic Air Command bomber he sends in. A belligerent political scientist advising the Pentagon ignores the millions of corpses but insists on the retrieval of corporate records from the melted city. 'Our economy depends on it,' he points out. At least this catastrophe is an accident, lamented by both sides. More cynically, Jean Renoir amused himself in 1974 by imagining a conference on the hot line between the White House and the Kremlin, with the two chief executives matily agreeing to spark a diversionary war in some expendable country to revive their sluggish industries. Once some ruins had been created, the lucrative business of rebuilding could begin. 'The aim of warfare,' Renoir pointed out, 'is no longer conquest but construction.'

In *The Power Elite*, published in 1956, Wright Mills described an America run by its own Comintern, with the captains of industry and their military clients keeping a 'permanent war economy' stoked up. The purpose was and apparently still is to enrich contractors at home: the Pentagon chronically over-pays its suppliers, and it was recently reported that a $7 hammer cost $436 by the time the Navy took delivery of it. *White Collar*, Wright Mills's earlier study of the American middle class, claimed that well-paid office workers at their desks or salesgirls behind their counters were just as disempowered as the Soviet proletariat in its factories. The only difference was the American insistence on cheerfulness – banter around the watercooler, family picnics on Labor Day, Christmas parties in the office. But that cheerfulness did make a difference, as Lee Harvey Oswald found when he defected to the Soviet Union in 1959. Oswald hinted that he had secret information about America's U-2 spy planes, which he believed would entitle him to special treatment. The KGB interrogators called his bluff and, having no further use for him, peremptorily assigned him to an electronics factory in distant Minsk, where he was put to work as a lathe operator. He complained that the job was stupefying, with no nightclubs or bowling alleys where he could spend the pittance he earned. He began yelling American slogans that were meaningless in the society he had elected to join: when union organizers hustled him out of bed early in the morning to vote in an election at the factory, he made the mistake of shouting 'This is a free country!' Eventually he took to exemplifying freedom in a uniquely American way. His fellow workers gaped as he relaxed by putting his feet up on a table, as if stretching out in a Western saloon. Eighteen months after his arrival in Moscow, Oswald begged to be repatriated, and the United States Embassy ill-advisedly loaned him funds for the trip back to Dallas.

In theory, communism aimed to reform human nature and chasten its possessive vices. Despite Henry Luce's admonitions, most of us have no wish to be angels, and the Cold War was won in the shops not on the battlefield. Popular culture cannily predicted the outcome. Vincente Minnelli's *Silk Stockings*, released in 1957, exults in the surrender of a prudish female commissar who has been sent from Moscow to Paris to recapture some ideological strays. At first she resists the decadent Western underwear that ought to weaken her rectitude, and says that silk should be reserved for parachutes. She succumbs, however, to a pink-ribboned girdle, a frilly petticoat, and a pair of jewelled slippers with high heels. The story patronized women, but it made a legitimate point about the corruptibility of communists with travel privileges. In George Axelrod's script for the 1962 film *The Manchurian Candidate*, a sinister Chinese mind-controller slips into the United States to check that his patient – an American war hero whose brain he washed clean and reprogrammed in Korea – has been primed to kill a presidential candidate at a Madison Square Garden rally. The Chinese envoy squirms uneasily when a top-up session of hypnosis over-runs. His wife, he says, has given him a shopping list, and he needs to spend the afternoon at Macy's.

In Billy Wilder's *One, Two, Three*, James Cagney does his best to undermine the USSR by dosing it with Coca-Cola. Cagney, who runs the company's office in Berlin, is charged with setting up bottling plants behind the Iron Curtain. The farcical plot has the pace of a military exercise, and Cagney's business methods, like his rat-tat-tat delivery of the repartee, are as drilled and drastic as the heated-up war his cold drinks are supposed to be preventing. 'General alarm, complete mobilization!' he barks to his underlings in the office. Wilder began filming on location in Berlin in 1961; soon afterwards, the wall that bifurcated the city went up and the set representing the Brandenburg Gate had to be rebuilt in Munich so that filming could continue. Laughing off the international crisis, Wilder saw little difference between divided Germany and the disunited United States. In the film, the nubile, stupid daughter of a Coca-Cola executive takes up with a leather-jacketed communist agitator and helps him launch balloons stamped with the slogan YANKEE GO HOME. This is not anti-American, she explains; she is from Georgia, where Coca-Cola has its corporate base, and down south everyone hates Yankees. Cagney, a northerner, retaliates by describing Atlanta as 'Siberia with mint juleps'.

The Russians in *One, Two, Three* sneer at Cagney – who refuses complimentary tickets to the Bolshoi and instead demands cash before he will divulge the secret of the esoteric black syrup – as 'the ugly American'. For them the phrase is a slur, though it was coined, only three years before, as a compliment. In 1958 the retired naval officer William J. Lederer and the political scientist Eugene Burdick published *The Ugly American*, a flimsily fictionalized tract about the communist threat in Southeast Asia. Their hero is an engineer called Homer Atkins, whose ugliness is purely allegorical, a credential of plain, earthy democratic virtue. With blackened nails and calloused palms, Homer sets out to 'show the idea of America to the people'. In remote areas of a country that is obviously Vietnam, he supplies villages with water pumps that are powered by broken-down bicycles; having designed a prototype, he turns out some samples, then recruits a sales force with the promise of a 10 per cent commission. 'In America,' a collaborator explains, 'one of the best things that can happen to engineers . . . is to be allowed to sell what they make.' Homer's wife Emma simultaneously lightens the chores of village women by cutting slender bamboo reeds to make long-handled brooms, which can be used without slavishly kneeling. Once the showdown with Asian communism began in earnest, these modest innovations had to be upgraded, and in the film of *The Ugly American*, made in Thailand in 1963, the Atkinses were moved closer to the front lines. Homer, renamed Horace, emerges from the jungle to become the foreman on a military highway known as Freedom Road, and Emma runs a children's hospital for the casualties of war. Spending their own money, they are dealing with what they call 'unfinished world business'.

The American ambassador in Lederer and Burdick's book expects the Soviet Union to gain from colonial uprisings against the French in Indochina, and predicts that 'The Russians will win the world by their success in a multitude of tiny battles.' But they did not, in part because they could not compete with the entrepreneurial ingenuity of Americans like Atkins. Lederer and Burdick even discern a trace of their ideal type in a Chinese envoy – not, admittedly, from the mainland: he represents Chiang Kai-shek – who is 'as American as a tractor salesman'. This is a bizarrely partial but precise definition of what then seemed to be the American national character, and it goes some way towards accounting for the country's recovery from its military defeat in Vietnam. The Chinese and Russian communists had tractors, but they lacked personable salesmen; they produced no equivalent to Ronald Reagan, the son of a commercial traveller who traipsed around Illinois with a sample case stocked with shoes. During his presidency Reagan was praised as the 'Great Communicator' and, whatever the constitution may have said about the duties of the executive branch, his primary function was to communicate the idea of America's glossy, commodity-rich greatness. Arthur Miller's obituary for salesmanship was premature.

Technologically, the Soviet Union gained an advantage after launching Sputnik in 1957. Radio engineers on Long Island were the first to pick up the satellite's signal, and they rushed the tapes into Manhattan so that NBC could broadcast those cheeky beeps: the capsule was performing for an American audience. In 1959, a Soviet rocket called Lunik II, loaded with scientific instruments, landed on the moon; the feat was timed to coincide with Khrushchev's first visit to the United States, which began a few days later. Otherwise the Russians were shamingly aware of their backwardness. Material prosperity gave Americans a gilded allure, felt even by Khrushchev when, at the Geneva summit conference in 1955, Eisenhower introduced him to Nelson Rockefeller, then serving as Special Assistant for Foreign Affairs (or, in a variant of his title, Special Assistant for Psychological Warfare). Giddy in the presence of a multimillionaire, Khrushchev wanted to touch Rockefeller but did not dare. Eventually he got up the courage to give him an awkward hug, with his arms – since he was so much shorter – encircling the plutocrat's stomach.

During the late 1950s, Khrushchev's son Sergei worked as an engineer on preparations for what one of the State Department's experts in the *Ugly American* novel calls 'the final crisis'. Sergei's speciality was guidance systems for missiles that in theory were to be launched from submarines and aimed at the United States; he also tinkered with lunar vehicles and boosters for space rockets, as the conflict was expected to ricochet around the cosmos. Looking back after the disassembly of the Soviet Union, he saw this bellicose posturing as a feint, even a fraud. Sergei remembered assuming, like most Russians, that Eisenhower's election in 1952 was an implicit declaration of war: why else would the Americans have wanted a general as president? Then in April 1953, a month after Stalin's death, Eisenhower delivered a speech to newspaper editors in which he recalled the accord between east and west in 1945 and regretted that the alliance had subsequently been split apart by ideology. 'The result,' he said, 'has been tragic for the world, and for the Soviet Union it has also been ironic.' The irony was that the Russians, feeling threatened by what Eisenhower called 'the free nations', had terrorized themselves; they wasted resources on armaments that could never be used, and chose to live in 'perpetual fear and tension'. Sergei recalled farcical duck-and-cover drills at school in Moscow, when children were told to wrap themselves in something white to deflect radiation. Eisenhower appealed for an end to this mutual mistrust, and asked 'What is the Soviet Union ready to do?' Its first response was to reprint the speech immediately in *Pravda*, which intimated that a dialogue might be possible.

Even so, when Khrushchev became First Secretary of the Communist Party later in 1953 he challenged Eisenhower to a competitive display of aeronautical toys. He was piqued when he arrived in Geneva for the 1955 summit on a two-engine Ilyushin 14, code-named 'Crate' by NATO, whereas Eisenhower disembarked from a Lockheed Constellation that had four engines. Khrushchev fought back during a week-long visit to England in 1956. He wanted to fly in on a Tupolev 104, the first turbo-powered jet, but the plane often bucked and caused pilots to lose control, so he was persuaded against it; he therefore sailed to Portsmouth by warship, but had his mail flown in from Moscow every day on a noisy Tu-104. For his trip to America in 1959, honour demanded that he use the long-range Tu-114, despite warnings from his son about the skittishness of the engines. Unfortunately he over-reached himself: the plane was so tall that the steps wheeled out after it landed at Andrews Air Force Base fell short of the forward door, and he had to lower himself clumsily down an emergency ladder.

On his tour of Washington, Khrushchev glowered at the Lincoln Memorial. Photographed from behind by Burt Glinn, he and the Great Emancipator, who is raised high on his throne, are two immovable objects. Khrushchev's bald, ballistic skull, seen close up by Glinn's camera, is a thick, dense weapon: might he be about to head-butt the statue? In New York, he was grumpily gratified when an elevator in the Waldorf-Astoria Hotel stalled while taking him to his suite on the thirty-fifth floor: to prove his case against capitalism, the technology on which the vertical city relied had failed. His gloating was cut short by the indignity of his exit from the stationary box. Perched on the operator's stool, he squeezed out onto the floor above, with the American ambassador to the United Nations pushing his bulbous rear end. A huffing and puffing walk up the remaining five flights of stairs ensued. When taken to the viewing platform on the Empire State Building he was unexhilarated, and remarked that once you've seen one skyscraper you've seen them all. Short of accepting American superiority, all he could do was boorishly grumble.

Khrushchev could not deny that Americans were more productive than Russians, and he worried – according to Sergei – not about the arms race or the space race but about the food race. Even before his American visit, he sent a delegation to study the cornfields of Iowa, and invited a seed manufacturer called Roswell Garst to bring his wares and his expertise from Coon Rapids for a consultation in the Kremlin. Garst was scathing about the inflexibility of Soviet practices. On a collective farm, he found that sacks of fertilizer had been left unopened because to spread the contents on the fields would have interfered with the sowing schedule imposed by the bureaucrats. Nor did the farmers dare to use hybrid seeds, which produced the best harvest, because this contravened the genetic orthodoxy of the Soviet agronomist Trofim Lysenko. American agribusiness impressed Khrushchev, who made a detour to Des Moines in 1959 to study swine nutrition. He also enviously sized up America's labour-saving devices: he inspected coin-operated luggage lockers in railway stations, and admired the trucks that scooped up garbage and churned it into swill in San Francisco. He admired the efficiency of the IBM cafeteria in San Jose more than the company's computers: executives toted their own trays, and Formica surfaces made it easier to keep the tables clean. Watching the apparatchiks who accompanied his father queue at the self-service counter, Sergei tartly noted that 'most of them had not moved food from stove to table in a good many years'. In practice, this seemed to be a less hierarchical society than Russia. Yet none of these novelties unsettled Khrushchev's faith that socialism would ultimately prevail; he assumed that it was possible to imitate American methods while somehow prohibiting the ambitious, acquisitive drive that lay behind them.

When his tour reached Los Angeles, he was entertained to lunch at Twentieth Century Fox. Reagan saw an opportunity for ideological grandstanding and refused his invitation, but Marilyn Monroe accepted after the studio bosses assured her that she was as popular as Coca-Cola in the Soviet Union. They also asked her to wear one of her tightest dresses, and as she wriggled into it, showing off her body for patriotic reasons, she told her maid that she guessed there was not much sex back where Khrushchev came from. All went well until the guest of honour was informed of a change in arrangements for the afternoon: because the city could not guarantee his safety, his scheduled trip to Disneyland had been cancelled. Although Sergei claimed that his father possessed 'only a very vague idea of what a "Disney country" consisted of', Khrushchev had a tantrum, which is how babies and despots react when contradicted. His disappointment was touching, since it confirmed that America's wonders can elicit childish rapture from even the mightiest; it also revealed his cultural dependence, as his reported rant at the end of the lunch drew on the alarmist scenarios of American movies, muddling genres with angry absurdism. Had there, he wondered, been an outbreak of cholera in the magic kingdom, or a putsch by gangsters? Were rocket-launching pads concealed behind Sleeping Beauty's castle?

Still fuming, he was led off to watch Walter Lang directing *Can-Can*, a Cole Porter musical about the revival of the prohibited dance in Montmartre. Lang wondered why such saucy 'Frenchy stuff' was being shown to the Russian visitors. Given the plot of *Silk Stockings*, someone may have calculated that the Cold War would be won by a titillating glimpse of underwear – or of its absence, since Shirley MacLaine rehearsed but did not deliver a speech telling Khrushchev that in the interests of international friendship she intended to perform her high kicks without panties. Instead, when she jabbed her leg into the air, a male dancer disappeared beneath her skirts and emerged waving her red knickers. Khrushchev and his frumpy consort Nina scowled, perhaps musing about the puerile delights of Disneyland; the next day, he made the incident serve the purposes of propaganda by telling reporters that in Russia the human face was considered a nobler and more beautiful sight than a bare behind. Sergei, who had recorded the display with his own movie camera, refused to be doctrinaire about MacLaine's exhibition. 'It was just American life,' he shrugged – a good comment on the cheerful flagrancy of this unregulated, happy-go-lucky society.

During his harangue at the United Nations the following year, Khrushchev denounced Americans as 'surfeited and depraved people'. But despite his disapproval of surfeit he could not help employing the language of affluent gluttony, as he did when threatening that Russia would manufacture rockets 'like sausages'. What could be less menacing than a sausage? And in any case, after sampling his first hot dog in Iowa in 1959, he had deferentially confessed to Henry Cabot Lodge that 'We beat you to the moon, you beat us at sausages.' With his rages and his repartee, Khrushchev was performing a war dance, not making a declaration of war; Saul Bellow – who was amused by his boisterous extroversion and preferred him to the stiff, timid politicians of the West – actually described his misbehaviour as a can-can, executed 'with a deep and gnomic joy', its tempo set by banging a bunched fist or a shoe on a table.

While abusing America in the General Assembly, Khrushchev periodically refreshed himself by taking a swig from a glass on his podium. 'Borjum, excellent Russian mineral water,' he explained: when not pretending to be a vituperative tyrant, he was happy to play the American role of salesman. He dodged between the bullyboy tactics of the school playground and sly, seditious teasing. Not long before his trip to the United Nations, during a visit to the American installation at the World's Fair in Moscow, he doubly embarrassed Vice President Nixon by asking first whether he wanted to fight and then proposing 'Let's kiss'. Such shadow-boxing was necessary, because he was trying hard not to be over-awed by what he saw inside the golden geodesic dome in Gorki Park that housed America's wares.

The structure designed by Buckminster Fuller was global, and so were its contents. A film entitled *Glimpses of the USA*, projected onto seven suspended drive-in screens, showed images of milk deliveries on doorsteps, backyard swimming pools, romping family dogs and heavy-laden supermarket shelves – Rockwellian banalities that in Russia were literally fabulous. Disney's Circarama outdid Cinerama by providing a 360-degree tour of American cities, monuments and national parks, and the Museum of Modern Art sent *The Family of Man*, a photographic inventory of humankind. Six separate editions of this show had been on tour since 1955 under the supervision of the United States Information Agency, and it eventually travelled to thirty-seven countries on six continents. Documenting ordinary lives, it aimed, as the curator Edward Steichen put it, to establish 'the oneness of the world'; it did not always succeed, and when it reached Paris, Roland Barthes snidely suggested that the parents of Emett Till – a black teenager who had been tortured, shot and dumped in a river in Mississippi as punishment for supposedly flirting with a white woman – should be asked 'what *they* think of *The Great Family of Man*'. Steichen, in Moscow for the opening, attested to the show's friendly persuasiveness by taking snapshots of Russians who smiled happily at photographic equivalents of themselves in other countries. His title, however, came from a speech made by Lincoln in 1861 about the dissolution of the Union, in which the family of man referred to is the American people. At this universal meal, the United States inevitably sat at the head of the table.

Next to Fuller's planetary bubble stood a glass pavilion designed by Welton Becket, best known for a Disney World hotel pierced by a monorail and for the Capitol Records Building in Hollywood, which is modelled on a pile of thirteen vinyl discs stacked on a turntable and has a stylus with a spike-shaped needle on its roof. Becket's pavilion contained a full-scale ranch house prefabricated by a Long Island builder and fitted out by Macy's with a colour television set and a TV dinner to eat while watching it, a hi-fi, closets of fashionable clothes, bathroom cabinets of cosmetics, packets of cake mix, and a fridge containing a supply of Pepsi-Cola, which had outmanoeuvred Coca-Cola to obtain the soda concession at the Fair. Scattered on tables were glossy magazines in which visitors could browse, admiring advertisements for the same products by which they were surrounded. Detergent flakes and scouring pads were on hand to ensure that everything remained immaculate, and a lawnmower was parked in the garage in case the Astroturf decided to grow. A gangway bifurcated the house so that crowds could troop through: this earned it the nickname Splitnik, and without leaving the earth it successfully countered the orbital triumphs of Sputnik. Unaware that shops had more appeal than laboratories or factories, *Izvestia* scoffed that the Americans had chosen to display 'a branch of a department store' rather than their scientific achievements or the industrial techniques that the Bolsheviks admired. Khrushchev, wrangling with Nixon in the house's kitchen, defended the Soviet economy by outrageously claiming that all Soviet housewives had washing machines like the General Electric model on view.

Steichen's photographs pretended that all men were brothers; the Splitnik was a reminder of abiding inequalities. This Platonic idea of an American home convinced the Russians, as Sergei Khrushchev said, that they lived in 'a sacrifice society', which denied them the consumerist boons Americans took for granted. While the politicians wrangled, *Life* lined up their womenfolk for a cover photograph that wordlessly resolved the argument between the two economic systems. Pat Nixon, tall, thin, elegant, wearing a cool floral dress with pearls at her neck, is flanked by the drab but evidently contented wives of Khrushchev and Anastas Mikoyan. To one side stands the wife of Frol Kozlov, a Hero of Socialist Labour who at the time was touted as Khrushchev's likely successor. Solid but shapeless, wrapped in a prickly synthetic shawl, Kozlov's consort grips an incongruously dainty lace hand-kerchief and a handbag that looks as if it might double as a cudgel; a rope of beads lolls on her ample chest. The other women smile at the camera, but she has swivelled sideways, and the camera catches her training downcast, covetous eyes on Pat Nixon's clothes.

When the Soviet bloc finally collapsed, it did so to the accompaniment of an American soundtrack. In October 1989 Gorbachev's spokesman Gennadi Gerasimov announced on American television that the Kremlin would not intervene to curtail separatist movements in Poland and Hungary. He was, he said, replacing the Brezhnev doctrine of compulsory adhesion with 'the Sinatra doctrine': the socialist republics were free to do it 'My Way'. It was a bold pronouncement, since the song, as declaimed by Sinatra, is an anthem for self-betterment and laissez faire. In 1991 Sergei Khrushchev did it his way by giving up his position at the Control Computer Institute in Moscow and migrating to Rhode Island; in 1999, shortly before acquiring American citizenship, he explained his new allegiance in an interview with the *Los Angeles Times*. He made no magniloquent statements about freedom, but praised Kansas steaks and remarked 'I love Home Depot – it pushes you to some creation', adding that he had panelled the basement in his personal Splitnik with supplies bought there.

The kitchen debate between Khrushchev and Nixon in Moscow had an epi-logue in Beijing in 1983 when Arthur Miller went to China to direct *Death of a Salesman*. At the time of the play's first performance in 1949, Miller thought that the woebegone Willy Loman disproved Luce's view of Americans as indomitable achievers. Decades later, with America less buoyant, Willy's dissatisfaction seemed to confide the unease of a society that had begun to question its go-getting values and to recognize the tormenting complexity of its problems. Miller now deemed it better 'to admit our suffering than to show the world our bathrooms and ceaseless success' – better, that is, for Americans. The Chinese cast, living under a communist regime, did not share his scepticism about the American dream.

The actors asked Miller why Willy moaned about being a failure when he owned a car and a house. He also owned a fridge – a Hastings rather than a more reliable General Electric, which was bought on hire purchase and (as he and his wife Linda lament) has taken so long to pay off that it will be superannuated by the time it is rightly theirs. That fridge occupies a place of honour in the play's kitchen; it is hard for us to realize now how totemic such a possession once was. The cultural treason of the runaway Dickie in Patricia Highsmith's *The Talented Mr Ripley* is all the more shocking because, despite his wealth, he refuses to have a fridge in his house near Naples, and perversely chooses to drink warm Martinis. When at last his girlfriend Marge bullies him into buying one, he views it with disdain, as a trophy of the bloated society he has quit: the door has 'so many shelves . . . that it looked like a supermarket swinging out at you every time you opened it'. In Graham Greene's *The Quiet American*, the very idea of such an appliance antagonizes the British journalist Fowler, who fears losing his Vietnamese mistress to a soft-spoken American rival. In Joseph Mankiewicz's film of the novel, Fowler sneers that the American offers 'a deep freeze and a television set'. Later he repeats the point, saying that Phuong has betrayed him in exchange for Canasta lessons and frozen food. Why the vendetta against refrigeration? It preserves freshness and retards decay, which for Greene the Catholic was an almost blasphemous interference with natural law: his dislike of America had the force of an ecclesiastical anathema.

In Beijing, the luxury of Willy's kitchen made it almost inconceivable to the play's designers. Trying to reproduce the directions in the script, they made it absurdly elegant: the chairs and table were mahogany, with unfunctional curvy lines more suitable for a sitting room. During early rehearsals the fridge remained an abstraction, represented by a tall cardboard box with a sheet of white paper draped over it like an altar cloth. Then one day Miller arrived to find that the box had been replaced by a 1940s fridge – actually made of papier mâché, he saw when he looked closer, but fitted with working hinges that allowed Willy to open it and take out a bottle of milk. Modelled on a vintage magazine advertisement, it had been created by a craftsman who specialized in funerary replicas, reproductions of a dead person's treasures that were burned at the funeral to signify their transference to the next world. That gave the fridge an appropriately supernatural aura, as the open door revealed a shining igloo, a glimpse of a cool, expensive paradise.

Miller was irritated by the way his play's meaning had been confounded, but also a little abashed. How could he begrudge the Chinese their modest craving for goods that would improve their lives? It was, he realized, easy to disparage consumer capitalism when you were enjoying its benefits.

12 | Little America

Europeans adjusted to America in their own time, absorbing its culture without having to renounce their political arrangements and ingrained social habits. Japan's case was more drastic: after 1945 it was transformed by decree into Little America. With General MacArthur as Supreme Commander of the Allied Powers, the occupying forces administered the country until 1952, imposing a new constitution that required the Emperor to forfeit his divinity, prohibited rearmament, established parliamentary government, broke up business conglomerates, changed the menial status of women, and improved the lot of tenant farmers. MacArthur licensed a free press, although it was forbidden to publish criticism of the occupation; among other petty acts of censorship, *Citizen Kane* – which started the young Truffaut's love affair with American culture – was banned, because it gave an unflattering account of plutocracy at home.

Donald Richie first visited flattened Tokyo in 1947 as an employee of the occupying American shogunate, and except for the years from 1949 to 1953, during which he was enrolled at Columbia University, he lived there until his death in 2013. His first house had no running water or gas, with a pit outdoors instead of a flush toilet. He pronounced these rudimentary arrangements 'ideal – so different from the comforts with which I grew up'; it was his choice to live in a 'poor, defeated island' where, for the time being, spirit mattered more than making and spending money. The Japanese, like Arthur Miller's Chinese actors ogling the fridge, did not understand such self-spiting acts of renunciation, and Richie's high-mindedness soon came to seem perverse. By the end of the 1950s, the free market set up by the Allied Powers enabled the Japanese to buy the imported amenities Richie eschewed, and Yasujiro Ozu's film *Good Morning* records the unstoppable advance of Americanization in a modest suburb outside Tokyo. A door-to-door salesman distributes leaflets that advertise such untranslatable appliances as toasters and blenders, along with pencils and brushes. One householder has acquired a washing machine on the instalment plan, and in another family a debate rages about investing in a television set. The children clamour for it so they can watch baseball, but the father worries that it will produce a nation of idiots. He finally gives in to this latest foreign intrusion, which acclimatized itself rapidly: a few decades later, everyone in the world coveted sets made by Sony or Yamaha.

The Japanese learned their economic lesson only too well, and in the late 1980s, when they began buying up American corporations, there were hints of revenge on the complacent West. A Japanese trade minister, according to Gore Vidal, privately predicted that in the near future the United States would be his country's granary and Europe its boutique. Retaliating, Americans took to what Richie called 'Japan-bashing', and in 1992 the United States Postal Service planned to issue a stamp with an image of the atomic blast at Hiroshima, commemorated, according to the inscription beneath the mushroom cloud, because it hastened the end of the war and thus saved American lives. On the Tokyo subway, Richie was eyed with hostility. To pacify the other passengers he 'tried to look European' – perhaps by affecting an air of world-weariness? – and ruefully remembered a time when Japanese strangers glowed with delight after exchanging mute glances with him.

Through these ups and downs, Japan preserved its separateness, and Little America remained incorrigibly un-American. Its psychological insularity perplexed the anthropologist Ruth Benedict, who began to study the country during the war. Her initial aim was to understand the psychological stamina of Japanese soldiers in the Pacific, after which she tried to make sense of their unexpected surrender. The moment the Emperor gave the order, the troops laid down their arms and cooperated with the victors, quietly astonished that they had not been made to atone for the nation's humiliation by committing suicide. Benedict was puzzled by this obeisance to a higher power, an instinct that had been bred out of Americans. Hence the startling first sentence of her book *The Chrysanthemum and the Sword*, published in 1946: 'The Japanese were the most alien enemy the United States had ever fought in an all-out struggle.'

Benedict assumed that Americans exemplified what she called 'integrated behaviour': emotionally honest, they said what they felt and acted accordingly. For the Japanese, however, a public front concealed private consciousness. When they lost face they felt ashamed but not guilty, as their morality was concerned only with maintaining external decorum. Having made this distinction, Benedict had to admit its relativity. In the America of the 1940s, psychiatry began to ease the burden of puritanical guilt, and shame was now the regulator in a newly acquisitive society where keeping up with your neighbours mattered more than following the crabby dictates of conscience. In another dichotomy, Benedict linked psychological norms to financial practice. Every American, she suggested, believes in the originality of his or her own existence, whereas the Japanese think of themselves as an extension of those who preceded them. This makes them debtors from birth, piously obliged to pay tribute to the ancestors to whom they owe their lives. Benedict likened the onus the Japanese assumed to the American respect for budgets, settling accounts promptly and not defaulting on loans: that was all very well until, decades later, the United States began to live on credit.

To explain Japanese conduct, Benedict cited analogies from American subcultures that were either outmoded or disreputable – further proof that her own country had set the standard for civilized behaviour. Feuds were surely a relic of feudalism, so that the Japanese 'sensitivity over trifles' reminded her of the tribal wars stirred up by insults among the hillbilly clans of the Kentucky mountains, or of rivalries between adolescent gangs in the urban slums. This tetchy readiness to take offence also recalled 'case-histories of neurotics', perhaps like Robert M. Lindner's rebel who had no real cause for his actions. On occasion she did question Western values. The cult of ritual suicide persuaded her that the Japanese would rather do violence to themselves than to others, as Americans regularly did when refusing to take the blame for a personal disaster. For the Japanese, self-discipline – as in the hard physical training of judo – was good in itself. Americans, Benedict realized, thought of this moral chastening as self-sacrifice, found it painful, and expected some kind of reward for their voluntary suffering:

charitable donations, for instance, demonstrated to the world that they were rich enough to give money away, which compensated for their loss. Even when, much later, Americans began going to the gym, their motives were not ascetic: the subscription was meant to buy a good body that could be narcissistically placed on display.

The Japanese in their turn thought of Americans as lawless creatures, and were bewildered, Benedict said, by their 'emphasis on freedom as a prerequisite for achievement'. Before the political creed that was haltingly transliterated as 'demokurashi' could work, the Japanese had to be made more selfish, taught to pursue their 'rightful happiness' as individuals, which entailed getting ahead and making money. As a corollary, they were now entitled to be sexually happy, like uninhibited Americans. The military government considered Japanese reticence to be antisocial and potentially dangerous: were they bashful, or sly and deceptive? The Civil Information and Education Section therefore encouraged film-makers to violate a traditional taboo and show characters kissing, as Akira Kurosawa shockingly did in 1950 when the bandit in *Rashomon* molests the veiled lady. Improprieties were preferable to the impenetrable rigour of the mask.

As in post-war Germany, baseball was crucial to the process of indoctrination: the Americans believed that heckling the referee would wean spectators from automatic deference to an Emperor or a Führer, and the trading of players – or, among young fans, of baseball cards – like stocks in the financial market was a lesson in the volatility of capitalism. 'Besoboru' was already popular in Japan, although during the war the Patriotic Baseball Association covered up its American origins by renaming it 'field ball', and players, always referred to as 'warriors', wore khaki uniforms and saluted each other according to rank. Even with this camouflage, questions were asked about baseball's slippery American ethics. The diplomat Inazo Nitobe denounced it as a pickpocket's pastime because it was about stealing bases, and contrasted it with rugby, a worthy exercise for brave men who risked injury to prove their mettle. The very idea of sport was problematic for the Japanese, who lacked a word for it and had to borrow and re-pronounce the English term. Athletic activity in America was a reflex of bodily enjoyment,

a way of burning off physical energy; the Japanese thought of it more solemnly, as an exhibition of spiritual virtue like the sword-wielding code of
bushido. In 1954 Roger Angell regretted the bland professionalism of current
American baseball players and pined for the scrappers, haters, loudmouths,
roughnecks and screwballs of yesteryear. The Japanese, on the other hand,
always cared more about the team's unity than the starry exploits of individual players. Batsmen relegated to the bench looked remorseful about being
sidelined, whereas Americans nonchalantly joked while they awaited their
chance. And if their team lost, the Japanese did not cheerfully shake hands
with the winners and look forward to getting even next time. Instead they
slunk away in mortification; one coach, Suishi Tobita, expected losers to cry
in the changing room as proof of their disgrace. Even the spectators were
depressingly self-controlled, and threw back foul balls rather than seizing
them as souvenirs.

Slowed down by an inbred caution, this version of baseball was anything
but playful. The Japanese were equally earnest in their economic activities,
and lacked the buccaneering panache of American capitalists. Life and
liberty never became synonymous here, and happiness remained a trivial,
ignoble goal.

In 1956 in *The Teahouse of the August Moon*, Marlon Brando, cast as an
impish Japanese harlequin, sniggers at an experiment in Americanization
that has already failed. The film, based on a novel by Vern Sneider and a
subsequent Broadway play by John Patrick, is about the effort to re-educate
villagers in Okinawa immediately after the war. Brando – orientalized by his
inky hair dye, his mouthful of prosthetic teeth, and his mashed and mangled
consonants – plays the interpreter Sakini, who mischievously misinterprets
the army's directives. Mirthlessly grinning, Sakini talks about 'benevolent
assimilation of democracy by Okinawa'; the island has, however, been
successively overrun by Japanese warlords, Chinese pirates, English missionaries and American Marines, and despite eight centuries of invasion has
contrived to remain the same.

Okinawa is far from the mainland, so the film tactfully omits any mention of the war, the firebombing of Tokyo and the destruction of Hiroshima. Sneider's novel, published in 1951, was closer to those events and could not ignore them. The village geisha here only wears her kimono on Sundays: it was made in Tokyo, and because the city is ashen rubble there is no chance of replacing it. The novel also admits that the occupying army had a Plan A, devised to deal with sabotage by the disgruntled Japanese, which never had to be put into practice. The film concerns the milder provisions of Plan B, which provided for the welfare of a dependent population. Glenn Ford plays Captain Fisby, a specialist in Psychological Warfare transferred to Okinawa to establish a monetary economy by training the peasant farmers to mass-produce chopsticks and tourist trinkets. His cheerfully bigoted commanding officer Colonel Purdy notes that as a civilian Fisby was an academic who taught Humanities, and hopes he will now teach the Okinawans to act like humans. The human species, however, comes in many varieties, and men do not all belong – as Steichen's photographic exhibition contended – to a single family with Adam as its patriarch. The American occupiers were at first forbidden to associate with 'indigenous personnel'; when they edged closer, they discovered that the Japanese were human beings of a different kind, who saw the world in their own idiosyncratic way.

Following orders, Fisby begins to build a schoolhouse in the shape of the Pentagon, inside which the pupils are trained to sing 'God Bless America'. He also delivers lectures on democracy, which he defines – to the polite befuddlement of his audience – as 'the right to make the wrong choice'. A fracas in the rice queue calls the American bluff. When the local geisha trots to the head of the line with her bowl, there are protests from the villagers she has bypassed. Each of them wants the same favoured treatment: if everyone is equal, shouldn't they all be the same? Democracy in effect means a jostling chaos. Alternatively, it means giving in to the will of the majority, which is why, as Fisby announces with a resigned smirk, 'Uncle Sam is going into the teahouse business.' Allowing the villagers a vote, he uses lumber sent for the pentagonal schoolhouse to build a pavilion in a pine grove where the Americans and Japanese can relax together and drink jasmine tea as they watch the sunset.

In Sneider's novel, Fisby reconciles himself to this dereliction of duty by remembering that, after disputes with the rulers of colonial Virginia, Jefferson, Monroe and their colleagues retired to the Raleigh Tavern in Williamsburg to drink while discussing 'the yet unborn American nation'. He also solemnly imitates Lincoln by setting free the two geishas he theoretically owns. In the film he makes no such sanctimonious attempts to exemplify patriotic principles. The teahouse is his antidote to America; as he sips his tea, he says that this way of life ought to prevent the ulcers and nervous break-downs from which his striving compatriots suffer. The contemplative idyll is subsidized by an illicit still that produces sweet potato brandy, with profits from sales diverted to a bank in Seattle. Purdy at first assumes that Fisby has siphoned off this money for himself, which would be the American way. When informed that the village has formed a co-op to give everyone a share, he thunders 'That's communism!' and orders the demolition of the teahouse. Then he belatedly changes his mind, and asks the subordinates who carried out his orders 'Whatever happened to the American spirit of rebellion?' The wily Sakini preserves the distillery, which earns him Purdy's most heartfelt compliment: 'He's really an American – he's got get-up-and-go.'

On his way home, Fisby says that in Okinawa he has learned 'the wisdom of gracious acceptance. See, I don't want to be a world leader. I've made peace with myself, somewhere between my ambitions and my limitations.' It is a gloriously unlikely speech for an American officer to make: here power is rebuked by comedy, which coaxes us to admit our common frailty. But international relations are not governed by such wise, smiling precepts, and in 1955 Samuel Fuller's *House of Bamboo* exposed persisting frictions. This was the first film made on location in Japan after the country regained its independence; although it notices ancient points of orientation – Mount Fuji, the all-seeing statue of Buddha at Kakamura, the moated Imperial Palace which is the seat of an invisible and now ineffectual sovereign – the Tokyo in which it takes place is a smoggy anthill of small trades or a floating shanty town of barges connected by bouncy gangplanks, its shrines supplanted by pachinko parlours where worshippers feed alms into clattering machines that may or may not answer their prayers.

In *House of Bamboo*, the occupying force has not retreated, merely changed its function. As the gangster Dawson, Robert Ryan commands a private army of former soldiers who were hoodlums before they were drafted, among them an ordnance sergeant with a cache of stolen weapons. Dawson 'runs his outfit like a five-star general', and military discipline prevails during his raids on factories and offices. Wounded gang members, for instance, are shot dead to prevent them from blabbing under interrogation. In Dawson's villa, discreet, shuffling servants serve tea and look after the caged birds in the garden, but this traditional Japan is a papery screen for rough, raucous America: at a party the delicately tottering geishas suddenly throw off their kimonos and start jitterbugging. In a few sideways glances, Fuller documents the new helotry of an abased population. Outside a theatre, two GIs complain about the tardiness of their dates – with whom they won't be able to converse because they don't share a language – while an old woman bends before them, polishing their boots. Dawson struts into a Japanese house without removing his shoes and roughs up an elderly uncle to obtain information, then makes gruff amends by telling one of his goons to give the victim a cigar. The old man, who cannot afford to be offended, accepts the donation.

This meekness is painfully characteristic, since the Japanese had been warned to blame no one but themselves for their predicament. Recriminations were banned, and writers dealing with the war were not permitted to refer to the Americans as 'enemies'. When in 1954 an embodiment of the destroyer finally emerged from the collective imagination, it did not take the form of two American planes loaded with atomic bombs; instead it was a saurian throw-back whose breath could melt electric pylons like wax. The mutant lizard in *Godzilla* is an instrument of Japanese self-castigation, and the flustered politicians in the film fuss about keeping its earliest rampages secret because the news will imperil the country's international alliances. What they mean is that it might encourage criticism of the United States, whose bomb tests in the Pacific have resurrected the extinct creature by disturbing its underwater tomb. Even this fantastical tale was defused by being retold under American auspices. In 1956 the Japanese film was chopped about by an American producer, with Raymond Burr inserted into the pre-existing footage as a reporter who happens to be visiting Japan when the lizard rears up from beneath the sea. While Godzilla lays waste to Tokyo, what matters for Burr is ensuring that the line to his news service in Chicago remains open; the disaster only has significance if it is witnessed by and reported to Americans.

When Kurosawa resumed his career after 1945, he had to secure the approval of the Civil Information and Education Section's censors, who insisted that films must applaud the new moral order. In 1948 he submitted a synopsis of *Drunken Angel*, about a slum doctor who treats a gangster with tuberculosis. His summary made no reference to the doctor's despair as he tries to cope with an epidemic in the infested Tokyo slums; instead he pretended that the story was a critique of 'feudalistic loyalty' among criminals, who lived in 'an old world which runs in the opposite direction of democracy'. This clever evasion bamboozled the overseers, and freed Kurosawa to present the yakuzas in *Drunken Angel* as exemplars of American free enterprise who affect American fashions – loud floral shirts, zoot suits, a Bogeyesque fedora. He even flouted a decree that forbade films to show Roman lettering, which was supposed to ensure that the occupation stayed out of sight. The signage in *Drunken Angel* keeps up a sarcastic peripheral commentary on the misery of the doctor's sickly, scavenging patients. The black market is identified as THE HAPPY MARKET, and a lewd dance hall has a painted placard over its door saying SOCIAL CENTER OF TOKYO, even though it is located in a dusty unpaved alley beside a festering sump where bacilli germinate like microscopic Godzillas.

    Stray Dog, made in 1949, brought Kurosawa into open conflict with a self-appointed American guardian of humane values. The titular mongrel is metaphorical: it stands in for a gangster who commits murders using a gun stolen from a young policeman. Kurosawa cast the dog after a visit to the pound, then had it made up to look ill, with white rims painted around its eyes and grease smeared on its patchy fur. An assistant riding a bike took it out for some brisk exercise in the summer heat, after which it was filmed as it panted, tongue lolling over its teeth. An American woman who saw the film was convinced that Kurosawa had injected a healthy dog with rabies, and threatened to sue; he had to defend himself by swearing a legal deposition. This, he later said, was the one occasion on which he regretted that Japan had lost the war.

Although he pretended to deplore feudal deference in his synopsis of *Drunken Angel*, Kurosawa continued to revere the ancient relationship of master and disciple: in *Stray Dog* an older policeman restrains and counsels the younger colleague who is dishonoured by the loss of his gun. He was sceptical as well about the virtue of acquisition, so zealously recommended by the victors. The canine thug Yusa steals a diaphanous Western dress for the dancer Harumi, who says she would have purloined it herself if she had been brave enough. She adds that shop owners deserve to lose their stock, and have no right to put such temptations on display. Her logic may be ditzy, but the accusation has a sharp edge: consumerism is a crime because it incites desire. Were the Americans corrupting not reforming Japan? That – according to James F. Davidson, a State Department official, in an essay written in 1954 – was also the seditious implication of *Rashomon*. Davidson saw the bandit played by Toshiro Mifune as a surrogate American, coarse and oversexed; the nameless woman he allegedly rapes is Japan, a veiled and exalted goddess whom he drags down to the ground.

Kurosawa's most explicit quarrel with Americanization is *High and Low*, released in 1963, an adaptation of *King's Ransom*, a novel by Ed McBain about detectives at the 87th Precinct in New York. The story concerns a kidnapping. McBain's tycoon Doug King refuses to pay the ransom when he discovers that the son of his chauffeur has been snatched, not his own boy. King despises the way that capitalism in what he calls 'the big country' has turned from a doctrine of hard work into a fantasy of instant enrichment. Criminals cannot be bothered to rob a bank; they simply borrow a child for a few hours, then set an exorbitant price for his return. Hence King's decision not to reward them, even at the cost of the victim's life. For Kurosawa's character – a Yokohama shoe manufacturer called Kingo Gondo, played with seismic fury by Mifune – the choice involves a more agonizing self-inquisition and a comparative test of American and Japanese ethics.

The boys in McBain's novel are playing hide-and-seek when the muddled kidnapping occurs. In the film they are dressed for an American game, alternating the roles of sheriff and outlaw and sharing the costume: one has the pistol, chaps, tin star and cowboy hat, the other the boots. The medical intern who does the kidnapping lives beside a scummy canal in a fetid alley, with a shop on the corner that incongruously sells television sets and kitchen appliances, the trophies of Americanized modernity. Yet despite the fancy dress and the electrical novelties, the Japanese have not undergone the required psychological re-education. 'Ask humanity to commit suicide for a brother!' scoffs McBain's King, for whom capitalism is about the primacy of the thrusting, grasping ego. In the film it is precisely because Kingo is not asked to behave with such mad altruism that he chooses to do so, voluntarily and ruinously. As the chauffeur begs Kingo to save his son's life, the feudal decorum of the household cramps him. He bows, prostrates himself, begs to be excused for his presumption; then, as if acknowledging his worthlessness and trampling the vexatious self, he tells his master not to worry about the boy. When Kingo resolves to bankrupt himself by paying the ransom, he is not acceding to this grovelling request: his magnanimously tragic gesture is acclaimed by the newspapers because it exhibits his sacrificial sense of honour – the very spirit the Americans wished to eliminate. Tsumoto Yamakazi, cast as the kidnapper, was astonished by Mifune's throttled, wrenched intensity in the scenes where Kingo struggles with himself while attempting to keep his distress secret. He likened his colleague to a soldier on the battlefield at the end of the war, aware that he was losing (to America, of course) and mortified by his survival.

Demilitarizing Japan, the occupying forces prohibited films that glorified the samurai, the warriors who, until Commodore Perry arrived with his steamships in 1854, defended aristocratic power and preserved the country from foreign adulteration. In the 1870s the samurai were replaced by an army of conscripts, and forfeited their right to summarily execute commoners who offended them. Their ideal of valour had a revival during the Pacific war, when it was recommended to kamikaze pilots, and they retained a distinct identity as a military clan, called shizoku, until the 1947 constitution officially eliminated the caste and its title. As soon as self-government returned,

Kurosawa made *Seven Samurai*, released in 1954. Here some poor farmers whose harvest is threatened by bandits hire the unemployed samurai as a militia. The situation has a teasing relevance to recent history: are the villagers resigning themselves to the American protectorate, or teaming up to fortify Japan? One of Kurosawa's characters flouts the hieratic deportment of the group, and in this medieval setting anachronistically behaves like an American. Kikuchiyo is wild and rambunctious, sometimes drunk; he fishes in a loincloth, scratches his backside, sounds the village alarm as a practical joke, and pokes his tongue out at his disapproving colleagues. Mifune, playing the role, is as scandalously relaxed as the slouching, mumbling Brando, as flurried and suddenly violent as James Dean (though less neurotic), and his roustabout antics are accompanied by a jazzy score – bongo drums, piccolo, and a snarling bassoon that mimics his snoring when he collapses – not by ancestral Japanese instruments like the keening flute. The villagers are as taken aback as the factory workers in Minsk when Oswald put his feet on the table: power expresses itself in unbuttoned, easy-going relaxation, not the stiff rigour of the imperial regime with its precisely calculated genuflections.

Kurosawa's oblique criticism of America became more pointed when his samurai films were remade as Westerns. John Sturges used *Seven Samurai* as his source in *The Magnificent Seven*, and Sergio Leone adapted *Yojimbo* – in which Mifune plays another unkempt, skittish communal bodyguard, who rejects a pistol and dispenses justice with his sword – in *A Fistful of Dollars*. The two later films are set near the southern border of the United States, and cannot avoid noticing the inequality of the countries and cultures that face each other there. Sturges made *The Magnificent Seven* on location in Mexico, where the authorities worried that the story about villagers who travel north to recruit Texan gunmen implied that Mexico was feebly dependent on its brawny neighbour. Sturges therefore initially sent the deputation to buy guns, not to hire a squadron of foreign gunmen. The Japanese origins of *The Magnificent Seven* may be responsible for its pessimism, rare in American Westerns. Here there is no possibility of clearing away pesky natives, laying rails from coast to coast, or implanting civilization. One of Kurosawa's samurai says that, no matter how many swordfights he has won, he is always on the losing side: what keeps him going is his infatuation with death and his determination to die stylishly. He passes on that fatalism to the character played by Yul Brynner in *The Magnificent Seven*, who as he rides away with his two remaining comrades dismisses their success in routing the bandits and freeing the villagers from fear. 'We lost,' he says. 'We always lose.'

In *Yojimbo* Kurosawa medievalized Dashiel Hammett's novel *Red Harvest*, about union busting in a Montana mining town called Personville, nicknamed Poisonville. He muffled Hammett's cynicism and allowed the ronin played by Mifune to eliminate the rival gangs of bandits without returning power to the ruthless magnate who runs the place, as the private eye does in the novel. Hammett's Continental Op, like McBain's self-serving Kingo, is reformed by the austere Japanese code of conduct: the ronin negotiates a high fee for his services, then gives the money away to demonstrate his contempt for mercenaries. The character played by Clint Eastwood in Leone's *A Fistful of Dollars* – a nameless gringo in a town south of the border where guns and liquor are bought for resale to Indian tribes in Texas – has no such selflessness. 'I don't work cheap,' he warns an employer. Unlike the ragged ruffian in *Yojimbo*, Eastwood arrived on set in Almeria in southern Spain with his own wardrobe and props – jeans from Hollywood Boulevard, a hat from a Santa Monica costume shop, cigars bought in Beverly Hills, and a gun belt and spurs left over from his television series *Rawhide*. He looked, as Leone intended, like a foreign star disdainfully slumming.

One of Eastwood's jobs is to escort some Mexican soldiers to the Rio Grande, where they are to hand over bullion to the US Cavalry in exchange for a consignment of weapons. At the rendezvous, the Americans turn a machine gun on the Mexicans and make off with the gold; they even shoot the horses. The incident is not altogether explained away when we learn that the murderous, larcenous Americans were members of a Mexican gang wearing stolen uniforms. Kurosawa, constrained by the Japanese belief that disagreement is bad form, kept his opinion of the victors to himself. Leone, however, showed them behaving with treacherous rapacity, then excused himself by passing off the disclosure as a case of mistaken identity.

Only in 1964, when Seijun Suzuki made *Gate of Flesh*, could a film acknowledge how the Japanese – represented by a pack of prostitutes inhabiting the ruins of Tokyo in the sweaty summer of 1945 – truly felt about the occupying army. Suzuki had a personal grudge: he could not forgive the Americans for sinking both the cargo ship that was taking him to the front and the freighter on which he later fled from Manila to Taiwan. The street-walkers in *Gate of Flesh* spit at the American flag that breezily surmounts their squalid midden while honouring a tattered Japanese battle standard. One of the women is pursued by a military chaplain, who wants to save her soul; instead she lewdly incites him to have sex, then smirks as he stumbles off to kill himself. A cocky black marketeer randomly knifes GIs, and raids an army supply store to steal penicillin for resale. The women and their starving neighbours grab tins of pineapple or Carnation powdered milk, also stolen from the army's warehouse – but a man in the mob queueing for a bowl of American stew retches when he finds a distended condom afloat in the squelchy brown mess. This, according to Suzuki, is how power expresses its contempt for those who are supposedly in its care.

Kurosawa settled into stoical acceptance, without forgetting his resent-ment of the American takeover. In *Rhapsody in August*, released in 1991, some children go on a tour of Nagasaki with their grandmother, who still has nightmares about a flaming eye that stared out of the sky when the bomb fell. In a school playground, they look at a rusty climbing frame warped by heat from the detonation. During a brief vigil, the children remove their baseball caps – one of which is emblazoned with the logo of an American college football team, the SMU MUSTANGS – and near the site of the blast they inspect sculpted tributes to the dead set up by the governments of China, the USSR and its satellite states. One of them remarks on the absence of any American memorial, but the older girl says 'What do you expect?' The conquerors will not apologize for their victory, and the conquered must accept what cannot be altered.

Yukio Mishima was appalled when the Emperor accepted his demotion to equality with other human beings. 'More imperial than the Emperor', as

Donald Richie said, Mishima **refused** to accept Little America's legitimacy: he resented the disarmament **that was** forced on Japan, and also the moralism that condemned the love of comrades when the country's morals were, in Ruth Benedict's word, first 'Westernized' after the 1870s. In an interview on French television in the early 1960s, Mishima insisted that homosexuality was 'a more ancient feeling and more natural in Japan than heterosexual love', and accused American missionaries of chastening the privileged intimacy between samurai. He revived the military caste when he formed his Shield Society, a literal national guard – 'like soldiers in Switzerland', he said – that would protect the political and spiritual integrity of Japan; the solidarity of his brothers in uniform was to be cemented by sexual contact.

A neurotic personal drama underlay Mishima's militancy. Despite his sword-waving, he surrendered to American dominance with an almost feminine frisson. He claimed that peace was for him 'the most difficult and abnormal state', yet he did not fight in the Pacific war, faking symptoms of fever at his medical examination so that he was declared unfit for service. In retrospect, he tried to atone for this cowardice by his bodybuilding and his training in the martial arts. But he continued to make submissive gestures, acting out rituals of capitulation. Faubion Bowers – a scholarly expert on Japanese theatre, who served as MacArthur's interpreter during meetings with Emperor Hirohito in 1945 and dissuaded the Supreme Commander from banning kabuki because of its feudalism – indiscreetly reported in *The Village Voice* that Mishima once 'flew over to America just for sex' and set off into the downtown night in New York and San Francisco to satisfy his urgent 'need for a white man'.

Mishima fretted about his literary reputation in America, and was hurt when colleagues like Tennessee Williams, whom he entertained in Tokyo, failed to bolster his stock in that larger, more lucrative market. Yet this desire for American esteem did not block his aesthetic distaste for the country; his secret susceptibility only strengthened his self-loathing. His story 'Thermos Flask' is about this attraction to and revulsion from America. A salaryman on assignment in San Francisco meets a former geisha who had once been his mistress. He is on his way home to his family, she is preparing to open a restaurant financed by her new protector. She recognizes his nationality from a distance because he walks as if he had a pair of swords at his belt, but he registers her Americanization with a shudder. He compares her shapeless, ferally shaggy mink coat with the 'stiff, clean austerity' of the obi he remembers her wearing, and in his mind it is 'as if the great, vermilion-lacquered, black-riveted gate of some noble lady's mansion' had changed into 'a slick revolving door'. The metaphor measures the distance between two cultures, setting courtly ceremony against democratic accessibility, painted layers of prohibition against glassy confidentiality, anticipation against forgetfulness, a palace against a commercial hotel.

There is a corresponding gap between his memory of hushed, decorous Ginza coffee shops and the Californian equivalents, with their 'peculiarly American odour' – half medicinal, half carnal, mixing disinfectant and cheap perfume. In the San Francisco café described in 'Thermos Flask', female customers are 'consuming machines' who gorge on 'large sweets and open sandwiches'. Largeness and openness are offensive in principle to the Japanese, and when a milkshake is brought to the table for the woman's daughter, the salaryman calculates that 'The glass must have held a pint.' Given that the national diet traditionally excludes dairy products, a pint of milk is repellent enough; perhaps the slopping glass also hints at Mishima's loathing for matriarchy and the cult of Mom, the provider of edible, drinkable joys. Those who dislike America generally emphasize the loud, aggressive machismo of Uncle Sam (and one American, the epicene Truman Capote, turned unexpectedly virile to denigrate Japan during his visit in 1955, when he announced that 'I do not like a country that has little cocks'). Mishima's anti-Americanism, by contrast, was misogynistic. For him, the Japan of tempered steel and hard male musculature had been rendered flabby, feminized by the pampering upholstery of wealth. The man in the story appreciates the impeccable evenness with which the geisha applies her make-up. American women appal him by taking out their compacts in public and showering themselves with powder, stirring up storms of pink dust that always leave 'bare spots . . . beside the nose'. That praise for an impervious mask, like the white, almost enamelled faces of kabuki actors, is political as much as cosmetic: Americans have a slapdash, sloppy informality, and Mishima's eye, noticing the spots beside the nose, seeks out undefended crevices where he can make an attack.

Despite having recruited his militia and designed its uniforms, Mishima knew that Japan's actual shield was its security treaty with the United States. In 1969 a Canadian television interviewer asked him whether American withdrawal from Vietnam would increase the danger of a left-wing takeover in Japan. He said that it would, and recalled the error made by the United States in 1939 when it backed the wrong side in the Manchurian war – a snub to Japan, then the most steadfastly anti-communist country in the region. In 1970, during street riots protesting against the renewal of the security treaty, Mishima and his followers staged a coup at the Tokyo Garrison, hoping to rally support for a new constitution and the rearming of Japan. The assembled troops jeered at his sermon about the country's corrupted soul, after which Mishima ceremonially sliced open his stomach and was decapitated by an accomplice. His end was not elegant, as he expected it to be: the floor of the garrison commander's office was puddled with entrails and squirting blood, the room stank of excrement, and it took several fumbling efforts to sever his head. For Mishima, 'the most appropriate form of daily life . . . was a day-by-day world destruction'. Understandably enough, the Japanese people chose a world that had been providentially recreated on the American model, filled with a material plenty that eased and sweetened daily life.

13 | Astronauts and Assassins

After enduring appraisal by so many Europeans, America was scrutinized in 1951 by an extraterritorial critic of a new kind – a visitor from outer space, who accused the country of offences against the order of the universe. In Robert Wise's film *The Day the Earth Stood Still*, a shiny disc that resembles a fried egg flies over the Capitol, alarms crowds outside the White House, and touches down on the National Mall. Out steps a figure in a silver jump-suit, who removes a plastic bowl from his head and identifies himself as Klaatu. He tells the President's envoy that he comes from 'another planet', which means that 'we're neighbours'. The envoy says that it is difficult to think of another planet as a neighbour: he speaks for an America that is entrenched between two oceans. Klaatu points out that, in the present situation, some rethinking will be necessary.

'Holy Christmas!' gasp the British sky-watchers who track the unknown flying object as it crosses Hong Kong on its way to Washington. The bowdlerized exclamation is apt: Christ here returns to earth to judge human faults, and Klaatu rebukes mankind – meaning America – for its motorized madness, warning that the overheated planet will be eliminated if there is no return to a slower, more temperate way of life. To demonstrate that he means business, he brings all the machinery on earth to a temporary halt. Wise based his film on a story by Harry Bates, published in 1940, which contains no critique of America and no ultimatum to its government. Bates's Klaatu is shot by a deranged onlooker and buried in a marble mausoleum in the tidal basin of the Potomac. The story then follows the vindictive ravages of his companion, the robot Gnut, who escapes from a prison of fortified glass and, after resisting a bombardment of fire, acid, radiation and a barrage of tank guns, announces 'I am the Master'. Bates was warning that the human body would soon be superseded by heavy engineering, the brain by electronic circuitry. The film ignores these prognostications; it is a religious parable – a plea for divine intervention to humble overweening America.

In 1956, in his play *Visit to a Small Planet*, Gore Vidal sent a supercilious alien called Kreton to Washington on a different mission. Kreton is a satirist, not a saviour like Klaatu, and he blinks in amazement at the trivial speck of matter on which he lands. The house he invades belongs to a television host, who appears onscreen addressing homilies to Mother-and-Father America, with pauses to extol the merits of the 'milkier milk' his sponsor sells. Kreton observes that these infantilized people openly enjoy violence, which is why the television set resounds with gunfire, but they are secretive about sex. When the daughter of the household sneaks off to a motel with her boyfriend, they take care to bring luggage – a suitcase stuffed with phone directories – so they can bluff their way past the censorious check-in clerk. Convinced of his own superiority, Kreton wants to take charge of the world. 'Of the United States?' asks a general, aghast. 'Oh, no,' replies Kreton, wearily correcting America's self-centredness, 'everything. The whole world. All of it.' But unlike the Good Samaritan in Henry Luce's editorial, he does not want to alleviate the world's ills. He prefers to help it destroy itself, and he therefore irritates the Russians in the hope of provoking a world war. Just in time, his keeper Delton 4 arrives in another spaceship to bundle Kreton off home. Before leaving, this sober functionary explains that his manic patient is actually no better than the Americans. 'He is morally retarded,' says Delton 4, 'and, like a child, he regards this world as his plaything.' Vidal felt he had compromised by allowing a god to alight from a machine and save the situation. In a first draft of the play, he ignited a nuclear war at the end, as Kreton wishes – a satirical judgement on mankind and therefore, in Vidal's opinion, 'the perfect curtain!'

For Kreton, Americans resemble lower primates, oafish blunderers who are less than human. To others, they were somehow post-human – stupidly innocent, cleansed of the faults and quirky complexities that humanize the rest of us. In Graham Greene's *The Quiet American*, published in 1955, it is the undercover CIA agent Pyle who looks and behaves like an alien, touching down in Vietnam from some distant and more sanitary galaxy. He has an 'unused face' and a 'wide campus gaze', and his bristly crew cut brands him as an overgrown adolescent.

Greene had been declared a politically undesirable alien by the United States because he belonged to the Communist Party during his student days, and in 1954 he was deported from Puerto Rico when he stopped there on his way home from Haiti; awaiting expulsion, he took his revenge by charging the drinks in his San Juan hotel to Uncle Sam. He was debarred by what he called 'the plastic curtain' – flimsier than the iron one, but unpleasantly slick and synthetic. In *The Quiet American*, his scorn extends to all Pyle's compatriots, who live in a sterilized and therefore inhuman society, like a larger version of 'those bright clean little New England grocery stores where even the celery was wrapped in cellophane'. The novel's narrator Fowler, a London journalist, says that an attaché at the embassy in Saigon has a face that looks as if it should be on television: an extraordinary comment, which assumes that a head grinning from a cathode ray tube inside a box has been detached from the human body, its brain surgically extracted. Another womanizing boor is described by Fowler as 'an emblematic statue of all I thought I hated in America – as ill-designed as the Statue of Liberty, and as meaningless'. The metaphor lurches illogically from a sleazy drunkard to the upright matriarch with the torch; although Fowler calls the statue meaningless, its meaning is only too clear, which is what irritates Greene. For a Catholic, liberty is a denial of our sinful origins: the poster for Luis Buñuel's film *Le Fantôme de la liberté* therefore reduced the Statue of Liberty's body to a pair of ripe pink buttocks and had her hold up a torch that droops like a dead flower or a limp penis. With the same defamatory glee, when Fowler sees some American girls primly eating ice cream, he wonders whether 'they take their deodorants to bed with them'. Cleanliness is not next to godliness; Greene treats it as an insult to God, because it enables us to shed our fig leaves.

What vexed Greene most was the American determination to make the world better. That counted as another denial of original sin; it also showed an ignorance of the history from which Americans removed themselves when travelling to their new continent. Pyle takes guidance from a spurious chronicle called *The Rise of the West*, although – given the subsequent history of Vietnam – he might have been better off consulting *The Decline of the*

West, with its prediction of inevitable doom. Racked by baronial feuds and territorial disputes, Indochina is for Fowler a version of medieval Europe, and he mocks Americans for parachuting in from the future, unaware that 'Columbus hadn't discovered their country yet': worse than childish, they are not even embryonic. Inexperience makes them dangerous, even deadly, like Pyle when a diversionary bomb blast he organizes for the CIA results in civilian casualties. Fowler, offering no evidence, tells Pyle that 'Most of your GIs who were hanged for rape in the war were virgins' and goes on to say 'We don't have so many in Europe. I'm glad. They do a lot of harm.'

When an American edition of *The Quiet American* appeared in 1956, critics assumed that Greene's venomous tone was a reaction to Britain's forfeiture of its empire, and a review in *The New Yorker* upbraided him for accusing his country's 'best friends' of murder. Fowler is certainly a xeno-phobe, who remembers when people talked about 'sterling qualities' and asks whether, now that America manages the world, there is such a thing as 'dollar love', which is presumably what persuades his mistress Phuong to leave him for Pyle. Such calumnies were prudently erased in Joseph Mankiewicz's film of the book, released in 1958. Pyle also lost his smutty or blockish surname and became a generic 'young American', who saves Fowler's life when they are attacked by guerrillas. Fowler, unimpressed by the risks Pyle takes, snaps 'We're not Marines in the movies', but it is foolish of him to ridicule the movies when – in the person of Michael Redgrave – he is appearing in one. His comment is especially offensive because the role of the American was played by Audie Murphy, an accredited hero who had won the Medal of Honor, along with a slew of other decorations, for bravery in combat in 1944. The film could hardly link someone with Murphy's repu-tation to the CIA, and after performing his good deed he dies in an ambush, betrayed by the ungrateful Fowler.

Greene fumed about these changes to his plot, but by selling the rights he had tacitly consented to the whitewash. The virginal aliens had outwit-ted him, and turned his book into propaganda for virtuous America. In the film, Fowler gives a clever reply when the American accuses him of lying to hold onto Phuong. 'European duplicity,' he says. 'We have to make up for our lack of supplies.' Mendacity, which multiplies the truth, is a response to American superfluity – but even in this department the floundering Europeans could no longer claim priority.

'What kind of place is America?' This is the question that Don DeLillo has Lee Harvey Oswald's Russian wife Marina ask in *Libra*, his novel about the Kennedy assassination. Still in Minsk with Lee, the pregnant Marina reads a book by Dr Spock in which he assures an expectant mother that her infant will be 'a reasonable, friendly human being'. She is taken aback: surely that is only true of American babies, who apparently do not scream, squall or make urgent nocturnal demands to be fed? When she and Lee leave for America, her relatives view it as 'a trip into space'. So it proves to be. The real Marina's only information about Texas came from having seen the film of *Oklahoma!*, which hardly prepared her for suburban Dallas. Looking around, she saw no cowboys and fringed surreys, no golden-hazed meadows and towering corn stalks; she found the city to be a torrid desert. In the novel, friends 'show her how to shop' – a weirdly contracted infinitive, which makes it a devotional act – and she is enchanted by 'the cool smooth musical interior' of the Montgomery Ward department store with its cathedral-like aisles of merchandise. Actually, as Marina herself told Norman Mailer and Lawrence Schiller, the plethora soon palled. Supermarket shelves were stocked with two hundred varieties of cereal, interchangeable except for their packets. Freedom was the right to choose between sober Quaker Oats and ebullient Cheerios. Either way, she had to make a purchase: consumption was a civic obligation.

Two years after arriving, Marina discovered what freedom meant and what kind of place America was. It was the kind of place where her husband was free to buy a rifle and use it to kill the President; it was also the kind of place where a seedy nightclub operator who may have had Mafia connections was free to wander into a police station and murder Lee. Historical tableaux did not usually look like this – absurdly contingent, a mockery of law and order yet also a demonstration of civil liberties in action, further democratized by the raw and disrespectful candour of the cameras that caught Jacqueline Kennedy scrambling to get out of the bloodied limousine as it sped away or Oswald gaping in outrage as Ruby fired at him. Those chaotic happenings startled people everywhere into realizing that America was an alarming, unknowable, implosive place. Church bells tolled in Moscow, and Khrushchev hurried back from the Ukraine to sign a book of condolences at the American Embassy. In Dallas, however, in some quarters at least, there was jubilation. John Peel, later a BBC disc jockey, was working as a filing clerk in a life insurance company there: he remembered the employees applauding when they heard the news, pleased that Kennedy had got his comeuppance for threatening Texan oil revenues. That afternoon in New York, Andy Warhol calmly went on painting, irritated by 'the way television and radio were programming everybody to feel sad'. By 1978, a decade after the President's brother had been added to the necrology, a San Francisco punk band adopted the flippant, uncaring name Dead Kennedys.

Mailer rejoiced in 1961 when a majority rejected the 'psychic security' of Nixon and elected Kennedy: the choice was a sign that Americans knew they must become 'more adventurous, or else perish'. For a few days, during the standoff over the missiles in Cuba, the second option seemed possible, but it was Kennedy who perished while adventurously riding into an unfriendly city in an open car. Abroad, the assassination was a shock; Americans had less reason to be surprised. In *Suddenly*, a 1954 thriller about a plot to assassinate the President as he passes through a country town in California, Frank Sinatra plays the hired killer who takes over a house above the railway station, from where he will have the best line of fire. The home is a wholesomely American haven, with a kitchen from which Sinatra seizes a wedge of cake for himself and a glass of milk for a crony with a stomach ulcer, but it also contains a small arsenal. The grandfather has been trying to repair the television so that he can watch baseball, and once the back of the set is off, the five thousand volts the box contains gives him a weapon to discharge against the intruders. He also has a gun left over from his days in the secret service, and the eight-year-old son, whose father died in Korea, receives a cap pistol from the cop who is to become his stepfather. The toy is his initiation into manly violence, preparing him to fight 'when his time comes'. And although his mother disapproves, she gets over her liberal quibbling in time to shoot Sinatra. The society is combustible, sparking with potential violence.

John Steinbeck incorporated the assassination of Kennedy into his patriarchal theory of the presidency. 'To all the other rewards of this greatest office in the gift of the people,' he wrote in 1966, 'we add that of assassination.' It is a reward because it is a hero's fate, even if the man of power is brought low by a nonentity like Oswald; failing this, the incumbent is expected to destroy himself – provoked to commit high crimes and misdemeanours like Nixon, or to behave foolishly like Clinton. At the time of Kennedy's election, Gore Vidal said that 'the job today is literally killing, and despite his youth, [he] may very well not survive'. After the assassination, Vidal commented that Kennedy's 'death in public' satisfactorily completed a primitive ceremony, with the community assembled to witness the sacrifice of the 'man-god'. Ancient civilizations slaughtered their selected victims to ensure that the sun continued to shine or that crops sprouted each spring; Americans after the 1960s began to dismember celebrities because their culture required perpetual novelty, which meant that politicians like pop singers had to be hauled from the heights and replaced by fresher versions of themselves.

Writers understood their role in this mythological cycle, either as self-dramatizing victims or as waspish killers. Mailer, briefly imprisoned during a march on the Pentagon in 1967, wondered whether the warders would arrange 'a piece of petty Oswalderie' and have him gunned down in a corridor. That, he thought, might be better than incarceration, which would surely leave him incubating a cancer like Jack Ruby. In 1968 in Miami, while waiting for Reagan's arrival at the Republican National Convention, Vidal preened as he was inspected by secret servicemen who could see 'the imaginary gun in my pocket'; he survived their scrutiny because he performed his executions with words, deadly but bloodless. In 1971 in *Our Gang*, Philip Roth provided the same service for Nixon, who in the novel is murdered by a posse of Boy Scouts while in hospital for the removal of a sweat gland. No arrest can be made, because everyone in the crowd of supposed mourners proudly confesses to the crime. In *Libra*, DeLillo describes a video game designed by a Scottish company which casts the player as Oswald, challenged to match the three shots fired at the motorcade as it passes. Stephen Sondheim's musical *Assassins* stages a fairground contest in which any contestant in a shooting gallery earns the right to take aim at whoever happens to be President. Assassination is a collective fantasy, as much an expression of popular will as an election. There had been many previous killings, and there were to be other attempts – Squeaky Fromme threatening Gerald Ford with an unloaded gun in Sacramento in 1975, Sara Jane Moore firing at him and missing in San Francisco three weeks later. When Reagan was shot by John Hinckley in 1981, he acknowledged that this was a scene he expected to play, and at the hospital he joked about his lack of rehearsal by remarking that he should have ducked. Hinckley prepared more carefully for what he called, in his explanatory letter to Jodie Foster, his 'historical deed'. He practised his impersonation of Travis Bickle in Scorsese's *Taxi Driver* by going to see the film fifteen times. Even so, he fumbled, and tragedy degenerated into black, bloody farce.

At the time of Kennedy's death, *Pravda* speculated about a coup by militarists opposed to the Nuclear Test Ban Treaty that had been signed a few months before. But the balance of terror and the prospect of annihilation suddenly seemed less relevant: from now on, the spectacle that engrossed the world was the volatility of American society and the precariousness of its political system.

The Cold War accustomed Americans to thinking dualistically. Eisenhower called the United States 'the greatest power on God's footstool that has been permitted to exist', and specified that it was 'a power for good, among ourselves, and in all the world'. The country's opponents therefore had to be demonized, as when Reagan denounced Russia's 'evil empire' and George W. Bush aligned the sponsors of terrorism on an 'axis of evil'. Such a division had its risks. In 1964 Jean Genet pointed out that 'America the Good' had dreamed up its antithesis, 'a sort of gangster who is an almost total incarnation of Evil'. This outlaw was a public enemy, the antithesis of national values, but he was resident in the United States, secretly cherished by his fellow citizens because he disrupted the God-fearing timidity of a society that Genet – who admitted that he knew next to nothing about America – assumed to be 'very boring'.

In 1959 in his *Independence Day Manifesto*, Allen Ginsberg worked the same Manichean reversal. He declared God's own country to be the devil's resort, a 'crossbone skullbone jailhouse' where an industrial Moloch feasted on human flesh, and thought that this 'police-state America', lacking both sex and spirit, was 'prepared to battle the world'. 'I'll show you how ugly the Ugly American can be,' brags The Intolerable Kid – a personified virus, programmed to infect and derange human beings – in Burroughs' novel *Nova Express*. He makes good his boast by exhibiting images of atrocities like Hiroshima; Burroughs often quoted the line when drawing attention to the latest news photograph of carnage in Vietnam. The good works of Homer and Emma Atkins in the novel by Lederer and Burdick counted for nothing.

Mailer too believed that America had been overtaken by an 'irredeemable madness', and imagined that it was readying its own 'concentration camps' and 'liquidation centers' for those who dissented. The massed gatherings of protestors against Vietnam revealed 'a growing sense of apocalypse in American life', as if these crowds had gathered to see the sky fall in and the earth rent asunder. While the 'plasticized mass' of toilers slaved away, bromided by television, bureaucrats in 'air-conditioned vaults' were preparing to transfer their headquarters to some other planet, where they could 'comfortably phase nature in and out'. Ginsberg diagnosed a national nervous breakdown, while Mailer identified the ailment as schizophrenia, a schism induced by the contradiction between the Christian benevolence of the average good-natured citizen and the impersonal brutality of 'the American corporation'. Samuel Fuller's film *Shock Corridor* compresses the country into a mental ward, whose inmates – a would-be Confederate general who is still fighting the Civil War, a self-hating black man who fancies that he founded the Ku Klux Klan, and a scientist driven to derangement by his responsibility for nuclear weapons – represent communal psychoses.

Hysterical as all this sounds, it became received wisdom. In 1966, Thomas Pynchon concluded an essay on the Watts riots in Los Angeles by describing a sculpture pieced together from the wreckage which served as an American totem, a voodoo doll for use during the last rites: it was a gutted television set containing a human skull, entitled 'The Late, Late, Late Show'. In the same year Susan Sontag, in her answers to a *Partisan Review* questionnaire, concluded that 'This is a doomed country', and only hoped that its 'elephantine agony' would not 'drag down the rest of the planet'.

In 1968 three literary eschatologists – Genet, Mailer and Burroughs – were dispatched to Chicago to witness another stage in the republic's demise during the Democratic National Convention. Genet's criminal record made him ineligible for a visitor's visa, so he flew to Quebec where French Canadian separatists helped him to slip across the border into the United States, which, he announced, resembled 'Switzerland flattened by steam-rollers', a dreary hiding place for money. Arriving in Chicago, he sniffed the gore from the stockyards and thought he scented 'the decomposition of America'. Mailer, ensconced in the Hilton on Michigan Avenue, fancied that the hotel's jittery elevators and overstressed switchboard did not work because they were symptoms of an imminent breakdown of the social machine. Genet chose to imagine the city putrefying, though he also called for the rest of the country to be 'demolished, . . . reduced to powder'.

As the radical revels got underway, Burroughs was embarrassed to be participating in a peaceful march against the Vietnam War: he much preferred violence, and cheered himself up by imagining massacres and mutilations. Rather than reporting on actual events, which is what *Esquire* had hired him to do, he devised his own scenario. In his version of the political process, a purple-arsed baboon is nominated as the Democratic Party's presidential candidate; the ape is promptly assassinated, after which he 'ejaculates, excretes and dies'. Genet likewise interpreted his commission from *Esquire* as a licence to fantasize, although his reveries were less scatological. Mixing with the demonstrators in Lincoln Park, he paid tribute to the hippies as a race of hirsute Adams, who cultivated flowers on their own 'new continent'. Soon enough he was sprayed with tear gas by the police, then hosed down by a solicitous doctor; delighted by this double martyrdom, he announced that the clumsy Americans 'tried to burn me and a few minutes later to drown me'. When he recovered, he fixed an appreciative gaze on the muscular thighs of the police, their polished boots, and especially on their billy clubs, which they gripped in the way he would himself 'hold a black American's member'. Mailer noticed the ironically sky-blue cloth of the police uniforms; Genet went further, gasping about a 'Mallarméan blue' and treating the azure helmets of the police as a sign that they had floated down from heaven. In his aphrodisiac reverie he forgot that Mayor Daley's enforcers were supposed to be the enemy, and felt tempted to tumble girl-ishly into the arms of one particularly handsome cop. Mailer likened Daley's crowd control to the tactics of the Gestapo and heard the 'beer-hall bleats' of an incipient American fascism, but at least he was dismayed not aroused by the spectacle of muscled brutality.

Esquire balked at publishing the conclusion to Genet's article, in which he urged the star spangled land to wind up the Vietnam War by discharging the nuclear bombs that were hatching like 'monstrous eggs' in its missile silos. In 1970 he returned to America, again illicitly, to make speeches in support of the Black Panthers, who were described by the activist Tom Hayden as an indigenous Vietcong. Genet was now excited by the possibil-ity of a racial war that would eliminate 'the whole white world'. The Panthers, he thought, had dreamed up 'an imaginary Africa that combined Islam and spirit worship' – just as Genet himself dreamily imagined an America that combined milky-white Protestantism and the worship of dollars – and he praised the call for armed reprisals made by George Jackson, an armed robber who had undergone a political conversion while in San Quentin. When Jackson was killed by guards during an attempted prison break in 1971, Genet declared his death to be an assassination and traced responsibil-ity back to Reagan, then governor of California.

The revolution Genet hoped for turned out to be a fad, a transitory fashion. The Black Panther leader Eldridge Cleaver, exiled in France, designed a pair of trousers with a padded codpiece, 'to solve' – as he said – 'the problem of the fig-leaf mentality', as if the magisterial penis could dispense social justice; the Panthers came to be more concerned with Masonic handshakes and accessories like berets and steel combs than with racial recriminations. Undaunted, Genet continued to assail an America that he now universalized. 'By "America"', he wrote in 1971, 'I mean Europe too', along with anywhere else that was controlled by 'the European and Anglo-Amerikan capitalist', including the 'Union of South Africa (U.S.A.!!)'. It did not matter that the Union of South Africa had been renamed the Republic of South Africa a decade earlier, when it ceased to be a British dominion. The fortuitous initials enabled Genet to score another victory, signalled by his exclamation marks, in a war that consisted exclusively of words.

Among the tourists who came to Chicago to see a society disintegrate was Michelangelo Antonioni. Like Genet, he was gassed in the free-for-all that Mailer observed from the nineteenth floor of the Hilton, but the mishap counted as research: Antonioni regarded the United States as 'the most interesting country in the world', because there 'some of the essential truths and contradictions of our time can be isolated in their pure state'; in practice it served as a laboratory in which he could set off a controlled explosion. *Zabriskie Point*, on which he was then working, ends in a desert like that where the Los Alamos physicists concocted a formula for ending the world, and organizes its own terminal blast by detonating a cantilevered house and atomizing the commodities it contains. MGM hired the property, which jutted from a rock outside the town of Carefree near Phoenix, then built a replica nearby that could be spectacularly demolished. Seventeen cameras multiplied the blasts from every possible angle, while the owner of the original house sat on his deck to watch the show. Americans have an enviable capacity to enjoy Armageddon, which reveals both how safe from harm they have always been and how excited they are by imagining their come-uppance. When a devastating California earthquake was predicted in 1969, Warhol's punk crony Danny Fields rented a house beside the San Andreas Fault and waited for the earth's crust to split apart. 'I want to be in a disaster,' he told Warhol. 'I've been seeing so many movies about them for so long.'

Zabriskie Point begins on a campus in Oakland, California, where Eldridge Cleaver's wife exhorts students to riot. Then, like Genet and Burroughs in their fantasies about the affray in Chicago, Antonioni advances from a political debate to an orgy: in Death Valley, the members of Joe Chaikin's Open Theatre romp through a revolution of another kind by making polymorphous love among the dunes. One extra claimed she had been directed to perform fellatio, and a grand jury was convened in Sacramento to consider whether Antonioni had been guilty of white-slave trafficking. There were rumours of other enormities, including the desecration of an American flag, though at worst the flag that hangs sideways on a cracked bedroom wall in Mark Frechette's Venice bungalow was dipped in red dye so that its bleeding stained the white and blue. Antonioni wanted to end the film with a skywriting plane that would puff out 'Fuck You America' across a blue horizon; he was of course overruled by the studio. Landing his stolen plane in the desert, Frechette paints the fuselage green and leaves it looking like a pterodactyl, with bare breasts on its wings and a pink nose cone. The slogans on its underbelly denouncing war and the dictatorship of the dollar are almost an afterthought. In any case, the geological mortuary of Zabriskie Point demonstrates that human beings can never engineer change. Chaikin's copulating actors resemble calcified Pompeiians as the dust stirred up by their frisking encrusts their flesh and whitens their hair; the knobbly spines of purple rock, the sculpted mounds that might be the feet of raptors, the dried river bed that is a hot granular glacier – these are reminders of the convulsions that the abraded American earth has already lived through.

Antonioni chose Zabriskie Point as his film's defining location because it was 'so primitive, like the moon', and he thought of his characters as astronauts, not political radicals. Frechette, the director explained, helps himself to the plane because 'America for him coincides with "the earth", from which "he needed to get off"'. In the summer of 1969, that lift-off occurred, and a few days later two Americans set foot on the moon. After awkwardly hopping about in the grey waste, they planted the national flag, even though there was no hill to set it on and no breeze to make it flutter. Lyndon Johnson, who once said that he disliked the idea of going to bed by the light of a communist moon, must have slept easier. Congratulating Neil Armstrong and his colleagues, Nixon passed on the latest baseball scores, then summed up their achievement by declaring that this had been 'the greatest week in the history of the world since the Creation'. If so, it was less a sequel to Genesis than an attempt, fuelled by jet engines and controlled by a barrage of computers, to go beyond it. God made the earth, pronounced the result good, then rested. America continued the story, which had no necessary conclusion. Ginsberg described the 1960s as a 'mutant moment' for the human race, or at least for the American segment of it – the time when some ultimate transformation might occur, with interstellar transit extending the ocean voyages that led to the discovery of the western continent. Perhaps now it would be possible to leave the superannuated earth behind and set off, as Mailer said in his account of the moonshot, to 'govern the universe'?

Tom Wolfe made sense of Nixon's hyperbole by interpreting the NASA missions as an evolutionary peak, not merely the culmination of American scientific endeavour. His pilots in *The Right Stuff* indignantly protest against the plan to send chimpanzees into orbit. Demanding manual control of their instrument panels, they refuse to be experimental animals and instead become 'olden knights', probing empty space with their chivalric lances. They are righteous, in Wolfe's estimation, because they ignore the graft and greed of civil society and conserve 'the most important values of American life' – discipline not hedonism, honour not opportunism. Mailer saw the adventure less heroically: in an allusion to Spengler's account of the West's catastrophic cult of progress, he called it 'Faustian'. That hurtling mental ambition flared on the launching pad at Cape Canaveral to thrust the rocket upwards, freeing it from gravity and leaving it to orbit until it passed out of sight on the far side of the moon. Here was an ultimate abstraction, which separated the West, as Mailer put it, from the 'materiality of forms' and from matter itself. Suited up, the astronauts represented to Mailer 'some magnetic human force called Americanism, patriotism, or Waspitude'; the 'spiritually anaemic land' from which they came was as blank as the planet where they made the first human landfall. Mailer contrasted their lonely voyage through black silence with the massed conviviality of the rock concerts attended that same summer by oceanic crowds whose shared emotion, he said, was 'Oriental'.

In Europe, the best joke about the flaming velocity of American rocket science was a mimed suggestion that it led backwards not forwards. During a frantic, mishap-ridden road trip from Paris to Amsterdam in Jacques Tati's *Trafic*, people along the way are glimpsed watching the television relay from Apollo 11. Tati's convoy, bound for a motor show, has to stop overnight for repairs at a rustic garage in Holland, where the mechanic keeps one eye on the astronauts in their puffed-up suits floating or bouncing over the lunar surface, as if on decelerated pogo sticks. The spectacle is comic because so beautifully inane and childishly futile. It is also an unexpected reproof to the high-speed Americanized efficiency of the factories and highways in Tati's film: when the lazy mechanic returns to the job, he and his helpers adopt the rhythms of Armstrong and Buzz Aldrin and pretend to be working in zero gravity, so they handle their tools with excruciating slowness and bob in unsteady jerks across the floor of the garage. So much for the indefatigable industrial tempo of what European admirers once called 'Fordism'.

Astronauts in the years after 1969 were coached to refute criticism like Mailer's by denying their alienation from the earth or their alien status in outer space. James Irwin, who spent three days on the moon in 1971, said that he 'felt like an alien' on the way there, but added that after touchdown 'I felt at home . . . precarious but comfortable'. Eugene Cernan, a member of the final mission in 1972, justified his presence on the moon by invoking the theory of 'terra nullius', often used to justify imperial invasions. He pointed out that there were no signs of previous ownership, so he was not expropriating anyone else's terrain. Resuming the Faustian quest, Cernan added 'Man must explore.'

One earthling was saddened by those explorations, not wryly amused like Tati's moonwalking workers. In Tom Stoppard's play *Jumpers*, first staged in London a few months before the last moon landing, the heroine Dorothy complains that astronauts have reduced the universe to a backyard and the remote, palely luminously orb to a pockmarked golf ball. She is a singer, who values the moon as a versatile trope, 'well-known in Carolina, much loved in Allegheny, familiar in Vermont'; along with the once-popular songs about moonlight in such locations, she might have mentioned the moon of Alabama, serenaded by the brothel girls in Weill's opera *Mahagonny*. She takes care not to be fashionably anti-American – the spacemen in Stoppard's play are British, which is one of the comedy's best jokes – but she cannot help being depressed by their lumpen exploits, and she removes from her repertory all songs that refer to the demystified moon. It was a charmingly silly self-denial, because the songs she deletes are not about an Americanized moon. Instead they describe its reflected light in a scattering of American regions – Carolina where the moon keeps shining on someone who waits for whoever is singing, Allegheny where its silver beams lead the way to golden dreams, Vermont where the moonlight brightens the snow on ski trails. The sentiments are always the same; only the regions differ, and all of them, if you live somewhere else, are exotic. To govern a mere universe is an exhausting chore. Americans may be better off in the abundant, variegated multiverse they have at home.

14 | 'I Want it to Come *HERE*!'

Vietnam, in which the United States had so few allies, became a world war by adoption. 'I want it to come *HERE*!' yelled Glenda Jackson in *US*, an agit-prop performance directed by Peter Brook for the Royal Shakespeare Company in London in 1967. 'I WANT IT TO GET WORSE!' she added. Jackson was challenging another character who longed for the war to end; she played a harpy who hoped it would spread to Thailand, Chile, Alabama and eventually to England, establishing a salutary reign of terror and disrupting forever the pretence of social order. Brook's actors apologized to the audience for being Londoners who had never been 'burnt with jellied petrol'. They meant to express solidarity with the napalmed Vietnamese, but it sounded as if they were also making a muffled request for an invitation to the party. This was a time of psychedelic jollification: hoping to combat the mind-control that persuaded Americans to support the war, the satirist Terry Southern had called for a campaign 'to bomb out the entire public consciousness of the US with LSD or some therapeutic equivalent'. Love may have been an alternative to war but drugs were a substitute for it, harmlessly recreating its excitements as they exploded in the brain or the bloodstream.

Right-thinking Europeans applauded American setbacks. Italo Calvino was pleased that 'the greatest military power in the world' had been tripped up by 'a population of rice-growers', and Isaac Deutscher, the biographer of Trotsky and Stalin, enjoyed watching the unexpected outcome of a 'war between palaces and huts'. Others accused the aggressors of reneging on the new moral dispensation they propounded in 1945. The dramatist Peter Weiss denounced America as 'the inheritor of Guernica, Lidice and Majdenek', claiming that its troops had massacred Vietnamese civilians or bundled them into concentration camps, and Bertrand Russell declared that this 'universal empire of evil' told lies about the communist menace 'to justify cruelties equalling those of Hitler'. On balance Russell preferred

Hitler to President Johnson and General Westmoreland: the Führer 'seldom professed humanity', whereas the Americans prated about 'human brotherhood' while prosecuting a 'war of annihilation'.

Sartre called American policy genocidal. Ignoring demographic facts about the percentage of African-Americans in the US Army, he imagined that the war pandered to the racism of Southern whites, goading GIs to express their annoyance about the Civil Rights Act of 1964 at home by shooting Vietnamese women for target practice and slicing the ears off dead men as souvenirs. In 1967 he amplified the charge when he defined Vietnam as a 'war of example', which admonished 'the whole of humanity' to 'submit or face extermination'. But what exactly had humanity been asked to submit to? The answer, inevitably, was America's greed for raw materials and commercial markets, though the evidence in this case was skimpy. Eisenhower, explaining the assistance given to the French in Indochina during the 1950s, spoke of protecting supplies of tin and tungsten, just as Johnson later lamely boasted of having introduced television to the culturally laggard Vietnamese. Joking about the imperial quest for new customers, the pilots of a helicopter company deployed on the battlefield sprinkled the ground with business cards announcing services that included Defoliation. Vietnam, however, lacked oilfields, and Sartre admitted that American corporations had 'negligible interests' there. Yet this, he claimed, was why Vietnam could be destroyed with impunity, as a warning to others who might oppose American expansion.

Westmoreland believed that 'the Oriental doesn't put the same high price on life as does the Westerner'; he meant that the Vietnamese would fight to the death, but also that they could be put to death without misgivings, since for them 'life is not important'. Johnson railed against a symbolic 'yellow dwarf with a pocket knife' who had dared to threaten the United States. He dreaded being thought 'an unmanly man' if he backed down, and vouched for his virility with a seamy, incriminating metaphor when he described the bombing of North Vietnam as a 'seduction' which, he promised, would never be upgraded to 'rape'. The distinction between persuasion and coercion is tricky, especially when you are talking about bombing raids not roving hands, and in either case Johnson was picturing Vietnam as a woman who had no choice but to give in to lustily male America. Sartre speculated about whether the warmongers were conscious of what they were doing, then shrugged: 'We would have to plumb the depths of their consciences – and the Puritan bad faith of Americans works wonders.'

At home, Johnson extended Kennedy's New Frontier by passing legislation to forbid racial discrimination and amending social security provisions. Abroad, he was less liberal and compassionate. He wanted, he told Congress in 1964, to make 'war on poverty', but could not afford to do so because he was preoccupied with expensively making war on impoverished Vietnam. Here, perhaps, was the kind of tragedy that Europeans in the 1950s thought Americans were incapable of comprehending – a conflict between high ideals and the harsh necessities of power. In 1972 the critic Robert Brustein reacted to that earlier European criticism by taking a bizarre pride in the Vietnamese mess and the domestic upheavals it caused. Brustein, having founded a repertory theatre in New Haven, was at the time working as a drama critic in London; he disliked a National Theatre production of Eugene O'Neill's *Long Day's Journey into Night*, and attributed its failings to what he diagnosed as a local lack of the tragic sense. Brustein blamed the welfare state for making life too safe for the cosseted British, though he suspected that sectarian troubles in Northern Ireland might soon treat them to some of the danger and disturbance that gave his own agitated society its edge. In 1941, Henry Luce had described America as 'the most powerful and vital nation in the world'. Now the proof of its vitality was the virulence of its problems.

In the title of a novel published in 1967, Mailer asked *Why Are We In Vietnam?* The story is about using a helicopter to hunt for a grizzly bear in Alaska, which suggests that the war was an outlet for a mechanized assault on nature that could no longer be conducted at home – and indeed Walt Rostow, Johnson's Special Assistant for National Security, advised using Vietnam as an 'experimental area' for testing new weapons. It did not occur to Rostow that he was arming dissidents as well as patriots: black conscripts often said they were pleased that Vietnam taught them the techniques of guerrilla warfare, which they intended to use in the ghetto when they were demobbed. *F*** the Army*, a film documenting the political vaudeville that Jane Fonda and Donald Sutherland performed outside army bases throughout Asia in 1971, ends with Sutherland reading a poem about an activist who refuses to kill the designated enemy and instead targets the government that has sent him into battle. He could be describing Rambo, the Green Beret first played by Sylvester Stallone in 1982 in *First Blood*. Trained to wreak havoc, Rambo exercises his skills in a Washington town whose sheriff harasses him; he tosses a rock to bring down a helicopter, slaughters some tracking dogs, hijacks an Army truck, and shoots up a sporting goods emporium with a machine gun. 'You want a war you can't win?' a colonel from Special Forces asks the sheriff, advising him to order a fresh supply of body bags. The unwinnable war was America's effort to contain the frenzy it had generated.

In a culture where freedom had come to mean causeless rebellion and the pursuit not of happiness but of thrills, Vietnam offered the addictive excitement of mortal peril. Michael Herr, reporting for *Esquire*, occasionally travelled on military helicopters that needed to fly sideways, and could never resist looking at the ground as it lunged up towards him from a few feet away. He was not remembering his professional obligation to be a witness; like Warhol's friend waiting for the San Andreas Fault to open, he genuinely wanted to have that stomach-churning, bowel-loosening experience. The heroes of Herr's book *Dispatches* are two rogue journalists for whom the war was an existential escapade, 'apolitically radical, wigged-out crazies' who were not fighting the Vietcong but daring themselves to die. Errol Flynn's son Sean atoned for his father's swashbuckling antics in films like *Objective, Burma!* by riding a motorcycle into communist-controlled territory in Cambodia, where he was captured by guerrillas and never seen again. The photographer Tim Page ended the war full of shrapnel, with a two-inch shard in his skull that paralysed him on one side. He was treated at a military hospital outside Washington DC, which, as Herr marvelled, 'took some doing' because he was 'a civilian and a British subject'. During his rehabilitation, Page wept, according to Herr, as he remembered 'how happy he and all of us had been' in Vietnam.

In *Air America*, which in nonchalant retrospect treats the war as a farce, Mel Gibson plays a pilot on the CIA's private airline, ferrying guns and drugs around Laos in 1969. When he explains why he is in 'the wild wild East', he revises the old argument about defending the American way of life and says he is standing up for 'the politics of Saturday night', with its chicken barbecues, weenie roasts and bottles of Southern Comfort. Saturday night, he has been told, is not much fun in Moscow or Peking. He later admits that this was a slick rationalization: actually he is a 'trouble-junkie, mainlining on danger'. The prospect of American withdrawal does not bother him, and he predicts that 'There'll be another new war opening soon in a theatre near you.' A theatre is a place for the enactment of fantasies, and that was Vietnam's function for a country that needed to vent its own uncomfortable tensions. Did Americanization mean saving the world or dominating it? Were science and technology alleviating life or devising efficient ways to destroy it? And why did the idea of disaster so engross a society that should have been pacified by its material plenty? Vietnam gratified a national death wish; the cult of progress expected a moment of impact when the juggernaut would crash and burn. In 1967 Mailer suggested that the United States should use some of its economic surplus to buy up a few million acres of useless land in the Amazon, send in Seabees to clear it, then stage a rite or riot to which the whole world – 'the Chinks and the Aussies, the Frogs and the Gooks and the Wogs, the Wops and the Russkies', and so on – would be invited. Mailer imagined a playground of pyrotechnics featuring war games that used real bullets, 'amateur war movie film contests for the soldiers, discotheques, Playboy Clubs, pictures of the corpses for pay TV'.

Three years after the war ended, Francis Coppola recreated it in the Philippines in *Apocalypse Now*. His title chimed with the deranged extravaganza dreamed up by Mailer: the film is a sensory bombardment, from the half-heard scything of propeller blades at the beginning to the ceremonial slaughter at the end, supplemented by a tropical thunderstorm and the voice of Jim Morrison sepulchrally wailing about insanity as The Doors play what the scriptwriter John Milius called 'the music of war' and surges of fire decapitate palm trees. Coppola's actors treated the filming as an uninhibited, amoral joyride. 'A war is fun, shit,' said Lawrence Fishburne, who was four-teen when he lied about his age at an audition to secure a role in the film, 'you can do anything you want to.' Fishburne remembered a friend who returned from the war with a dope habit, for which he gave thanks to Uncle Sam: 'Vietnam,' he bragged, 'was the best thing they coulda done for my ass!' Sam Bottoms, cast as a drugged surfer, begged Coppola to include a scene like the My Lai massacre, when the soldiers of 'Charlie' Company killed several hundred unarmed Vietnamese civilians. 'We wanted to experi-ence something like that,' said Bottoms. Coppola admitted that his film was 'not about Vietnam, it *is* Vietnam, it was crazy – we were in the jungle with too much money and too much equipment, and little by little we sank'. He expected that Donald Rumsfeld, then Secretary of Defence, would recognize him as a comrade in arms and rent the production some Chinook helicop-ters; he was briefly put out by Rumsfeld's refusal, but obtained his military hardware from the Marcos regime instead. The helicopters, however, were sometimes recalled for use against communist rebels on the pearl farms of the southwestern Philippines, and the automatic rifles carried by extras had to be kept under guard, for fear that they might be stolen by guerrillas hiding in the hills.

Coppola's wife Eleanor called his office 'command headquarters', and noted that he had set up 'his own Vietnam with his supply lines of wines and steaks and air conditioners'. At work Coppola occasionally wore an Australian army hat, dressed for his role as a general whose personal war aimed, like the Pentagon's opening salvoes in Iraq in 1996, to induce shock and awe. After a squadron of F-5 jets streaked past and torched the jungle during the surfing episode, Eleanor noted in her journal that 'The big effects are really dangerous' and shivered deliciously at the mood of 'excitement and antici-pation'. When the temple infested by Kurtz's private army was napalmed, the concussed earth shuddered underfoot and a hundred suns blindingly exploded in the darkness. The production designer Dean Tavoularis said 'God, you couldn't buy a ticket to a show like that anywhere in the world.' Coppola agreed: 'They'd never let you [do it] in the United States. The envi-ronmentalists would kill you. But in a war, it's okay.' He meant that it was permissible in the Philippines, thanks to the welcome of President Marcos, Washington's cherished ally: America had exported the apocalypse.

Critics complained during the 1950s that Americans lacked the capacity to see themselves as others did. Keyes Beech, reporting on the fall of Saigon for the *Chicago Daily News* in April 1975, suddenly understood what this meant. With the city on fire, all remaining Americans received the order to evacuate. Beech's car was turned away from the airbase; he managed to reach the embassy, only to find it besieged by panicking Vietnamese. He had to fight his way through the crowd and scale a ten-foot wall to get into the compound. In the scrum, he knocked down a woman clutching a baby. Her husband angrily struck him, but the woman begged Beech to take their child to safety. Now, he thought, he knew 'what it's like to be a Vietnamese. . . . But if I could get over that wall, I would be an American again.' A Marine, otherwise engaged in pushing back Vietnamese climbers, reached down and hoisted Beech out of the grappling mob. He was soon aboard a helicopter bound for an aircraft carrier, with his national identity restored but not, perhaps, his sense of entitlement or his self-respect.

During the war, a few renegade Americans made common cause with the other side. Jane Fonda travelled to North Vietnam in 1972, sang for the troops, and tactlessly posed on a gun emplacement that was aimed at American planes – an act of treason, or a publicity stunt? Godard mistrusted her motives, and in his filmed essay *Letter to Jane* he spent an hour examining and analysing a news photograph of her encounter with some bombed civilians. Her expression in the grainy still may be sympathetic, but she is an actress, so she knows how to look concerned. And although the caption in *L'Express* said that she was questioning the Vietnamese, her mouth is closed; she is non-commitally listening, and we have no idea what she truly thinks or feels. Godard concludes that any snapshot of a film star is 'ideological merchandise', bought and distributed by Western media that share the capitalist's determination 'to trick the customer about the product'. Despite Fonda's militant intention, she cannot escape from the economic and political system she unwittingly served.

During her own visit to Hanoi in March 1968, Mary McCarthy grappled more conscientiously than Fonda with divided loyalties. In 1967 McCarthy had been to South Vietnam, where she found it wickedly enjoyable to act as a saboteur. 'I was looking for material damaging to the American interest,' she told her readers in *The New York Review of Books*, 'and . . . I found it'. Often the incriminating data was fed to her by guileless military spokesmen, although she accumulated evidence about the use of napalm simply by sniffing the air, which stank of incendiary gasoline. That journey confirmed her liberal prejudices; her trip to Hanoi, however, provoked 'an identity crisis'. She was at ease when conversing in French with Vietnamese intellectuals, but her meetings with American prisoners of war – mostly 'pathetic cases of mental malnutrition' – were painful. She studied them across a gaping cultural distance, suspecting that they saw her as a traitor; she relied on words to widen this gap not abridge it, and for the same reason she regretted that the second language of the Vietnamese was not French, as in colonial days, but English – and specifically '*American* English' not 'the language of the BBC', which McCarthy, 'liking frills', would have preferred.

Inevitably she denounced 'Americanization, a creeping disease', only to realize that she herself was one of its symptoms. In theory she shared the local disapproval of consumerism: she preferred the bicycles people smoothly pedalled around Hanoi to the cars that had overrun the West, and thought that the bamboo and straw from which the Vietnamese had woven their world stood for elasticity and lightness of being, as opposed to the bellicose bulk and weight of American engineering. Then she winced as she remembered the personal baggage train of suitcases she had brought along, evidence of her 'unenvied freedom'. Yet she still hankered after one precious boon of that freedom, the opportunity to go shopping: was there nothing to buy in Hanoi except spare parts for your bike? 'The very name Silk Street,' she confessed, 'sends a pang through the luxury-loving passer-by.' A gift of jewellery at the War Crimes Museum caused her a twinge, because the ring had been made from the melted aluminium of a downed American plane. Did she refuse to wear it, she asked herself, because she felt remorseful about receiving handouts from the enemy, or because she the humble trophy did not match her other, costlier ornaments?

The bombing raids excited McCarthy, as if she were enjoying the factitious emotions stirred by a film or a play; each departure on a field trip, 'smacking of danger, was an adventure'. She applauded the revolution through which North Vietnam was living as a kind of Chinese opera, with reality suspended in favour of 'a delightful magic show, complete with movable scenery, changes of costume, disguises'. The 'lyricism' of this turbulent society thrilled her, and its shrill excitability reminded her of the Risorgimento choruses composed by Verdi during Italy's war against the Austro-Hungarian Empire. She treated the American debacle ironically by describing it as 'a cowboys-and-Indians story, in which the Indians, for once, are repelling the cowboys'. That left the rules of the genre intact, except in this single instance. McCarthy belonged, she knew, among 'the fossil remains of the old America', privileged by a detachment from European quarrels that obliged its citizens to be just and fair-minded in their treatment of other societies. The identity crisis began when her sense of her 'supreme authority as an American' faltered. Could she go on identifying herself in this way after she heard her hosts refer to 'the neo-colonialists' or 'the Johnson-McNamara clique'?

Susan Sontag, who travelled to Hanoi later in 1968, lacked McCarthy's sense of connection with the 'old America' and its verities. She knew she was opposing her country's interests and challenging its power, and half-expected to be prosecuted on her return to New York. She flinched when a North Vietnamese writer described her as 'the very picture of the genuine American'; Ho Chi Minh's respect for the Declaration of Independence – which he quoted when proclaiming the Democratic Republic of Vietnam in 1945 – implied that the primal American idea now belonged to the enemy. To Sontag's frustration, the meek Vietnamese were slower than she was to vilify Americans: instead they spoke of the atrocities visited on them with 'gentle sorrow'. But she acknowledged the wisdom of this stoicism, and these people who apparently lacked the affliction of ego offered her an antidote to the greedy, dissatisfied mentality of the West. The war was not an effort to resist what General MacArthur called the 'play for global conquest' being made by communism. Sontag saw it as a philosophical contest, with America's manias – its 'principle of "will"', its 'self-righteous taste for violence', its rampant technology – unleashed on a country whose social life resembled, in her eyes, an 'ethical fairy tale'. Like Mailer in his comments on the moonshot, she praised the drop-outs, protesters, Hare Krishna converts and hirsute androgynes at home for adopting 'Oriental thought and rituals'. Sontag shared McCarthy's notion of revolution as a contagious delirium whose purpose went beyond political change; it had to release 'energies of all kinds, including erotic ones' – though perhaps this was only true of San Francisco love-ins and performances of *Hair* on Broadway.

Sontag warmed to the 'moral beauty' and 'physical grace' of the Vietnamese. Pulchritude should not have made a difference, but it enabled her to characterize her countrymen as ugly Americans: she was disgusted by President Johnson, who had once been spotted scratching his itchy groin in public. Yet in her journal she castigated the Sartrean 'bad faith' of her responses to the country and its 'handsome people'. She marvelled, for instance, at the elegant, ingenious conversion of an unexploded bomb's casing into a bell, a crater into a pond for breeding fish, a parachute into a canopy for a hospital operating room, then blamed herself for aesthetic observations that made her the detached spectator of a suffering she could never share. She was at fault as well when she admired Vietnamese gestures: this way of seeing interpreted existence as a ballet, mute and therefore merely decorative. Her predisposition to think of the Vietnamese as refined, pure-hearted creatures led Sontag to report that they treated American prisoners of war as honoured guests and gave them extra portions of food because they had bigger bodies – a solicitude not confirmed by McCarthy's interviews with those 'gaunt, squirrel-faced' men, or by the recollections of imprisoned pilots like John McCain. The internees actually thought of their detention as a post-mortem existence, and when referring to their lives before capture they spoke of the time 'before I got killed'.

McCarthy brought America with her, stuffed into her compendious luggage. Sontag travelled lighter, and even wore Vietnamese trousers and sandals made from recycled tyres. But despite her camouflage, she found herself pining for aspects of America that might have annoyed her at home. Unlike McCarthy, it was not the shopping that she missed. Hanoi, she said, lacked the 'strident noise' of Manhattan, and the Vietnamese, 'over-extended ethically', were not good haters. Did this make them virtuous, or 'simple-minded, naïve'? The scruple demonstrated Sontag's reliance on the aggression and even acrimony of public debate, a symptom of America's divisiveness. The conclusion she reached was that she did not deserve to live in the politically correct society of Vietnam, because her 'mental appetitiveness' left her with a 'lust' for New York, its picturesque inequalities and hyped-up vigour. Her phrasing is self-disgusted: the pleasures to which she was addicted made her 'spoiled, corrupt, decadent', as if she were gorging on chocolate or alcohol, not the arts and contentious ideas.

In the short term, Sontag's reaction helps to explain why this was the first war America lost. Its mobilized machinery was no match for a society in which personal whims were overruled by the collective effort of ensuring survival. In the long term, it explains why the later, larger war against communism and its economic theories proved easier to win. After Vietnam, America gave up threatening. Instead, the rowdy pleasures of its culture and the seductions of its commerce persuaded the rest of the world to postpone revolution indefinitely.

Almost enviously, Europeans helped themselves to the Vietnam War. They had every right to reclaim it: its origins lay in the efforts of France, supported by the United States, to suppress an uprising in its Indochinese colony, and history, of which Europe has so much, is about endless recurrence. Studied from a distance, this war had analogues in the past, or else its absurdity could be defined by raiding the past for alternative scenarios. Godard, editorializing on the soundtrack of *2 ou 3 Choses que je sais d'elle*, asks 'Dear George Washington, what madness made you want to play the role of William Pitt?' – a reference to the British prime minister who declared war on revolutionary France in 1793. Bertrand Russell reminded Americans that in 1776 they were in the position of Vietnamese peasants fighting for independence with pitchforks, and Graham Greene gauged the folly of American intervention by suggesting that it was as if Britain had sent armed support to the Southern states during the Civil War (which, because Lancashire mills relied on American cotton, at one point seemed possible).

In 1974, Marco Ferreri's satirical film *Touche pas à la femme blanche* brought Vietnam back to France. Without jungles or rice paddies, Ferreri squeezed the war into the hole gouged out in the centre of Paris after the demolition of the market at Les Halles. Beside the sandy gulf is the disused Bourse de Commerce, whose painted dome contains scenes of commercial transactions with American Indians, along with sections illustrating trade in Asia or Africa; the economic pirates in all cases have military backup. Vietnam is prefigured on the frontier where the West was bloodily won: the 'trou des Halles' doubles as Indian Territory, in which the flaunting dandy General Custer, played in the film by Marcello Mastroianni, makes his last stand. The native tribes have been corralled in reservations to clear the way for the iron horse, and Buffalo Bill, played by Michel Piccoli, disposes of another encumbrance, boasting that he has slaughtered four thousand buffaloes at the behest of the Kansas Pacific Railroad. Bill easily acclimatizes himself to Ferreri's Paris, along with his trollopy mistress Calamity Jane: his Wild West circus toured Europe after 1890, travelling, as the publicists put it, 'From Prairie to Palace' or 'From the Missouri to the Danube' and regaling audiences with dramatizations of the civilizing process – displays of synchronized rifle fire, choreographed round-ups of wild animals, a staged assault on a mail coach (which of course failed), and dances by tamed natives. As the centuries overlap, Custer and the other commanders take their instructions from a cadre of grey-suited political advisers employed by Nixon's White House. The war they are fighting generalizes itself by analogy. A CIA spook camouflaged as an anthropologist passes round snapshots of the dead Che Guevara and of Lumumba, another battler against colonial servitude, dragged into court in the Congo. Custer's scout remarks that the Indians are interchangeable with Algerians, who played a correspondingly vexatious role in French history, but when they hide in the rubble of the bulldozed market to ambush the American cavalry, they become Vietcong guerrillas.

The trench where the iron-pillared market buildings of Les Halles once stood is referred to in *Touche pas à la femme blanche* as 'the big hole of the Black Hills', as if the diggings were in South Dakota not Paris. The excavation did turn out to be a mimicry of America, filled in with an underground shopping mall. In line with this supposed progress, the war has a peaceable, profitable sequel. Captive Indians work on tribal trinkets in a sweatshop above a fancy boutique, with a glowering portrait of Nixon on the wall to monitor their productivity. One of Custer's colleagues complains when the chieftain Sitting Bull fails to bring tribute to their pow-wow: his daughter was hoping for some moccasins.

In Ferreri's film, Vietnam is a repetition of the past, bogged down in that freshly dug abyss; for Godard it was a playlet acted out in the present. His characters project themselves into the geopolitical dispute because it allows them to experience sensations of strutting power or deliciously painful impotence otherwise absent from their pacified society. In 1965 in *Pierrot le fou*, Belmondo and his fellow runaway Anna Karina improvise a charade for an audience of American sailors. Belmondo in naval costume is Uncle Sam's nephew, Karina in a coolie's hat is the niece of Uncle Ho. He swigs whisky and waves a gun, she simpers and gabbles mock-orientally, pleading for mercy. Then he torches her jungle by using a book of matches to char a strip of cardboard. As agit-prop the performance fails, because the sailors are amused not aghast, but that hardly matters: like the war games of children, it is an assault on dreary, dutiful adult life, which Belmondo and Karina have rejected. In *2 ou 3 Choses que je sais d'elle*, released in 1967, Marina Vlady's husband treats the war as entertainment. He listens gleefully to a short-wave radio broadcast in which LBJ announces that he has extended his bombing campaign to Peking and has missiles aimed at Moscow: what a blitz of light and sound that will be! Johnson may not have said such a thing, but Reagan did. In 1984 he jokily remarked in front of an open microphone that Russia would be bombed in ten minutes – one of several occasions during his presidency when he confused reality with fiction. In Godard's film, Vlady and another part-time prostitute are hired for the afternoon by an American reporter, recently returned from the war zone. He wears a T-shirt emblazoned with the stars and stripes, which one of the women says represents 'Amerika über alles'. All he requires is that they parade around his hotel room naked, with TWA and Pan Am flight bags covering their heads; since carnality and carnage are interchangeable, the session is illustrated with magazine layouts of wounded Vietcong. Back at home, Vlady's young son tells her that he has had a dream about two twins jostling on a cliff path that is only wide enough for one. The twins resolve the argument by merging, so he deduces that they must be North and South Vietnam – a neat, trite political solution but also a scary metamorphosis. Godard's war is a trauma, and it rages inside the minds of those who remain on the sidelines.

'Maybe we need a war,' Mailer suggested in 1967. A conflict in Asia was too remote to satisfy his desire for flaming uproar and howling aggression. 'Let us, instead,' he proposed, 'have wars which are like happenings. Let us have them every summer.' That summer in London, Peter Brook and his team of actors rehearsed *US* – a 'happening' whose ambitious aims, according to Brook's collaborators Albert Hunt and Dennis Cannan, included 'ending the war, deepening human consciousness, restructuring society, creating new aesthetic experiences'. As she explored the streets of Hanoi, Mary McCarthy – using the existentialist catchphrase employed by William Barrett in his commentary on Europe in 1945 – wondered about 'the scramble of extreme situations' when a crowd had to squeeze into cramped shelters during an air raid. Cannan broadened McCarthy's point by claiming that 'we all *want* extreme situations . . . we yearn for invasion, apocalypse'. The North Vietnamese, however, did not share that craving. Over there, a Buddhist monk immolated himself in public to dramatize his country's sufferings, and a police chief, too impatient to bother with legal protocols, summarily executed a handcuffed Vietcong prisoner in the street. The monk sat at prayer in the lotus position as the flesh burned from his bones; the bound prisoner toppled to the ground with blood squirting from the hole in his skull. On stage in London, excruciating episodes like these were simulated, which may have been a new aesthetic experience but did not necessarily deepen consciousness, restructure society or end the war. At another moment in *US* a naked actor was pelted with red pigment and rolled in a sheet of paper that he smeared as if with blood. This human action painting was meant to represent the agony of manhandled Vietnam, but the scene remained an infantile tantrum, messy and painlessly gory. Brook imitated Johnson's 'escalation' of the war by organizing two shouted crescendi for opposed teams of actors, who might have been the rival gangs from *West Side Story*. It was all somewhat mild-mannered when set against the theatre of cruelty acted out by amateurs in Vietnam, where GIs allegedly performed obscene tableaux of their own – urinating into the open mouths of Vietcong corpses or cutting out their hearts and feeding them to village dogs.

At the end of *US*, Glenda Jackson tongue-lashed a young man who was intending to set fire to himself like the monk, and challenged him to describe the America he hated. The actor who played the part had never been there, and could only envisage a chrome-trimmed car as long as a house with a number plate saying 'California, Garden State' (though that is New Jersey's pet name, California being the Golden State). In the car he placed a family on a shopping trip, which prompted Jackson to ask what they were buying. 'Everything,' her colleague replied, unaware that he was describing a blandly generic television commercial, set in a second-hand America. Although Brook instructed his performers to 'search deeply for the idea of being dead', he did not intend the young man to incinerate himself. Instead a butterfly was taken from a box, held up to view, then singed with a cigarette lighter. 'We cannot tell if it is real or false,' said the script for *US*: of course it was false, hardly matching the reality of scared, blackened skin.

When Brook adapted *US* for a film, he toyed with the idea of calling it *Vietnams – A Story of London*. Grosvenor Square, the site of the American Embassy with a wide-winged, sharp-beaked stone eagle on its roof, stood in for the Pentagon, while Soho and its sleazy nightclubs deputized for Saigon. Jackson's tirade concluded by calling for a local Vietnam, with gas grenades poisonously fuming at a flower show in the genteel Home Counties and an English dog frisking on an English lawn with a scavenged human hand in its mouth. But was this hallucinatory scene a protest against America's conduct of the war, or – like Karina's comment on the distant explosions in *Made in USA* – a lament about being stranded on the peaceful periphery in Europe?

15 | Nether Americas

America's founding myth is about the pilgrimage to a promised land, and if the land defaults on its promise, the pilgrim has good reason to spurn it. Or the promised land can eject the unbeliever: hence the Nixon-era slogan 'Love America or Leave It'. Either way, citizenship is a contract that binds both parties. Europeans expect little of the state and nonchalantly shrug at the shabby conduct of politicians, but Americans regularly consider disowning or divorcing their country when a government betrays its ideals.

Gore Vidal predicted in 1967 that exploits like Vietnam would destroy America, 'along with a large portion of the human race'. As a satirist, he had few regrets about the elimination of mankind, which could well be a bonus for the other species we have trampled. More immediately, sounding for once more like a principled American than a weary Europeanized cynic, he warned that if the war continued after the next presidential election, 'a change in nationality will be the only moral response'. Vidal did not make that scornful gesture, though he established residence on the Italian coast at Rapallo, where he wrote a series of historical novels in which the downfall of the Roman Empire served as a prototype for the inflation and demise of American power. During the affray in Chicago in 1968, Mailer also pondered self-exile. But he foresaw a problem, now that the rest of the world consisted mostly of America's abject clients. 'There might not be any foreign lands,' he warned, 'not for long.'

In William S. Burroughs' fantasia about the Democratic Convention, the ape nominated as a presidential candidate condemns the treason of 'queers, dope freaks, and degenerated dirty writers . . . living in foreign lands under the protection of American passports'. The rant targeted Burroughs himself: long before young men dodging the draft crossed into Canada, he began scouting for exits from the censorious United States. In his novel *Naked Lunch* the puritanical Freeland Republic announces a scheme to retool humanity, and a lobotomizing psychiatrist proudly shows off his master-work, '*The Complete All American De-Anxietized Man*'. Burroughs took flight because he treasured his anxieties; he was bothered less by the foreign policy of the United States than by the country's sanity and sanitariness. He loathed Palm Beach, where his parents settled after leaving St Louis, because it lacked slums and dirt. 'God,' he snorted, 'what a fate to live here!' Europe, the customary resort of malcontents, had a variety of demer-its. Burroughs found London 'God-awful', thought that Paris was 'pretty nowhere', hated Barcelona, and called Rome 'miserable'. Venice, notwith-standing the plethora of 'young ass', lacked the requisite quality of 'horror'. Sweden was unacceptable because of its laws rationing hard liquor. Further afield, he advised a friend against Thailand and Japan, 'both Americanized'. Where else was there? For a while he fancied exile in Beirut, where drugs were easy to come by: the trips he took were not only geographical, and he relied on chemicals to speed him through space-time.

Promoting his restless itch to a cosmic urge, Burroughs summarized 'the Spenglerian Cycle routine' as a conflict 'between the East – represent-ing spontaneous, emergent life, and the West – representing control from without, character armor, death'. On the American continent, those polar opposites were north and south rather than west and east. The pale-faced, over-policed slice of the United States was not young but 'old and dirty and evil', as it had been 'before the settlers, before the Indians'; Burroughs left the fantasy of the newfoundland and its manifold novelties to bemused Europeans, and travelled south in quest of a nether America. Mexico, for him, qualified as 'an oriental culture (80% Indian)', and after moving there in 1950 he wrote almost blasphemously to Kerouac, saying 'What a relief to be rid of the U.S. for good and all, and to be in a fine free country!'

'Thank You, North America' – that was the refrain of a song Carmen Miranda performed in the Broadway revue *Sons o'Fun* at the end of 1941. Accompanied by Brazilian percussion and wearing the customary tropical fruit salad on her head, she effused about the hospitality of the United States and, rhyming 'splendour' with 'surrender', swooningly capitulated to its handsome men in their military uniforms, with a special mention for Tyrone Power. North America, she concluded, was 'very OK'. To return the compliment, in 1942 Walt Disney was asked by the Office of the Coordinator of Inter-American Affairs to go on what he called 'a handshaking tour of the ABC countries' – Argentina, Brazil and Chile. Disney demurred, saying he had no interest in shaking hands; instead he led a team of artists to collect sketches of native costumes and folk dances and research 'picture ideas'. Animated, the results appeared in *Saludos Amigos*, which transformed South Americans into semi-human cartoon characters – snooty llamas wearing professorial spectacles, a parrot with tropical plumage dressed up as an urban dandy brandishing a furled parasol, a horse from the Argentine pampas that sheds tears when serenaded – and dispatched Donald Duck in a sailor's suit and Goofy in cowboy gear as tourists to sample these exotic oddities. It was an odd way to make friends.

After the war, the countries that the State Department hoped to ingratiate with did not always behave like good neighbours. When Vice President Nixon was sent on a goodwill mission in 1958, he was heckled in Uruguay, stoned in Peru, and in Venezuela had his car besieged by demonstrators wielding metal pipes. A floral wreath representing Old Glory was torn to pieces in one of the scuffles. Travelling in Bolivia and Peru in 1960, Ginsberg celebrated Castro's assumption of power in Cuba and cheered as he listened to local communists jeering at the United States.

There was a single, notable precedent for the north's unexpected submission to the south. In 1913, after a farewell tour of the Civil War battlefields on which he had fought in his youth, the American journalist Ambrose Bierce, then aged seventy-three, crossed into Mexico and disappeared. 'To be a Gringo in Mexico,' Bierce had written to his niece, 'ah, that is euthanasia!' Imagining what might have happened to him, Carlos Fuentes suggests in his novel *The Old Gringo* that his journey was a symbolic act of expiation, a cultural suicide. Bierce is shot – according to Fuentes – by Pancho Villa's revolutionaries, after which an American woman brings his body back across the border, where she is asked whether she supports a war to 'save Mexico for progress and democracy'. She says she prefers 'to live with

Mexico in spite of progress and democracy'. Patrick Chamoiseau, born in Martinique, more trenchantly urges resistance not coexistence. His novel *Texaco* is set in a Fort-de-France shantytown, named after the oil refinery on which it abuts. Here Christ has a second coming, returning to earth as a modernizing city planner whose new dispensation involves bulldozing the slum's illegal hutches as well as stamping out the superstitious muddle of local folkways. Protected by a matriarch who is its founder and the keeper of its swarming, polyglot history, Texaco outwits the imperious religion of progress.

In these latitudes, the technocratic United States encountered cultures with their own reserves of occult power. Chamoiseau recommended confounding flat-minded Americans by 'rubbing the real with the magical', as happens in voodoo. Pablo Neruda described Mexico as 'the last magical country', and Fuentes called for the use of magic as 'a national resource', ultimately more valuable than the oil the northern profiteers wished to siphon off. Truman Capote had a first-hand experience of this sorcery during a visit to Haiti in 1948. Before Mardi Gras, he attended a ceremony at which a wizard wearing a pearl earring officiated, with tongues of flame and the hypnotic beat of a drummer provoking an ecstasy during which 'the spirit (god and demon) opened like a seed and flowered in his flesh: unsexed, unidentifiable, the magician gathered in his arms man and woman'. After handling fire and remaining unburned, he hurled himself against an unopened door that led to 'truth's secret'. Having witnessed these transformations, Capote saw the limitations of realism and reality. In the house of fiction, no door need remain closed.

Kerouac summed up Mexico as 'a frenzy and a dream', which made it a respite from the unfrenetic United States: the trouble with the American dream was that it did not resemble the exciting irrationality of the scenarios that agitate our brains while we sleep. In *On the Road* he describes leaving Texas at Laredo in 1950 and crossing into Tamaulipas, which to his gratification 'looked exactly like Mexico', with loiterers wearing straw hats and white pants lounging against seedy storefronts in the middle of the night. Travelling down to Mexico City, he exulted in the cheapness of the beer and the teenage prostitutes, the profusion of marijuana, and the amiable incompetence of the police. Ginsberg remembered him stretched on the roof of a car at night, 'allowing mosquitoes to seep into his body' in a kind of communion, mixing bloods as they bit him. Dysentery completed Kerouac's acclimatization. Undeterred, he declared that only in Mexico was the effort of being born and dying worthwhile; there life was still seen as a journey between two eternities, not a self-promoting career.

Burroughs, who led the way into Mexico in 1949, crossed the border as a fugitive, decamping from an indictment for possessing narcotics and a slew of other legal embarrassments. After amateurishly farming cotton in Texas, he had settled for a while in New Orleans, where he was enraged by rent controls that forbade him to evict sitting tenants from a property he bought: this, he complained, was '*Un-American Socialism*'. When he quit the United States, he symbolically rejected 'the obscenity "Welfare State"' and 'a Socialistic police state similar to England, and not too different from Russia': for all his flagrant perversity, Burroughs was a traditional libertarian, who scorned governmental interference with his instincts. He had his own version of the pledges that daily affirm the loyalty of American citizens, and offered to show his patriotism by sucking the flag, so long as it was first soaked in heroin. He did his best to subvert Truman's attempt to save Central and South America from communism – a supplement to Marshall's scheme for Europe, called the Point Four Plan – when he tried, without success, to seduce a Point Four chauffeur. In Colombia a policeman showed him scars obtained during a tour of duty in Korea, to which the country's conservative regime had sent troops. 'I like you guys,' said the cop. 'No good ever comes from these America lovers,' Burroughs growled.

Mexico appealed to Burroughs because of its chaos, the result of two millennia of 'disease and poverty and degradation and stupidity and slavery and brutality and psychic and physical terrorism', all of which on balance counted in the country's favour. Cockfights and bullfights were to his taste, like the venomous scorpions. Mexico City's murder rate was, he boasted, the highest in the world, and he made his own contribution to the statistic in 1951 when he shot and accidentally killed his wife during a drunken party game. Released from custody on bail, he hastened to resume his travels, moving first to Panama. After his arrival in Peru he learned that he had been tried for murder in his absence, sentenced to two years in prison, and classed as a 'pernicious foreigner'. Clearly it would not be prudent to return. 'I feel like a Roman exiled from Rome,' he said: a snub to the other empire across the northern border, since for him the latter-day Rome was Mexico City. Expatriation also served as a kind of self-exorcism. Late in the 1950s, when the title of the book by Lederer and Burdick had become a catchphrase, Burroughs placed the blame for pointing the gun at his wife on his own indwelling ugly American, whom he called 'the Ugly Spirit'. This fiend was the embodiment of 'American acquisitive evil', although it is hard to see how Rockefeller, Vanderbilt, Hearst and the CIA, named by Burroughs as other manifestations of the demon, had any responsibility for his wife's death.

In Lima, disbursing 'the Yankee dollar' in return for sex, he felt that he was undoing the Spanish conquest, which served as a model for the subsequent American economic invasion. The street boys he picked up represented a sappy, unashamed 'South American Potential', and he was 'a new Bolívar': their liberator, not their exploiter. He understood the inequity of this sexual commerce, but was glad that the deals could be finalized in the open, with no need for concealment. In the United States, he had to define himself as a deviant, or else accept the 'dreary boredom' of normality. Here in Latin America, as he later said of Tangier, he found 'no weight of disapproving "others", no "they", no *Society*'. Could the American West have been like this before law-enforcers pinned on their badges and fence-builders domesticated the plains? For a while, Burroughs planned to establish what Kerouac called a 'Hipster Colony' on a farm in Ecuador, where his fellow renegades would be safe in the event of a Soviet victory in the Cold War.

In Bogotá he was comically mistaken for an imperial plunderer, an agent of the Texas Oil Company, which had recently given up prospecting in the area. In an odd anticipation of Chamoiseau's plot, he received royal treatment, since his presence seemed to foretell the oil company's return, 'like the second coming of Christ'. But for Burroughs the elixir was not oil: he spent months in the jungles beyond the Andes hunting for yagé, a vine with hallucinogenic and supposedly telepathic powers, which he described as 'the final kick'. In the process he made his own valiant contribution to the Cold War and its competitive scramble for raw materials. The Russians had preceded him, shipping quantities of yagé back to Moscow where supposedly they hoped to brew a potion that would invigorate or sedate factory workers according to need; Burroughs instead expected the drug to deliver an ecstatic derangement, and gleefully reported on the 'convulsions of lust' it induced. No wonder a starchy missionary from Oklahoma informed him that yagé was an invention of the devil. During his search, Burroughs found other remnants of a culture that was buried or submerged in the white north. On a jukebox in Colombia, he heard a snatch of music from the mountains, and was reminded of the tunes that shepherds played on pipes in Albania, 'where pre-Greek, Illyrian racial strains linger. A phylogenetic nostalgia conveyed by this music – Atlantean?' Sunken Atlantis, the missing link between Europe and America, here re-emerged from beneath the water and shimmered for a moment in the air. Later Burroughs dabbled in Mayan priestcraft, imagining witch doctors who could perform rites that made the bodies of male lovers merge to create 'bio-energetic fusion' and 'orgonotic penetration'.

In 1963 Mailer distinguished between two kinds of novelists – those who studied society, and those who embarked on a 'trip up the upper Amazon of the inner eye'. Mailer wrote this with a wrinkled lip, since the upper Amazon, in his view, might just as well have been the lower digestive tract; but Burroughs explored the dense, dank rainforest both metaphorically and actually. Then, as old age approached, his wanderings ended. After long periods of residence in Paris and London, he began spending time in New York, and in 1964 he travelled back to his birthplace, St Louis. At Grand Central Station he requested a private drawing room on the train. The astonished clerk, offering a roomette instead, asked 'Where've you been?' 'I have been abroad,' said Burroughs, as genteelly out of touch with demotic America as Henry James. By 1972 he had been away long enough to consider the United States 'the most exotic country of them all', and after 1974, established as a downtown celebrity, he occupied a series of lofts and grim bunkers on the Lower East Side of Manhattan. Forced out of New York by rising rents in 1981, he settled in Lawrence, Kansas, not far from St Louis. He told a local newspaper that the town appealed because it was quiet and cheap. In a mumbled reconciliation with his native land, he said that America was 'about as easy a place to live in as you can find'; it had distinct advantages if you needed triple bypass surgery, as he did in 1991. He died in Lawrence six years later.

Burroughs genuinely hoped to discover an alternative America, an open range not yet closed down by moralists. Hunter S. Thompson, by contrast, went south in search of a vantage point from which he could reconsider the United States and understand, as he said, 'why it will never be what it could have been, or tried to be' before it was taken over by bosses, fixers, and slimy writers of advertising copy. In his early twenties, the bilious Thompson had proved to be unemployable at home. *Time* hired him as a copyboy, then fired him for impertinence. A newspaper in upstate New York let him go when he wrecked the candy machine in the office. In 1960 he shipped out to the tropics, and in Puerto Rico took a job on a rag called *El Sportivo*, glad to be away from 'the slick strivers and jingo parrots . . . of the Luce empire'. But the America he detested caught up with him, and he reported that Luce's busybodies and do-gooders were spreading 'like a piss puddle' now that the Caribbean islands had been annexed by the Marines for target practice and by Conrad Hilton for resort hotels. In his novel *The Rum Diary*, a tourist ship disgorges businessmen 'from somewhere in the middle of America, some flat little town', while another 'fearsomely alike' group consists of 'shapeless women in wool bathing suits' and 'dull-eyed men with hairless legs' who should never have been allowed to leave their local Elks Club.

Despite these vexations, Thompson succumbed happily to 'tropic rot' in muggy San Juan. All he missed was Kools: the vending machines in Puerto Rico were stocked exclusively with Salems. But he displeased the local police, who accused him of drunken rowdyism and encouraged him to move on. He got as far as Bermuda by working as a deck hand, then returned to New York with the help of funds donated by a friend. He next hitchhiked to California, where he soon began to plan another escape. With no interest in the Atlantean reunion of sundered cultures, he refused to consider a trip to Europe. 'Who the shit cares whether England sinks or swims?' he asked. Mexico, the nearest getaway, was also out of the question, since Baja California had become an 'abortion hospital' for knocked-up teenagers, which made it 'the coccyx bone of the universe'. Thompson decided on 'the biggest outest place I can find on the map – South America'. Before departing in early 1962 he joined the National Rifle Association, as he planned to go jaguar hunting in Colombia: wherever he went, he looked for his own version of the Wild West.

Disillusionment set in soon after he disembarked from a whisky-smuggling sloop in Colombia. 'These latins are all whores,' he observed on the way to Bogotá; as a result, 'the U.S. is looking better and better'. He disposed of Ecuador and Peru by suggesting that both should be dynamited. Bolivia initially seemed promising, and he saw 'definite humour in the rape of nuns'. After sampling Uruguay, Argentina and Paraguay, he arrived in Rio de Janeiro, witnessed a voodoo ceremony on the beach at Copacabana, and declared projects for 'civilizing these people' to be absurd. He laughed at Kennedy's Alliance for Progress, which 'imported ping-pong and the Twist to combat the Red Menace'. 'For god's sake,' he recommended, 'bring MAGNUMS.' Like a mercenary, he thought of dodging sideways to Angola to enlist in a colonial war that was Portugal's little Vietnam: 'I think I could kill humans as easily as deer or wild pigs, which probably makes me good timber for Africa,' he bragged. Luckily his violence remained windily rhetorical.

As an adolescent, Thompson had lovingly typed out the entire text of *The Great Gatsby*, hoping to absorb its style though not expecting to be persuaded by its romantic hopefulness. He complained repeatedly that Gatsby's 'goddam green light' – the beckoning, teasing prospect of a new start on an unspoiled continent – had been extinguished; Lee Harvey Oswald, he said in 1965, had written a new ending to Fitzgerald's novel. Now in Rio he picked up a copy of *O Grande Gatsby* in a bookshop and found it refreshed by the unfamiliar language. Brazilians, he said, were as double-faced as Gatsby – devious, shady, yet somehow beguiling. If Fitzgerald had lived down here, 'they'd have made him an emperor' and called him Dom Scott I, a jazzy potentate who 'played everything off-key except the high white note'. The United States no longer monopolized the American dream.

Before Thompson's return home, a young woman in Bolivia asked him to help her find a job as a maid with an American family; she was sure, she told him, that all Americans were good people. 'Where did she get that idea?' the mortified Thompson asked a friend in the United States Information Service: what she took to be a truism ought to be true, but was not. Eventually he settled in the Rockies, admitting – from inside his fortified alpine hermitage – that in other countries someone who vilified successive governments as he had done would be in prison, or dead. Instead, with his right to vituperate protected by the constitution, he wrote a drunken letter to President Johnson declaring his willingness to be appointed Governor of American Samoa. Johnson ignored the offer, which Thompson indignantly withdrew after the escalation of the Vietnam War. He also protested when Johnson sent extra troops to the Dominican Republic, where a communist coup seemed possible: he demanded to know why there had been no diplomatic warning, which meant that American responses were jumpy and belated. As a taxpayer, he felt entitled to grumble about the embassy's inefficiency.

Recalcitrant and ferociously independent, defending his liberty with a private arsenal, Thompson was true to America's original principles. In 1970 he ran for sheriff of Pitkin County, Colorado, as a Freak Power candidate, and when he shot himself in 2005, Senators George McGovern and John Kerry attended his funeral, at which – in a last act of noisy fulmination – his ashes were fired from a cannon. America, despite Thompson's early attempts to find somewhere else, is territorially and morally large enough to accommodate the most ornery of misfits.

Ginsberg too experimented with the southern trajectory. In 1954 he spent six months in Mexico, where he visited the pyramids with Kerouac and laughingly mimed Aztec sacrifices. Like a Mayan prophet protesting against the Spanish conquistadors, Ginsberg addressed a doom-laden diatribe to 'the Iron Hound of America' – yet he and Kerouac were themselves invaders, legatees of Columbus: they spent much of the time planning their literary conquest of New York, and when they returned to Texas they celebrated their renewed access to its creature comforts by buying softie ice creams.

In 1962 Ginsberg set off in a different direction, on what became the hippie trail through India. He studied Tibetan Buddhism during long sojourns in Benares and Calcutta, after which he travelled to Japan, where a Zen abbot inducted his fellow poet Gary Snyder into monastic discipline and entrusted him with priestly functions. Ginsberg was following a course plotted by Whitman, who sent his soul but not his body on a passage to India. Ginsberg's philosophy of fraternity owed as much to Whitman's creed of democratic blood-brotherhood as to Krishna Consciousness and Mantra-Rock, just as the bardic expostulations of *Howl* were a franker, more ribald version of Whitman's 'barbaric yawp'. He also carried with him a photograph of a plaster cast of William Blake's face, and in Bombay he wrote a *H*Y*M*N* T*O* U*S** that was his response to Blake's revolutionary poem *America*. The asterisks were not a typographic equivalent to the stars stitched onto the national flag: they joked about the deleted letters of dirty words, and the obscene hymn warns 'Mother Democracy' that 'I fuck thee piously in the Image of America, O Formless One'. America here is neither a virgin, nor – like the Statue of Liberty and the goddess Columbia – a respectable matron in a ball gown. Instead she resembles the Hindu demon Kali, a dominatrix whose foot tramples the corpse of Uncle Sam. Elsewhere she enters into 'Amorous play with the United States of the Universe' while also androgynously managing to be 'Spouse of Europa' and 'Husband of Russia'. By demonstrating what he called 'international concern', Ginsberg separated himself from 'appreciation of America and homeyness and family and normal values', the shibboleths of the small-minded suburbs. Yet despite such animadversions, he could not sever the umbilical cord that attached him to 'Mother U.S.'. Personified in that way, the country stood in for his own mad mother, who died in an insane asylum in 1956. This matriarchal America 'dreams of the wild embrace of world masculinity', and seems to want Ginsberg himself to satisfy her. Homosexuality was his safeguard against incest, with expatriation as a secondary precaution.

Ginsberg's hymn aptly defines his homeland as the globally promiscuous 'Imagewife of Mankind'. He meant that America had become what the
rest of mankind dreamed about, the fecund source of the shared stories
that are called myth, and the further from it he got, the more inescapable he
found it to be. Sometimes, with startling primness, he noted India's diver-
gence from America's sedate social norms. He was taken aback to see that
people in India walked around in their underwear, 'shorts with open flies
like Americans have nightmares being caught in the streets in'. His reaction
is less liberated than contemporary ads for Maidenform bras and foundation
garments, which took a flushed pleasure in the fantasy – not a nightmare
at all – of being underdressed in public: Ginsberg carried with him an odd
strain of provincial prudery. Confirming Mailer's suspicion, he also found that
foreignness was hard to come by in an Americanized world. As he watched
the holy city of Benares revive at dawn, with radios blaring, rickshaws circulating, food stalls opening for business and householders carrying their pots
to the river, he noted in his journal that he felt 'like An American in Paris in
1920', with sitars replacing Gershwin's saxophones.

The American enthusiasms Ginsberg brought with him proved revelatory
when he considered Indian religion. The cosmic dances of creation, he said,
would have amazed 'Fred Astaire . . . in his grey age'. The remark was not
disparaging. Whether in a Hindu temple or in the gleamingly laminated Art
Deco nightclubs where Astaire's films are set, dance is the art that expresses
the revelry of living creatures, who were equipped by whatever deity first
made them with sinuous arms, strutting legs and, in Astaire's case, percussive feet. Nor was Ginsberg insulting Hinduism when he described it as 'a
huge cartoon religion with Disney gods'. In Mankiewicz's film of *The Ugly
American*, Michael Redgrave's Fowler makes a detour to Tây Ninh, near the
border between Vietnam and Cambodia, where he visits the headquarters
of Cao-Dai, a nationalist cult invented in 1926. As he strolls through the Great
Divine Temple to cool off, he dismisses it as 'a Walt Disney fantasia of the
East', a zoo of fiery-breathed dragons and rubberized serpents. Ginsberg
was amused by Hindu representations of an elephant balanced on a mouse
or of Ganesh with his 'big Disney Dumbo feet', but unlike Greene he meant

no disrespect, either to Hindu gods or the friendly monsters in Disney's cartoons. After his trip to Hollywood in 1930, the Russian director Sergei Eisenstein praised the 'divine omnipotence' of Disney, referring to the animator's ability to enliven bodies at the rate of twenty-four flickering frames a second. In the same spirit, Ginsberg saw that America's popular culture was a new theology, catering to the same credulous needs as longer-established religions.

While Ginsberg's quest took him east, Burroughs continued to travel south, though he exchanged the jungle for the desert by venturing to Morocco, where he lived from 1954 to 1958. The novelist Paul Bowles, born in New York, was already resident there, having followed the example of the Touareg people who disappeared into the Sahara so as not to be civilized by the Roman Empire. It pleased Bowles to think that the desert could absorb and obliterate America. 'With an area considerably larger than the United States,' he wrote, 'the Sahara is a continent within a continent.' Bowles was fond of a song that looked back without regret at what he had left behind:

> Il y a une chose magnifique,
> C'est la bombe atomique.
> Ça vient de l'Amérique,
> Ça arrête le trafic,
> C'est leur bombe pacifique.

Bowles's bolt-hole was in Tangier, which existed in a legal limbo known as the International Zone – abbreviated by Burroughs, who saw the city as a dizzy extra-terrestrial playground, to Interzone. Under a protocol that lasted until 1956, Tangier belonged to no country and was jointly administered by France, Spain, Britain and later a consortium of other powers. Its residents were excused from patriotic bigotry and from any other moral discipline, and Burroughs reported that there was 'no lower age limit on boys', with forty cents as the going price for sex. Here, with no God or government in charge, everything was permitted; as a corollary, nothing was provided, since a city that did not levy taxes or charge customs duties could hardly supply the usual social services. Bowles called Tangier 'a transition from one way of being to another', and for Burroughs too it was a frontier of dreaming, 'the prognostic pulse of the world'.

At first Bowles complained that American tourists saw it as a displaced Utah. Then after 1951 he reported sighting newcomers of another kind – bearded, 'belligerently informal' in dress, the advance guard of a '"lost generation" which America turned loose after the recent war', their explorations subsidized by the Veterans' Administration. Bowles characterized these seekers as 'nihilist mystics', who with the help of drugs pursued 'an absolute detachment from what is ordinarily called reality'. Alcohol, the fuel of what he called 'Judeo-Christian civilization', inflames the drinker and inclines him to fight, whereas kif or hashish or cannabis, freely available in Tangier, makes the smoker contemplative, quietly solitary. Bowles knew that his scented Eden was under threat. In the 1960s he complained that Turkey had Westernized itself by banning cannabis, and he deplored the 'deculturizing programmes' that the United Nations had brought to Africa, showing 'the little nations' how to be modern – that is, how to be wistfully pseudo-American.

Ginsberg visited Burroughs in Tangier in 1957, then after a tiff left for Spain and Italy: in this new bohemian version of the Grand Tour, Europe was an afterthought or a second best. Other refugees from moralistic America cruised the fringes of the Mediterranean. While touring the Greek islands, Tennessee Williams made a side trip to Istanbul, which Elia Kazan, who was born there, had recommended as 'delightfully evil'. Williams found it dirty but insufficiently wicked, so said 'There's Asia' and retired to his hotel bar for a drink. He was even more unexcited by Tangier, which he called 'Miami Beach thrown in the middle of some ghastly slums'. But Capote liked being in this limbo, because 'the average Arab . . . thinks America and Europe are the same thing and in the same place, wherever that is' – an amusing replica of the average midwesterner's myopic world view. The self-containment of Tangier made Capote compare it to a monastery, luckily with no staid rules about celibacy. At a nocturnal feast during Ramadan, he overheard chanting voices that were 'sweet and sultry as kif smoke'. As teasing as ever, he stopped short of saying that he or anyone else smoked marijuana, and instead let the metaphorical fumes invade his prose.

Despite its narcotics, Tangier did not have a soothing effect on Burroughs. He enjoyed the city's 'end-of-the world-feeling', by which he meant that it was both an outpost and a terminus, not quite Bowles's anteroom to eternity. He also approved of its all-encompassing mercantilism: nylon shirts, Swiss watches and methadone were all available over the counter. But Burroughs had no intention of vegetating with a hookah or a perfumed cigarette; his preference was to raise hell. In 1952, enraged by the stupor of Florida and its population of doddering retirees, he called for a revival of bomb-throwing anarchism to liven up the place. Residence in Tangier brought him closer to the idea of a holy war that took no prisoners. He approved of jihad, 'the whole-sale slaughter by every Moslem of every unbeliever', which had started with the riots against French colonialism; it did not occur to him that he might be one of the casualties. 'I simply must see some of this bloodshed,' he said in 1955 when the disturbances resumed. He reassured Kerouac about his safety by loudly insisting that 'ARABS ARE NOT VIOLENT. . . . They *do not attack people for kicks or fight for kicks like Americans*.' Yet he exemplified the American way – psychotic mayhem rather than a zealous, purgative ire – when he joked that he had bought a machete and intended to wrap himself in a sheet and rush outside to yell 'I killa everybody.' He had his own interpretation of Islamic fatalism, and assumed that 'It Is As Allah Wills' meant that 'whatever I want comes to me': as if telepathically, his spasms of lust caused boys to knock on his door. This American creed of instant gratification was not quite what the prophet Mohammed had in mind. Soon, wishing to defame all sanctimonious principles, Burroughs turned against Islam, and elaborated a satirical routine about charging into a mosque, emptying garbage cans on the floor, unloosing a herd of hogs, urinating on the relics, and yodelling in a parody of the call to prayer.

This orgy was meant to conclude, with the help of the scandalized Muslims, in a satisfying self-destruction. 'What a beautiful way to commit suicide, to get yourself torn to pieces by Arabs,' sighed Burroughs, extending Bierce's comment about euthanasia in Mexico. He was free to indulge such a fantasy because at the time there was no prospect of it actually happening: he remained a conceptual terrorist, who in an emergency could count on the protection of the Pax Americana.

Kerouac made the obligatory trek to Tangier in 1957, hoping that its 'Fellaheen world' of peasant farmers would rescue him from 'this modern America of crew cuts and sullen faces in Pontiacs'. To his dismay, he found that Moroccan teenagers played jukeboxes and loitered around pinball machines as if they were in the Bronx; it was in New York that Ginsberg in *Howl* had seen, or at least imagined, 'Mohammedan angels staggering on tenement roofs', which made the detour to North Africa unnecessary. A bad experience with some suspect hashish prompted Kerouac to admit that all he wanted was a bowl of Wheaties in 'a pine breeze kitchen in America' – comfort food in the motherland, fed to him by the fiercely protective, comforting Mom to whom he gave the Québecois nickname Memère. On the way home, he visited Paris and London, which presented further evidence of a worldwide monoculture. The Rive Gauche was Greenwich Village all over again, and Piccadilly Circus was a shabbier Times Square.

By 1968, the pilgrimage in quest of spiritual truth had narrowed into a hunt for ethnic trappings, which could be satisfied in the flea markets of downtown Manhattan: Andy Warhol commented on the popularity of 'the Pakistani-Indian-international-jet-set-hippie look – all embroidered and brocaded'. Despite this smattering of exotic influences, on his own travels Warhol was comforted by the universality of America, now as omnipresent as its currency. After a show of his work in Paris, he noted in his diary 'It was the Dollar Signs and they looked pretty good.' He was referring to his silk screens of the globally honoured financial icon, in which the curvaceous S writhes around the upright bar, pulsing with expansive energy, and the pigment oozes like ketchup. Wherever he went, Warhol mingled with a floating population of celebrities like Liza Minnelli and Jerry Hall, who constituted, he said, 'a nationality without a nation'. He seldom ventured beyond the round of interchangeable hotels, restaurants, galleries and discotheques, and when he did go further afield he usually regretted it. In Kuwait in 1977, he liked just one building, 'a copy of the Ford Foundation'. If he behaved more like a wider-eyed tourist, it was only to be ironic: on a trip to London in 1986, he amused himself by photographing 'Big Ben and things. All the funny English spots.'

Once, waiting to board Concorde in Paris, he ran into the trumpeter Dizzy Gillespie, who had just returned from Africa. Warhol was taken aback when Gillespie reported that in Africa 'there was a lot of dirt on the ground': on one continent at least, culture had not yet supplanted nature. Otherwise Warhol lived contentedly in a global continuum, like a wrap-around America. In 1982 in Hong Kong – where he described the swampy humidity as 'Florida-type weather' – he was pleased to be told that the local time was twelve hours ahead of New York, 'so you didn't have to change your watch' (or adjust your ideas). Returning home from Beijing, he realized he had forgotten to bring back trinkets for friends. But there was no need for embarrassment: he sent an assistant down to Chinatown to buy some souvenirs of his trip.

16 | B-Day and Other Invasions

Young people driven by ambition have always travelled from the outlying provinces to the city: it is an imperative of natural selection, a means of establishing your place in the pecking order. In an Americanized world, this journey of self-promotion extends beyond national borders and vaults across oceans.

David Bailey and the model Jean Shrimpton travelled to New York in 1962 to photograph a *Vogue* feature entitled 'Young Idea Goes West'. The young idea was English, sent west to tease or startle a New World that was feeling its age. Bailey, who caused a stir by wearing his scuffed leather jacket at the St Regis Hotel, had an unfoppish, truculently proletarian manner that marked a new fad in artistic conduct, and the gawky angularity of Shrimpton refashioned the female body. *Esquire* cited her as a forbiddingly aloof example of what it called 'The New Sentimentality', which was not an American style: her haughty remoteness was accentuated by her outsize dark glasses, later to become essential equipment for celebrities who exist to be looked at but return no one's gaze. At the airport in New York, Bailey photographed Shrimpton with her pile of cases on the edge of a BOAC landing jetty that protrudes into empty space. The gap between continents remains, and she may have to jump from the modish future into the stuffy past. Accompanying her is a teddy bear: Americans had a monopoly on youth, but the English knew how to be childish. Once Shrimpton crossed that yawning gulf, suspicious customs inspectors rummaged through her luggage, and removed some worming pills – to be used on her pets, not including the teddy bear – for chemical analysis.

To the annoyance of the *Vogue* stylists, Bailey took Shrimpton slumming. He refused to photograph her with the sculpted lions outside the Public Library on 42nd Street, arguing that he could have done that in Trafalgar Square. Instead he posed her on the littered sidewalks of Harlem or Chinatown and in noisy amusement arcades around Times Square. She squeezes her reflection into the soiled window of a cigarette machine, or leans against a lamp post that warns of a $25 fine if you fail to curb your dog when it defecates; her gloved hand dangles the bear in the gutter, but since it has no digestive system she can disregard the law. When Bailey photographed her on a rooftop with the foggy outline of the Empire State Building behind, the image emphasizes bizarre foreground details – the lid on a chimney, its flap shaped like a human head, or a television antenna alert to receive messages from the sky – that make Shrimpton look unearthly, a mannequin from Mars. The United Nations secretariat appears, robbed of symbolic significance. In one photograph it retreats behind a rusty chain-link fence that the bear is climbing, in another it is an anonymous oblong box, an example of the drab functionality that Bailey and Shrimpton were mocking. Despite their impudence, Diana Vreeland, who edited American *Vogue*, declared the upstart pair 'adorable', and in an over-punctuated series of gasps and gushes announced that 'England. Has. Arrived.'

Exactly two years later, in February 1964, the Beatles followed Bailey and Shrimpton to New York. Before leaving the airport they presided at a press conference, wittily affronting earnest America. Asked if they would sing, John Lennon replied 'No, we need money first.' Asked if they were wearing wigs, Paul McCartney replied 'Yeah, I'm bald', and Lennon added 'We're all deaf and dumb too.' Asked if they were going to get haircuts, George Harrison replied 'I had one yesterday.' Shrieking female fans banged on the windows of their car as they left to drive into Manhattan, and they arrived at their hotel with an escort of mounted police. That evening on the television news, Walter Cronkite likened their landing to D-Day – though it was no secret, which accounted for the hysterical crowds – and suggested calling the raucous invasion B-Day. For once, Americans were experiencing a cultural assault as disruptive as their own impact on the wider world had been.

A few years earlier, the music of American teenagers had provoked moralistic fury in Europe. The film *Rock Around the Clock* set off a riot in Dortmund, even though Bill Haley and his unincendiary Comets looked staid and paunchy, dressed in clothes that would now qualify as smart-casual on corporate Fridays. In Britain the official attack on the film appealed to racist fears: the politician Jeremy Thorpe denounced it as 'musical Mau Mau', alliteratively evoking a recent colonial uprising in Kenya, and the *Daily Mail*, paraphrasing the Nazi critique of jazz, called rock 'n roll 'the Negro's revenge'. Was America a ruler policing global order, or an unholy, unhinged tempter? In *Jailhouse Rock* Elvis Presley behaves like a more violently irate version of James Dean: he kills a man in a bar-room brawl, slugs some guards during a food fight in prison, smashes his guitar when the night-club patrons ignore his singing, insults the guests at a fancy cocktail party, and punishes a record company executive for infringement of copyright by slapping him in the face. Added to all this, Presley's sulky mouth, insolent slurred drawl, rotating hips and thrusting pelvis made his body a weapon.

The Beatles, by contrast, were flippant not obstreperous, impudent not lewd. In 1970 Presley – by that time middle-aged, drug-addicted, and corpulently attired in Las Vegas spangles – told an FBI agent that the 'filthy unkempt appearances and suggestive music' of the Beatles set a bad example to American youth. At worst, however, they incited a squealing frenzy, and Ed Sullivan declared them to be 'four of the nicest youngsters' who had ever appeared on his television show. Although McCartney remarked that they were treated as 'exotic beasts', shaggy pixies with tight trousers and elfin pointed boots, they were never truly bestial; he added later that they found America 'a bit backward. It was old-fashioned, they had a lot of catching up to do' – the first time, perhaps, that anyone had been cheeky enough to say this about the futuristic United States.

For a while, American bands affected quaintly Olde English identities, calling themselves the Byrds, the Town Criers or the Beau Brummels. This mimicry overlooked the fact that the Beatles too were cultural copycats, who had brought their own version of America with them. They played music influenced by the Memphis sound, and despite their Liverpool accents their diction was transatlantic: they swallowed the dental consonants when they sang 'I *wanna* hold your hand'. The better-educated Rolling Stones used American idioms even more insistently, irritating in a society where pronunciation was still an indicator of social status. In 1965 Brian Jones's father, a church organist in respectable Cheltenham, said 'There's enough of these Americanisms around. Couldn't you just sing "I Can't Get *Any* Satisfaction"?' No, they could not; the ungrammatical monosyllable 'No', to which Mick Jagger gave such thunderous emphasis, sounded more blunt and coercive. A single American word could cast a spell, while a place name functioned like a magic carpet. In 1967, during a trip to New York, the Bee Gees wrote a song called 'Massachusetts', about going back to a state they had actually not yet visited: the trite lovelorn situation was their excuse to use the ethnically alluring, unBostonian name. In 1968, across a longer and more estranging distance, the John Phillips song 'San Francisco', about dropouts wearing flowers in their hair, became the anthem of the Prague Spring – an appeal for release or change that ended when Russian tanks reasserted the will of a dogmatic empire.

On their first tour, the Beatles cavorted through a square and sober America. Travelling by train to Washington, they served drinks to passengers in the club car, wore hats cadged from porters, and pretended to nap on the luggage racks. The Rolling Stones, who followed a few months later, were not content with pranks, and did their best to outrage local propriety. They looked unkempt, even fearsomely ugly – especially Keith Richards with his carious teeth, pimply skin, and the piratical sliver of bone that dangled from his ear – and made pronouncements that sounded scornful not cheeky. At a press conference in the Rainbow Room high above Rockefeller Plaza, a journalist asked Jagger whether he was more satisfied now than when he wrote his urgent, yelping song. 'You mean sexually or philosophically?' drawled Jagger. He then confirmed that the answer was sexually yes, financially likewise, whereas philosophically he was still trying. Jagger dressed to offend, sometimes sporting a flashy crucifix, and for a concert at Madison Square Garden in 1969 he wore an Uncle Sam hat accessorized with a long purple chiffon scarf and jewelled belt as he romped through 'Jumping Jack Flash'; the year before in London, a Confederate flag fluttered from the band's Bentley as they drove away from the court after Brian Jones's drug trial. This misuse of American pennants and totems outraged the Solicitor General Erwin N. Griswold, who denounced Jagger as 'this prancing Britisher in our midst' and warned against his inflammatory effect on 'our children'. The promoter Bill Graham sarcastically called Jagger 'this god' and asked what right he had 'to descend on this country in this way'.

The Stones almost complacently assumed that their appearances would incite a pandemonium. On one occasion they arrived late in Boston after an affray at the airport; rushing to their concert in a convoy of police cars, they noticed a distant blaze from a racial disturbance in the Public Garden. 'We do that?' asked Jagger, who was probably disappointed to be told that the Stones were not responsible. At their 1969 concert in Oakland, a broadsheet distributed to the audience addressed the band as 'comrades' and hailed their music as an incitement to 'deadly acts' aimed at 'the maniacs who hold power'. That December they gave a free concert at the Altamont speedway outside San Francisco. It was meant, Jagger said, as an attempt to create 'a microcosmic society' where people could 'get together and talk to each other and get stoned'; it ended as a diabolical bacchanal, not a blissed-out seminar. Leathered bikers were hired to keep the peace in exchange for free beer, and earned their pay by grabbing fans who scrambled onto the low stage and hurling them back into the scrum. Film of the event shows naked women having seizures, drunkards epileptically flailing, babies bawling, stray dogs scrapping. A hippie Christ carrying an American flag trudged through the mud on the way to Golgotha, while collectors with buckets sought donations for a fund to defend the Black Panthers. When the jostling turned to fisticuffs, Jagger, dressed as a harlequin, made a whiny appeal to the mob: 'Why are we fighting, and what for? . . . If we are all one, let's show we're all one.' He then added 'We need an ambulance and we need a doctor by that scaffold there.' Before the band began 'Under My Thumb', he pleaded with his audience of three hundred thousand to sit down, like an overwrought schoolteacher trying to restore discipline in a classroom. Somewhere in the heaving crowd, a man who was high on methamphetamine brandished a gun; one of the Hell's Angels stabbed him and stomped on him when he fell, killing him. There were reports of three other deaths, balanced by four births. The Stones made a prudent retreat by helicopter, like evacuees from a war zone. When it was pointed out that they had envenomed the murky atmosphere by performing 'Sympathy for the Devil', Charlie Watts unregretfully apologized for their flirtation with Satan by saying 'Oh dear, what a shame.'

Beatlemania, by contrast, was not at all maniacal, although 'Yellow Submarine' was sung at an anti-war rally at Berkeley in 1966, and in 1969 the Manson gang used quotes from 'Helter Skelter' as cues for carnage. But Lennon, domiciled in Greenwich Village with Yoko Ono after the band broke up, did flirt with the protest movement. He befriended Bobby Seale of the Black Panthers and composed a song condemning the imprisonment of the marijuana-smoking activist John Sinclair, whose release it secured. Lennon and Ono campaigned for peace in Vietnam by spending a week in bed in hotel rooms in Amsterdam and Montreal, demonstrating the virtue of disarmed passivity. By way of retaliation, the federal authorities declared Lennon an 'undesirable alien' and spent four years attempting to deport him. Impish as ever, he joked that it was like being in trouble at school in England, except that the Immigration and Naturalization Service had not yet caned him.

In 1973 he and Ono reacted to this harassment by dreaming up their own private America, an immaculate version of the messy microcosm Jagger hoped to convene at Altamont. Called Nutopia, it was a conceptual state with 'no laws other than cosmic' and a flag that was pure white, even more blameless than Jasper Johns' bleached specimens. As the ambassadors of this landless, unbounded country, Lennon and Ono made a plaintive request for diplomatic immunity. They also petitioned for Nutopia's admission to the United Nations, which only recognized states that actually existed. Eventually the INS lost its case and Lennon was granted a green card. Accepting it, he uttered the Black Panther catchphrase 'Right on, brother' with flat Lancashire vowels: it was his way of asserting that he belonged in this nation of immigrants and idealists, whether or not he was a native son.

Christian fundamentalists fumed when Lennon joked that the Beatles were more popular than Jesus Christ, and accused him of corrupting American morals. For another English visitor, the transaction was the other way around. David Hockney paid his first visit to the country in 1961, hoping that America would corrupt his gawky provincial timidity. He recorded the stages of his supposed self-degradation in a series of etchings that he entitled, following Hogarth, *A Rake's Progress.*

With its strumpets and gin mills, London pauperizes and deranges Hogarth's Tom Rakewell. Hockney found the soft, sensual enticements of New York to be harmless, and never risked relegation to the madhouse at Bedlam. The etchings show him to be a bespectacled innocent abroad – the role Americans used to assume in Europe – who happily sheds his inhibitions in this brash, brazen society. Arriving, his first stop is a penile skyscraper that semaphores pleasure, not power or ambition: its length is taut like knobbly, vibrant flesh, its tip is suggestively rounded, and its pinnacle sends out a climactic jet of light. Hockney, who lands in an aerodynamic blur with the legend FLYING TYGER trailing behind him, seems to have been fired directly at it. Next to the skyscraper is a long shadowy box: the package it came in, like a sex toy? Or perhaps this is the deathly barrier of denial through which the would-be rake must crash. Hockney's alter ego begins his tour by confronting 'the Good People' – icons of republican virtue in Washington, a gospel singer at Madison Square Garden. The statuesque Lincoln is a darkly disapproving father figure, and Jefferson stands beneath his dome with his hands behind his back like a drill sergeant on the parade ground. The monument to George Washington, however, is another tapered phallic shaft, and in the evangelical revels at Madison Square Garden the hallelujahing singer has unclad breasts shaped like nonmetallic missiles. Her followers wear ties announcing that GOD IS LOVE, and the lightly pencilled word HEAVEN sketches Hockney's preliminary definition of America: a place where heaven descends to earth, from which Hogarthian hellfire is banished.

The initiation of Hockney's rake – a splash that corresponds to the immersive delight of the swimming pools he painted later in California – comes when he applies peroxide to his lank, mousy hair. The etching is captioned 'The Start of the Spending Spree' and should mark the onset of dissolute self-destruction, but the bottle of Lady Clairol that he balances on his head is cheap, and it works wonders. The image testifies to instant gratification:

a door swings open, palm trees gyrate in a tropical breeze, an excited sun rises out of the ocean. Once his hair is dyed Hockney overcomes his shyness. He stares appreciatively at two male joggers, the cartoonish halo of dashes around his head signifying both sweat and desire, and he learns about Whitmanesque fraternity in a bar where he watches couples matily clutching each other.

The downfall that follows is a fate that Hockney, so hedonistically fulfilled by America, never had to experience. Prison, drunkenness, destitution, a sordid demise in Harlem – such endings are better suited to edgy, flagrantly neurotic Abstract Expressionists. The madmen in Hockney's etching roam free in what Crèvecoeur called 'the great American asylum', a permissive playground not a disciplinary enclosure. Not locked in the cellular mind like Hogarth's lunatics, they are sedated into conformity, attuned to the same frequency: their back pockets are fitted with transistors that pipe treacly mood music into their heads, and they wear identical T-shirts proclaiming I SWING WITH W ABC. Perhaps a private Bedlam is resounding in their ears, but its aim is soothingly medicinal.

Returning in 1964, Hockney advanced to California. Because he could not drive he was advised to go to San Francisco, but he chose motorized Los Angeles, lured by John Rechy's novel about its underworld of male hustlers, *City of Night*. On arrival he cycled fifteen miles from Santa Monica to Pershing Square – which was deserted, not aswarm with cruising sexual opportunists as Rechy's book promised – and then back. Once again, his experiment in rakery fizzled. He adjusted to the city by applying for a provisional licence, buying a car and heading east. Not daring to use the off-ramps on the freeway, he kept straight ahead until he reached Las Vegas; by then he found he knew how to drive.

He prepared to transcribe his new surroundings by stocking up on acrylic paint, which suited the smooth enamelled skies of southern California, its pastel-coloured houses, and the grass that might have been and sometimes was Astroturf. Because acrylic dried quickly, it also kept up with his breezy drive-by vision. His first Los Angeles painting, *Plastic Tree Plus City Hall*, simply manoeuvres two touristic emblems into proximity, though Hockney allows the dwarfish tree to be taller than the building, which then kept a domineering eye on the official centre of the centrifugal city. His early lithographs of Wilshire, Olympic and Washington Boulevards are interchangeable except for the street signs: in each case the image contains a blank building like a cardboard carton, with frayed palm fronds as a decorative afterthought. These were happy, casual acts of appropriation, less dutifully comprehensive than the photographic inventories of twenty-six gas stations, thirty-four parking lots and thirty-eight apartment houses made by Ed Ruscha on his treks around Los Angeles in the early 1960s. Ruscha let a machine do the observing for him, and attached an automatic camera drive to the rear of a pickup truck so he could snap every building on either side of the Sunset Strip without needing to look closely. Hockney, however, never lost the newcomer's amazement at this lush oasis, conjured from the desert with stolen water. His Los Angeles is fluent, liquefied: water dribbles from hoses, hangs in vaporous clouds above irrigated lawns, and sketches calligraphic designs on the surface of backyard pools. He cared more for these domestic tributaries than for the ocean, although he often remarked that the Pacific deserved its name, since it mostly behaves with peaceful languor. The city was like an outdoor extension of the luxuriously plumbed American bathrooms that Edmund Wilson preferred to sombre, uplifting European cathedrals.

American sublimity interested Hockney less. In his 1965 painting *Rocky Mountains and Tired Indians* the mountains are a striped wave, no longer rugged or precipitous, and a bucket chair has been provided for the benefit of the footsore Indians, who in any case do not belong in this vicinity. Eventually he did face up to a grander, less domestic America. His photocollage of the Brooklyn Bridge in 1982 takes the structure to pieces and then reassembles it: thanks to Hockney's placement of his Polaroids, the central arch now bulges outwards, not shuddering with shocks of energy as it does in John Marin's paintings but comfortably widening to admit the walker whose expensive polished shoes are positioned at the bottom edge of the composition, politely waiting on America's doorstep. The poet Hart Crane called the bridge both harp and altar, its aesthetic and religious functions fused by the welding that made its steel cables malleable. Hockney had no need for such over-heated metaphorical engineering, and the boardwalk and the steps ahead of him are cleared for his advance.

He tackled the Grand Canyon in another fan-shaped collage, and in 1998 painted *A Bigger Grand Canyon* by dividing that scarcely comprehensible emptiness into a grid and distributing it over sixty canvases. As Arnold Schwarzenegger put it, the phenomenon of America is about power, which – before power took the form of money or of skyscrapers and rockets – meant the potentiality of open space. On the rim of the canyon, Hockney prepared himself for the intellectual feat of confronting 'big space' by reflecting on the cosmological speculations of Carl Sagan, who thought that 'God must be even greater than we dreamed of. Much bigger. The universe, bigger. Grander. Vaster. More spacious.' This made Hockney's task harder, because he now had to conceive of infinitude, not just a hole in the ground. Nevertheless, despite those straining comparative adjectives, God does not make an appearance in his flushed mural. The painter looks across rather than down into the canyon, avoiding the crevasse in which space measures the time it took for the Colorado River to slice its way through those cross-sectioned cliffs. Almost in self-defence, Hockney beautifies the scene: purple bluffs, a distant rim that is orange, red tree trunks and green foliage. The canyon, which has many ways of killing you, here looks almost liveable, with lookouts fenced off for safety and paths and trails that suggest routes for a leisurely stroll. Rather than aiming to conquer America, Hockney simply wanted to make it a home.

17 | Dialogues with Consumer Products

In 1957, in a study of the advertising industry, Vance Packard quoted the jubilation of an American sales executive, who defined a new economic era when he announced 'Capitalism is dead – consumerism is king!' This was not the finale to history that Marx had predicted, and the new state of affairs prompted the social theorists Theodor Adorno and Max Horkheimer to meet in Frankfurt in 1956 to discuss a book in which they intended to update *The Communist Manifesto*. Adorno and Horkheimer had escaped to the United States from the Third Reich, then returned to Germany after the war. In 1944, in their *Dialectic of Enlightenment*, they foresaw a collapse into barbarism. Instead humanity was reprieved by an Americanized affluence, evident in the fabled economic recovery of Germany, which began in 1948 when Economics Minister and future Chancellor Erhard abolished price controls on consumer goods. But Adorno and Horkeimer were less than overjoyed by this happy ending. Their priority in 1956 was to decide whether they should be 'for or against America' – the country that saved their lives, and of which Horkheimer was now a citizen. Historically, they agreed with the philosopher Ernest Bloch, who took refuge in the United States in 1938 but moved back to Germany in 1949: American society, Bloch said, was a neon-lit impasse, offering no solution to the inequities analysed by Marx.

When Adorno reviled America, Horkheimer reminded him of its positive benefits, such as 'the reliability of the legal system, the drugstores, etcetera', after which the list petered out. With a little more enthusiasm, he declared that 'the USA is the country of argument', a place of good-humoured debate with no trace of German authoritarianism. But both men were vexed by this leisured society, where the grinding logic of their dialectic had come to a halt. Either machines performed the hard labour, which left the workers with no chains to lose, or else resources were wasted, as Adorno said, in 'production for its own sake'. David Riesman's *The Lonely Crowd* argued that the nineteenth-century American model of economic man – striving, diligent, good with his hands – had been replaced by 'a new "plastic man"', a passive and perpetually famished consumer whose tastes heeded the dictates of the market. Adorno and Horkheimer worried that America's cascade of covetable goods had bribed workers to forget their grievances; rather than identifying themselves as members of the proletariat, they aspired to suburban prosperity, bolstered by the latest appliances. It bothered Horkheimer that 'the opposite of work is . . . nothing more than consumption', though he admitted that people enjoyed advertisements and were content to obey their commands. Adorno abhorred mass culture and wished he could get rid of rubbishy television programmes – but how, and by what right? Already omnipresent in American households, television served, in Riesman's phrase, as a 'tutor in consumption'; the media, as C. Wright Mills said, were 'mass persuaders' and kept the economy functioning by inciting 'artificial frenzies'. Packard's study of advertising went further, narrowing the gap between the two sides in the Cold War. With their mnemonic jingles and their sly subliminal suggestions, the copywriters had turned Americans, he believed, into 'the most manipulated people outside the Iron Curtain'.

For Adorno and Horkheimer, the spectre that stalked Europe was not Gary Cooper on horseback but Marlon Brando on his motorbike in *The Wild One*. The brain-weary savants worried at length about the significance of this modish form of transport, which had become essential for American rebels. Horkheimer decided that the true proletarian pleasure in riding a bike lay in 'the anal sound it emits', an impertinent fart. A few days later, after pondering the phenomenon, he added that the rider was simply the captive of ideology, seduced by a sales pitch. Adorno disagreed, and saw the bike as 'congealed labour power', allowing workers to bestride the machines that enslaved them.

The longer Adorno and Horkheimer talked, the more remote the prospect of an uprising by the underclass became. Perhaps capitalism had indeed expired; certainly it had advanced beyond their comprehension. Transferred to Europe, the problem was placed on show in Godard's *Tout va bien*, released in 1972. At a Carrefour supermarket in Lille, shoppers load their trolleys with outsize packages of American detergents like Palmolive, Persil, Skip, Ajax and Omo, while a communist agitator tries without success to sell discounted copies of a party tract near the check-out lanes. Abuse is exchanged and punches thrown; the police sent in to control the mob help themselves to the merchandise stacked on the shelves, so Marx loses out.

Horkheimer grumbled that the commodities distributed so wantonly in supermarkets like this were 'pseudo-consumer goods', because 'exchange value is substituted for use value', which has become steadily truer in the last half-century. Fashion demands that clothes must be bought all over again every season whether or not they are worn out, and it is shameful to be seen with last year's version of the currently most coveted electronic toy. The frenzies referred to by Wright Mills are no longer artificial: Nike's release of its Foamposite Galaxy shoe provoked riots at a Florida mall in February 2012, and stampedes are customary when shops open for Black Friday sales after Thanksgiving, with one or two shootings every year. Revolutions today do not begin when crowds storm a prison like the Bastille, or empty consignments of imported tea into the Boston harbour. The mobs that took to the streets throughout London in August 2011 looted shops stocking branded footwear or Apple electronics, and scooped up grooming products from the shelves in pharmacies. The police classify such acts as 'acquisitive crime'.

During the 1950s, Wright Mills described a bazaar like Macy's as a cathedral, whose rituals accompanied customers from the cradle to the grave. The institution that now discharges that function is larger and more all-embracing than any single department store. The Mall of America, also known as the Megamall or the Sprawl of America, opened in 1992 in Bloomington, Minnesota; it has room for seven Yankee Stadiums and 258 Statues of Liberty, although it actually contains 520 shops, an aquarium, an amusement park and an indoor forest, with facilities for hosting birthday parties, weddings, family reunions and 'senior outings', though as yet no funeral parlour. To patronize such establishments counts as a solemn civic duty. In October 2001, just before New York Fashion Week, Mayor Giuliani urged his constituents to defy Al Qaeda and show off America's valour and its values by returning to the emporia of Fifth Avenue or to their local malls.

'Freedom to shop,' he said, 'is one of the fundamental liberties the terrorists want to deprive us of.'

The impetus of this economy was invested in a new sector of the population, unknown before the American 1950s. Baby boomers, born immediately after the war, grew up to be the world's first teenagers. No longer children yet not quite adults, they enjoyed a certain independence, made possible by pocket money from their indulgent parents and later by after-school jobs as babysitters, shelf-fillers in supermarkets and employees in fast-food restaurants. In 1968 the film *Wild in the Streets* speculated, at first humorously and then with hysterical foreboding, about what might happen if their precocious purchasing power made them demand political representation. The voting age is lowered to fourteen, and as a consequence an adolescent demagogue is elected President; he revenges himself on the oldies who imposed the Vietnam draft by sentencing them to euthanasia or internment in camps where they are force-fed LSD. A senatorial candidate is aghast to discover that his son supports this juvenile despot. When the boy is advised to trust his father's wiser head, he replies 'That's what George III told the American people in 1776.' Another newly enfranchised teenager delivers a druggy address to Congress while banging her tambourine: her message is that 'America's greatest contribution has been to teach the world that getting old is such a drag.' Revolution, for which Adorno and Horkheimer still tenuously hoped, had been replaced by rejuvenation.

In January 1969 *Fortune* examined the way in which American youth was 'changing the world'. By 'the world' it meant the American economic system, represented in a double-page advertising spread by a square-jawed allegorical figure labelled 'The American Capitalist', who with funds from Chemical Bank has 'parlayed . . . smart money management into a growing empire'. The magazine's editors were troubled by students who questioned careerist values, scoffed at the law, rejected military service, and therefore hardly qualified for membership of society: *Time* nicknamed them YADs, meaning Young American Disaffiliates. Menacing ads paraded the might of the America these dissenters challenged. The aircraft carrier *Enterprise*, at sea with a loaded deck of fighter jets, appeared twice in *Fortune*, first illustrating the hydraulic and pneumatic capacities of Aeroquip Corporation and secondly vouching for the computer systems developed by Univac. One of the articles reassuringly argued that there was no danger of social break-down, as in France during the riots of May 1968; the American problem was merely the threat to commerce. *Fortune* therefore proposed treating the dis-affected generation as a marketing opportunity, and suggested that General Motors might relaunch its Oldsmobile as the Youngmobile. J. C. Penney had already treated its salesmen to a crash course in 'Youth Concepts' and psychedelia, issued them with samples – including an empty marijuana pouch – and encouraged suppliers to design clothes in colours like purple and fuchsia that might appeal to young people who lacked 'brand loyalties'. IBM adapted and modified the rhetoric of the dissidents, inviting its custom-ers to 'make the world *a better place to live in*', which meant that it was to be made more comfortable, not necessarily more equitable.

As they aged and outgrew their radicalism, the teenagers of the 1960s revised the new American creed proclaimed by the tambourine-wielding girl in *Wild in the Streets*. On American television today, senior citizens in commercial breaks remain in a permanent prime thanks to vitamin sup-plements, surgical nips and tucks, cosmetic dental implants, discreet flesh-toned hearing aids, doses of Viagra, and adult diapers. Even disability can be made to look sporty and agile. A folding walker sold to immobilized afternoon viewers is punningly called a Hurry Cane, which gives its tottering user a gale-force velocity, and a range of motorized wheelchairs goes by the name of Jazzy. The superannuated film star Lorne Guyland in Martin Amis's *Money* is ridiculed for his 'tan-and-silver sheen', which makes him look as if welded from 'zinc and chrome and circuitry coolant'. But Amis's go-getting British protagonist John Self is not averse to eternal youth, and after a binge in New York he plans to replace or renew his over-taxed body, hoping that in California his scalp can be sown with synthetic turf and his mouth made to gleam afresh with 'cobalt and Strontium 90'. Death, like the revolution, must be postponed, so that the career of consuming can continue indefinitely.

Travelling through Pennsylvania, the Austrian hero of Peter Handke's novel *Short Letter, Long Farewell* listens as a woman he has met regales him with an account of her household appliances. She has a dishwasher, though she complains that some of her cooking pots are too large for the machine and must be scrubbed by hand. With only herself and a small child to feed, he wonders why she needs such huge pans. She explains that she cooks in bulk and stores the food in her deep freeze; she is about to depart on a road trip, and wants to have a vat of soup ready for defrosting when she returns. Handke's narrator understands her magical thinking: 'I had the feeling that nothing could possibly go wrong before the fall came and she would thaw out that soup.' She lives in an American future with which Europe has not yet caught up. Subsistence has been replaced by surfeit, and a full freezer, like the contents of a safety deposit box, guarantees that happiness will last forever.

In time, American youth did change the rest of the world – or at least it altered the tastes of young people everywhere. Advertising agencies identified the group with the hungriest appetite for consumer goods as 'New World Teens', who lived in Europe or Asia but modelled themselves on their brand-conscious contemporaries in the United States. In 2001 the journalist Mark Hertsgaard found the species thriving in South Africa, where a bus driver wearing a Jack Daniel's baseball cap told him about two rival gangs who were permanently at odds in the country's urban townships. The Young Americans (named after a David Bowie song that mentions Ford Mustangs and Barbie dolls in its survey of accelerated, immature teenage life) concentrated on copying the clothes they saw in music videos; the Ugly Americans wanted to acquire the guns used by their prototypes in Detroit or Los Angeles. Hertsgaard asked whether the generation to which the driver's parents belonged was equally infatuated by the United States. 'No,' his informant replied, 'they are more Christian.' The non sequitur was startling but logical: people who have been Americanized want paradise now, and are unwilling to wait for the resurrection.

In 1965 in *Masculin féminin*, Godard defined these picky faddists as 'the children of Marx and Coca-Cola'. In the film they drift between such unParisian institutions as a bowling alley or a laundromat, attend events like the

'100% Soirées Rock' announced in pidgin on a placard in the street, and learn English in the remote hope of making movie deals in Hollywood. A young woman says she is practising birth control with 'a gadget from America', brought back for her by an Air France pilot: are the Americans intent on sterilizing France, or practising genocide by stealth? The most rebarbative episode in the film is captioned 'Dialogue with a Consumer Product'. The personified commodity – interviewed by Jean-Pierre Léaud, who relays questions transmitted to him by Godard through an earpiece – is a harmless girl who has won a teen magazine's contest to identify Miss 19. Complacent, unintrospective, not very articulate, she squirms through an interrogation that lasts for six gruelling minutes. Asked whether she would rather live as the Americans do or be a socialist, she says she does not understand the difference. Asked to define 'la vie américaine', she comments that it is very fast and very free. Léaud refrains from inquiring what America frees you to do; the answer would be that you are free to consume, or to present yourself as a fatuously glamourized article for consumption in the market, like the girl he browbeats.

Godard's paradoxical slogan glossed over a dispute between Marxists and those who placed their faith in fizzy drinks, and on the soundtrack of *Masculin féminin* gunshots – perhaps the first round of a revolution – inconclusively alternate with the chirping of cash registers. 'Do vacuum cleaners sell? Do you like cheese in tubes?' asks Godard in one of his rebarbative voice-over editorials. The two questions call for different answers: Hoover and Electrolux had universal appeal because they saved labour, but they posed no threat to Brie, Camembert, Roquefort, Pont l'Evèque, Tomme de Savoie, Époisses and the other varieties of ingeniously metamorphosed milk that the French consume. Godard defined the agitator played by Léaud as a European whose world has been redefined by America, calling him 'a descendant of Werther . . . lost somewhere between the Negroes and Vietnam'. The sorrowful poet Werther in Goethe's novel could vent his distress in nature, moaning to compete with its tempests; Léaud's acts of protest are never more than practical jokes, ineffectual whether their outcome is absurd or deadly. He paints peace slogans on a car driven by an American military chauffeur and, less amusingly, donates a match to a passer-by who then splashes gasoline on his clothes and sets himself alight outside the American Hospital in Neuilly. In a mood of angry isolationism, Léaud maintains the integrity of France by pretending not to know who Bob Dylan is. A friend explains that Dylan is a Vietnik but adds, with a hint of envy, that he sells ten thousand records a day: Marx is once more trounced by the lucrative attraction of retail.

Masculin féminin is set during the run-up to a presidential election between de Gaulle and François Mitterrand, and Léaud anticipates the outcome by sadly intoning the prayer of the French people, which is 'Give us a television set and a car, but deliver us from liberty.' Yet those who had saved up for their first television set and car – taken for granted in America, still extravagances in post-war Europe – surely felt liberated by their purchases, given access to a larger mental and physical world. Arthur Miller allowed the Chinese to covet Willy Loman's refrigerator, but Godard regarded French people who aspired to own such appliances as robotic ads for Americana. At a cocktail party in *Pierrot le fou* the characters sing the praises of their possessions, the men rhapsodizing about the Oldsmobiles or Lincolns they drive while a woman testifies to the sleek fit of her Maidenform girdle. In another of his commentaries in *Masculin féminin* Godard reports that 'American scientists have succeeded in transferring ideas between one brain and another by injection.' In fact no syringe was necessary: the transfusion was already underway, thanks to the desires implanted by the writers of advertising copy. Godard regarded advertisers as pimps, with all of us as their compliant whores; in *Made in USA*, Anna Karina calls advertising a form of fascism – a means of mind control, pulping individuality and making everyone a second-hand American.

Travelling late at night on the Métro, Léaud in *Masculin féminin* eavesdrops on an argument between a French woman and a black man, presumably an American. They are performing a scene taken from LeRoi Jones's play *Dutchman*, in which the conversation occurs on the New York subway. He ridicules her for imitating a Hollywood hooker, and sneers at whites who praise Bessie Smith's cracked, careworn voice without understanding that her songs are about the plight of her race. *Dutchman* ends with the woman coolly killing the man, whose body is thrown off the train like garbage, but the brief extract in *Masculin féminin* stops short before she can fire the gun she conceals in her lap. Out of context, relocated to Paris, the argument is between continents not races, and the bigoted, homicidal woman is now charged with a different crime – not murder but a craven obsession with America.

The mismatch between Marx and Coca-Cola produced no offspring but, a few decades later, personifications of Europe and America did copulate in public. The representatives of the two cultures were Jeff Koons and Ilona Staller, professionally known as Cicciolina. He was a commodities broker on Wall Street who reinvented himself as an artist while believing, in an adroit summation of Reagan's career, that 'salesmen are today's great communicators'; she was a Hungarian chambermaid who spied on American diplomats in a Budapest hotel before moving to Italy and reinventing herself as a porn star. Cicciolina had ambitions to be a global unifier. She offered to make love to Saddam Hussein if it would help to ensure 'universal peace', specifying that she would hold her nose and keep her eyes closed for the duration; after 9/11 she remarked that her breasts had harmed no one whereas Osama bin Laden had killed thousands, though this time she refrained from offering her body to defuse the war on terror. She married Koons in 1991, and their union produced a son, together with a series of soft-porn tableaux documenting their lithe-limbed sex life, grouped together under the title 'Made in Heaven'.

The marriage made in heaven merged utility and sanctity. Koons's contribution was the American domestic gadgets and leisure toys that he exhibited as sculptures: a two-tiered array of Hoover vacuum cleaners, a deep fryer, a coffee percolator, an electric broom, a shampoo polisher for floors, and a Spalding basketball that hovered in mid-air inside an equilibrium tank like a foetus swimming in its amniotic ocean. Cicciolina brought with her a venerable European dowry, enabling Koons to claim that he was 'in the realm of the spiritual'. She connected him to the ecstatic eroticism of the baroque, exemplified by Bernini's swooning St Teresa, and to the ornamental excess of the rococo, which melted down gold and dribbled it on altars for the glory of God. They split up after a year, but the marriage of continents, joined by a consumerist cult that had replaced the ebbing Catholic faith, was by then indissoluble.

The journalist William Allen White once described Coca-Cola as 'a sublimated essence of all that America stands for'. That makes it sound as mysterious as the quintessence sought by the alchemists, and it is indeed brewed from a secret formula guarded in a vault in Atlanta and has a brand name that alludes to coca, the plant whose leaves, when chemically treated, can be turned into cocaine. As a bonus, sublimation suggests that it has the power to change the drinker's mood, administering an almost spiritual afflatus. Thanks to Coca-Cola, America is a potion as well as a place. In the 1956 film *Invasion of the Body Snatchers*, interstellar spores rain down and replace ebullient Californians with affectless duplicates hatched in pods. A travelling salesman quickly spots the difference between the real thing, so vitally bubbly, and this flat, stale simulacrum: 'You can hardly even buy a Coke at most places,' he grouses.

After 1941 Coke helped America to win the world, and conquered new markets along the way. Technical Observers attached to the army in Europe and the Pacific ensured that the GIs were reliably supplied with carbonated drinks, which were said to boost their morale. Empty bottles did a secondary service as weapons, dumped from the air onto Japanese landing strips so the shards could rip the tyres of planes taking off. In Fritz Lang's *American Guerrilla in the Philippines*, a local boy congratulates Tyrone Power on the surrender of the Japanese by presenting him with a Coke, wrapped in a hat because there is no ice. Power, raising the bottle in a salutation among a sky of flags, says 'For three years I'd have sold my soul for one of these!' The remark perhaps had a sardonic undertone: many of the characters in the films Lang made in Berlin before he quit the Third Reich sell their souls for cocaine, and despite the director's professed loyalty to his adopted country he may have remembered a comment by Otto Dietrich, Hitler's press chief, who said in 1942 that America's only bequests to world civilization were chewing gum and Coca-Cola. Still, what other drink could be used to toast victory?

During the post-war occupation of Germany, Eisenhower dosed his Russian colleague Georgy Zhukov with Coca-Cola, and even commissioned a contraband version with the caramel dye removed and a red star stamped on the bottle so that Zhukov and his intimates could enjoy it without incurring ideological disapproval. This arrangement was not so remote from the satirical invention of Billy Wilder's *One, Two, Three*, where James Cagney, on a mission to disseminate 'the blessings of democracy', offers to spare the deprived Russian masses from having to drink Kremlin Cola, which is used in Albania as sheep dip. He stamps his foot when he is refused permission to install a Coke machine in the Berlin Reichstag, angrily asking 'Who won the war anyway?' A snub at the end of the film teases those global ambitions: Cagney plugs a dispensing machine with coins at Tempelhof Airport and receives in return three Cokes and a Pepsi. A few years earlier, Wilder mocked the rival brand in *Love in the Afternoon*, where Maurice Chevalier plays a Parisian private detective whose client has been cuckolded by Gary Cooper, an American businessman with a financial interest in Pepsi-Cola. 'The pause that refreshes?' asks the horned husband. Chevalier manages an even more salacious innuendo when he explains that the slogan of Coke's competitor is 'Pepsi hits the spot'. These American drinks are silly but somehow indecent, which is why Chevalier's daughter, played by Audrey Hepburn, has been kept in ignorance of them. Enticed by Cooper to sip champagne, she tipsily asks 'Is this Pepsi-Cola?'

The foreign brand emerged from underground in Eastern Europe in 1990: after the breaching of the Berlin Wall, the corporate ensign of Coca-Cola – red in colour, but not because it had been dipped in the blood of communism's martyrs – was symbolically raised above the former STASI headquarters in Leipzig. Only in Vietnam did Coke cross sides, in an ultimate proof of the war's moral mayhem. Crates stolen from the army's commissaries were distributed to peasants who sympathized with the Vietcong; they set up roadside stalls and resold Cokes to passing GIs at the then-shocking premium rate of 50 cents a can. When trade slackened, they returned to laying landmines which were intended to kill their thirsty customers. By the time of the first Gulf War there were no doubts about the brand's patriotic credentials, and Coca-Cola sponsored General Schwarzkopf's homecoming celebration in Tampa in 1991.

Coke served as a kind of currency, liquefying transactions between Americans and the populations with whom they had dealings. The refrain of a calypso from Trinidad – bowdlerized by the Andrews Sisters, who recorded it in 1945 – remembered the way it helped GIs in the West Indies to extract sexual favours from local girls:

> Drinkin' rum and Coca-Cola
> Go down Point Koomahnah
> Both mother and daughter
> Workin' for the Yankee dollar.

Yves, the young French lover of the American hero in Baldwin's *Another Country*, recalls a family history of compromise with the invaders. His slatternly mother kept a Paris bistro in which she fraternized first with German soldiers, then with the Americans who ousted them. In the 1950s she re-outfitted the place by junking its wooden chairs and tables in favour of squeaky laminate and acquiring a jukebox to replace the 'metal football players of the *baby-foot*', a bar game that bewildered the ham-fisted GIs. Along with flickering neon strips, Yves remembers that 'there were Coca-Cola signs, and Coca-Cola'. The signs have priority in his recollection because they proclaimed modernity, so that the drink itself was almost an afterthought. Out of sight, the bar's lavatory – a hole in the floor with foot rests on either side and a supply of tattered newspaper pinioned by a nail – remained gruesomely unAmericanized.

Time summed up the ambiguity of Coca-Colonization on its cover in May 1950. An anthropomorphized globe clasps a Coke bottle in its hand, plugs the rim into its face, and empties the contents through an orifice in the South Atlantic. Did this imply that the brand had turned the world into a guzzling infant? The sweaty globe is goggle-eyed, its pursed lips fastened around the bottle like a nipple. Paraphrasing the company's protestations of goodwill, the illustration is headlined 'WORLD & FRIEND', but underneath is a smarmy summary of profits from new markets in the Middle East, Europe and South Africa – 'Love that piaster, that lira, that tickey, and that American way of life'. For the Chilean poet Pablo Neruda, the new global order proclaimed by the Coke drinkers amounted to nothing less than a revision of Genesis. Looking up from what he described as the sweet waist or succulent girdle of America, he described Jehovah ceremonially dividing the world between Coca-Cola, Ford Motors, the Anaconda copper mining corporation and United Fruit, which had exclusive rights to the produce of Neruda's juicy homeland.

Effervescing internally, Coke conjures up America's mythical promise. At corporate headquarters in Atlanta, an exhibition inside a gigantic vending machine that illustrates 'the Coca-Cola side of life' is called the Happiness Factory. A television commercial in the 1970s described Coke as a benefaction to humanity: a multicultural crowd of youngsters romped on a hilltop with lighted candles and sang of their desire 'to build the world a home and furnish it with love'. On the occasion of Coca-Cola's centenary in 1986, twelve thousand bottlers from 125 countries were invited to Atlanta, where the company's chief executive asked them to join hands. 'The United Nations can't do it,' he said. 'We're not mad at anybody. Can you feel the energy? Can you feel the love?' As well as accomplishing wonders beyond the power of diplomacy, Coke vouches for American egalitarianism. It is a leveller, averse to the snobbery of wine connoisseurs: Andy Warhol was pleased to think that the high and mighty – by which he meant Elizabeth Taylor and the President of the United States – drank the same Coke as everyone else. The lookalike bottles in his silk screens celebrated a society that mass-produced people, simplifying the human prototype and standardizing tastes to increase economic output.

At the end of *2 ou 3 Choses que je sais d'elle*, Godard constructs a toytown that is his own version of Europe's newly Americanized cities. Laid out on a manicured lawn, it consists of cartons containing detergents like Tide, Ajax and Dash, boxes of cigarettes and batteries, and – presumably to vouch for the presence of culture – a packet of Hollywood Chewing Gum. These are our age's cardboard monuments, supplanting the arches, towers and steeples of more eternal cities. What if the mementoes our civilization leaves behind are the Coke bottle with its light-emitting diodes that glows above Times Square, or perhaps a Coke can squashed in the gutter on Broadway? Coca-Cola, an elixir of liveliness, almost inevitably finds its way into stories about the end of our world. In Nevil Shute's *On the Beach*, the only evidence of life in the northern hemisphere after a nuclear war is a signal tapped out by a radio transmitter near Seattle; it turns out, when the noise is investigated, that it is made by a Coke bottle jolted onto the telegraph keys in an abandoned power station when a breeze blows through an open window. In Cormac McCarthy's equally apocalyptic *The Road*, a father pushing a grocery cart through depopulated America finds an unopened can of Coke and solemnly offers it to his son. The boy sips it slowly, aware that this is his first and probably last chance to taste the fabled drink. Which is sadder – a drained but indestructible bottle left behind as an archaeological relic, or a full can that represents the life we expend as we do the compulsory work of consuming?

Consumerism refers to an alimentary process, though the idea is now so crucial to the world's economy that it serves as an omnivorous, infinitely adaptable metaphor. Hence the redefinition of appetite, turning an ancient vice into a modern virtue. In 1986 in a commencement address at the Berkeley Business School, the stock speculator Ivan Boesky – imprisoned a year later for insider trading – announced 'I think greed is healthy. You can be greedy and still feel good about yourself.' Being or doing good now mattered less than feeling good, the glow of self-satisfaction that derives from a full belly.

The exemplary consumer of that glutted era was Patrick Bateman in Bret Easton Ellis's novel *American Psycho*, who during the daylight hours works as an investment banker on Wall Street, idolizes Boesky, and summarizes his mastery of the universe by revising the conventional boy-meets-girl plot of Hollywood movies. 'The world of most of us,' he says, consists of 'big ideas, guy stuff, boy meets world, boy gets it.' Gorged on pornographic videos, Bateman kills the women he seduces, and in one case cooks and attempts to eat the corpse of a victim. On another occasion, neatly completing the cycle of consumption and excretion, he unpacks a cake of disinfectant meant for a urinal, coats it in chocolate, and serves it to a female dinner guest, who finds the taste a little minty. Bateman's only emotions are 'greed and, possibly, disgust', which in the lingo of consumerism is known as buyer's remorse. He blabs confessions, but no one wants to believe him. A date wants a decaff au lait; absent-mindedly – perhaps remembering his habit of hacking off a victim's head, scooping out the eyes and covering the unsightly cavities with expensive Alain Mikli sunglasses – he asks the waiter to bring her 'a decapitated coffee'. He tells another woman that he's 'into, oh, murders and executions'. She thinks he means mergers and acquisitions, and Ellis's verbal play makes the activities interchangeable. The frivolity of it all suggests that his outrages may be merely the indulgence of ravening fantasy – an example of the malign and morbid American 'cult of entertainment' which the Czech novelist Ivan Klíma blamed in 2002 for peddling 'violence, horror and perversion' to the rest of us.

Bateman's problem is disposal: he chops up the bodies of his women, dumps them in a bathtub, sprinkles them with quicklime, and waits for them to decompose. Here too he is exemplifying the contradictions of an affluent economy, which produces more than can ever be consumed and has to find ways of discarding the indigestible surplus. Warhol, so instinctively attuned to the way this society functioned, once remarked that whereas Europe's mercantile tradition directed people to 'buy and sell, sell and buy', Americans preferred to 'buy – people, money, countries', and would 'rather throw out than sell'; he then proved his point by going off to Macy's to stock up on unnecessary underwear. Given these spendthrift habits, the United States, despite possessing only 5 per cent of the world's population, churns out 25 per cent of its garbage. It is, as Robert Frank realized during a walk in Manhattan in 1969, a proud statistic. On his ramble, Frank catalogued the mattresses, record players, television sets, furniture, clothes and toys left on the streets of the Upper West Side to rot, or to be gathered up by passers-by. 'What a fantastic country,' he said, genuinely awestruck. Since this was the summer of Apollo 11, he wondered whether Neil Armstrong and his fellow astronauts might set up shop on the moon to redistribute the overflow throughout the galaxy.

During the next quarter-century, the automobile population of the United States increased six times faster than that of its human citizenry. What could be done with all those obsolete, unloved vehicles? In Robert Altman's *Nashville* a BBC reporter played by Geraldine Chaplin traipses through a graveyard of crushed metal located beside a busy freeway, like a hidden valley where elephants go to die. 'Oh cars,' she says, pointing her microphone at the hills of twisted tin, 'are you trying to tell me something?' Such dumps became monuments to the bulimia of the boom years. In DeLillo's *Underworld*, Ishmael and his Bronx gang scavenge cars that have been joyridden to death and ferry them to a scrap dealer in Brooklyn, who presides over 'a junkworld sculpture park'. Art – here and in the parking lot in the western desert where Klara Sax in DeLillo's novel paints flights of grounded Cold War bombers – is the reification of refuse, the detritus of our dreams. Klara says that J. Robert Oppenheimer gave his bomb the nickname shit, 'because it's garbage, it's waste material'. Another character in *Underworld*, employed in the government's nuclear missile programme, calls waste the 'devil twin' of creation, the archive of our 'underhistory'. DeLillo describes a mound of garbage at Fresh Kills Landfill on Staten Island as America's own pyramid of Giza, and the same metaphor occurs in Philip Roth's *American Pastoral*, where some gutted New Jersey factories beside a railway viaduct are 'the pyramids of Newark: as huge and dark and hideously impermeable as a great dynasty's burial edifice'. In the future, these accretions of waste may form a new topography, and DeLillo imagines a neck-craning tour of the peaks and crevasses of Plutonium National Park. Meanwhile we have seen actual American cities turned into waste lands, at least temporarily – the smoking ash heap of Ground Zero in Manhattan, from which debris was taken to rat-infested Fresh Kills; New Orleans awash after Hurricane Katrina; bankrupt Detroit left to moulder.

Others remain hungry for whatever America discards. The poorest

African nations still receive charitable bequests of pesticides that have passed their expiration date, and countries with nothing else to sell trade carbon credits, bestowing their own right to pollute on the United States. The Turkish novelist Orhan Pamuk remembers his fascination with the Coke cans, known as 'kukas', that he and his friends scavenged from rubbish tins in Ankara in 1961. Stamped flat, the metal skin could be turned into a sign that advertised anything but Coca-Cola; the finger-sized tabs, discarded after the top was ripped open, served as play money, a fantastical alternative to the dollar. In the Chinese province of Guangdong there is a city of electronic junk known as Laser Jet Town, a cemetery of defunct Hewlett-Packard technology where traces of gold are separated from electrical contacts in acid baths and circuit boards are heated on braziers until the solder leaks out. Ships sent to Bangladesh and other Asian scrap yards are broken up, then sunk to form reefs of tarnished metal. To supplement this non-organic coral, new floating continents of sludge and coagulated polymers thicken as they drift to and fro in the Pacific and Atlantic Oceans. Sometimes the rest of the world looks like America recycled.

18 | The Campaign to Free America

In 1941 Henry Luce rallied Americans to raise the spirits of the world by spreading 'joy and gladness and vigour and enthusiasm'. After the lethal fiasco of Vietnam and Nixon's disgrace, observers saw less evidence of the nation 'conceived in adventure' whose 'magnificent purposes' Luce extolled. Occasionally it seemed as if America needed to be rehabilitated. During George W. Bush's Gulf War, Lars von Trier was refused permission to have the American national anthem played as he mounted the red-carpeted stairs at Cannes for a screening of *Dogville*, an anatomy of sexual enslavement and economic exploitation in the Rockies that was the first film in a satirical trilogy he intended to call *USA, Land of Opportunities*. Fuming, von Trier said he would like to start 'a Free America campaign'. To free it from what? From its government, from a history that propagandists like Luce had misrepresented, and from the images of itself that had beguiled the world.

The other Europeans who joined von Trier in undertaking that work of liberation had forgotten the miserable dependency of 1945 and recovered their sense of historical pre-eminence. The German artist Joseph Beuys, for example, called the United States 'a totally destroyed country', where the 'West Principle', obsessed with the manufacture of goods, had reached its terminus. Beuys refused to cross the Atlantic until the American government signed a peace treaty with North Vietnam, apparently imagining that his absence would make Henry Kissinger more eager to negotiate; in January 1974 he decided that his conditions had been met, and undertook a ten-day lecture tour of New York, Chicago and Minneapolis. As the battle for control of the world's oil resources began, Beuys announced his own 'energy plan', which proposed replacing fossil fuels with the power of spirit, to be transmitted by magic not pumped into petrol tanks. He offered himself as a forerunner of the 'New West Man', a shaman able to undo the damage inflicted on America by the predatory individualists – specimens of 'Old West Man' – who ravaged the land and killed off its native inhabitants. On a second visit to New York in May 1974, Beuys performed this cure by bedding down with a coyote.

Intent on his mission, he preferred not to look at America, and groped through Kennedy Airport with his eyes covered. Nor did he set foot on the abused, trampled soil: swaddled in a blanket, he was carried on a stretcher to a hired ambulance that transported him, siren keening, to a gallery in downtown Manhattan. He entitled the performance he gave there *I like America and America likes Me*, though not much mutual esteem was evident. The Gothic script chosen for the poster was as prickly as barbed wire; behind it, a photographic negative of Beuys's head made him look like an ectoplasmic messenger from the beyond. Entering a wire-fenced enclosure in the gallery, with a turbine humming or roaring to voice the city's clamour, he 'made contact,' as he said, 'with the psychological trauma point of the United States' energy constellation'. The traumatized victim he endeavoured to heal was a coyote called Little John – a descendant, supposedly, of the Eurasian wolves that accompanied the wanderers who first crossed a land bridge from Siberia into empty America. Beuys could have shared the cage with an eagle, symbol of the 'abstract powers of the head', but the bird had been conscripted as a national symbol. A coyote suited him because it had escaped the massacre of indigenous species, a cull that recalled 'the Europe of the pogroms'; it deputized as well for the tribes exterminated or corralled into reservations as the settlers pushed west.

For three days, Beuys and the beast engaged in 'a silent dialogue', conducted through gestures. They relaxed on a bed of straw, and had a pile of *Wall Street Journals*, luckily refreshed each day, to soak up bodily emissions. To discharge his hieratic function, Beuys wore a wizard's cloak and hat of felt; he also carried a triangle, which he tapped to teach the coyote the harmonizing agency of music. A section of the video that documented the event shows him encased in the felt, no longer recognizably human, with a hooked stick protruding like a wand from his carapace. The coyote, eager for sport, nuzzles the cape and bites the stick. A title card interprets the scene as a re-enactment of the moment when the first white trespassers in America were offered 'the right hand of fellowship' by the trusting Indians, who saw the palefaces as celestial envoys. The skittish coyote, however, did not shake hands, or treat the intruder with superstitious reverence. Beuys rearranged the stack of newspapers beside its water bowl and advanced to another stage in the reconciliatory rite: according to another title card, this signalled that 'The Medicine Man . . . prepares the pit for the heated stories.' The coyote, not a good listener, scampered away; later it shredded the newsprint. It seemed not to recognize Beuys as its 'elder brother', which is how he thought that the bears and buffaloes regarded the Indians.

At last Beuys enfolded his squirming patient in an embrace and returned by ambulance to the airport. In 1979 he displayed some props from the New York performance at a gallery in Berlin. When the show closed, the gallery was gutted and the rubble – along with Beuys's toenail clippings, the hay bale, those grubby copies of *The Wall Street Journal*, and some hair shed by Little John – were packaged in sixty crates, shipped back to New York, and exhibited under the title *News from the Coyote*. The news was that the coyote, despairing of an accommodation with America, had gone into exile in Europe.

On his initial lecture tour, Beuys searched for traces of some relatives who had immigrated to Chicago early in the century to work in a bakery. As he explored the neighbourhood in which they had lived, he happened to find himself outside the Biograph, the cinema near Lincoln Park where the bank robber John Dillinger was ambushed by FBI agents in July 1934. On a whim, Beuys adopted Dillinger as an avatar, a potential superman led astray by 'negative energies', and re-enacted his death scene for a video, running out of the lobby to collapse in the street as if shot. Caged with the coyote, he ministered to America's victims; in this case he played one of its public enemies.

Dillinger was already established as an unofficial cultural hero, an outlaw and therefore an honorary artist. Burroughs cited him as a fellow martyr in *Naked Lunch*, admiring the nonchalance with which he ignored warnings to remain hidden and ventured out to the Biograph with the brothel-keeper who tipped off the FBI. Famous for his prison breaks, Dillinger was praised in 1948 by the critic Harold Rosenberg as an 'artist of escape', belonging in a tradition that extended from Odysseus to Houdini. Rosenberg had to admit that Dillinger's 'self-extrication' did not really qualify as a revolutionary act, but he remained a model for those who defied American power or wanted to free the country from its false values. Hence his reappearance in Marco Ferreri's 1969 film *Dillinger Is Dead*. The Milanese protagonist Glauco, trapped by his work and his marriage, listens to a colleague paraphrasing Herbert Marcuse on the plight of man in industrial society, affluent but unsatisfied; personifying that predicament, he drives home through streets ablaze with neon inducements to discontent – a sign advertising PAN AMERICAN, another that says CALIFORNIA. As he prepares dinner, Glauco fumbles in a kitchen cupboard and pulls out a dusty parcel tied with string. It contains newspapers reporting on Dillinger's death, wrapped around a gun that may or may not have belonged to America's most wanted man. Glauco studies the gun, lubricates its chamber with olive oil, takes it to pieces, spray-paints it red, then dabs on some white polka dots. Is it a piece of Pop art, even more harmless than the wooden pistol with which Dillinger bluffed his way out of an Indiana jail? Inducements to violent action dangle from the kitchen ceiling: *Time* with a cover story on 'The Gun in America', *Espresso* with an article about America by Alberto Moravia, illustrated by a fist that grips and squeezes the Statue of Liberty. Prompted by Dillinger's legacy, Glauco uses the gun to shoot his sleeping wife, then absconds on a yacht bound for Tahiti.

The conclusion is a dream of impunity, an extension of the home movies Glauco projects onto the wall of his apartment. It may explain why Dillinger went on his fatal outing to see *Manhattan Melodrama*, in which Clark Gable cheerily strolls to the electric chair, glad to be spared the tedium of long-term imprisonment. In 1977 Ferreri described the movies as a global village, and claimed that America, a society like 'a multicoloured caramel', would never have cohered if immigrants from so many nations had not found in this new art something they all loved and could share. It was their substitute for going to church – preferable, according to Ferreri, because they were not required to stand or kneel, and could make love in the discreet darkness of the back rows. Inside the Biograph, Dillinger was safe; when he stepped back onto the sidewalk, American reality took aim at him and killed him.

In 1978, like Beuys making restitution to the coyote, Ferreri commiserated with another victim of progressive America, the ape that scaled the

Empire State Building in *King Kong*. The film had recently been remade, with Kong now climbing the new World Trade Center, and Ferreri's *Bye Bye Monkey* was a footnote to this latest instalment of the myth. On a sandy landfill, Gérard Depardieu stumbles upon an inflatable rubber version of Kong. Having slumped to earth, it is sadly shrivelled, but out from under the tattered canopy crawls a live monkey, which Depardieu adopts. In both *King Kong* films, the ape on the skyscraper is toppled by gunfire from fighter planes, punished for its threat to a society that had stormed the heights vacated by the gods. Depardieu hopes to defuse the conflict by returning to our common evolutionary origins. He dresses his pet in baby clothes, installs it in a crib beside his bed, and registers its birth to ensure that it qualifies for American citizenship. But history cannot be rewritten: the monkey falls victim to a plague of rats that have been expelled into the streets by excavations for the corporate palaces of lower Manhattan.

Ferreri completes the story by setting fire to America – or at least to a facsimile of it, represented by a wax museum that supposedly commemorates the Roman Empire but in fact records America's inheritance of Rome's imperial role. In the museum's display, the head of Caesar, the victim of assassins, is replaced by that of Kennedy, and Nero acquires the mirthless smirking face of Nixon. Among the exhibits is the crucified Spartacus, said by Marcello Mastroianni – who plays a refugee from Italy, where he expects a communist takeover – to have been more valiant than Sitting Bull, and more nearly successful in his challenge to the army sent against him. The owner of the museum says that New Yorkers, like the Romans, are living in a 'time of decadence', and warns that once again 'the barbarians are at the gates'. As it happens, there is no need to wait for them to break down those gates: the wiring of the display that dramatizes Nero's urban arson crackles, sparks, then blazes up to melt the wax figures and kill all the human occupants of the place. In the background throughout the film loom two sculptural blocks with no discernible purpose and no apparent summit. In daylight scenes the towers disappear into the wintry fog, and at night they are ladders of light, like a pair of compressed and tidily stacked galaxies. Less than a quarter of a century later, they too were toppled.

The wax museum in *Bye Bye Monkey* probably derives from Umberto Eco's 'Travels in Hyperreality', an essay about America published in 1975. Eco noticed that the United States was 'spangled with wax museums', and made a point of visiting as many as he could, starting with Movieland in Buena Park, California, where stars like Jean Harlow returned to an eerie simulation of life and the charioteers from *Ben-Hur* rode again. Michael Jackson turned up for the unveiling of his likeness here, raising the question of which was more authentic, the original or the fake; Vincent Price once impersonated his own wax model, twitching and grinning to alarm the customers. With such ghoulish jests about what theologians call the real presence, American entertainment takes the place of religious revelation and makes the afterlife materialize here and now. Eco believed that wax museums also expressed a nostalgic guilt, remorsefully recalling what had been condemned by the haste of the society's 'futuristic planning'. Americans, he thought, had faith in such fakes because they offered some consolation for 'a present without depth'. The downtown Manhattan vistas in *Bye Bye Monkey* illustrate his point. Here ruins are not allowed to crumble at their own elegiac pace, as in Rome, and the recent past – office blocks redundant after a few decades, piers left empty because commerce no longer uses maritime routes – is briskly swept away. On the man-made beach where Depardieu encounters Kong, a bulldozer searches for natural outcrops to flatten, and a sign on a wire fence announces the sale of apartments that have not yet been built in what was presumptively called Battery Park City.

Eco noted that American wax museums dispensed not only fun but terror, by which visitors were clearly titillated. These palaces of amusement were surely built for reassurance, like Italian cathedrals: why then, pretending to honour heaven, did they extend an invitation to the inferno? Eco asked this question at the end of his essay but did not answer it, so America was left to its fate of spontaneous combustion.

When Wim Wenders first visited the United States in 1972, he felt like a pilgrim arriving at a desecrated shrine. His mistake was to turn on a television set. 'I loved American cinema, John Ford for me was holy, *Young Mr*

Lincoln was a holy film,' he said. He undertook the journey from Germany because Ford's pastoral idyll – in which Henry Fonda lolls on the grass beneath a tree beside a river with his law book open, as if its edicts were absorbed directly from nature, written on the paper by light – had made him a believer in the beauty and nobility of the American dream. Yet when he saw *Young Mr Lincoln* on television, it was chopped up every few minutes by chirpy commercials for used cars and fast food, and ended by merging with those sales pitches. Wenders bestowed this experience on the hero of his road movie *Alice in the Cities*, released in 1974. Philip, the German tourist played by Rüdiger Vogler, rambles morosely up the east coast; in one of the shoddy motel rooms he occupies, Ford's cinematic gospel blearily flickers on television. Outraged by the blasphemy, he bashes the box, knocking it over and leaving it to smoke on the floor. Wenders was less of a vandal, and prudently unplugged the set whenever he checked into a motel.

Did the director and his alter ego imagine, like Adorno, that they could free America from television, whether by passive resistance or vindictive aggression? Philip fumes that the medium has a 'boastful contempt' for its audience; the truth is that it ingratiates only too successfully. As for the mercenariness of televisual images, which as he says 'all want something from you', that is a give-and-take in which the viewers are mostly content to engage. Philip is a frustrated director, who imagines that he can give orders to obdurate America, as he does when he plays a practical joke on Alice, the waif who is left in his care. He walks into their Manhattan hotel room as she gazes out the window at the illuminated Empire State Building. He arrives at midnight, knowing that this is when the floodlights will be switched off; timing the moment exactly, he blows a puff of air at the spire to snuff it out like a candle.

The Empire State Building mimes obedience by instantly going dark, but otherwise America does not live up to Philip's fantasies. *Alice in the Cities* begins with him on a beach – supposedly in Florida, actually in Far Rockaway, beneath a strident succession of jets on their way in to land at Kennedy Airport. Crouched under a boardwalk, he tunelessly chants the Drifters' 'Under the Boardwalk', even though he is not, like the singer, sharing a blanket with a girlfriend and making love in the sun. He amuses himself by taking Polaroids of the tired waves that slump onshore, then wanders away on the sand through wind-blown litter. He goes home to Germany without regret, and is only reconciled with America when he attends a Chuck Berry concert in Wuppertal. He smiles while drinking a Coke and listening to Berry perform 'Memphis, Tennessee', about a long-distance call that does not go through; he finds it easier to maintain the love affair at a distance, as if telephonically. Finally, on a train from Duisburg to Munich, he reads John Ford's obituary in a newspaper. The article is entitled 'Verlorene Welt', but Philip's reaction is oddly joyous: he opens the window and salutes the Rhine. Has Ford's death freed him to think well of his own country?

Wenders, however, continued to grieve for the loss of a world that only ever existed on a screen. As late as the 1990s, he shed tears when he returned to a corner of Utah to visit Monument Valley, whose whittled clumps and teetering stacks of red rock had been the setting for Ford's epics of quest and heroic fortitude. The valley for Ford was coterminous with America: in *Cheyenne Autumn* he elasticized geography to make it stretch from the plains of Oklahoma to the rugged heights of Montana. Now, Wenders found, it had been redefined as Marlboro Country, and the glamorous urban cowboys who posed against its buttes or on its mesas were selling cigarettes. 'The Las Vegasization of America is taking place rapidly,' he declared, adding that he considered Las Vegas to be 'that place where hell is on earth'.

In 1984 in *Paris, Texas* Wenders staked his own claim to the West and was accused, as he put it, of 'sacrilege'. The film's title seemed tactlessly ironic, especially since it is not set in the Texan version of Paris, a small town north of Dallas which justified its claim to the name by building an Eiffel Tower of wood, only to see it toppled by a passing tornado. The actual locations chosen by Wenders are alternately primitive and futuristic. Travis, the drifter played by Harry Dean Stanton, staggers through a mountain range ground down to knobbly vertebrae at Big Bend in Texas, and briefly visits a truck stop on the California border which has a concrete dinosaur rearing on the tarmac; his brother Walt, by contrast, lives in the barbered hills of suburban Burbank, where walking in the street rather than driving is considered to be an eccentric, faintly shameful habit. The washed-up doctor who treats Travis at a grubby clinic in the Texas scrub is a German with a thick Bavarian accent, and although Walt has never travelled abroad his wife is French. Their presence here, far from home, is left unexplained, so they must be deputies for the disoriented Wenders. A billboard beside a Los Angeles freeway, installed by Walt's company, advertises Evian mineral water, and on the edge of a desert burbles about its source deep inside the French Alps. But such psychological props cannot save the characters from being belittled or effaced by America: Texas turns Paris into a flurry of dust.

Walt looks at roads or railway lines that taper towards a heat-blurred vanishing point on a featureless plain and says in dismay 'There's nothing out there.' Houston, site of the Space Center, could be in outer space: Travis's young son is dumbfounded by a silver-roofed parking lot with metal stumps that ingest or regurgitate money as you drive through, and asks 'This is a bank?' In Port Arthur, a building that houses a brothel is decorated with a mural of the Statue of Liberty, who with pouting lips and frizzy hair is more of a voluptuary than the colossus in the New York harbour. The stone book she grips contains a secretive back entrance, her upraised arm is a ventilation duct, and electric wires snake up to her torch somewhere on the roof. The film's America does not keep the promise made by this permissive hostess. On the drive from Burbank to Houston, Travis's son summarizes the history of the universe: a compressed dot exploded outwards, its gaseous fragments floating in limbo until the sun hardened them. He might be describing the gestation of the unstable, unfinished country they see outside the car, with vagrant people hustled by some cosmic gale.

Europeans reserve the right to be selectively anti-American. The Finnish director Aki Kaurismäki, for instance, detests Coca-Cola and hamburgers but approves of jukeboxes and Cadillacs, and is especially keen on Harley-Davidson motorcycles, since he and a friend opened a dealership in Helsinki during the 1990s. In 2003 he said that he admires the America of FDR, 'not that led by the clown George Bush': breadlines and hoboes hopping freight trains were preferable, apparently, to glutted crowds at shopping malls. Kaurismäki's *Leningrad Cowboys Go America*, released in 1989, is about a deluded Russian rock band whose members are cover versions of Americana, with quiffs that resemble Elvis's pompadour uncurled and stiffened into a prong. The film was a response to the dismemberment of the Soviet Union, Finland's bear-like, overbearing neighbour, and it begins in the starveling tundra in a village so backward that it even has a resident idiot. But when the Cowboys arrive in New York – on a tour promoted by a cultural commissar who assures them that they will succeed in America, where lack of talent is no hindrance to stardom – they find the rival empire to be just as down-at-heel. On Queens Boulevard, Jim Jarmusch, cast as a sleazy used-car salesman, makes patriotic propaganda by recommending a battered checker cab rather than the Japanese vehicle the Cowboys want to buy. When they decide on a Cadillac, he tells them they will be able to drive it through World War III unscathed. What they encounter when they set off is an unfabulous America of boarded-up storefronts, discount supermarkets and dead-end bars. After stops in Memphis, New Orleans, the swampy Everglades and Natchez, the golden land reaches its terminus on a soiled beach at Galveston.

The goal for these latter-day immigrants may be freedom, but like many newcomers they immediately join the underclass. Their manager Vladimir feeds them raw onions and sends them out to beg while he swills Budweiser and adds to his cache of dollars; in *Leningrad Cowboys Meet Moses*, released in 1994, the Cowboys give the American dream a last chance during an out-of-season sojourn in the Russian ghetto at Coney Island, after which they are shepherded back to Siberia by Vladimir, who now calls himself Moses and takes with him the Statue of Liberty's sawn-off nose. They drag the souvenir back through the former colonies of the Soviet bloc, pursued by a CIA agent who is trying to recapture the precious proboscis. They club him with a statuette of Lenin – a knockout, but not for communism: both sides in the phoney war have reneged on their ideal agenda.

Jarmusch is a natural ally for Kaurismäki, because his own films look at America through alienated eyes. Jarmusch is the child of immigrants – Czech, German and Irish – who for artistic reasons chooses to remain unassimilated. As a New Yorker, he is not quite an American: he prefers to think of the city as 'the capital of Europe', or perhaps as an autonomous city-state – 'like Berlin, an island', as he said in 1985 before the Wall fell. He also considers New Orleans to be a separate country (and the same could possibly be said of Los Angeles or San Francisco, perched on their precarious tectonic plate). In these marginal, contingent places, Jarmusch adopts the viewpoint of newcomers: Eva from Budapest who bumps down to earth in New York in *Stranger than Paradise*, Bob the Italian card sharp on the loose in New Orleans in *Down by Law*, or the Japanese teenagers, Italian widow and Lancashire Elvis imitator adrift in Memphis in *Mystery Train*.

Stranger than Paradise begins with Eva standing, like Eve ejected from Eden, in a field of churned rubble as a Pan Am jet prepares to take off from an airport runway. As it departs, she picks up her suitcase and walks into America. A travelling shot tracks her down bleak streets past scrofulous walls and the lowered grilles of shops, one of which has sprayed across it a slogan that sums up Jarmusch's opinion of the lumbering, blundering America beyond New York:

US OUT OF EVERYWHERE

YANKEE GO HOME.

When Eva and her male companions take a road trip, the vista is obscured by fog on the highway or smoke from the Cleveland steel mills, then whited-out by a blizzard. It hardly matters, because as one of her fellow travellers puts it, 'You come to some place new, and everything looks the same.' She develops a taste for Chesterfields; accustomed to the regional patchwork of Europe, she hopes that these will be available in Cleveland and that they will taste as good. Her cousin Willie (John Lurie) assures her that they are the same all over America: such is the poverty of affluence, standardized and tediously predictable. Disappointed by Lake Erie, Eva proposes a detour to Florida, where she expects to see alligators. On arrival, stranded in a shabby motel, she echoes Walt in *Paris, Texas*: 'This is nowhere.' Yet America in this case does reward the ingenuous immigrant, thanks to the comic benevolence of Jarmusch. Walking on the beach, with no alligators in prospect, Eva is mistaken for a drug dealer and has a wad of cash foisted on her, which changes her mind about returning to Hungary. Likewise in *Down by Law* the puckish tourist Bob – an Italian who adores Hollywood movies and has read Whitman and Frost – is at heart a better American than Jack and Zack, a pimp and a DJ with whom he shares a gaol cell. Bob leads their escape from prison, and then hunts and cooks a rabbit for their supper as they wander famished through a bayou. He deservedly goes to ground in the Louisiana backwoods at the end of the film, enjoying the life hereafter that is the immigrant's cherished dream.

Wenders, grumbling about the mistreatment of *Young Mr Lincoln*, complained that in America there is 'nothing sacred'. Jarmusch envies those seeing the country for the first time, for whom the aura of sanctity has not worn off. In *Mystery Train*, a random assortment of pilgrims converge in Memphis, the site of Graceland, Elvis's celestially ornate mansion with its gold piano, its ceilings of twinkly lights, its Tiffany-tented pool table, its green-carpeted jungle room, and its cornucopian pantry that was kept stocked during the owner's lifetime with cigars, chewing gum, Pepsi, peanut butter, fudge cookies, banana pudding and brownies. The Italian widow is consoled by a vision of a ghostly Elvis. Almost as wondrously, the nondescript streets supply the Japanese teenagers with a revelation at every turn – a barber's striped pole, a Cadillac, a diner with laminated banquettes, a hotel with an infernally crimson neon sign, the obligatory graveyard of crushed cars. They keep repeating 'This is America', hardly able to believe that they are actually here. At night, the Japanese girl unpacks her scrapbook, in which portraits of Elvis are pasted beside images of Buddha and the Statue of Liberty. As she points out, the singer, the sage and the anthropomorphized political principle all have the same face, and her triptych redefines America: in this strange paradise, celebrity and divinity are fused, music is a means of liberation, and a watchful, protective den mother permits her children to do whatever they feel like.

Raging against Bush, von Trier was trying not to free America but to free himself from it. He spoke as if Denmark were an occupied country: 'We are a nation under a very bad influence. . . . America is sitting on the world.' But he could hardly raise a barrier against invasive images, and even his refusal to set foot in the United States did not preserve his immunity. *Dancer in the Dark*, released in 2000, takes place in the Pacific north-west, though it was made in Scandinavia – yet its pine forests, lakes and houses with steeply pitched roofs look like Minnesota, settled by Nordic immigrants who found there a reminiscence of the landscapes they had left. America, not content to be everywhere, also contains equivalents of all other places.

The dancer in the dark is Selma, a Czech immigrant with failing eyesight who lives in a trailer and works in a factory that makes metal sinks. Despite her drab circumstances, she thinks of America as a dreamland where people eat candies out of pink tins and, as in Hollywood musicals, 'nothing dreadful ever happens'. In fact those manufactured fantasies are as exigent and exhausting as her dreary job. At the cinema, she watches Ruby Keeler collapse in Busby Berkeley's *42nd Street*, worn out by the drilled, clattering repetitions of a tap dance; likewise in *The Pajama Game* the chorines at their sewing machines, harassed by a time-study expert, give a singing, dancing demonstration of industrial efficiency. Selma and her colleagues put on *The Sound of Music* in the factory, and when performing Maria's song about her favourite things they haul on a cumbrous succession of props – copper kettles, woollen mittens, a plate of schnitzels with congealed noodles – that literal-mindedly ridicule this prescription for banishing depression. At last, sentenced to death for a murder she did commit, Selma regrets her credulity and realizes that 'communism was better for human beings'.

In *Dogville* the location changes to a settlement near a mine in the Rockies, although von Trier obliterates alpine America by reducing the town to diagrammatic markings on the black lacquered floor of a machine hall in Sweden, where he made the film. His alienation effects – dry rain, notional doors in non-existent walls – are his critique of an art that usually depends, like America, on expensive illusions. The people of Dogville, supposedly 'good, honest folks', collar, chain and serially rape the heroine Grace when she strays into town. She is rescued by her father, a Chicago gangster, and as he takes her away she orders his henchmen to massacre her persecutors. Watching them die, she announces that she has shed blood for the sake of humanity and to make the world a better place, which is what American presidents say about their wars. In von Trier's sequel *Manderlay*, Grace moves to a plantation in Alabama, where she liberates some anachronistically enslaved field hands while fettering their former white masters, who are made to pass an exam to qualify as 'graduate Americans'. Her rectitude is no remedy for inherited ills. When a grizzled, weary servant asks Grace to decide on mealtimes for the household, she replies that free men eat when they are hungry – advice which, as the film's narrator remarks, is of little use to America's under-nourished underclass. Finally the former slaves chase Grace away, and the camera withdraws to look down on a stark, simplified map of the United States, an empty space with fences between the states and the Statue of Liberty – the only icon in a desert of lines and letters – diminished to a crude, tacky statuette.

Manderlay suggests that the very idea of freedom is anathema to von Trier, who as a European believes that it is impossible to shrug off the burden of history. He is just as sceptical about the pursuit of happiness, because in his view it condemns the poor to think of themselves as failures rather than blaming society for their misery. Yet American happiness is congenital, which may be why it annoys resigned, enervated Europeans. After settling in America, Louis Malle made two documentaries for public television – *God's Country* in 1979, followed by . . . *And the Pursuit of Happiness* in 1986; and in both cases he found that the catchphrases he took as his titles were simple truths, for ordinary Americans and for those who aspired to become American.

God's country is the small town of Glencoe in Minnesota, which ought to be von Trier's Dogville at a lower altitude. But here Malle encounters Miss Litzauer, an old biddy of eighty-five in a pioneer's bonnet, who is bending over her vegetable patch as he passes. Asked whether it is hard work, she shares out the responsibility for her chores: 'God takes care of the garden, the devil takes care of the lawn.' This is a land where Manichean battles are fought out in suburban yards, and Malle notes the 'devastating passion' with which the townsfolk mow their lawns – a memory of clearances on the frontier, or perhaps a way of prosecuting the fight against the devil, whose rank, pullulating crop is weeds? 'I'm going to cultivate the potatoes over there,' says Miss Litzauer, 'and radishes and onions.' Her old-fashioned verb is apt: gardening is culture at grass-roots level. Her sisters, she tells Malle, want her to move; they worry about the frigid rural winters, even though she keeps herself busy doing crochet work, braiding rugs, and cooking three meals a day. She is adamant about staying put: 'I would not go to the cities,' she declares. The plural sounds unidiomatic until you realize that she is referring to the so-called twin cities of Minneapolis and St Paul, an hour away, but her statement could be a rejection of all cities, which for Americans in the heartland are not synonymous with the civilized life. 'It's so nice out here,' says Miss Litzauer, inviting Malle to watch the flowers grow.

Passers-by at a Bavarian fair ask him why he is filming. He says it is for television, and adds that he is French. They reply that everyone in town is of German descent but they welcome him just the same, and their greeting makes America the solvent of abiding European antagonisms. Malle and his crew are so touched by this hospitality that they forget their fastidious Gallic tastes and uncomplainingly eat at Dairy Queen, the only local 'gastronomic resource'. Briefly nostalgic for civilization, Malle asks the assistant police chief 'Could we get mugged in Glencoe?' The cop, whose most recent case concerned a noisy car alarm, has to disappoint him. When Malle returned a few years later to add an epilogue to his film, he found that little had changed. A farmer in the sequel grumbles vaguely about 'the Jewish people' who control the market for his grain; a draft protestor, jailed during the Vietnam War and absent in California as a busking musician in 1979, has returned home, rejoined society and made a fortune selling computer software. But Miss Litzauer, now ninety-one, is still pickling vegetables and doing her own housework. The last word goes to a lawyer who condemns the cupidity of the Reagan era, then affirms that 'There is a lot of good in this country and a lot of good people.'

Hence the eager influx documented by Malle in ... *And the Pursuit of Happiness*. Some Cambodian refugees are soon compensated for their loss of a precious tub of rice, confiscated at the airport in New York when they arrive. In their English class, they chirpily repeat the mantra 'Let's go to

Wendy's and have a hamburger.' What better way to assimilate? The teacher, with a lilt of excitement in her voice, lists the multiple choices available in the land of the free: 'You can go to McDonald's, Burger King – anywhere!' Communion feasts proliferate. A Cuban woman in Miami pets her Alsatian dog, a fellow asylum seeker and a replacement for the daughter she had to leave behind; asked whether the dog likes America, she replies 'He loves the food!' A Laotian teenager praises pizzas and burgers, wrinkling her nose at the smelly curries of her native land. Everyone Malle interviews has attained happiness, or expects to do so. An ageing Russian actor, the proud proprietor of a Stanislavskyan studio, announces 'Now is beginning my second life', aware that at home the allowance is single not plural. A cheeky detainee who slips across the border into San Diego grins at the immigration officer who deports him and says 'I promise you I will be back! Maybe in half an hour.' The only dissenter is the Caribbean poet Derek Walcott, who while lounging on the promenade in Brooklyn Heights speculates about the conditions attached to the Statue of Liberty's offer of asylum. The process of becoming American, he rightly says, is more revolutionary than any left-wing doctrine, because it emphasizes the individual's rebirth, not just a change in social and political arrangements. This makes the United States 'an aggressive democracy', which as Walcott points out is a contradiction in terms. He resists this mandatory levelling: 'I don't always want to be equal. I want to feel superior sometimes – or inferior.' Malle does not ask the Nobel Prize winner why or when he favours the latter option.

Atlantic City, made on location in the resort late in 1979, is Malle's study of personal resurrection and urban renewal, and against all the odds it validates the national creed of new beginnings. Atlantic City counts as one of America's artificial paradises, an island off the New Jersey shore surrounded by swamps, as marginal to the sober United States as the Manhattan or New Orleans of Jarmusch. It began in the 1870s as a homeopathic resort for sedate strollers on the boardwalk, with brine and salty air as its selling points; its street plan served as the prototype for the Monopoly board, the relic of a staid era when wealth depended on property and being sent to gaol counted as a disgrace, not an inconvenience to be evaded with the help of a fancy lawyer. After New Jersey legalized casino gambling in 1976, Atlantic City's ancient hotels were demolished – Malle's film begins with the implosion of the Traymore, a baronial sandcastle that instantly crumbles into powder – and replaced by temples that glorified the speculative capitalism of the Reagan years. The Marlborough-Blenheim gave way to the Trump Taj Mahal: English aristocracy now seemed dowdy, so the architectural ideal became Asiatic extravagance. Far from trusting in the recuperative power of sea breezes, the new tycoons worried that nature might distract the gamblers they had lured indoors, and instead of ozone they pumped extra oxygen through the air-conditioning ducts to keep their customers alert. Fresh air and sea bathing were replaced by the use of recreational drugs.

In Malle's film, posters on building sites promise a comeback, but behind the ocean front is a ghetto littered with abandoned cars where welfare recipients loll in dented armchairs and hand their scarce funds to Lou (Burt Lancaster), a retired gangster who is now a runner for the numbers racket. Still, people earnestly accredit the blather of the promoters. Susan Sarandon plays Sally, who has come to Atlantic City from dull Saskatchewan to train as a blackjack dealer, and hopes to move on – in a further reincarnation – to work as a croupier in Monte Carlo. Her husband Dave, tracking her, has paused on the way from Las Vegas in an older America: he is seen stealing a consignment of drugs from a phone booth on Walnut Street in Philadelphia, just outside the Norman Rockwell Museum. He and his pregnant girlfriend then hitchhike the rest of the way to Atlantic City, carrying all they own in bags and knapsacks across a bridge above the coastal marsh; they might be peasants trudging through the Russian steppes, bound for America.

Dave is killed by the drug dealers whose stash he purloined. Lou then shoots the dealers and pockets their money, only to have it stolen from him by Sally, who uses it to finance her next life on the French Riviera. Having got away with two murders, Lou takes her treachery in good part, and as the film ends he jauntily promenades on the boardwalk with his mistress, a superannuated showgirl, formerly bedridden, who has now inexplicably regained the use of her legs. A wrecker's ball stubbornly concusses the facade of another condemned hotel; it bruises the masonry and dislodges a cloud of plaster, but the valiant structure resists. Deaths in America, as *Atlantic City* demonstrates, are merely preludes to rebirth, and Malle's characters remain inveterately, incorrigibly happy.

A few months after Beuys made his one-sided peace with the coyote, another European magus came to New York to cast a spell on technocratic America. One morning in August 1974, the French aerial acrobat Philippe Petit stepped from the roof of the unfinished World Trade Center onto a cable he had strung between the towers and spent an hour nimbly treading across the gulf. Sometimes he skipped, and once he sat down on the wire to rest. He wore no safety harness: treading on the wind, with only a quivering horizontal pole to maintain his balance, he placed his trust in the benign energies of a nature that vertical Manhattan ignored.

Petit engaged in subterfuge and espionage to plan his entry to the site, and with helpers as sly as guerrillas he smuggled the kit he needed past the guards. This entitled him to call his feat 'le coup', although the word had no political or military connotations. He left the conquest of the World Trade Center to King Kong, who in the 1976 film leapt from one tower to the other to mark out his territory. For Petit, the true ape was New York, which he called 'the most savagely gigantic city of the Americas', and his own role was that of an angel, afloat in mid-air. He treated the mercantile building tenderly, placing a strip of carpet on the parapet so that his thick steel wire would not grate. In his eyes, the cable was umbilical, or perhaps Atlantean: as if dredged up from that submerged landmass, it linked two slabs of steel and concrete that looked, when he first stood on the roof, like continents that had split apart. After an earth tremor far below, he felt the towers shudder and was sure they emitted a cry, though they immediately fell silent, ashamed of 'having expressed secret feelings'. He was their single auditor, the confessor who allowed them to ventilate the unease that travelled up from the American bedrock.

Having scampered to the summit, Petit did not look down to enjoy his triumph, as one of Ayn Rand's supermen would have done. Instead he gazed up at the sky, and on his way from the south tower to the north he paused to converse with a bird that hovered near him. The transit became a transfiguration: he chose to spend the night of 6 August in hiding on the roof because this was the date of the church festival that celebrates Christ's mutation into bodiless radiance, and Petit expected to be 'flooded with light' when he began his walk across the top of the world in the morning.

The moment he reached the north tower, he was taken into custody and charged with a pettifogging series of misdemeanours. But those who had watched from below acclaimed his courage, grace and ingenuity, and his eventual reward was a lifetime pass to the observation deck of the World Trade Center – good, as it turned out, only for the lifetime of the towers, which he outlived.

19 | 'Why Do They Hate Us?'

Henry Wallace warned Americans in 1947 about the hard hearts of ungrateful Europeans. Not wanting to sound so emotionally needy, President Johnson preferred to describe the country as the object of rankling envy. In 1966 he told soldiers at a camp in South Korea that 'There are three billion people in the world, and we have only two hundred million of them. We are outnumbered fifteen to one.' Unless the fort was held in Vietnam, Johnson predicted that those pullulating others 'would sweep over the United States and take what we have'. European condescension and Asian covetousness, however, were easier to deal with than a loathing fuelled by sacred rage. Addressing Congress after 9/11, President Bush said that he was voicing the mystification of the American people, who in response to the Al Qaeda attacks were asking 'Why do they hate us?' A few weeks later he plaintively added 'I know how good we are', probably wishing that the terrorists would take his word for it.

Bush was derided for naivety or hypocrisy, but his question marks a national blind spot, apparent as well, for instance, in John Updike. His 1978 novel *The Coup* is narrated by a deposed African dictator called Ellelloû, who while attacking American imperialism gradually discloses cherished memories of the time he spent in the 1950s at a college in Wisconsin, which flourished on 'the fertile and level moral prairie of American goodness'. Rather than estranging Updike from his homeland, the African persona enables him to see it with renewed amazement, as a child might. When Ellelloû remembers a football game during the harvest festival that his hosts call Thanksgiving, his exclamatory shorthand raises ordinary sights to the status of marvels – 'The pom-poms! The beer kegs!' – and even Islam is charmingly honoured, he thinks, by the 'dummy minaret' on the pitched orange roof of the local Howard Johnson's. Ellelloû admires a female embodiment of 'American freshness . . . born of fearlessness born in turn of inner certainty of being justly blessed with health and love'. That comment is more perturbing now than when Updike wrote it: Americans share this self-certainty with those who hate them, who are fearless because it is not their lives but their deaths that are justly blessed.

Later, when Ellelloû is installed as his country's president, the Nixon administration sends an envoy on a goodwill mission. Chomping a cheroot, Klipspringer expatiates on American benevolence: 'America is downright lovable, America loves all peoples and wants them to be happy, because America loves happiness.' Despite the syllogisms, this is not an estimation with which Updike disagreed. In a volume of stories published the year after the novel, he defined America as 'a vast conspiracy to make you happy'. Never mind that the conspiracy may be commercial: who would prefer to be glum and grudging, like the British? Updike found the principled hatred of this blithe way of life scarcely conceivable, which explains the abrupt reprieve at the end of his 2006 novel *Terrorist*, when a young Muslim fanatic on his way to set off a bomb in Manhattan has a change of heart after he watches an American family quietly pursuing happiness in a car he passes on the highway.

History has no interest in such miraculous conversions, and discredits the myth of fresh, innocent beginnings. Islam's abomination of America's secular delights long pre-dated 9/11, though it went unremarked as the process of Americanization continued, apparently without hindrance. Between 1948 and 1950 Sayyid Qutb, later a leader of the Muslim Brotherhood, studied in Washington DC, Colorado and at Stanford. The experience was purgatorial; he found the campuses to be brutish jungles, or cauldrons of sweltering sin. American men had the bodies of oxen, and were especially bestial when playing football: since the foot was not permitted to touch the ball, the game required no skill and simply invited them to bludgeon each other. American women, Sayyid Qutb reported, possessed disgracefully frank eyes and thirsty mouths, supplemented – as he irresistibly lowered his gaze – by round breasts, full buttocks, shapely thighs and dangerously limber legs. Such physiques had no room for 'windows to the world of the spirit or the heart or tender sentiment'. A glance at the recently published Kinsey

Report persuaded him that Americans were goaded exclusively by carnal hunger, along with their proverbial love of money.

Sayyid Qutb was executed in 1966 after being convicted of a plot to assassinate President Nasser, but he bequeathed his holy fury to a succession of Egyptian or Palestinian moralists, who were horrified when they observed the Great Satan at close hand. Hisham Sharabi claimed that female students at Northwestern University worked their way through college as striptease dancers at a bar in a non-existent town south of Chicago, and Muhammad Hasan-al-Alafi joylessly declared that the Halloween masks worn by children testified to the blood-sucking vampirism of American culture. For Jadhibiyya Sidqi, dressed salads were as repellent as the undressed women from whom Sayyid Qutb backed away in dread: during a stint as a lecturer in the midwest in 1960–1, she refused to eat lettuce drowned in 'a sluggish sauce with its lethal fat that can simply kill you', and in an outburst of dietary fundamentalism she called for vegetables to be served 'the way they were created by God'. The satirist Mahmud al-Sadani also made it God's responsibility to deal with the hubristic United States. 'Oh merciful, oh compassionate Lord,' he prayed in 1990, 'deliver us from the American era.'

When the reckoning arrived, many of those who sympathized with stricken America did so only partially. Jean-Marie Colombani's editorial in *Le Monde* on 12 September 2001 declared 'We are all Americans!' but immediately qualified that effusion by specifying 'We are all New Yorkers.' Foreigners shared the wound because they thought of New York as in part their turf, belonging – as Mario Vargas Llosa put it in an essay on 9/11 – 'to nobody and everybody', set apart from the rest of America by its 'Babelic' nature and its messy pluralism. While Colombani grieved over the toppling of the World Trade Center, he castigated the United States for failing to embrace the world and eliciting from certain parts of it 'nothing but hate'. The cynicism of the country's foreign policy had tripped it up: the Pentagon originally armed the Taliban to help drive the Russians from Afghanistan, and Osama bin Laden's brother owned a mansion in Florida, not far from Disneyworld.

Canadians may not hate the United States, but they look at it quizzically, and in Québec they are inclined to roll their eyes in disbelief – at least that is how the Montréal hedonists in Denys Arcand's 1986 film *Le Déclin de l'empire américain* regard their potent, self-important neighbour. Despite its Spenglerian or Gibbonian title, geopolitical prophecy is incidental to Arcand's sex comedy; even so, the pampered affluence and promiscuity of the characters are symptoms of a forthcoming end. Dominique, a historian, argues that the preoccupation with so-called personal growth occurs only in societies that, like Rome under Diocletian or contemporary America, are disintegrating because the collective conscience has weakened. Hers is an abrasively conservative creed, which hankers after a time when life was about labour not enjoyment, and sex was productivity by other means not a leisured amusement. But at the empire's margins, decadence is agreeable enough. Arcand's frivolous nihilists hope that the anticipated apocalypse will be a good show, and as they stare at the night sky, they wonder whether they will see the barrage of nuclear missiles – meant to detonate in the stratosphere, according to Reagan's Strategic Defense Initiative – pyrotechnically colliding above them. As a second best, they wish for a Russian attack on the Strategic Air Command base at Plattsburgh, just across the border in upstate New York. Smoke from there should be visible in Montréal, with perhaps the extra thrill of a mushroom cloud.

After 9/11, Arcand brought the same characters back in *Les Invasions barbares* to reflect on the empire's fall. Older and even more cynically resigned, they conclude that civilization is intermittent and temporary, inevitably overtaken by a barbarism that is the moronic norm. Their examples of the exceptional moments in history are Athens in the fifth century BC, Florence during the Renaissance, and Philadelphia in 1776 – although they note in an afterthought that Florentines currently vote for Berlusconi and Philadelphians for Bush. A cop in a parked car watches heroin traders do business, but makes no arrests: it is, he says, an invasion, by gangs of Iranians, Libyans and Turks whom he tactfully refrains from calling barbarians.

The hero Rémy, fecklessly self-indulgent in the earlier film, now has cancer, and for his sessions of radiotherapy is driven from a squalid nationalized hospital in Montréal to a shiny establishment in Burlington, Vermont. Old Glory flutters as the ambulance enters God's country, the anthem plays, and a beaming helper who opens the door of the vehicle says 'Welcome to America.' 'Praise the Lord,' replies Rémy, sarcastically adding 'Hallelujah'. He has no patience with the palliative sentiments that get Americans through their lives and ensure that they feel good, even in extremis. His son Sébastien wants to move him to a clinic in Baltimore, where he will have a private bathroom and a bedside CD player. Sébastien – a financier who works in London – is a puritan and a capitalist, whereas Rémy in healthier days was a voluptuary, which means, according to Arcand's logic, that he is a socialist. He voted for state-subsidized medicine because he expected society to look after him, and he now feels obliged to put up with what Québec provides. Unregenerate and therefore un-American, he does not pursue a happiness that lies ahead, over the rainbow. Happiness was something he attained during his days as a libertine, and he refuses to complain when it is taken from him.

During *Les Invasions barbares* a liberal academic reviews television footage of 9/11 and watches the second plane open a fiery gash in the World Trade Center. He refuses to commiserate. three thousand dead is a negligible total, compared with the fifty thousand who died on a single day at Gettysburg. Rémy likewise corrects a pious nurse when she says they are living in terrible times. He denies that the twentieth century was particularly bloody, and reminds her that in the sixteenth century the Spanish and Portuguese conquistadors, without the benefit of modern military hardware, managed to exterminate 150 million Latin Americans. The English composer Thomas Adès had already given a voice to those forgotten victims in his cantata *America: A Prophecy*, in which a keening Mayan seer describes falling cities while a choir repeats the prayers of the militant Christians who expunged the natives in God's name. The cantata was first performed in New York in 1999; two years later the singer's keening prediction, which calls for flames to scorch the infidel and level their dwellings to dusty mounds, acquired an extra relevance. In 2008, when Adès conducted the piece in Los Angeles, the city was encircled by wildfires, with clouds of ash suffocating the orange sky. 'It's not my fault,' he told the audience before he raised his baton.

Bush and his colleagues expected that international sympathy after 9/11 would be followed by approval of the Iraq War. When that did not happen, Chancellor Schröder and President Chirac were said to have formed an 'axis of weasels', a European counterpart to the 'axis of evil' along which Bush aligned Iran, Iraq and North Korea in 2002. Wim Wenders noticed that his neighbours in the hills above Sunset Boulevard now ostentatiously refused to buy German cars and poured their stores of French wine into the gutter. In response Wenders designed for himself a T-shirt with the slogan 'Proud to Be a Weasel'; for the first time in his life, he said, he was glad to be German. The America he so admired had turned dislikeable, twisting its liberal principles into 'anti-Christ messages'.

Land of Plenty, directed by Wenders in 2004, is his muddled attempt to comprehend this menacing patriotism. Its two central characters, though native-born, look at America as if they were immigrants, or perhaps – like Wenders – cultural orphans seeking adoption. Paul, a paranoid Vietnam veteran, conducts a personal vendetta against the terrorists. His mobile phone chirps the national anthem, and in a van papered with WANTED posters for Osama bin Laden he drives around Los Angeles collecting water samples that he tests for toxins and raising the alarm about unattended luggage. 'This is my country,' he says. Drunkenly assuaging his guilt for not having been a passenger on one of the hijacked planes, he adds 'This country's been good to me . . . this beautiful country.' The sentiments do not quite fit his personal history, since America was not good to Vietnam vets, who were the embarrassing evidence of a national calamity; it is Wenders who silently mouths these lines. The situation of Paul's niece Lana is even more extraneous. She is a missionary, who has spent 9/11 on the West Bank and remembers Palestinian crowds cheering as the World Trade Center's towers sank to their knees. 'They hate us,' she tells Paul. As her plane descends into smoggy Los Angeles, she thanks God for bringing her home, although she later admits that she has no idea 'why I'm here, in America'.

Both characters have an indirect, mediated relationship with the society to which they are supposed to belong. Their chosen medium, like that of Wenders, is photographic. Paul keeps watch on the city with a surveillance camera, and Lana uses a digital camera to document the city's woes. Her lens does more than merely uncover illicit truths, like the snooping devices in Paul's van. As she surreptitiously snaps homeless people camped under a bridge, she says that although they may be lost to the eyes of the world, for God 'every one of them is just as worthy as the President of the United States'. The camera confers value on these social rejects, and reconvenes an inclusive democracy. Intent on his own mission, Wenders forgets that Lana should have fed them instead of taking photographs of their encampment.

A subplot about a suspected Pakistani terrorist takes Paul and Lana to Death Valley, which here is the rusty site of a borax mine that may have supplied potash and nitrous explosives for bombs, not the prehistoric place visited by Antonioni's dropouts in *Zabriskie Point*. They then set out on a cross-country road trip, a pilgrimage to the ruins of the World Trade Center. On the way they check off the compulsory talismans, even though Las Vegas, which appears first, is for Wenders an inferno, and in Monument Valley, which comes next, some immobilized trailers and a herd of listless goats messily clutter the base of John Ford's weathered, stoically enduring cliffs. In Washington, the Capitol with its Roman dome is a rude reminder of imperial pomp. A flag, somewhat tattered, flaps from a mast on the back of Paul's van, which at one point passes a whitewashed rock with a rhetorical question painted on it: 'WHAT WOULD AMERICA BE WITHOUT GOD?' The answer, probably, is that it would be truer to the enlightened principles of its founders.

At last comes a glimpse of the Manhattan skyline, followed by the plunge into the Lincoln Tunnel. A roller-skating youth who zigzags through traffic on Broadway near Astor Place shows off the anarchy and exhibitionism that are as much a testament to American liberty as any national monument. Then, on a rooftop near Ground Zero, Paul and Lana close their eyes and try to experience a healing calm. But all they can see is a pit being dug for another commercial skyscraper, with tragedy buried beneath a new, insentient cladding of concrete.

The mourners in *Land of Plenty* are looking at what Spengler thought of as the cemetery of the West. He called New York a 'daemonic desert of stone', and said that its 'soulless material' mocked the 'spirit-pervaded' uplift of Gothic architecture. Here, with the skyscrapers as tombstones, was civilization's dead end.

Spengler never saw the city he was describing, so his prognosis could easily have been ignored. But *The Decline of the West* recurs throughout the decades after 1945, either as a memento mori for America or an assurance that a new culture would emerge when the next phase of the cycle began. The hopeful liberals in Trilling's *The Middle of the Journey* repudiate this 'great black volume' that foresaw only decay, but Kerouac used the book as a guide to what he called America's 'High Civilization phase', and the Beat poet Lawrence Ferlinghetti took up Spengler's theory that a 'second religiousness', exemplified by the woozy spirituality of the hippies, often emerged in empires that were falling apart. Ferlinghetti jokingly explained the Vietnam War by citing Spengler's law about 'the natural Westward spin' of the globe: Maoist China had reversed this rotation, and America was relying on armed intervention to restore the proper momentum. Even in the 1980s, the preppie socialist in Whit Stillman's film *Metropolitan* sleeps with a copy of *The Decline of the West* beside his bed. Presumably it warns him that New York is in decline and about to fall – at least in the eyes of the patrician class that was ousted from Park Avenue by venture capitalists who owed their instant wealth to Reagan's economic policies.

Spengler divided the history of civilization into three phases, each with its own territorial base and governing philosophical precept. The culture of the Greeks and Romans was grounded by an equilibrium that Spengler associated with the lucid god Apollo; its token was the firmly planted Doric column. Next came the Arabs, who relied on 'magian' or wizardly powers to balance the warring principles of light and darkness. In the third and final phase, the Europeans and their American successors are neither harmoniously humane nor unworldly and mystical. These modern men owe their dominion over the material world to a force of will that for Spengler was diabolical: he saw them as followers of Faust, who was promoted to superhuman status by his pact with the devil. In industrial Europe, that driving volition became visible in steam power; in contemporary America,

Spengler's Faustian impetus takes the form of oil. Voraciously consuming energy and negligently expending it, this is a society that moves faster so as to accelerate its own decline.

Americans consume 25 per cent of the world's diminishing supply of oil; essential to keep the country's motors running, it is visible only when wasted, as in the *Exxon Valdez* spill in Alaska in 1989 and the explosion of the BP well in the Gulf of Mexico in 2010, or when bubbles of methane gas pucker and slurp on the surface of the La Brea tar pits in Los Angeles. Oil is the secret source of vitality, warmth, wealth, even – as Umberto Eco pointed out when he visited the Getty Museum in 1979 – of culture. At the time J. Paul Getty's collection was still housed at Malibu in a villa from Herculaneum, destroyed when Vesuvius had a coughing fit in 79 AD. The ruins reconstructed on the Pacific coast guarded the magnate's tapestries, Persian rugs, marquetry furniture, baroque clocks and specimens of rock crystal, along with a smattering of classical busts, Renaissance altarpieces, and keepsakes salvaged from Versailles after the French Revolution – the flotsam and jetsam of Europe's convulsive history, washed up on what Eco called 'the Last Beach'. In Malibu, as at the Cloisters in Manhattan, the New World reproached the Old World for its failure to sustain civilized society. But the villa's cool colonnades and trickling fountains concealed the origins of the money that paid for this salvage operation from Europe's democratized palaces and desanctified churches. In Eco's judgement it was 'entrepreneurial colonization by the New World . . . that [made] the Old World's condition critical', and Getty Oil – which first sunk wells in the red dirt of Oklahoma, then took over a neutral zone between Saudi Arabia and Kuwait – helped create the problem to which the villa was supposedly a solution.

At a time when oil seemed to be an inexhaustible resource, it was orgiastic stuff. Upton Sinclair in his novel about the industry, excitedly entitled *Oil!*, hears a 'Homeric laughter' in the spouting of a gusher, which reminds him of Niagara, of a lava flow, and of 'an express train shooting out of the ground'. In the film of Edna Ferber's *Giant*, James Dean bathes in a viscous cataract when his Texas well blows its top. Circulating in its underground pipelines like blood or seminal fluid inside our bodies, generating life in the machines it fed, oil inevitably came to be eroticized. In *Why Are We in Vietnam?* Mailer refers to it as a febrile current of 'fucklust' beneath the American earth, and Tennessee Williams once likened himself to a prospector whose erection probed for black gold: 'Never sunk my shaft in sweeter ground,' he wrote in his notebook after having sex with Frank Merlo. The metaphor recurs in the 1976 *King Kong*, where the ape is captured by a Houston petrochemical company for use as a corporate logo, the definitive answer to the tiger in Exxon's tanks. An archetypally ugly American played by Charles Grodin first wants to drill on an unspoiled Pacific island, and then after ecological protests settles for kidnapping Kong, whom he stows in the hold of the Petrox tanker as a substitute for the lake of oil he expected to bring home. Jeff Bridges accuses Grodin of being an 'environmental rapist': his treatment of nature is indeed more ruthless than Kong's clumsy fondling of Jessica Lange. In *W.*, Oliver Stone shows Vice-President Cheney – in the apoplectic, bullet-headed person of Richard Dreyfuss – jabbing a map on the wall of the White House situation room as he plans the annexation of Iranian oilfields. 'Control Iran, control Eurasia, control the world,' he barks, like Nero in a business suit not a toga. 'Empire, real empire. No one will ever fuck with us again!' Cheney doubtless never said anything so crass or choleric, but perhaps he did not need to: he could rely on a tacit consensus.

For Ayn Rand, oil was demiurgic, like the ignition that crackles from the finger of Michelangelo's God on the ceiling of the Sistine Chapel, and in *Atlas Shrugged* drilling converts the 'primeval ooze' into a mental impetus. The mucky sludge is less of an embarrassment if it is seen as an unmoved mover, like the God of enlightened philosophers in the eighteenth century. The hero of Joseph O'Neill's novel *Netherland* is a Dutch equities analyst for a merchant bank in New York, who dabbles in Texas crude. His special expertise is to speculate about the future of 'large-cap oil and stocks', and he can give an informed estimate of 'the oil-production capacity of an American-occupied Iraq'; the substance has been replaced by numbers, as intangible as the exponential zeros of the money he moves around. But for Mark Wahlberg, who plays a US Army sergeant in David O. Russell's *Three Kings*, there is no denying oil's connection with appetite and ordure. When he is taken prisoner in Iraq, his tormenters test his capacity for guzzling gas by ladling motor oil into his mouth and making him swallow. That indigestible glut may be preferable to the depletion foreseen in McCarthy's *The Road*, where a scavenger in a desiccated petrol station decants a few drops from quart bottles and sniffs one of the pipes that led to the bowsers. 'The odour of gas,' he finds, 'was only a rumour, faint and stale.'

Dribbling decline like this is too slow and shaming: better a sudden, star-blazing finale. In recent decades, evangelists, politicians and professional fantasists have come together to imagine a grand climax for the American century. In 1981 the television preacher Jerry Falwell predicted that a Russian raid on Middle Eastern oil would soon provoke 'nuclear holocaust on this earth', followed by Christ's long-awaited comeback. Two years later President Reagan told an Israeli lobbyist that he had been consulting the terminal predictions of the biblical Apocrypha, and was confident that 'we're the generation that's going to see that come about'. No matter how often they are disappointed, American millenarians remain elated by the imminence of the end, and in May 2011 they eagerly prepared for an earthquake that was due to slice the ground open and swallow the ungodly. The Rapture, as believers call it, is a comforting delusion; the end will surely not depend on a divine timetable. In 2010 Gary Shteyngart's novel *Super Sad Love Story* speculated about 'the Rupture', a not so remote future when a bankrupt United States may have to be bailed out by the International Monetary Fund. As Shteyngart imagines it, the IMF chops the country into concessions handed over to be exploited by Norway, China and Saudi Arabia, with Manhattan set apart as a retail Mecca, a 'Lifestyle Hub and Trophy City', out of bounds to all but the biggest spenders. Aiming to eliminate subversives who do not belong here, the totalitarian regime in Washington sends fire-spitting helicopters to sink the Staten Island ferry. 'It's the fall of the Roman Empire out there,' says Lenny, the novel's panicked protagonist. After a financier explains the long-incubated IMF plan for subdivision and devolution, Lenny gasps 'No more America?' 'A *better* America,' his friend assures him.

Bush asked the wrong question. The conundrum is not why others hate Americans, but why Americans are so violently dissatisfied with their own society, eager to be rid of it in order that the adventure of discovering and creating the ideal state can happen all over again, whether in this world or the next. Films have become a medium of babbling prophecy – agents of a jocose terrorism, forever devising newly ingenious ways of taking out symbolic targets. Those that do so most spectacularly are known as blockbusters: although the word suggests that they are busting box-office records and amassing block-like piles of profit, it actually refers, more frighteningly, to a kind of aerial bomb deployed during World War II, valued because it could bust or demolish an entire city block at one go. Such explosive feats now count as entertainment for the enraptured masses.

Missiles loaded with poison gas are aimed at San Francisco from a launching pad on Alcatraz in Michael Bay's *The Rock*, released five years before 9/11. The Statue of Liberty's head, apparently sliced off by a guillotine, bounces down a Manhattan avenue in *Cloverfield*, and the Empire State Building freezes to a jewelled icicle in Roland Emmerich's *The Day After Tomorrow*. In Emmerich's *Independence Day* the White House is atomized by a ray from a spaceship that hovers overhead. When the earth's crust splits in the same director's *2012*, the fragile mansion is destroyed a second time, shattered by an aircraft carrier that is flushed out of Chesapeake Bay by a tsunami and transformed into a projectile. Later in the same film, Air Force One is swilled around in a flood that swamps the Himalayas; it sinks, taking the government with it. For *Battle: Los Angeles*, about an alien invasion, the designer Peter Wenham coated the sets with bone ash, explaining that '9/11 is kind of a look if you like that I wanted to try and sort of take through the movie from a texture point of view'. Wenham's verbal fumbling perhaps masked his embarrassment at having used the charred, smoking burial plot of Ground Zero as a stylistic aid.

In 2008 a new version of *The Day the Earth Stood Still* brought back Klaatu, now played by Keanu Reeves, to issue a starker ultimatum than in the 1951 film: our pestilential species is to be exterminated, though specimens of all other animals and plants will be carried off in a biosphere to regenerate elsewhere. Klaatu's arrival in Central Park is treated as a breach of national security, and the Secretary of Defense, played by Kathy Bates, wants to know his intentions in invading 'our planet'. He replies 'It is not your planet', and asks whether she speaks for 'the entire human race'. 'No,' she says, 'I speak for the President of the United States.' Unimpressed, Klaatu shuts down the nation's power supply, even causing the derricks on oil wells to nod more sleepily and then stop altogether. The Secretary remorsefully reflects on the early history of settlement in the Americas, realizing that when contact occurs between a technically advanced civilization and one that is more backward, the latter will be wiped out. Pizarro did away with the Incas; this time her compatriots are due for elimination. At Klaatu's command, locust-like nanobots munch their way through New Jersey and reduce a sports stadium in the marshes to a whirl of flimsy implosive pixels. 'They're not afraid of us,' the Secretary concludes – an almost unspeakable thought, now uttered aloud by the chief executive officer of the Pentagon.

'Are you a friend to us?' Klaatu is asked by a woman whose husband, a military engineer, was killed during one of America's oil wars. Her phrasing is awkward because the pronoun chokes on the truth: 'us' really means 'US'. He responds by declaring that he is a friend to the earth. 'You're an alien, you don't understand,' says the woman's cheeky son, who is accustomed to zapping extra-terrestrials on his game console. Again the accusation misfires: the government of the United States invidiously classifies earthlings with different passports as aliens, and even applies the term to foreign nationals who reside inside its borders. Klaatu takes pity on the widow and her son, and on their account lets Americans off with a stern warning. But as he departs he uninvents electricity, the fire stolen from the gods that made it possible for human beings to wreck their own natural habitat.

Emmerich resumed his spectacular offensive in *White House Down*, where a paramilitary group knocks the dome off the Capitol and blows up Air Force One. Previews for the film intercut this mayhem with quotations from a speech by Abraham Lincoln, first the assertion that 'America will never be destroyed' and then, illogically, a jump to an obituary that admits 'We destroyed ourselves'. Lincoln meant that America would never be destroyed from outside; destruction could happen, he thought, only 'if we falter and lose our freedoms'. By isolating his final phrase and using it as a tag line, the preview for *White House Down* obscured the hypothetical nature of Lincoln's warning and implied that the self-destructive act had already occurred. Given this eschatological mood, America's avowed enemies hardly need to employ propagandists. In April 2013 North Korea reacted to criticism of its missile tests by circulating images of the White House fierily strafed by fighter jets, which smote the apex of the Washington Memorial as they veered down the National Mall. Although this alarming scenario counted as a retaliatory threat, the vision of retribution came from trailers for an American film, *Olympus Has Fallen*, in which a North Korean terrorist takes the President prisoner and plans to blow up America's nuclear missiles in their silos, irradiating the entire continent. Kim Jong-un's scaremongers ignored the unpropitious fact that the terrorist in the film is killed by being stabbed in the head. In Pyongyang, it looked as if the United States had obligingly written the script for its own downfall.

20 | 'Thanks, America'

Soon after 1776, Crèvecoeur reported on the renovation of humanity in an annex to the known world. Now as then, Americans are people of a new kind – original, with the dew of origins moist on them. The ABC network starts the day with a programme called *Good Morning America*. The salutation not only greets viewers but, like the campaign ad for Reagan in 1984 that celebrated a fresh start by declaring 'It's morning again in America', it suggests that this is the most American time of day – vigorous, brightly expectant, far from the vespertinal mood of Spengler's Europe, which is defined in the German title of his book as the 'Abendland', the land of evening.

What keeps the country new is the fact that every American has a personal contract with its founding idea: those whose birthright it is remind themselves daily of their good luck, while those who have attained citizenship express their gratitude for having been accepted as members. In his autobiography, Frank Capra – who was born in a Sicilian village and taken to America in steerage at the age of six in 1903 – remembered his thrill when he was chosen 'out of hundreds of little dagos, niggers, cholos, and Japs' at his school in Los Angeles to recite the pledge of allegiance on Independence Day, and he described the films he directed as 'my way of saying "Thanks, America"'. In a country whose most solemn, non-sectarian festival is about giving thanks, the phrase was more than a casual formality, and it has particular resonance because Americans never allow the process of thanking to remain a one-way transaction, a measure of indebtedness and therefore of inequity. That is why they say 'You're welcome' or 'You're most welcome' or 'It's my pleasure' or 'Enjoy' when thanked for some small, probably automatic courtesy: the catchphrase ensures that the goodwill goes on circulating.

Capra spoke to America with affectionate familiarity, and the Presidents who personify America speak to their compatriots with the same colloquial ease, as if across a back fence. Franklin Roosevelt thought of his wartime addresses on the radio as convivial fireside chats with his fellow Americans; Jimmy Carter even wore an unbuttoned cardigan as he delivered a homily about conserving energy on television in 1977. Such informality is rare and precious. When Queen Elizabeth II broke her customary silence on the night before Princess Diana's funeral in 1997 and requested her disaffected subjects 'to show to the world the British nation united in grief and respect', it was respect for the institution of monarchy that she had in mind; she spoke, she specified, 'as your Queen' – a reminder of hierarchy and its gradations. America, even when shaking its fist, is able to employ a different vocal register. 'We are the United States of America,' said President Obama when threatening Syria with reprisals for its deployment of chemical weapons – but he was not using a royal plural: the plurality in his statement was the fifty states, which make up a chorus that seldom thinks or utters in unison. As Obama said on the night of his re-election in 2012, 'the task of perfecting our union moves forward', by which he meant that it was still far from complete. A republic is a jostling forum where public things are open to debate, and democracy is many-headed, polyphonic, and in contemporary America also polylingual.

That, however, creates a problem. Although the nation is supposed to be indivisible, what can unify such a motley place, where liberty and justice are guaranteed to all but each individual pursues those goals in his or her own way? Certainly not God, inserted so belatedly into the pledge of allegiance. The quarrelsome consortium is held together by what the founders called 'propositions', schemes for future realization. Britain, like other European nations, still claims to be a family, which is why the Queen in her admonition about conduct at the funeral said that she was addressing her people 'as a grandmother' – a matriarch, everyone's presumptive parent. America has no such genealogy. Made up of those who did not want to go on belonging to their national clans, it was from the first not a natural growth but a concept, a conceit, an act of imagination – or what we might call a fiction (and a supreme one). Europeans unaccustomed to this way of thinking have trouble with such presumptions. The poet Hans Magnus Enzensberger initially felt grateful for the food packages and Benny Goodman records the GIs handed out after 1945; then during the Vietnam War he came to believe that the America by which he and other young Germans were fascinated was 'not the real thing, it was a projection'. Yet that is precisely how Americans themselves have always seen their country. Looking at it from the view-point of his Kenyan father, Obama once called America 'this magical place', distant and dreamy: a common denominator for Americans is this belief in the transformative powers of their society. After the 2008 primary election in New Hampshire, Obama invoked the Promised Land and a new frontier in outer space; he hinted that these were purely mythical destinations, but said they were inseparable from 'the unlikely story that is America'. In his speech on Independence Day in 2013, he made the obligatory reference to the United States as the greatest country in the world, but just before doing so he also called it 'this improbable nation'. His favourite adjectives are at once messianic and ironic, catching both the defiant novelty of the American idea and its precariousness.

In 1954 the cultural historian Jacques Barzun – who was sent from France to be educated in New York at the age of thirteen, and stayed for the rest of a very long life – published a book with the proudly possessive title *God's Country and Mine*, qualified only slightly by a subtitle that glossed its contents as *A Declaration of Love, Spiced with a Few Harsh Words*. Barzun would never have expressed such blatant ardour if he had remained a French citizen. France did not need flattery from him: like a parent, it expected a love that was dutiful and lawful, no more and no less. America excites emotions closer to what you feel for the person who becomes your lover – intense, demanding, but also, despite wedding vows, querulous and conditional. Hence the spice in Barzun's book: he was mildly flustered by the 'mechanic pace' of American life, ridiculed the silliness of advertising, and deplored the puritanical habit of prohibiting certain kinds of pleasure. Having got these provisos out of the way, his book then toured the American regions – those antipodal zones, east and west, north and south, which are as distinct as European nations – and concluded by quoting two beauti-fully effusive attempts to define the emotional climate that pervades these sundered parts. The first is William James's remark that America should be loved 'for her youth, her greenness, her plasticity, innocence, good intentions, friends, everything'; the second, Scott Fitzgerald's definition of America as 'a willingness of the heart'. It would be a pity to ignore James's admonition, or to dismiss Fitzgerald as a sentimentalist.

In the first decade of America's century, Barzun understood its commanding and exemplary role in the world's history. 'We have here a complete Europe,' he announced – a Europe that had managed (so long as you overlook the war between the American states) to live in peaceful cohabitation, without the flare-ups along borders that provoked the old continent's wars. In the 1950s it was still possible to think of the United States as a cooperative microcosm, 'an epitome of the whole world' as Barzun said: no longer just a refuge for disadvantaged or persecuted Europeans, it had become 'the testing ground of the possibility of mankind living together'. Now that the liberal coasts and the conservative interior have drifted apart, this view is sadly dated. Today the golden door referred to on the base of the Statue of Liberty is at best ajar. In 2011 Herman Cain, a candidate for the Republican Party's presidential nomination, returned from a trip to China and a stroll on the Great Wall to propose raising the barricade along the Mexican border to a height of twenty feet and topping it with electrified barbed wire. For good measure, he joked about a moat filled with snap-happy alligators. And although the poor, tired, huddled Latino masses yearn to breathe free, the most they can hope for on the other side is a better-paid servitude.

Parables improve the reality. On rare occasions, admission to America is automatically conceded to the virtuous, like entry into heaven: in *Moscow on the Hudson*, Robin Williams plays a saxophonist from the Russian circus who defects in Bloomingdale's near the end of the Cold War and is officially assimilated when he is offered a free hot dog by a former Soviet apparatchik, now happily plying his trade behind a food cart. Along the Rio Grande, it is trickier to arrive at an acceptable version of events. Tony Richardson's *The Border*, released in 1982, begins by retelling a biblical story of flight and refuge: a young Mexican mother crouches with her child beneath a statuette of the Virgin in a tumbledown hut as she waits for her chance to scurry into the United States. Jack Nicholson plays a guard who is supposed to keep out such surreptitious immigrants, even though the economy depends on them and employers subsidize the illegal traffic; when the woman's child is stolen by baby-traders, he turns against his corrupt colleagues. But how far could Richardson, himself an immigrant, allow his uniformed hero to go? Nicholson can hardly eliminate his compatriots. A lecherous people-smuggler therefore trips and blows his head off with his own gun; Harvey Keitel, pursued by Nicholson, wriggles beneath a truck that skewers him when its tyres deflate. In a preliminary version of the ending, Nicholson fire-bombs the border patrol station in disgust. After editing the film, Richardson changed his mind and reshot the conclusion, making Nicholson – an unlikely fairy godfather – restore the stolen baby to its mother, who whispers 'Gracias' as he watches over her with misty eyes. Alejandro González Iñárittu shows less compunction to Brad Pitt in *Babel*. The Mexican nanny he employs in San Diego takes his children across the border for the weekend, with their passports but with no letter of permission from the absent parents; she is arrested on re-entry. Pitt declines to press kidnapping charges, but he either cannot or will not prevent her deportation. She will be easy to replace.

In 2004 Joshua Marston's *Maria Full of Grace* tried hard to rehabilitate the myth of America as Bethlehem – a sanctuary for the persecuted, the birthplace of a new hope. Its Colombian Maria is another pregnant Virgin, who on her flight to the United States carries with her not only an embryo but sixty-two packets of cocaine she has been forced to swallow. She has an unseemly miscarriage on the plane, when some of the packets stowed in her stomach squeeze out prematurely, and she has to re-ingurgitate them; her companion Lucy dies after a pellet of cocaine she has not yet excreted ruptures inside her. Despite these misadventures, Maria chooses to stay in America: where else can the woman who is full of grace deliver her holy infant?

Cherien Dabis's *Amreeka*, released in 2009, concerns migrants from the actual, disputed Bethlehem on the West Bank. Muna and her son Fadi move to Michigan during the second Gulf War and are taken in by her sister, whose neighbours assume she is an Iraqi because, militantly homesick, she refuses to hang Old Glory outside their house. As they leave the airport in Chicago and drive over the frigid plains, Muna asks how far it is to Disneyland. The answer is disappointing, but the suburbs look to her like a magic kingdom: silver bags of potato chips in the supermarket are no less weird than the tabloid beside the checkout counter, which reports on a woman adopting an orangutan. Fadi assimilates, after receiving consumerist advice from his female cousins, who ban his pleated plants and issue him with a hoodie and a beanie. Muna, a bank teller in Palestine, has to settle for a job as a fast-food cook in a White Castle diner, a turreted, mock-medieval box of enamelled porcelain. 'Couldn't you have chosen Wendy's?' sighs her tiny but scathingly brand-conscious niece. Nevertheless Muna does her bit to make the midwest more ecumenical, and convinces her employers to put falafel burgers on the menu. Near the diner, a sign encourages customers to SUPPORT OUR OOPS – a patriotic command that has lost some crucial letters, or an exclamatory apology for the ill-advised war?

A similar sign appears in Thomas McCarthy's 2007 film *The Visitor*, draped on a bridge over the highway along which Walter Vale, played by Richard Jenkins, drives into Manhattan to attend a conference on global policy and the developing nations. The banner on this occasion says SUPPORT OUR TROOPS AND BRING THEM HOME, inadvertently expressing America's muddle: why have troops at all if you're so reluctant to let their boots touch foreign ground? McCarthy's plot criticizes the paranoia of the home front, where Americans who worry about immigration feel they are fending off an invading army from the Third World – and 'Vale' means 'farewell' in Latin, so perhaps he personifies decline, or the loss of white hegemony. When Walter arrives at the Greenwich Village apartment he has left vacant while teaching in Connecticut, he finds a black woman soaping herself in his bathtub. Though he is the rightful tenant, she regards him as an intruder, and shrieks 'You get away from me! You leave me alone!' A double-dealing agent has sublet his apartment to the woman, a Muslim from Senegal, and her Syrian boyfriend. They expect Walter to expel them; instead he invites them to stay. When they get to know him, they are startled to learn that he has never visited the Statue of Liberty, but he hardly needs to make the trip: he is liberality itself, hospitable to the point of self-abnegation. It helps that his guests are impeccably cultivated, speaking perfect French as well as English. She designs jewellery, he is a jazz drummer on the African djembe, which he teaches his stilted, cerebral host to play. Walter is told to place his feet flat on the ground, grip the resonant skin between his legs, and stop thinking. The posture at last connects him to the American earth, deep below the tarmac or asphalt or tiles or carpet with which it has been overlaid.

Walter also has his tastes re-educated when his guests take him to a falafel café near Washington Square for a kebab. But World Music and ethnic dining do not ensure an amiable communion of cultures. The Syrian is arrested for jumping a subway turnstile (which he does with no intention of evading the fare: he law-abidingly swipes his MetroCard, and wriggles through the barrier after pushing his drum on ahead). When the police discover that he has overstayed his visa, he is deported, and his mother – quietly but also illegally resident in Michigan – chooses to return with him. Going to tortuous lengths to exculpate the immigrants, *The Visitor* leaves the problem unsolved. A conservative status quo is upheld by the repatriations; at the same time, liberal principles are flattered by the behaviour of the generous, solicitous Walter, who wordlessly protests against injustice when he performs a furious solo on the djembe on a subway platform.

Equally dejected conclusions are easy to imagine for *The Border*, *Maria Full of Grace* and *Amreeka*. The Mexican mother would give up hope of finding her child; the pregnant drug mule would return to Colombia to be miserable; the Palestinians would be treated as harshly in Michigan as they are by the Israeli soldiers who interrogate them at the checkpoints in Ramallah. Instead the poster for *Amreeka* showed mother and son resiliently pushing an overloaded luggage trolley down a suburban street between impeccable, interchangeable tract houses with freshly mowed lawns. They are smiling, as is the sky above them. Their largest suitcase, bulging like a hopeful immigrant's heart, has an American flag pasted to it, with another placard that cheers them on by shouting DREAM BIG. So long as America exists, salvation is in theory available to all.

The rest of us, dispirited residents of a fallen world, are inclined to snigger at American euphoria. Early in 2014 the dynastic politician Jeb Bush announced that he might be a candidate for his party's presidential nomination in 2016, so long as he was confident that he could run for office 'joyfully': will he be campaigning for the office of entertainer-in-chief? Mockery of this ebullience is easy, but it does nothing to mar the irrepressible national mood. The disposition to be cheerful goes deep. The purpose of American orthodontics, after all, is to keep everyone smiling, and no matter how lightly salutations like 'Have a nice day' are meant, they ease and sweeten daily life. Unlike the French, Americans do not use good manners as a way of regulating the distance between people; nor, like the English, do they regard others with a mistrust that politeness makes little effort to disguise. They genuinely believe that there is room for all of us and that in our pursuits we run on parallel tracks, as in an overcrowded but uncompetitive marathon, the goal being not to finish first but to achieve a personal best. At the same time they believe in the individual's untrammelled rights, cherish success and its spoils, and reserve a special contempt for so-called losers, which makes it difficult to maintain the balance. But they feel obliged to try. Accustomed to abundance, they are instinctive givers – of their surplus wealth (which explains their unEuropean tradition of philanthropy), of their hospitality (I was touched to realize, when invited to my first Thanksgiving meal, that strays and loners are entitled to a portion of America's bounty), and, failing all else, of their ebullient personalities. A pet word imparts a surprising truth: to tell someone something, anything, no matter how trivial, is to 'share' – a verb that in current American usage needs no object, since to make a gift of yourself and your personal experience is its own justification.

When Americans refer to themselves as 'We the people', they mean it. Collectively they are responsible for dreaming up and sustaining this society. Popularity matters to them because they belong to a populace and exert themselves to be of value within it. Willy Loman in *Death of a Salesman* talks about the importance of being liked and if possible well liked – not a reprehensible aim in life – and the sincerity of that yearning for acceptance or esteem, rather than for the genuflection that power expects, explains the puzzlement Americans feel when they notice that in some parts of the world they are venomously disliked.

The rallying cry of 'We the people' defines a population whose methods and modes of expression are unabashedly populist. The first syllable of that word, broken off and turned from a Latin prefix into a small vernacular explosion like that of a pop gun, may be the most potent word to emerge from loquacious America during its post-war decades of dominance. It named an artistic style, and a kind of culture that was not reserved for appreciation by connoisseurs. In 1964 in a radio discussion with Warhol and Roy Lichtenstein, Claes Oldenburg remarked that the kind of imagery called Pop – frames from comic strips, labels on soup cans or detergent packets, cheesy pin-ups, random scraps of newsprint – supplied the painter with something 'that you didn't create'. Here was relief from the modern artist's tormented rivalry with God. Does anyone create anything? Instead we continually rearrange and recombine the manifold contents of the world that already exists. In the same spirit, John Cage defined music as 'anything a man "makes"'; he placed the verb inside quotation marks because the music might be noise overheard through an open window, not man-made at all, like the taxi horns in Gershwin's *An American in Paris* or the wailing sirens and percussive thuds in Edgard Varèse's *Amériques*.

This new aesthetic theory, a gift to us all, defined man as a finder rather than a maker, like Robert Rauschenberg collecting urban flotsam – car tyres, number plates, light fixtures, a stuffed bald eagle, the inevitable Coke bottles – to use in the assemblages he called combines, or the photographer Walker Evans gathering and classifying driftwood, pull-tabs from tin cans, street signs and touristic picture postcards. Robert Frank compared his own keen eye to that of crows picking scraps of food out of the garbage. 'They get the good pieces,' he said admiringly. The found objects prized by these artists tend to be things that are downtrodden, dishonoured, like the Statue of Liberty's 'wretched refuse' or like what Whitman, referring to his own poems, modestly described as 'leaves of grass'. Irving Penn photographed cigarette butts found on the street: vegetative filaments of tobacco, paper delicately curling or moistly stained. Oldenburg manufactured some 'Giant Fagends' of his own, composed of latex, canvas and urethane foam, that spill from an ashtray and roll onto the floor, where – neither smelly, messy nor carcinogenic – they have a second life as soft furniture. The theory extends to literary language, so long as it is unedited and irrepressibly spontaneous. Ginsberg called Kerouac's automatic writing a 'junkyard' style, and he meant it as a compliment.

In 1969 Pauline Kael made a uniquely American contribution to aesthetics when, praising movies she liked but did not take too seriously, she argued that we could glimpse 'something good in trash'. This had little to do with what moviegoers thought of as art, which was refined, educative and probably subtitled: art, Kael said, 'is what America isn't, and especially what American movies are not'. The following year Warhol and Paul Morrissey proved her point in a film they unapologetically entitled *Trash*, with Holly Woodlawn as a transvestite who lives in an apartment furnished with curios salvaged from Lower East Side gutters. William Phillips, a founder of the *Partisan Review*, worried in 1947 that his country's culture might turn out to be only too popular, and feared that America would become 'the greatest exporter of kitsch the world has ever known'. That is what happened, but only because the rest of the world was glad to import what Phillips, using a haughty, untranslatable European term, called 'kitsch'. The high culture assaulted by the Nazis when they burned books, banned music and looted paintings was protected and preserved in America. That heritage is no longer at risk; there is no reason why it should not be supplemented, on the streets and in our houses, by a lowlier culture, as ephemeral as a popular song and as informal as the blue jeans coveted by Queneau's Zazie.

Despite Kael's terminology, foreign consumers of Americana do not usually think of themselves as scroungers feeding on rubbish. Eric Rohmer, writing in 1953 about Howard Hawks's Western *The Big Sky*, marvelled at its elegant, relaxed exemplification of courage, which testified to 'this world of physical ability in which the heroes of Yankee folklore live'. Rohmer called Hawks 'not the filmmaker of appearances but the filmmaker of being'. To watch John Wayne loping so casually down a dusty Western street, or Bogart warily negotiating dark alleys and crooked staircases, was existentially reassuring; these figures somehow seemed resolute enough to refute Sartre's

scary notion that being is predicated on nothingness. In America, even cinematic shadows still had substance, and over there, as Truffaut pointed out,
heroism retained some meaning.

Others had different but equally precious American epiphanies. During
his college days in London, David Hockney's imagination was ignited by
the under-the-counter magazine *Physique Pictorial*, in which young men
recruited on Los Angeles street corners posed as gladiators in G-strings
or as Greek warriors who were naked except for their plastic helmets.
'Very beautiful bodies,' Hockney thought, adding 'American', 'very nice' and
'the real thing'. The pin-ups supplemented his reading of Whitman, whose
delight in the 'adhesiveness' of male comrades suggested an unexpectedly erotic interpretation of the affinity that held this society – or one of
its subcultures – together. They also strengthened Hockney's attraction to
the unmodern idea of beauty, and reminded him that art might be a source
of pleasure, not anguish. The young Wim Wenders gaped as he leafed
through a different range of American magazines in provincial Germany:
'Incredible highway junctions! ... Women in bikinis! ... Cars!' When he
heard Little Richard, Chuck Berry and Elvis, Wenders thanked rock 'n
roll for giving him a concept of expressive freedom and saving him from
what would otherwise have been a joyless, Teutonically regimented life. As
a boy, he mistrusted the stories told in German films, which between
1933 and 1945 had served as fanatical propaganda. 'Only Americans,' he
thought, 'had the right to show and tell things', and he earned that right
by apprenticing himself to American culture. The Australian novelist Tim
Winton similarly discovered how to tell stories about his own society by
reading American books. English literature seemed to Winton to be remote
and witheringly superior, but he was encouraged by the example of non-
metropolitan American writers like Faulkner from Mississippi and Flannery
O'Connor from Georgia, for whom the region in which they lived was an
all-sufficient world. That gave him permission to write about his own corner
of Western Australia, which is – as the characters in his novels often scur-
rilously remark – very like Texas, only larger. Whatever we feel about the
ambition of successive presidents to spread the love of liberty around the

world, the idea of America certainly liberated people like these, and count-
less others as well.

In 2002 Harold Pinter sarcastically complimented the United States on the
'brilliant, even witty strategy' of its foreign policy, which preached freedom
while thuggishly conquering new terrain. Having helped to invent the United
Nations and installed it in New York, Americans now proclaimed their right
to make war without its authorization. Pinter scorned humanitarian excuses
for intervention in Iraq or elsewhere, and sneered at the fixed grins of successive presidents. The rest of us, he declared, were at the mercy of 'the
most dangerous power the world has ever known'.

President Bush, who said that those who did not support American policy
would be considered allies of the terrorists, dared the doubters to such out-
bursts. Yet the agenda of the American century was not a sly conspiracy to
attain global dominion. It was Churchill who appealed to the hesitant young
hero to come to the rescue of the fratricidal old continent; once this had
happened, there was no possibility of reversal or retreat. A war that wrecked
Europe inadvertently enriched America, and economic strength made possible the assertion of political will, as when Eisenhower in 1956 tripped up
the British government's attempt to secure what Prime Minister Anthony
Eden called its 'imperial lifeline' in the Suez Canal. Against American advice,
the British invaded Egypt. The United States then reminded Eden that his
country was a pauper: the International Monetary Fund refused Britain
further loans until its troops withdrew from Suez. Which side behaved badly,
or at least foolishly?

What Pinter saw as duplicity is in fact duality. Americans can be at once
innocent and ruthless, naive and cruel. Without such a combination of
opposite qualities, they could never have survived, let alone prevailed: the
country they thought of as paradise regained was a wilderness that had to be
subjugated by axes and guns, with faith backed up by force. Ingratiation has
been their preferred mode when approaching countries that are their clients
or dependants, with compulsion as a second best. Throughout these forays,
in Europe or the Middle East, Japan or Vietnam, power and its imperatives

have always been balanced by plans for lifting up the Statue of Liberty's torch to ensure, as Kennedy said at his inauguration in 1961, that the 'glow from that fire can light the world'. The success of their own society has made Americans keen to bestow its benefits on others, whether or not the recipients want it.

In that inaugural speech, Kennedy addressed both 'citizens of America' and 'citizens of the world': all were his constituents. He made pledges to 'new states whom we welcome to the ranks of the free', to people 'in the huts and villages of half the globe', and to 'our sister republics south of our border'. He then vowed to 'begin anew', as Americans have always done, and envisaged 'a grand and global alliance' that would lead mankind aloft. A little over fifty years later, such confidence about American centrality would enrage rather than comfort or inspire the hut-dwellers and benighted villagers. In O'Neill's *Netherland*, an Indian magnate laughs at the idea of televising a cricket championship from a stadium in Brooklyn, and declines to invest in the project: 'You don't need America. . . . America? Not relevant.' Hans, O'Neill's narrator, having returned to London, Googles his way back across the ocean by satellite, zooms in on the site of the proposed stadium, then clicks his way back into mid-air. What he sees from this imagined height is neutral, undiscriminating. 'There is,' he reports, 'no sign of nations, no sense of the work of man. The USA as such is nowhere to be seen.' Recognizing that a burden has been lifted, he also acknowledges a loss: the work of man, meaning culture as well as technology, is what the USA distributed to the rest of us. Perhaps our world is now so thoroughly Americanized that we no longer need to venerate the United States as what O'Neill calls a 'special, sealed-off zone of opportunity and freedom', the preserve of values and virtues that are honoured nowhere else. The narrator of *Netherland* is pleased to have outgrown his fascination with America, and O'Neill – born in Ireland, though still resident in New York – implies that we should all do the same.

Personally, I am not ready to be cured. My reason is explained by a character in DeLillo's *White Noise*, which is about an America of the near future where the air is thick with media-transmitted images that are the siren songs of consumerism, along with a load of fatal toxins. One of DeLillo's characters touts a new medicine called Dylar, which does not abolish death but takes away the fear of it, and says that the psycho-pharmaceutical potion makes her proud to be American. When a colleague queries her logic, she explains that the drug's ingredients tickle the brain's trillion neurons, switching on lights in the cortex and triggering sensations: she might be describing a cranial Times Square. Is this why Americans seem so lively and so competitively energized, fleeter of foot and often quicker-witted than the rest of us? 'We still lead the world in stimuli,' says the chemist. Indeed they do: a world without America would be a dull, constricted place, hardly worth living in.

The country is larger than whichever politicians happen to be self-interestedly singing its praises at the moment; it even exceeds the grasp of the millions who pitch camp on its tough, ancient terrain. Road trips here travel forwards in space but backwards in time, with glimpses, as at the Canyon Diablo meteor crater in Arizona, of interstellar traffic accidents. In 1953 the broadcaster Alistair Cooke said that a visit to Bryce Canyon in southern Utah should be compulsory for every American, 'if only to humble him in his new pride of world leadership'. The spectacle, Cooke explained, was sure to calm any trivial worries about the Russians: geopolitical ructions seemed trivial when you thought about those innumerable cathedral spires of striped rock, whittled into shape by drops of water over the course of 50 million years. America turns all of us into awestruck spectators, silently watching as – at Niagara Falls and the Grand Canyon, at Mount St Helens or in the midwestern corridor that is patrolled by tornadoes – nature simultaneously creates and destroys. The land itself obstructed the human advance from east to west: it was necessary to cross scorched or icy plains, swamps and mile-wide rivers, a spinal cord of mountains, a saline desert and a valley of death. But American engineering magnificently manhandles this heaving, unstable earth. The Hoover Dam blocks a crevasse of black rock with an elegant curved membrane of concrete and commands a river to stop flowing. The Golden Gate Bridge braces the headlands and corrects the craggy irregularity of the coast. The Lake Pontchartrain Causeway in Louisiana, losing sight of land for eight of its almost thirty miles, dances on the surface of the apparently endless water as if its anchoring pillars were playing leapfrog. The Arch above the Mississippi at St Louis commemorates westward expansion but also demonstrates how human ingenuity can bend steel into an elastic, resilient symbol of optimism. And the Empire State and Chrysler Buildings – the one stern and severe as it jabs the sky, the other jewelled and gracefully round-shouldered – jut out of the Manhattan granite to demonstrate that American cities are triumphs of art at its most outlandish, monuments raised to the idea of aspiration.

The architect Le Corbusier, craning his neck in awe when he visited New York, decided that Americans were gods; Sartre or Graham Greene thought they were robots, while Sayyid Qutb saw them as obscene savages. The dispute about their achievements and their motives is a quarrel about human possibility. Their society sets the individual free, and the removal of prohibitions and inhibitions has placed on view both the best and the worst of which we are capable.

America, which began as the surmise of visionaries, still produces idealists whose eyes are fixed on the horizon. During his days as a community organizer in the Chicago slums, Obama said he hoped that he could bring about a 'collective redemption', and when running for the presidency he announced that it was his aim to 'transform a nation'. Such feats are more often accomplished by dictators than by democrats, but America also produces ordinary people who, with no time to make noble pronouncements, find themselves behaving as altruistically as movie heroes – men like Stephen Siller, who on 9/11, loaded with fire-fighting gear, ran from Brooklyn to Manhattan through the Battery Tunnel to reach the World Trade Center, where he died, or Todd Beamer, who rallied his fellow passengers to seize control of a hijacked plane above Pennsylvania that day and achieved a moral victory by crashing it in a field. Then there are liberationists who were brave enough to act on the constitution's promise of freedom: Martin Luther King and Rosa Parks, or the conscientious objectors to the Vietnam War who were gassed in Chicago and killed at Kent State University; even the Beat rebels, in particular Allen Ginsberg, whose acolytes in Czechoslovakia crowned him King of the May in 1965 because he shaggily embodied 'sexual youth', a time of life and state of being which could be counted as one of

America's inventions. The secret police soon reversed Ginsberg's corona-tion and hustled him aboard a plane to London, which merely intensified the appeal of America and enhanced its value.

Henry Luce expected America to raise mere humans almost to parity with the angels. While attempting to do so, it has engendered more than its fair share of demons. Among them are Lee Harvey Oswald and Charles Manson, the unjustly revered Reverend Jim Jones, the Unabomber Ted Kaczynski and his fellow terrorist Timothy McVeigh, the cannibals Ed Gein and Jeffrey Dahmer. People commit murders everywhere, but some Americans believe that this is how they pursue happiness or exercise their liberty. Somewhere in purgatory there must also be room for Senator Joseph McCarthy, Governor George Wallace, Mayor Richard Daley and the rest of the political ogres, along with Bernard Madoff, who will never be forgiven for revealing that the lure of effortless enrichment was, in his own words, 'one big lie'. Innumerable celebrity criminals, talk-show show-offs and obnoxious pop idols can be added to the line-up. Henry Fonda's young Mr Lincoln on his lowly mule, the bashful idealists played by James Stewart in Capra's films, Rockwell's village sages, Steinbeck's abiding Okies – these are no longer the nation's ideal types. Carrie Fisher joked recently about our 'unof-ficial *American Idol*-ized world', where celebrity, even for a few minutes, is apparently a birthright. This is not, surely, what Mailer had in mind when he described America as an experiment in realizing 'the dynamic myth of the Renaissance – that every man was potentially extraordinary'. But the clamour and self-puffery of the wannabes must be tuned out; there is still no alternative to the self-evident truths set forth in the 1776 constitutional preamble.

America won the world by winning it over, sometimes with candy bars and jeans, mostly with images and sounds. Whether or not these benefac-tions broadcast an ideology, the rest of us have been the true winners. We were captivated rather than conquered – consensually Americanized, like Emily in the novel. At the start of what was meant to be its own century, America took pride in being the world's saviour. After that, it accepted an obligation to be the world's protector. Today it is probably best described as the world's designated entertainer – a role less exalted than that history wished on it after 1945, but also less meddlesome. In case this sounds like a diminution, it also has to be said that – quite apart from their unstoppable output of great, good and enjoyably bad art – Americans continue to do a disproportionate amount of the world's scientific and technological thinking: innovation is their national mission. But a slippage is occurring. By 2028, or perhaps earlier, the American economy will no longer be the world's largest. With the branches of government in Washington permanently at loggerheads and democratic accountability under assault from demagogic news media, the republic designed in the eighteenth century has ceased to be a model of rectitude. And now that the United States can no longer afford to take responsibility for a refractory world, its foreign policy has become muddled and indecisive. As Joseph Chamberlain said a century ago about Britain's flagging empire, the Titan is weary (which fortunately means, in America's case, that it has wearied of going to war). Before prematurely rejoicing, critics should ask themselves whether the Titan's successor will be so keen to make us happy.

As the globe resumes its westward movement, we ought to remember why it was that an old world wanted and needed to discover a new one, which challenged ancient estimations of human nature and historical rules about how societies function. Encounters in and with America can be baffling or bruising, but they are usually eye-opening and very often exhilarating. That is why this perpetually self-renewing place exists – to confound our assumptions, enlarge our ideas, and remind us that further west, tantalizingly out of sight and reach, there exists the possibility of somewhere better.

Index